Spectacle and Topophilia:
Reading Early Modern and Postmodern
Hispanic Cultures

HISPANIC ISSUES • VOLUME 38

Spectacle and Topophilia:
Reading Early Modern and Postmodern Hispanic Cultures

David R. Castillo and Bradley J. Nelson

EDITORS

Vanderbilt University Press
NASHVILLE, TENNESSEE
2012

This book is printed on acid-free paper.
Manufactured in the United States of America

The editors gratefully acknowledge assistance
from the College of Liberal Arts and the
Department of Spanish and Portuguese Studies
at the University of Minnesota.

*The complete list of volumes in the
Hispanic Issues series begins on page 275.*

Library of Congress Cataloging-in-Publication Data

Spectacle and topophilia : reading early modern and
postmodern Hispanic cultures / editors, David R.
Castillo and Bradley J. Nelson.
p. cm.—(Hispanic issues ; v. 38)
Includes bibliographical references and index.
ISBN 978-0-8265-1816-3 (hardcover : alk. paper)
ISBN 978-0-8265-1817-0 (pbk. : alk. paper)
1. Spain—Social conditions—1975–.
2. Latin America—Social conditions—1982–.
3. Cities and towns—Spain. 4. Cities and towns—
Latin America. 5. Human ecology—Spain.
6. Human ecology—Latin America.
I. Castillo, David R., 1967–.
II. Nelson, Bradley J., 1963–.
HN584.S66 2011
306.0917´56109045—dc2   2011014401

Contents

◆ Introduction:

Modern Scenes/Modern Sceneries

David R. Castillo and Bradley J. Nelson

The modern secularization or "disenchantment" of the social sphere that accompanies the rise of capitalism has been chronicled in classic works of social and cultural theory going back to Max Weber's foundational treatise *The Protestant Ethic and the Spirit of Capitalism* (1904). More recently, social historians have traced the roots of the economic and sociopolitical dynamics that we associate with modernity to the "expansive crisis" of the late Middle Ages and the early Renaissance. They have pointed out that some of the most significant developments of the 1400s and 1500s are the direct result of the increase in large-scale commerce and the emergence of the monetary economy. The modern city is both a consequence and a catalyst of economic, political, and social change. Urban spaces are fundamental contributors to the erosion of traditional systems of interpersonal relations allowing for the rise of the bourgeoisie (literally inhabitants of the burg), as well as the social type of the "uncoupled" or "unattached" ("desvinculado" according to José Antonio Maravall).[1] The geographical discoveries of the period, including the lunar explorations of Galileo Galilei and Giordano Bruno's speculations on the theoretical existence of the cosmic vacuum, as well as the Columbian encounter and the imperial dreams and nightmares that came with it, further eroded the economic, political, and cultural structures inherited from antiquity.[2]

Cultural historians have tied the modern *objectification* of the world to the disintegration of the Aristotelian universe. For James Burke, for example, the debunking of the Scholastic-Aristotelian cosmos resulted in the de facto emergence of a de-essentialized *world of objects* that would be subjected to direct human control. The objectification of the natural world would find a correlate in the rationalization of the sociopolitical sphere, insofar as the political order was thought to be grounded in the natural order. Thus, the progressive acceptance of mechanistic principles would end up reshaping natural philosophy, as well as the fields of political theory and moral thought in the works of seventeenth-century thinkers such as Descartes, Bacon, Boyle, Hobbes, and Gracián, among others.

The New Science's mechanistic conception of nature as passive, inert matter is considered central to the consolidation of the structures that continue to drive the global economy today. Carolyn Merchant (1980) has referred to the seventeenth-century shift in natural philosophy as "the death of nature" (193). Teresa Brennan (1993) focuses on the intersection between natural philosophy and economics in theorizing modernity as an era defined by a fundamentally psychotic drive "to dismember nature" in order to control it. She links this social psychosis to the exploitative practices of global capitalism aligning its "exploitation and alienation of humans with that of nature" (215n11).[3] Both Merchant and Brennan argue that the natural philosophers of the seventeenth century, who are considered the founders of the New Science, redefined man's interaction with nature as a Subject-Object dialectic in which the Subject aims to achieve absolute mastery over the Object. Merchant quotes from Francis Bacon's *Novum Organum*: "'By art and the hand of man,' nature can then be 'forced out of her natural state and squeezed and molded.' In this way, 'human knowledge and human power meet as one'" (171).[4]

For their part, art theorists and historians have argued that the *modern episteme* (to use the expression coined by Foucault) is rooted in a visually oriented structure of thought that privileges the single-point perspective. This is what Martin Jay has called "Cartesian perspectivalism," which he considers to be the dominant scopic regime of modernity. Erwin Panofsky and Philip Braunstein are also among the scholars who have underscored the role played by Renaissance perspective (the single-point perspective, in particular) in the appearance of the new sense of "self" that we associate with the *modern subject*. Braunstein is very explicit about this, noting that "self-consciousness is born when the individual can see himself in perspective" (536). Yet for all the attention scholars have paid to the primacy of the visual, as a structuring principle of modern subjectivity that is grounded in an objectifying view of the world, it is rare to find scholarly works that focus on the *spectaclist* dimension of modernity in connection with the "transformation of worldview from cosmos to landscape [which] came to mean a prospect seen from a specific standpoint" (Tuan 133).

This may be due, at least in part, to the fact that, as James Elkins has noted, Renaissance perspective was more about the correct representation of objects than the construction of a homogeneous space in which these objects would move: "The Renaissance artists had no conceptual equivalent for our term *space*, and when they juxtaposed *prospettiva* and *spazio* (or *perspectiva* and *spatium*), they usually had something decidedly scholastic or humanistic in mind" (14).[5] Elkins's 1994 study stands as an important corrective to works like those of Jay and Panofsky, which have insisted on the simultaneous development of the "correct" representation of objects and a homogeneous, mathematically organized space. Elkins provides copious textual and visual examples of how diverse perspective techniques are brought to bear on different objects and mathematical proofs, with or without an accompanying pyramidal grid. He also follows the parallel development of myriad perspectival techniques and an analogous proliferation of mathematical techniques motivated by different navigational, optical, astronomical, architectural, and military problems. In other words, "the Renaissance had things the other way around in regard to space and . . . artists and writers thought first of objects and second about what we call perspective space or fictive space" (15). From here it is but a short jump to our suggestion that space is itself an object that can be approached from an infinite number of perspectives, which, when understood according to Elkins's notions, are simultaneous with the plurality of spaces they configure. The places in which objects are displayed are not prior to, or the condition for, the communication of the meaning of objects but rather complex objects responding to a number of social, economic, political, and aesthetic tensions and desires.

Building on the work of Yi-Fu Tuan's *Topophilia* (originally published in 1974), and among the most intriguing contributions within the field of cultural studies of space, Denis Cosgrove has recently signaled the existence of an early modern link between theater and landscape: "[In the sixteenth century,] theater not only had the architectural meaning, derived from the ancients, of a playhouse and the performances staged there, but also meant a conspectus: a place, region, or text in which phenomena are unified for public understanding" (101). In his contribution to this volume, David Castillo takes note of this meeting place between scene and scenery in the spectacular panoramas that are characteristic of modern mass culture, going back to the theatrical productions of the Spanish Golden Age. These observations point in the direction of a path of inquiry into the *spectaclist* structuring of space in modern times that has yet to be mapped. Our collection of essays is aimed at sketching such a path within the fields of Hispanic studies. We believe that an exploration of the intersection between available theorizations of the modern spectacle—from José Antonio Maravall's conceptualization of the spectacular culture of the baroque to the Frankfurt School's theorization of mass culture, to Baudrillard's notion of the simulacrum, to Guy Debord's understanding of the society of the spectacle—and the findings of the emerging fields of urban studies, landscape studies, and, generally speaking, studies of space, will contribute to a better understanding of the cultural and sociopolitical configurations that continue to structure our perception of the world in the age of global communications and virtual selves.

The study of space, landscape, and place has recently gained currency in a wide range of fields, including physical and human geography, anthropology, architectural theory, sociology, cultural history, philosophy, and literary studies. The growing bibliography on the subject may be attributed, at least in part, to what Philip Sheldrake has called "a crisis of place in Western societies—a sense of rootlessness, dislocation or displacement" (2). It seems reasonable to attribute the current interest in our spatial surroundings, whether we think of them in physical or cultural terms (or a combination of the two), to contemporary anxieties about our place in the world. Indeed, at the very root of the *postmodern condition* (to use Lyotard's well-known expression) we can see a "decline in traditional systems of values and symbols—religious, ethical and social [that] tends, among other things, to inhibit a clear world-view" (Sheldrake 2) While the current "crisis of place" may, in some ways, be specific to our own time, we can nonetheless draw parallels between the "postmodern" sense of rootlessness and earlier experiences of dislocation and displacement beginning with the "European discovery" of America, the sixteenth-century split of Christianity followed by decades (or indeed centuries) of religious strife, and the scientific and cultural revolutions of the 1500s and 1600s. This connection between the epistemological crises of the sixteenth and seventeenth centuries and the modern and postmodern anxieties about rootlessness and emptiness (*horror vacui*) is at the heart of the present volume.

Recent scholarship on landscape and place may be said to stem from the phenomenology of Martin Heidegger (his concept of dwelling) and the work of postmodern thinkers such as Michel de Certeau, as well as the anthropologists Mircea Eliade and Victor Turner. Other important voices in place studies are

Marc Augé, Gaston Bachelard, Henry Lefebvre, Paul Ricoeur, John B. Jackson, Simon Schama, and the above-mentioned Yi-Fu Tuan and Denis Cosgrove, to provide a short list of foundational figures. They have pointed out that landscapes are composed of relational places that embody interpersonal emotions, perceptions, and memories. The places that form our landscapes are rooted in individual and communal memories that provide us with a sense of belonging. The memories attached to a place give historical meaning to our lives. This is why narratives are integral to our sense of place. Insofar as places are sites of competing memories within historically conditioned *systems of spatialization*, they are intricately connected with the dynamics of power (Lefebvre). In other words, human places are not just sites of interpersonal and communal encounters, but also sites of political, social, religious, and cultural conflicts.

Hence, in his contribution to this volume, David Castillo focuses on the construction of national spectacles and monumental landscapes. He draws from Tuan's exploration of the ideological structuring of topophilic sentiments in the context of nationalized landscapes and, simultaneously, from Guy Debord's theorization of the *society of the spectacle*. Castillo shows how national landscapes and monumental sites can become "landscapes of exclusion" (to use Sheldrake's expression [21]) structured by and imbued with the memories and values of hegemonic groups. He also explores alternative ways of marking the land and imagining human connections to and through place in his analysis of examples of anamorphic restructurings of highly symbolic places such as Rome and New York in works by Cervantes and García Lorca. Castillo links this type of anamorphic perspective with Sheldrake's call to rethink historical places as *multilocalities* and *multivocalities*.

William Childers offers an illuminating illustration of this notion in his exploration of the intersection between race and place in early modern Spain. He examines the different meanings that were attached to the place name "Granada" in the context of a multiphased colonial project that started in the 1400s and reached its zenith with the expulsion of the *moriscos* in the early seventeenth century. Childers studies how a complex, often antagonistic group of players, including the state, the population exiled from Granada, the new inhabitants of the city, and ecclesiastical hierarchs came into contact in the space, both imagined and real, of the cityscape: "In this complex process of negotiation, certain people and things associated with the place name 'Granada' were preserved as part of 'Spain' and others were cut off, lost, or destroyed" (29). The results of these encounters point to the exclusionary logic behind many of the pseudo-historical chronicles of the late Middle Ages and early Renaissance. While political genealogies flourished all over Europe in the fifteenth and sixteenth centuries, the cultural environment of Imperial and Counter-Reformation Spain was especially fertile for the proliferation of pseudohistorical legends and other historiographic myths of origin. These mythical chronicles (including those of Ruy Sánchez, Fabricio de Vagad, Margarit i Pau, Annius de Viterbo, Antonio de Nebrija and Florián de Ocampo, among others) attempted to redefine Spain as an essentially Christian nation, tracing its Christian origins to antiquity and even further back to the biblical times of Noah and his immediate descendants. As Robert Tate pointed out in his informative article "Mythology in Spanish Historiography of the Middle Ages and the Renaissance" (1954), the proclamation "Hispania tota sibi restitute est," with which Nebrija and his followers greet the conquest of Granada, implies in its context "not only the ejection of the Moors but also a reconstitution of the totality of the Peninsula, a recovery of self, a purification from external encroachments and alien influences" (14–15).[6] In this context, the work of cultural dissidents, such as the *morisco* doctor Miguel de Luna (author of *Historia verdadera del rey don Rodrigo* and mastermind, along with his relative Alonso del Castillo, of the famous Lead Book forgeries of Granada), must be understood quite literally as a desperate fight for historical time and space.

Cervantes seems to understand what is at stake in the cultural wars of the sixteenth and seventeenth centuries. In his references to the 1609 expulsion of the moriscos in *Don Quixote II,* and also in his posthumous *Persiles*, Cervantes holds to a different view of Spain as a *multilocality,* while striving to construct fundamentally polyphonic or multivoiced narratives. Childers has recently discussed Cervantes's countercultural views of the sociopolitical, religious, and racial landscapes of Imperial Spain in *Transnational Cervantes* (2006). In the book, as well as in his essay included in this collection, Childers draws simultaneously from archival sources and postcolonial theory, as he reexamines the Spain of Cervantes as a historical site plagued by conflicts that are in many cases tied to processes of internal colonialism.

In his chapter, Moisés Castillo also places Cervantes in a transnational context, albeit a Mediterranean one, adding to our view of the author as a critical voice in Golden Age Spanish literature. Castillo builds on the information provided by critics such as Jean Canavaggio, Michael McGaha, and María Antonia Garcés, among others, on the subject of Cervantes's experience of captivity in Algiers and its possible impact on his literary treatment of this theme in *Don Quixote*, *Persiles*, and several of his plays. Beyond the work of these critics, however, Castillo underscores the significance of the *oriental space* of Agimorato's garden in *Los baños de Argel*. He reinterprets this Cervantine *locus amoenus* and its metaphorical extension (the freedom boat) as a *hetero-*

topian place (Foucault) that reflects, as in an anamorphic mirror, Cervantes's own humanistic ideals of justice and human brotherhood. The Cervantine ideals of human bonding, compassion, understanding, and love are projected onto the landscape in this *place without limits* (one of the meanings of the Greek "outopos") symptomatically located in the space of the Other. As Moisés Castillo explains, this heterotopian drive has nothing to do with the regressive utopianism that José Antonio Maravall has rightfully attributed to pastoral literature, Chivalric and Christian romances, and mainstream Golden Age theater.[7] While conservative utopianisms uphold traditional nobiliary values and official Christian beliefs, the theatrical heterotopia that enables the *felice fin*, or happy ending, at the conclusion of *Los baños de Argel* is a place without (internal) limits or frontiers in which dramatic characters from different cultural and religious backgrounds rediscover their common humanity and their shared dreams of freedom.

Brad Nelson's contribution to the present volume is also anchored in an understanding of Imperial and Counter-Reformation Spain as a conflictive space, traversed by multiple vectors of historical meaning and desire. Nelson underscores the importance of the emblematical tradition in the context of modern and postmodern attempts to reimagine the place of humanity in an ever-expanding universe. In doing so he questions the traditional view of Golden Age Spain as culturally singular or "peculiar" in the context of early modern Europe, taking issue with Fernando R. de la Flor's interpretation of Counter-Reformation culture, especially Juan de Borja's emblems, as a nihilistic, anti-Cartesian critique of instrumentalist schools of thought accompanying early capitalism. In contrast to this focus on an exclusively Hispanic expression of unreason, one that R. de la Flor uses to place Spanish thought in a paradoxically postmodern position with respect to a hegemonic "European" modernity, Nelson reads Borja's use of the emblem as a "middle space or medium" in which conflictive definitions of reason (specifically Aristotelian natural philosophy versus Copernicus's mathematically based astronomy) are brought to bear on epistemological and ontological deadlocks that accompany early modern scientific discoveries.

One of the most volatile spaces that both produced and were subjected to these conflicting scientific ideologies was earth itself or, more properly, the cosmos. In his analysis of the vigorous debates concerning the status and validity of mathematical and geometrical modes of thought, Nelson argues that current developments in the genre of science fiction offer a useful frame for considering scientific debates in the baroque. Not unlike the 1982 sci-fi noir film *Blade Runner*, the baroque debates revolved around contradictory notions of free will, and the question of whether a mathematically based understanding of physical causes and effects results in knowledge that is hypothetical or real. It is noteworthy, for example, that Galileo's discovery of the moons of Jupiter and his explanation of the technical obstacles and meaning of the discovery in the *Sidereus Nuncius* become early modern sensations because of Galileo's emblematic framing of the discovery as a marvelous proof of the political legitimacy of the Medici dynasty (Biagioli).[8] Thus, not only is the nascent scientific community populated by contradictory fictions concerning the place of man in the cosmos, but its discourse is inexorably framed by aesthetic considerations as well as the political demands of courtly spectacles. In the end, given the multinational status of both absolutist alliances and predominant religious orders, it is impossible to map a singular profile of an emergent Hispanic identity, let alone do so in scientific terms.

One need look no further than the historical persistence of multiple national traditions and identities on the Iberian Peninsula itself for confirmation of the modern tension between the colonizer and the colonized that colors virtually every narrative of national space in the Hispanic world. Colleen Culleton's essay moves through a constellation that includes the 1375 *Atlas of Cresques*—a monumental *mappamundi* composed by an Aragonese Jew living in Mallorca—a 1975 scholarly volume dedicated to the study of this same artifact, a 1998 novel by the Catalan author Alfred Bosch *L'atles furtiu*, and a 2003 civic exposition called *Barcelona Conectada*. Culleton traces the tensions occasioned by the politically motivated desire of the three postmodern mappings of the 1375 artifact in order to frame the relation between the Jewish cartographer and his world map as a forerunner, or prototype, of the marginalized Catalan subject, as well as to recognize the resistance of any historical artifact to this kind of emblematization. If the map itself, even a monumental specimen like the *Atlas of Cresques*, provides but a partial perspective on a historically contextualized and thus contradictory worldview, then what are we to make of repeated attempts to fix the meaning of the absence-saturated text according to equally conflictive and contradictory definitions of cultural identity?

One is reminded of Merchant's and Brennan's notions concerning the early modern subject's need to master all objects *in sight* at the very moment in which a firm grasp on the meaning and place of Man in the cosmos is slipping away. Another image that occurs to us is that of the continual retracing of maps on an infinite series of palimpsests, each one motivated by the gaps and silences in the precursor and, just as importantly, leaving its own lacunae and deadlocks for the next cartographer to unravel. Since the mapmaker is hardpressed to account for his own ideological unconscious in the expression of his cartographical desire, a notion such as Walter Mignolo's "border thinking" helps bring into greater relief the colonizer-colonized dialectic at the heart of modern attempts to map the national space.

In his study of Argentine modernism, Justin Read foregrounds Mignolo's notion of border thinking, which emphasizes the constitutive relationship between modernity and colonialism, while underlining the historicity of an ideology that misrecognizes itself as universal. Like Culleton, Read brings into dialogue the efforts of a number of seminal thinkers to define and redefine a liminal habitus. In this case, the artistic and philosophical writings of Victoria Ocampo, Jorge Luis Borges, and Alberto and Raúl Prebisch are brought together within a national space informed by the concept of "total theater" as articulated by Walter Gropius: "the Total Theater envisioned both the creation of multiple chronotypes and the collapse of distinct chronotopes into one another" (101). The problem, as Read sees it, is that none of the Argentine thinkers whose work he analyzes can imagine the future of Argentina without first leaving behind the untidy residue—ethnic, architectural, economic, political—created by its dependency-rooted relation with Europe. Just as modernity seeks to cut its ties with the violence, both symbolic and real, produced in the colonial encounter at the heart of capitalist "advances," so, too, does Borges turn a blind eye to the more unseemly aspects at the heart of Buenos Aires's transformation into a quasi-European metropolis. This is not unlike Culleton's observation concerning the desire of modern Catalonia to become an inclusive, which is to say noncolonial, cosmopolitan space through the self-same gesture that posits Barcelona's constitutive centrality for imagining such a project. In Read's words, "this topophilic spectatorship is also a monumental act of misrecognition" (111).

David Foster continues this discussion of the relation between topophilia and misrecognition in his study of Horacio Coppola's urban landscape photography of 1930s Buenos Aires. Where Borges misrecognizes both the rapid modernization and accompanying ghettoization of Buenos Aires's port and peripheral shantytowns in his search for an appropriately masculine and epic national figure, Coppola's photography neatly cuts both of these untidy spaces completely out of his action-packed portraits of the ultramodern skyscrapers and bustling streets of an upscale financial and retail district and its accompanying governmental center. What is ironic about the photographs is that when Coppola is taking them, Buenos Aires's period of rapid growth and modernization had already been cut short by the 1929 stock market crash. Foster observes that "the objects of Coppola's photographic gaze in 1936 were more like a reflex of the more halcyon period of the 1920s (the so-called 'años de las vacas gordas')" (120) in much the same way that Borges's focus on the *gaucho* reflects the author's desire for an Argentina that had already disappeared. Foster's thesis that urban photography works to bridge Tuan's topophilic extremes of *the abstract* and *the specific* moves in two directions at once: on the one hand, Coppola's focus on a very specific microcosm of Argentinian modernity evokes a more abstract understanding of how Latin American dependency can be transformed into an energetic leap into the future; on the other, this narrow focus of the photographer's gaze, like Borges's bracketing of modern demographic and economic "progress," leads to an abstract ideal that turns a blind eye to internal dependency and poverty, a move that allows the Buenos Aires elites to set themselves apart from the regressive material conditions of their own affluence. Indeed, this willful misrecognition would seem to identify them as completely modern. If the rapid economic growth and expansion of Buenos Aires is what allowed the modern cityscape to take shape, then these photographs constitute a baroque-like simulacrum behind which lies Giordano Bruno's terrifying vacuum.

This quixotic disconnect between the desire to relive a bygone era of glory and an impoverished and conflict-ridden present is at the heart of Catherine Vallejo's study of the diverse receptions and interpretations of the spectacles that revolved around Spain's two royal delegates to the 1893 Chicago World Exhibition: the duke of Veraguas, Columbus's direct descendant; and Princess Eulalia, the young aunt of the future King Alfonso XIII. The exhibition's theme was the four hundredth anniversary of Columbus's discovery of America, and, as such, Spain would have a leading role in the fair, although the meaning of this role would be open to conflicting interpretations. Vallejo approaches the study of the fair through Mieke Bal's narratological apparatus and Tuan's proposal that an outsider's perspective on a cherished space offers the potential for critiquing the latter's shortcomings or contradictions. This is an intriguing conceptual pairing, in that Spain's narrative of its own historical importance and its desire that the former colony recognize her historical debt to Spanish imperialism collide head-on with the emerging imperialist narrative emanating from rapid US economic and political expansion. If the Spanish government's goal was to reassert its historical importance as well as its continuing imperial presence, the US hosts were more interested in showing how far they had come in the last four hundred years, including, of course, their own imperial aspirations regarding Cuba and Latin America. The desire of the Spanish dignitaries to strike a heroic, imperial pose is also undercut by the impoverishment of Spain's pavilion, located in the Agricultural Building alongside its former and soon-to-be-former colonial possessions in Latin America. According to the spatial organization of the fair, Spain has already been downgraded to a third-world by(gone) way. What is more, the US retinue surrounding the duke of Veraguas initiates a subscription campaign to help the duke recover financially from a disastrous series of investments, which made for a rather pathetic spectacle in a nation that prided itself on "lifting itself up by its own bootstraps." As for Princess Eulalia, in addition to offending exhibit organizers with her regal haughtiness and chronic tardiness, she dishonors her own country when she refuses to attend a ceremonial cannon salvo organized in her honor by the captain of the replica of the *Santa María*, which Spain had sent to the exhibition. In a moment reminiscent of Don Quixote's refusal to test his newly repaired helmet during his self-transformation from impoverished country gentleman to heroic knight errant, "Eulalia insisted on removing herself from the area as she did not trust the cannons. Indeed, there was an accident in which two sailors were wounded by shrapnel flying from the exploding cannon" (Vallejo 137).

This notion of a "crash" that explodes idealized narratives, and either launches the avant-garde subject into a futuristic nonspace (Augé) or returns the national subject to its inescapable rootedness, is at the center of Robert Davidson's study of Eduardo Zamacois Quintana's 1922 novel, *Memorias de un vagón de ferrocarril*. Davidson analyzes the Spanish avant-garde's celebration of European cosmopolitanism and concomitant deconstruction of narratives of Spanish national identity tied to the Castilian landscape by tracking the biography of the protagonist of Zamacois's novel, a railcar named Cabal. At issue is the conflict between the desire of the cosmopolitan subject to move freely through the disruptive changes brought about by modernity and the modern subject's love of particular, homely spaces. The novelist's decision to explore modern subjectivity through the construction, movement, and destruction of a luxury dining car shows, on the one hand, as Cervantes states—three centuries before Heidegger—that the subject is "made like this thing they call a place" (*Los trabajos* II, 12.363), and, on the other, that the movement of the subject through space shapes its experience in time and, thus, defines its contours and limits. Davidson follows the work of Díaz-Plaja on modern cosmopolitanism, which "acknowledges a more transcendent dimension to the concept by pointing to the way that the dynamic comes into tension with a nationalism 'confined by borders'" (148). Rather than focusing on Spain's idiosyncrasy vis-à-vis European modernity, so often metaphorically evoked by the inability of Spanish trains to travel outside of the Peninsula because of the distinct gauge of the tracks, Davidson studies how avant-garde cosmopolitanism becomes exhausted by its own dialectical relation with that which it rebels against and the accompanying ideological contradictions. In the end, the avant-garde subject, however cosmopolitan he or she desires to be, must always enunciate the break with tradition and history from an identifiable place in space and time and, as a result, constitute a new "literal and metaphoric center of the state that it had once traversed" (155).

Goretti Ramírez takes the notion of modernist exile one step further in her study of Luis Cernuda's poetic representation of urban, garden, and Spanish historical landscapes. Returning to the *topos* of "landscapes of exclusion" (Sheldrake) introduced by David Castillo and further developed by Childers, Ramírez focuses on the ways in which the Spanish exile dialectically engages Francoist attempts to link representations of Spanish monumental and natural landscapes to "a quest for *order* . . . an assertion of *authority* . . . and . . . a project of *totalisation*" (160). In contrast to Franco's identification of the fall of the Republic as the point of origin of Spain's heroic, epic, and *true* return to imperial triumphs and glory, Cernuda characterizes the lost Second Republic as an edenic space to which the Spanish nation should strive to return after the fall of the *true* Spain to the fascists. Like Childers's complex treatment of *maurophilia* in the context of the expulsion of the *moriscos*, Ramírez's analysis of Cernuda's landscapes demonstrates how "exiles resort to the creation of other atemporal myths to connect their existence to that of other exiles of history" (166). Similar to Américo Castro's notion of a "morada vital," the assemblage and erection of a historical space simultaneously constitutes a historical subject: "*un nosotros de la historia*" who inhabits the newly renovated historical landscape and defends its borders from incursions from other "mnemonic communities" (Beckwith xv). Seen in this light, Franco and Cernuda become rivals who engage each other in a fight to the death on and over the blood-stained terrain of Spain's imperial and modern history.

The last two essays of the volume reengage the question of the "historical *we*" through an examination of cinematic and media spectacles in Francoist Spain (Luis González) and in democratic Spain (Carmen Moreno-Nuño). González focuses on the Francoist reinvention of the rural landscape of Castile as the ancestral reservoir of Spanish values in the 1948 film *Un hombre va por el camino* (directed by Manuel Mur Oti) and the regime's demonization of the city space that is apparent in *Surcos* (directed by José Antonio Nieves Conde), first released in 1951. González shows how these films reconstruct Spain's historical landscape as the scene(ry) of a mythical struggle between the atemporal spirit of the nation and a soulless modernity that threatens to destroy it. While the urban center is often represented as an unredeemable space inhabited by monstrous crowds, the possibility of individual and communal salvation is still present in agrarian settings, which recall pastoral Arcadias. González's description of the urban scenery of *Surcos* may be said to evoke the imaginary of horror fiction, in particular a scene in which the father of the immigrant family, Manolo, gives candy to a child who approaches Manolo after he has set up his (illegal) kiosk in a park. Soon Manolo is surrounded by a veritable urban mob, much like the dystopian portrait evoked by José Ortega y Gasset's paranoid account of the loss of civilization beneath a flood of suddenly entitled proletariat masses in *La rebelión de las masas*. As described by González, this scene is reminiscent of countless horror classics dealing with evil children and also, more generally, with vampires and zombies.

While the city breeds anonymous crowds of soulless parasites, the traditional family structure of the countryside shows restorative powers for individual men, women, and children. As González writes, "It is in the countryside, untouched by the effects of Modernity, where Franco's regime will look for, and will find, the ideal subject of the New Spain" (175). From this perspective, we can see that the Francoist project of national reconstruction has much in common with the theatrical formula of "alabanza de aldea," or praise of the countryside, that had inspired such popular seventeenth-century plays as *Fuenteovejuna*, *El caballero de Olmedo*, *Peribañez y el comendador de Ocaña*, *El villano en su rincón*, and *El alcalde de Zalamea*, among many others. Thus, González's discussion of the Francoist program of monumentalization of the rural landscape of Castile brings us full circle to the issues discussed in the first chapter.

The role that monumental sites and national spectacles play in rearticulating communal memories is also the theme of the final essay of the volume. Carmen Moreno-Nuño notes that the temptation of identity closure leads to political and cultural battles over national memories and their meaning. She quotes from Castiñeira: "Lo importante en la memoria nacional del pasado, no es su verdad, sino su significación" (66) (What is important about a nation's memory of the past is not its truth but its meaning). Hence, in her interpretation of critically-acclaimed films such as *Soldados de Salamina* and *La ciudad sin límites*, Moreno-Nuño underscores opportunities to reconstruct historical places as dialogic, problematic, and conflictive multilocalities. As she writes, "By turning memory into a project Spanish cinema seeks to narratively represent a new hermeneutics of the nation through the link between personal memory, collective memory and historical memory" (200). With regard to current efforts to recuperate the historical memory of Spain, Moreno-Nuño calls for a self-consciously critical approach to the reconstruction of places of memory while cautioning against the current media frenzy that has turned historical traumas into national spectacles. Her analysis suggests that public acts of historical recovery and symbolic restitution must be accompanied by the recognition that places of memory do not have a single or univocal meaning but are subject to interpretation by individuals as well as small and large-scale communities. The essays included in this volume take this notion as their point of departure as they examine the politics and aesthetics of space and place in the *society of the spectacle* from early modern to postmodern contexts.

Notes

1. See Maravall's *El mundo social de "La Celestina"* and *La picaresca desde la historia social*, especially the introductory section.
2. For an explanation of the impact of Giordano Bruno's discovery of the vacuum and especially Galileo Galilei's recording of his lunar explorations in the context of a discussion of the epistemological shift of the sixteenth and seventeenth centuries, see Andrea Battistini's "The Telescope in the Baroque Imagination." Aníbal Quijano and Walter Mignolo have offered an important corrective to Eurocentric versions of universal history. They have placed the conquest and colonization of America at the very center of the modernity debates in arguing that the modern age is inaugurated by an act of imperial aggression and that European modernity is directly enabled by colonial violence, slavery and genocide (Mignolo, *The Dark Side of the Renaissance*).
3. See also Brennan's *Globalization and Its Terrors* (2003).
4. James Bono has recently pointed out that there is an alternative "modern" tradition of natural philosophy that questions the dominant mechanistic principles. He links this tradition to William Harvey's view of nature as "living matter" and also to the twentieth century work of Alfred North Whitehead. Bono quotes from Whitehead: "We are now so used to the materialistic way of looking at things . . . that it is with some difficulty that we understand the possibility of another mode of approach to the problem of nature" (3).
5. On the same topic, Elkins cites Peter Collins: "It is a curious fact that until the eighteenth century no architectural treatise ever used the word space" (24).
6. Much of the overview of Spanish historiography presented here comes from Robert Tate's compelling article. Tate's discussion underscores the emergence of propagandistic notions of Spanish integrity in the context of the Absolutist monarchy.
7. See Maravall's *Utopía y contrautopía en "El Quijote."* See also David Castillo and Nicholas Spadaccini's "El antiutopismo en *Los trabajos de Persiles y Sigismunda*: Cervantes y el cervantismo actual."
8. For a discussion of Galileo's *Sidereus Nuncius* in the context of baroque aesthetics and, generally speaking, European baroque culture, see Andrea Battistini's "The

Telescope in the Baroque Imagination." Not unlike Nelson, Battistini establishes a precise link between the philosophical and aesthetic yearning of the baroque, which is everywhere present in Galileo's reports, and the modern literary genre of science-fiction. As he writes, "the *Sidereus* provided an unintentional incentive for science fiction. . . . In reality, nothing at that moment was impossible, nothing incredible for those that, yearning for a freer and vaster world, were released from the laws of verisimilitude and able to reason in utopian terms" (27).

Works Cited

Adorno, Theodor, and Max Horkheimer. *Dialectic of the Enlightenment*. New York: Continuum, 1998.

Augé, Marc. *Non-Places: Introduction to an Anthropology of Supermodernity*. Trans. John Howe. London: Verso, 1995.

Battistini, Andrea. "The Telescope in the Baroque Imagination." *Reason and Its Others: Italy, Spain, and the New World*. Eds. David Castillo and Massimo Lollini. Nashville: Vanderbilt University Press, 2006.

Baudrillard, Jean. *Simulacra and Simulation*. Trans. Sheila Faria Glaser. Ann Arbor: University of Michigan Press, 1994.

Beckwith, Stacy N. "Introduction: Al-Andalus/Iberia/Sepharad: Memory among Modern Discourses." *Charting Memory: Recalling Medieval Spain*. Ed. Stacy N. Beckwith. New York: Garland, 2000. xiii-li.

Biagioli, Mario. *Galileo, Courtier: The Practice of Science in the Culture of Absolutism*. Chicago: University of Chicago Press, 1993.

Blade Runner. Directed by Ridley Scott. Warner Bros., 1982.

Bono, James. "Perception, Living Matter, Cognitive Systems, Immune Networks: A Whiteheadian Future for Science Studies." *Configurations* 13 (2005): 135–81.

Braunstein, Philippe. "Toward Intimacy: The Fourteenth and Fifteenth Centuries." *A History of Private Life*. Vol. 2 *Revelations of the Medieval World*. Ed. Georges Duby. Trans. Arthur Goldhammer. Cambridge, MA: Belknap-Harvard University Press, 1988.

Brennan, Teresa. *Globalization and Its Terrors*. New York: Routledge, 2003.

———. *History after Lacan*. New York: Routledge, 1993.

Burke, James. *The Day the Universe Changed*. Boston: Little, Brown, 1985.

Castillo, David R., and Nicholas Spadaccini. "El antiutopismo en *Los trabajos de Persiles y Sigismunda*: Cervantes y el cervantismo actual." *Cervantes: Bulletin of the Cervantes Society of America* 20:1 (Spring, 2000): 115-32.

Castiñeira, Ángel. "Naciones imaginadas." *Casa encantada: Lugares de memoria en la España constitucional (1978-2004)*. Madrid: Iberoamericana Vervuert, 2005.

Castro, Américo. "The Historical 'We.'" *An Idea of History: Selected Essays of Américo*

Castro. Eds. Stephen Gilman, Edmund King, and Roy Pearce. Columbus: Ohio State University Press, 1977.

Cervantes, Miguel de. *Los trabajos de Persiles y Sigismunda.* Ed. Carlos Romero Muñoz. Madrid: Cátedra, 2002.

Childers, William. *Transnational Cervantes.* Toronto: University of Toronto Press, 2006.

Cosgrove, Denis. "Spectacle and Society: Landscape and Theater in Premodern and Postmodern Cities." *Understanding Ordinary Landscapes.* Eds. Paul Groth and Todd W. Bressi. New Haven: Yale University Press, 1997.

Debord, Guy. *Society of the Spectacle.* London: Rebel Press, 1995.

Elkins, James. *The Poetics of Perspective.* Ithaca, NY: Cornell University Press, 1994.

Jay, Martin. "Scopic Regimes of Modernity." *Modernity and Identity.* Eds. Scott Lash and Jonathan Friedman. Oxford: Blackwell, 1992.

Lefebvre, Henri. *The Production of Space.* Oxford: Blackwell, 1991.

Maravall, José Antonio. *Culture of the Baroque: Analysis of a Historical Structure.* Minneapolis: University of Minnesota Press, 1986.

———. *El mundo social de "La Celestina."* Madrid: Gredos, 1986.

———. *La picaresca desde la historia social.* Madrid: Taurus, 1986.

———. *Utopía y contrautopía en "El Quijote."* Santiago de Compostela: Pico Sacro, 1976.

Merchant, Carolyn. *The Death of Nature: Women, Ecology, and the Scientific Revolution.* New York: Harper and Row, 1989.

Mignolo, Walter. *Global History/Local Designs: Coloniality, Subaltern Knowledges, and Border Thinking.* Princeton, NJ: Princeton University Press, 2000.

Panofsky, Erwin. *Perspective as Symbolic Form.* Trans. Christopher Wood. New York: Zone, 1991.

Quijano, Anibal. *"Coloniality of Power:* Eurocentrism and Latin America." *Nepantla: Views from South* 1.3 (2000): 533–80.

R. de la Flor, Fernando. *Barroco: Representación e ideología en el mundo hispánico (1580–1680).* Madrid: Cátedra, 2002.

Schama, Simon. *Landscape and Memory.* London: HarperCollins, 1995.

Sheldrake, Philip. *Spaces for the Sacred: Place, Memory, and Identity.* Baltimore: Johns Hopkins University Press, 2001.

Tate, Robert. "Mythology in Spanish Historiography of the Middle Ages and the Renaissance." *Hispanic Review* 22.1 (1954): 1–18.

Tuan, Yi-Fu. *Topophilia: A Study of Environmental Perception, Attitude, and Values.* New York: Columbia University Press, 1974.

Weber, Max. *The Protestant Ethic and the Spirit of Capitalism.* New York: Routledge Classics, 2005.

Part I
Foundational Landscapes

◆ 1

Monumental Landscapes in the Society of the Spectacle: From Fuenteovejuna to New York

David R. Castillo

The 1980 Radio Televisión Española (RTVE) production of Lope de Vega's classic drama *Fuenteovejuna* (1619) concludes with a suggestive visual montage that brings the landscape into the scene in spectacular fashion: the stone walls of the royal palace of Fernando and Isabel slowly open up and then fade away to reveal a panoramic view of the Castilian countryside. The significance of this climactic scene is underscored by an intense, seemingly supernatural luminosity, which transforms the fields beyond the architectural setting into an ethereal panorama. This spectacular montage may remind us of Yi-Fu Tuan's description of the convergence of the terms "nature," "landscape," and "scenery" in the early modern period. As he pointed out in his foundational work *Topophilia: A Study of Environmental Perception, Attitude, and Values* (1974), the convergence of nature, landscape, and scenery signals the demotion of the all-encompassing cosmos of the ancients, as well as the fundamental transformation of the original Dutch notion of *landschap* (farms, fields). The core of Tuan's thesis is that, in the sixteenth and seventeenth centuries, the landscape entered the realms of spectacle and make-believe (the world of the theater). In so doing, it claimed signifying centrality in official portraits and spectacles of power (133).[1]

The semantic charge of the Spanish word *paisaje* proves that the modern connection between landscape and spectacle goes beyond the English language. The definition of *paisaje* in the *Diccionario del uso del español* (1998) (compiled by Moliner) confirms the centrality of this link: "Extensión de campo que se ve desde un sitio. El campo considerado como espectáculo" (536) (Extension of terrain seen from a specific site. The countryside viewed as a spectacle). The entry for *panorama* is even more telling for our purposes, in that it reveals a link between the meaning of "paisaje" and the "total view" suggested by the etymology of the word (pan-orama): "Paisaje pintado en una superficie cilíndrica, que se contempla como espectáculo. . . . Referido a vistas o dibujos de algo, hecho a cierta distancia, de modo que se ve el conjunto de lo que se quiere representar" (557) (Landscape depicted on a cylindrical surface that is contemplated as a spectacle. . . . Referring to vistas or drawings of something from a certain distance so as to view the totality of what we want to represent).

Denis Cosgrove recently investigated this link between landscape and spectacle, beginning with Renaissance art and theater. He notes that the word *theater* acquired connotations beyond its ancient meaning that brought it remarkably close to the emerging notion of *landscape*: "In the sixteenth century, theater not only had the architectural meaning, derived from the ancients, of a playhouse and the performances staged there, but also meant a conspectus: a place, region, or text in which phenomena are unified for public understanding" (101).

Returning to the 1980 production of *Fuenteovejuna*, I would argue that the spectacular panorama at the conclusion of the film works as a portrait of the body politic, "unified for public understanding." Paraphrasing Tuan, we could say that the expansive landscape of the state becomes the background of the king's portrait—or better said, the scene of his pose. As the camera zooms in, we see that the citizens or "paisanos" of Fuenteovejuna are slowly moving through the scene(ry).[2] This "total view" of the body politic is strongly reminiscent of the illustration on the cover of Thomas Hobbes's foundational treatise *Leviathan* (1651), which represents the territory of the state as the body of the king, with his head rising over the landscape. On closer inspection, we see that the torso of the monarch is composed of countless human figures, whose own faces are turned toward the king's head.

The underside of this mythical portrait of monarchical omnipresence is the panoptic spectacle of vigilance, discipline, and punishment that is richly chronicled in the third act of Lope's play. I am thinking both of the graphic depiction of the brutal piercing and dismemberment of the medieval body politic allegorized in the figure of the *comendador* and of the compulsive repetition of scenes (near the end of the play) of inquisitorial interrogation of the king's subjects. It is important to recognize that this is not gratuitous violence but, rather, the price that must be paid for the establishment of the Absolutist order, the pound of flesh demanded by the emerging modern state. In the words of Fuenteovejuna's mayor, the exemplary voice of the new monarchical subjects: "Que Reyes hay en Castilla / que nuevas órdenes hazen / con que desórdenes quitan" (II, 1620–23) (For there are monarchs in Castile / who give [literally make] new orders / with which they eliminate disorders).

In erasing the history of social and political antagonism from the Castilian landscape, the mythical panorama of the pacified countryside, presented at the conclusion of the RTVE production of *Fuenteovejuna*, closely follows the monarchical metanarrative that is inscribed in the king's proclamation at the end of Lope's original text: "Y la villa es bien se quede / en mi, pues de mi se vale" (III, 2446–47) (And the town must thus remain within me, insofar as it has claimed me [as its legitimate ruler]). The implication is that the town of Fuenteovejuna, which allegorically represents all of Spain, voluntarily and heroically embraces monarchical absolutism as political desideratum and historical destiny. To be sure, Fuenteovejuna becomes a foundational *topos*, a monumental site that marks/commemorates/celebrates the birth of the Spanish State.

Tuan pointed out that topophilic spectacles extend the illusion of organic wholeness beyond local physiographic units inside the boundaries of the nation-state: "To enhance loyalty, history is made visible by monuments in the landscape and past battles are recounted in the belief that the blood of heroes sanctified the soil. Topophilia rings false when it is claimed for a large territory. A compact size scaled down to man's biologic needs and sense-bound capacities seems necessary" (99–101). The concluding montage of the RTVE production of *Fuenteovejuna* illustrates these notions in a deliberate and seemingly self-conscious manner. It makes it easier to grasp how Lope de Vega transforms an archival curiosity (a chaotic and contradictory story of local rebellion in a relatively insignificant rural area of fifteenth-century Spain) into a monumental *place of national memory*.[3] The spectacular mythology of *Fuenteovejuna* functions as a double screen that protects the nation from the traumatic and potentially disintegrating encounter with its own *historical real,* both in the past and in the present.[4] This may help explain why this seventeenth-century play has been used to promote self-celebratory images of the ruling order in political environments as diverse as Franco's Spain, the former Soviet Union, and revolutionary Mexico.

Today's spectators may feel a sense of déjà vu when watching this 1980 production of *Fuenteovejuna,* which, we should note, follows Lope de Vega's text very closely. Indeed, the climactic scenes of this baroque historical drama have much of the flavor of Hollywood epics and Disney productions. This should not be surprising when we consider that the modern world, *the society of the spectacle* according to Guy Debord, "was born from the world's loss of unity, and [that] the immense expansion of the modern spectacle reveals the enormity of this loss" (15). Insofar as the mass-oriented baroque spectacle is a public ritual of mourning (R. de la Flor) that offers consolation/compensation for the world's loss of unity (David Castillo, "Horror Vacui") in the language of the ruling order (Maravall), it makes sense to think of the baroque stage as a precursor of our own mass-oriented spectacles, from Hollywood to Disney-world.[5] The (re)constructive impulse that structures mass-oriented spectacles works on the same principle today as it did in the context of baroque culture, i.e., the principle of myth, which Roland Barthes aptly defined as a form of *naturalization* of history. As he puts it in *Mythologies* (1972): "Myth is neither a lie nor a confession: it is an inflexion. . . . We reach here the very principle of myth: it transforms history into nature" (129).

While a comparative analysis of baroque theater, vis-à-vis the productions of our own society of the spectacle, falls beyond the scope of this essay, I will review a few scenes from the popular animated film *Pocahontas* (1995) to illustrate how mass-oriented spectacles continue to rework history into a compact mythology, an easily digestible series of self-celebratory landmarks of the ruling order.[6] I will focus on the film's reconstruction of the American scenery as a transhistorical reservoir of the national spirit. I will also examine a music clip (included in the video release) that projects selected images of the film over the skyline of New York City. As in the concluding scene of the made-for-TV version of *Fuenteovejuna,* this video montage transforms the landscape (in this case the cityscape) into an ideological screen that protects the nation (the collective national fantasy) from a traumatic and potentially disintegrating encounter with its own historical contingency and its constitutive violence.

The storyline of *Pocahontas* is simple and familiar enough in its *naturalization* of colonial history. Pocahontas, the young daughter of Indian chief Powhatan, develops a romantic attachment with the courageous Captain John Smith, who, along with greedy Governor Ratcliffe, leads a shipload of British settlers into Virginian territory. As conflict breaks out between the local Indians and the British settlers, the Indian princess, always accompanied by animal friends, seeks the wisdom of Grandmother Willow. The ancient tree will help her understand her own personal destiny as part of a larger historical design.

We may be tempted to associate the film's mythical portrayal of Pocahontas as a free-spirited Indian living in perfect harmony with nature with new age ecological ideals. Yet images of close-to-nature (or nature-bound) Indians are but the gold standard of colonial discourse going back to Columbus's *Diaries*, as is the split of historical agents into noble idealists and greedy villains in such plays as Lope de Vega's *El Nuevo Mundo descubierto por Cristóbal Colón* (The New World Discovered by Christopher Columbus).[7] The familiar notion of "manifest destiny" justifies the conquest and colonization of the New World by linking the colonial order to providential designs or, in the case of the Disney film, to the will of Nature. Thus, when the confused Indian princess discusses her mysterious dreams about a spinning arrow with Grandmother Willow, the ancient tree encourages her to listen to the spirits of the earth, the water and the sky who will guide her toward the right path: "All around you are spirits, child. They live in the earth and water, in the sky. If you listen, they will guide you." Pocahontas will eventually find the path she is searching for with the help of Smith's lost compass (the spinning arrow). In the end the Indian princess becomes convinced that she and her people must embrace the Land's manifest destiny, which is inextricably tied to the predestined presence of the newcomers:

> Grandmother Willow: It's the arrow from your dream.
> Pocahontas: I was right. It was pointing to him [John Smith].
> Grandmother Willow: Let the spirits of the earth guide you. You know the right path, child. Now follow it!

This mythical version of "the encounter" is a foundational landmark that can be easily transferred to the present socio-political situation. Hence, today's (post)colonial landscapes, along with the socio-political structures contained in them, may be "naturalized" as the fulfillment of history: the shining city at the end of the "right path."

The music video version of the song "If I Never Knew You," which is performed at the conclusion of the film, reinforces this topophilic mythology. The central moments of the film are replayed against the night skyline of New York City as we listen to the nicely harmonized voices of Jon Secada and Shanice. On a few occasions the camera zooms in to give us a close up of an open door or window that reveals our own contemporaries looking up at the sky, seemingly mesmerized by the topophilic spectacle in which they play a part. We see ourselves in their eyes, sharing in the emotion of collective spectatorship. This is how we are integrated into the national landscape, not as "historical actors" but as "spectators" of the national drama.

The visual imagery provides a temporal and geographical bridge between the time and space of the mythologized Virginian "encounter" and the here and now of a cityscape that has been cleaned up to gloss over the daily realities of ongoing exploitation and violence. The mythologized meeting of a British captain with an Indian princess in sixteenth-century Virginia is explicitly offered as a metaphor for what/who we are as a nation: the world's beacon of freedom and opportunity. As the lyrics proclaim, "somehow we make the whole world bright." Remarkably, the city itself has been converted into a screen, an outdoor theater, for the continued projection of the ideological fantasies that sustain the trans-historical identity of the nation.

It is important to point out that this Disney version of the "Virginian encounter" (Pocahontas's path) does not differ a great deal from the historical narratives that are often pieced together in monument sites. The echoes of the self-justifying discourse of manifest destiny can be heard loud and clear in historical landmarks, museums, and monuments throughout the country. The End of the Oregon Trail Interpretive Center in Oregon City may be a particularly apt example, insofar as it taps into one of the most enduring figures of the national imagery: the American pioneer. We can literally touch the world of our ancestors as various relics from the time of the pioneers are passed from hand to hand across rows of spectators, who sit in front of a stage-like presentation area. To complete the visit, the audience is ushered into a stadium-seating theater for a film presentation featuring carefully selected quotes from the diaries of the first colonists to arrive at the West Coast, professionally recited over a series of dramatic shots of majestic mountains, lush valleys, and cascading waters. This documentary produces a narrative of American determination, resourcefulness, endurance, moral rectitude, unshakable faith, and compassion. The words of Simon Schama may come to mind as we watch this magnificent (very carefully framed) spectacle of nature: "Landscapes are culture before they are nature; constructs of the imagination projected onto wood and water and rock" (61).

The film concludes with an explicit call to new generations of Oregonians to follow the path of the pioneers—that is, to share in the quintessential American values as presented or constructed by the narrative. The Oregon landscape is thus elevated to the status of a *traditional monument* (Jackson), which invites us to celebrate a carefully edited version of the nation's past while mapping the proper road to the future, the "right path." In this context, a panoramic view of Mount Hood, to speak of a particularly recognizable Oregon landmark, may be considered an "ideological construction" as effective as any commemorative monument at Gettysburg. Hence, I would argue that Reuben Rainey's analysis of the function of monumental sites in "Hallowed Grounds and Rituals of Remembrance: Union Regimental Monuments at Gettysburg" applies to the End of the Oregon Trail Interpretive Center as much as to the self-consciously politicized landscape of *Fuenteovejuna* (in both Lope's original play and the made-for-TV production) and the New York cityscape at the conclusion of Disney's *Pocahontas*: "[The monument] not only instructs us about the great historical events of our culture but also reminds us of present and future social and political obligations. . . . [It] is a guide to the future as well as a celebration of the past" (69).

Rainey's observations on the social function of rituals of remembrance and monumental landscapes bring us full circle to Maravall's conceptualization of baroque culture (including secular as well as religious celebrations and spectacles) as a mass-oriented *culture of guidance* (cultura dirigida). Maravall follows Salomon and others in arguing that the utopian view of the countryside that is characteristic of baroque theater—he pays special attention to Lope de Vega's rural dramas, *Fuenteovejuna* among them—guides or coaches individuals to embrace a view of the world that is consistent with dominant values and beliefs. In their idealized representation of the countryside, Lope de Vega and his followers draw from the highly conventional tradition of pastoral literature going back to classical sources, including the Virgilian Arcadia and the poetry of Theocritus in the Alexandrian Age. However, Lope de Vega's "alabanza de aldea" (praise of the small town or countryside) should not be confused with a nostalgic longing for rusticity. Neither should we think of his frequent use of agrarian terminology as evidence of a down-to-earth perspective consistent with some sort of agrarian worldview in seventeenth-century Spain.[8]

Miguel de Cervantes makes this point contemporarily when he calls attention to the mystifying and manipulative dimensions of Lope de Vega's theater in his caustic interlude *El retablo de las maravillas* (The Magic Tableau). As I have argued elsewhere, Cervantes ridicules the mythical image of the countryside that is characteristic of Lopean theater, while also showing that this image is linked to institutional forms of political propaganda in seventeenth-century Spain.[9] Cervantes proposes a different model of spectatorship insofar as he invites or challenges us to make the connection between theatrical conventions and social conventions and to reflect on what is at stake in our communal rituals of self-affirmation. Hence, the meaning of monumental sites and sacred spaces is often "up for grabs" in Cervantes's texts. As Diana de Armas Wilson argues in her groundbreaking book on *Persiles*, even the sacred city of Rome takes on the characteristics of a barbaric land ruled by violence and exploitation in Cervantes's posthumous work.[10]

Cervantes's countercultural landscapes, and his anamorphic images of monumental sites and mass-oriented spectacles, are powerful reminders that places of memory are ideological battlegrounds. Philip Sheldrake may have said it best in *Spaces for the Sacred: Place, Memory, and Identity*: "The meta-narratives of those with secular or religious power at any given time take over public places and thus become stories of dominance and repression. . . . A strategy of resistance demands a critical engagement with contexts and the political will to transform the narrative and to redeem the place" (21–22).

Speaking of places of memory and redemption, I recently had the chance to visit the small mountain town of Viznar, northwest of Granada, where many believe Federico García Lorca is buried in an unmarked grave. A few years back, the town built a quaint commemorative park to celebrate García Lorca's cultural legacy. Just inside the monumental grounds, somebody had pasted a poem onto an olive tree.[11] The poem, signed "Anselmo," urged the visitors to let the dead rest in piece and *silence*. I reproduce some of its more "militant" verses (with my own translation):

El Olivo
Federico

¡Dejad el olivo!,
dejad el olivo,
que guarde sus secretos
en el hondo de la madre tierra.
Dejar los secretos que guarden
sus silencios en el alma del olivo,
que alma y alma universal
se abracen en el abrazo de la vida.
. . .
¡Que nos regalen la vida!,
de todos los cantes,
de la ciudad de Grana,
de la sierra de Grana,
del aire de Grana.
. . .
Dejad que los hombres mansos
reposen en la cama de la Tierra,
dejad que sus almas naveguen
por la blanca luz de los cielos.
Dejad que los muertos reposen en paz.

Dejad a los malditos abrazando
la muerte que un mal día sembraron.

The Olive Tree
Federico

(Leave the olive tree!
Leave the olive tree,
to guard its secrets
in the depths of the motherland.
Leave the secrets,
to guard their silences
in the soul of the olive tree,
so that soul and universal soul
may join together in the embrace of life.
  . . .
Leave the olive tree!
Leave the olive tree,
to guard its secrets
in the depths of the motherland.
  . . .
Leave the tame men
to rest inside the bed of the Land.
Leave their souls to navigate
across the white light of the heavens.
Leave the dead to rest in peace.
Leave the damned to embrace
the death they seeded that terrible day.)

The last two verses of the poem come remarkably close to the climactic scene of Guillermo del Toro's 2001 film *El espinazo del diablo* (The Backbone of the Devil). In the film, which has been widely acclaimed as an insightful commentary on the Spanish Civil War and its place in history, the ghost of Santi (Santiago) drags his killer down to the bottom of a pool where their bodies come to lie together, interlocked in an inert embrace. But the ghosts of the orphanage do not rest in peace, and will not rest in piece, until the narrative is transformed and the place is redeemed—to paraphrase from Sheldrake—by a generation of children who find the courage to face the past and join its victims in their quest for justice (22). At the conclusion of the film, the open door of the orphanage, which leads to a new horizon, is the polar opposite of the resting place that the poet Anselmo wishes for the dead Federico. The silent communion of the dead with the motherland in the depths of the earth might allow us to hear the dreamed "songs of Granada." However, the echoes of these "songs of the city of Granada, of the mountains of Granada, of the air of Granada" are likely to be as mystifying as the sounds of the Disney soundtrack that pour over the airbrushed landscape of New York City at the end of *Pocahontas*.

Looking at the park grounds, I could not help but wonder whether this celebratory *locus amoenus* might not be just the kind of silent "resting place" that the author of "El Olivo/Federico" seems to be endorsing, i.e., a monumental place where "hombres mansos" (tame men) may rest "inside the bed of the Land" as their souls "navigate across the white light of the heavens." Yet we know that García Lorca, who traveled to New York City right before the crash of 1929, was not interested in the songs inspired by airbrushed skylines and counterfeit dawns. This was not a "tame man" but the author of passionate and insightful denunciations of economic, social, and political violence, injustice, and exploitation. His "Grito hacia Roma" (Cry to Rome) is a moving indictment of the hypocrisy of the Roman Catholic Church, screamed from the top of the Chrysler Building. His nightmarish vision of New York City—a river of blood flowing through counterfeit landscapes and accounting offices—in "Nueva York: Oficina y denuncia" stands in revealing contrast to the bright skyline offered as dénouement at the conclusion of *Pocahontas*:

> Pero yo no he venido a ver el cielo.
> He venido para ver la turbia sangre,
> la sangre que lleva las máquinas a las cataratas
> y el espíritu a la lengua de la cobra. ("Nueva York, Oficina y denuncia," *Poeta en Nueva York*, 133)

> (But I didn't come to see the heavens.
> I am here to see the clouded blood,
> the blood that carries the machines to the waterfalls
> and the soul to the cobra's tongue.) (my translation)

This street-level cityscape seems to redirect our gaze toward other (often invisible) stories of the city: stories of colonialism, slavery, capitalist exploitation, frustrated desires, and broken dreams. At the same time, I can't help but think that the "river of blood" that "becomes money, cement, or wind in New York's counterfeit dawn" (133; my translation) is the humanity that continues to breathe, sweat, and bleed behind Disney screens, monument sites, accounting offices, and airbrushed panoramas. In this sense, Lorca's anamorphic cityscape seems to be doing the critical work that Philip Sheldrake calls for:

"We need to become aware of what might be called 'a longer narrative' in which 'the others' who have been made absent by those who control public and institutional histories are now being restored as people who are fully present. . . . The notion that place relates to issues of empowerment and disempowerment forces us to think of multilocalities (that actual locations are many different 'places' at the same time) and multivocalities (that there are a variety of different voices to be heard in a place)" (21).

As if to corroborate this assertion, we can find another poem, an *other vocality*, just outside the García Lorca park on the northern hills of Granada. A minimalist plaque marks the spot where the poet is believed to have been shot and killed (alongside a school teacher, Dióscoro Galindo, and two *banderilleros*, Francisco Galadí Melgar and Joaquín Arcollas Cabezas) by a fascist firing squad in August 1936. A short farewell, written by the poet himself, offers a distinctive alternative to the monumental logic of the García Lorca park: "Si muero, / dejad el balcón abierto" (García Lorca, *Canciones* 125) (If I die, / leave the balcony open) (my translation). The poet's dramatic plea to leave his balcony open if he should die signifies a desideratum for a fluid relationship between the dead and the living. The dying poet asks to remain a presence in the world of the living. He refuses to be laid to rest. We can say that he rejects "the depths of the motherland" and "the white light of the heavens," if only to stay put at his open balcony, watching over the living fields of the present and the future.

Del Toro's *El espinazo del diablo* comes to mind again. In the film, the ghost of another poet (Casares) refuses to abandon the Civil War orphans. The dead poet stands guard at the open window of the orphanage in ruins, ready to fight for the future alongside the victimized children. "I shall never leave this place," is Casares's promise. As an allegory of the cosmopolitan intellectual of the 1930s caught in the turbulent crossroads of the Spanish Civil War, the ghostly figure of Casares is determined to remain a historical agent, even in death (or perhaps more so in death). His dying words throw García Lorca's final plea to leave his balcony open in stark relief.

The dead poet's request reacquires a sense of historical urgency today, in the context of the controversial work of the Association for the Recuperation of Historical Memory (Asociación para la Recuperación de la Memoria Histórica), which seeks to reopen all unmarked graves of Civil War victims. What are open graves if not remainders and reminders of the multilocality and multivocality that monument sites and national spectacles are often designed to erase or cover over (literally bury)? And yet, open graves can also become public spectacles of national mourning, subject to the same ideological trappings as devotional sites. A recent article by the novelist and poet Manuel Vilas flippantly titled "Lorca Reloaded" touches on this seemingly unavoidable paradox:

> Federico García Lorca es por fin un espectáculo del siglo XXI, es nuestro Michael Jackson, o algo así. Necesitábamos encontrar la materia de que estaba hecho el poeta. Necesitábamos sus huesos, los huesos más amados de nuestra historia. Sin huesos, el cuerpo es ficción. El mito Lorca se agranda. Lorca nos alegra. Es nuestro hit internacional. Me fascina que no aparezcan sus huesos porque eso convierte a Lorca en una ilusión muy posmoderna, muy thriller, muy CSI. Pero amo los huesos de Lorca y quiero verlos antes de morirme. (*ABCD*, January 2, 2010)

> (Federico García Lorca is finally a twenty-first-century spectacle, our Michael Jackson or something like that. We needed to find the matter of which the poet was made. We needed his remains, the most beloved remains of our history. Without remains, the body becomes fiction. The myth of Lorca grows. Lorca makes us happy. He is our national hit. I am fascinated by the fact that his remains have not reemerged because this makes Lorca a postmodern illusion, a CSI-style thriller. Yet I love Lorca's remains and wish to see them before I die.)

What will we see if or when the remains of the poet are finally found? Will Lorca's remains become relics on which to build another monument site? Will the findings inspire mystifying songs or denunciations of ongoing injustice? Will the discoveries function as national or local landmarks, or will they reveal open wounds in the present historical landscape?

To conclude, whether we are talking about Lope de Vega's representation of the Castilian countryside as the moral and social reservoir of monarchical Spain in *Fuenteovejuna,* or the projection of the mythology of "manifest destiny" over the American scenery in Disney's *Pocahontas*, these types of mass-oriented spectacles (re)construct the national landscape as a series of monumental sites that celebrate dominant values and beliefs. We can say that the self-celebratory narratives of the society of the spectacle work as *landscapes of exclusion* (Sheldrake) that effectively colonize the past as well as the present and the future. From the perspective of cultural criticism, it is important to recognize that places of memory are irreducible multilocalities with alternative and often contradictory stories to tell. This is why we must call for self-reflective acts of historical recovery. In the absence of a certain degree of self-awareness and self-criticism, even the best-intentioned acts of historical remembrance and symbolic restitution run the risk of reifying the exclusionary logic they are meant to contest.

Notes

1. The following passages from Yi-Fu Tuan's book are especially relevant to the issues at hand: "The axial transformation in world view from cosmos to landscape may be traced in the changing meaning of the words 'nature,' 'landscape,' and 'scenery.' In modern usage the three words share a common core of meaning: scenery and landscape are often used interchangeably and both imply nature. However, the confluence is achieved at a sacrifice. Nature keeps company with scenery and landscape by ceding most of its semantic domain, and the last words are nearly synonymous through the loss of precision in meaning. . . . The slight differences in meaning they retain reflect their dissimilar origin. Scenery has traditionally been associated with the world of illusion which is the theater. . . .The difference is that landscape, in its original sense, referred to the real world, not to the world of art and make-believe. In its native Dutch, 'landschap' designated such common places as 'a collection of farms or fenced fields, sometimes a small domain or administrative unit.' Only when it was transplanted to England toward the end of the sixteenth century did the word shed its earthbound roots. . . . Landscape came to mean a prospect seen from a specific standpoint. Then it was the artistic representation of that prospect. Landscape was also the background of an official portrait; the 'scene' of a 'pose.' As such it became fully integrated into the world of make-believe" (133).

2. It is worth noting that the word "paisaje" (from the French "paysage") is closely related to the terms "pais" ("pays" in French) and "paisano" (nonmilitary person).

3. For a theorization of the notion of "place of memory," see Simon Schama's *Landscape and Memory* (1995). More recently Philip Sheldrake has elaborated on Schama's concepts with the works of Henri Lefebvre and, especially Paul Ricoeur in mind, he recontextualizes the discussion of places of memory in connection with the notion of "sacred space" in *Spaces For the Sacred: Place, Memory, and Identity* (2001).

4. What I call "the historical real," in the context of this essay, is the traumatic kernel of the nation, the history of state violence that our symbolic constructs are meant to cover over. This notion is loosely inspired in the Lacanian concept of the real. For a theorization of this concept see Jacques Lacan, *The Four Fundamental Concepts of Psychoanalysis* (1981). See also Slavoj Žižek, *The Sublime Object of Ideology* (1989).

5. Debord writes: "The spectacle is the material reconstruction of the religious illusion. . . . the ruling order's non-stop discourse about itself, its never-ending monologue of self-praise, its self-portrait at the stage of totalitarian domination of all aspects of life (*Society of the Spectacle* 20–21).

6. Bruce Burningham has recently followed this cross-cultural and cross-ephocal comparative path to propose interpretations of films such as *Fight Club, Brazil, The Matrix*, and *Toy Story*, as well as some of John Ford's classic westerns, in light of the baroque theatrical and literary production of the Spanish Golden Age. In chapter 1 of *Tilting Cervantes: Baroque Reflections of Postmodern Culture* (2008), Burningham argues that the baroque *comedia histórica* and the classic Hollywood western are

similarly structured by imperialistic drives, "fueled in part by similar ideological notions of Reconquista and Manifest Destiny" (9). He explains Lope's and Ford's reworkings of the national past in such dramas as *The Famous Asturian Damsels* (written 1610–1612) and films such as *Stagecoach* (1939) in light of Sheldon Hall's notion of "history as spectacle" (Burningham 10). The Marxist tradition of cultural criticism from Walter Benjamin to the intellectuals associated with the Frankfurt school has provided a series of insightful essays on the propagandistic nature of mass culture; see especially Adorno and Horkheimer's *Dialectic of the Enlightenment*. For a study of mass culture in the context of the baroque see Maravall's classic *La cultura del barroco* (1975). José María Díez-Borque has provided illuminating studies of the Spanish baroque theater as an institution. His sociological approach underscores the propagandistic function of mass-oriented theatrical spectacles in Golden Age Spain.

7.   For an interpretation of Lope's *El Nuevo mundo descubierto por Cristóbal Colón* in the context of a discussion of the propagandistic function of baroque theater, especially the so-called *comedia histórica*, see Moisés Castillo's article "Lope de Vega, inventor de América: El Nuevo Mundo descubierto por Cristóbal Colón."

8.   *Peribáñez y el comendador de Ocaña* (I, 41–65) provides excellent examples of Lope's construction of rural spaces and his frequent use of economic (agrarian) terminology in his *dramas rurales*.

9.   See Castillo, *(A)wry Views* (especially 125–30). See also Michael Gerli's "El retablo de las maravillas: Cervantes's 'Arte Nuevo de deshacer comedias.'"

10.   See also Castillo and Spadaccini, "El antiutopismo en *Los trabajos de Persiles y Sigismunda*: Cervantes y el cervantismo actual." This line of interpretation of *Persiles* as a countercultural text has recently engendered several books, including Childers's *Transnational Cervantes* (2006) and Armstrong-Roche's *Cervantes' Epic Novel: Empire, Religion, and the Dream Life of Heroes in* Persiles (2009).

11.   I would like to thank Carmen Moreno-Nuño, contributor to this volume and the author of *Las huellas de la Guerra Civil: Mito y trauma en la narrativa de la España democrática* (2006), for guiding me through the park and for discussing this poem with me. My comments here are, in part, a result of our conversations.

Works Cited

Adorno, Theodor and Max Horkheimer. *Dialectic of the Enlightenment*. New York: Continuum, 1998.

Anonymous. *The Olive Tree/Federico*. Unpublished.

Armstrong-Roche, Michael. *Cervantes' Epic Novel: Empire, Religion, and the Dream Life of Heroes in Persiles*. Toronto: University of Toronto Press, 2009.

Barthes, Roland. *Mythologies*. Trans. Annette Lavers. New York: Hill and Wang, 1972.

Burningham, Bruce. *Tilting Cervantes: Baroque Reflections on Postmodern Culture*. Nashville: Vanderbilt University Press, 2008.

Castillo, David. *(A)Wry Views: Anamorphosis, Cervantes, and the Early Picaresque.* West Lafayette, IN: Purdue University Press, 2001.

———. "Horror (Vacui): The Baroque Condition." *Hispanic Baroques: Reading Cultures in Context.* Eds. Nicholas Spadaccini and Luis Martín-Estudillo. Nashville: Vanderbilt University Press, 2005.

Castillo, David, and Nicholas Spadaccini. "El antiutopismo en *Los trabajos de Persiles y Sigismunda*: Cervantes y el cervantismo actual." *Cervantes* 20 (2000): 115–31.

Castillo, Moisés. "Lope de Vega, inventor de América: El Nuevo Mundo descubierto por Cristóbal Colón." *Bulletin of the Comediantes* 54, no. 1 (2002): 57–90.

Cervantes, Miguel de. "El retablo de las maravillas." *Entremeses.* Ed. Nicholas Spadaccini. Madrid: Cátedra, 1982.

———. *Los trabajos de Persiles y Sigismunda.* Ed. Carlos Romero Muñoz. Madrid: Cátedra, 1997.

Childers, William. *Transnational Cervantes.* Toronto: University of Toronto Press, 2006.

Cosgrove, Denis. "Spectacle and Society: Landscape as Theater in Premodern and Postmodern Cities." *Understanding Ordinary Landscapes.* Eds. Paul Groth and Todd Bressi. New Haven: Yale University Press, 1997.

Debord, Guy. *Society of the Spectacle.* London: Rebel Press, 2005.

Diccionario del uso del español. Ed. María Moliner. Vol. 2. Madrid: Gredos, 1998.

Díez-Borque, José María. *El teatro en el siglo XVII.* Madrid: Taurus, 1988.

———. *Sociología de la comedia española del siglo XVII.* Madrid: Cátedra, 1976.

El espinazo del diablo. Directed by Guillermo del Toro. El Deseo, 2001.

Fuenteovejuna. By Lope de Vega. Radiotelevisión Española (RTVE), 1980.

García Lorca, Federico. *Poeta en Nueva York.* México: Porrúa, 1986.

———. *Antología Poética.* Ed. Mauro Armiño. Madrid: Biblioteca Edaf, 2007.

Gerli, Michael. "*El retablo de las maravillas*: Cervantes's 'Arte nuevo de deshacer comedias.'" *Hispanic Review* 57 (1989): 477–92.

Hobbes, Thomas. *Leviathan.* London: Penguin Classics, 1985.

Jackson, John B. *A Sense of Place, a Sense of Time.* New Haven, CT: Yale University Press, 1994.

Lacan, Jacques. *The Four Fundamental Concepts of Psychoanalysis.* Ed. Jacques-Alain Miller. Trans. Alan Sheridan. New York: Norton, 1981.

Lope de Vega, Félix. *El Nuevo Mundo descubierto por Cristóbal Colón.* Eds. J. Lemartinel and Charles Minguet. Lille: Presses Universitaires de Lille, 1980.

———. *Fuenteovejuna.* Ed. Juan María Marín. Madrid: Cátedra, 2001.

———. *Peribáñez y el comendador de Ocaña.* Ed. Juan María Marín. Madrid: Cátedra, 1995.

Maravall, José Antonio. *La cultura del barroco: Análisis de una estructura histórica.* Barcelona: Ariel, 1975.

Moreno-Nuño, Carmen. *Las huellas de la Guerra Civil: Mito y trauma en la narrativa de la España democrática.* Madrid: Libertarias, 2006.

Pocahontas. Directors Mike Gabriel, Eric Goldberg. Walt Disney Home Video, 1995.

Rainey, Reuben. "Hallowed Grounds and Rituals of Remembrance: Union Regimental Monuments at Gettysburg." *Understanding Ordinary Landscapes*. Eds. Paul Groth and Todd Bressi. New Haven: Yale University Press, 1997.

R. de la Flor, Fernando. *Barroco: Representación e ideología en el mundo hispánico (1580–1680)*. Madrid: Cátedra, 2002.

———. "On the Notion of a Melancholic Baroque." *Hispanic Baroques: Reading Cultures in Context*. Eds. Nicholas Spadaccini and Luis Martín-Estudillo. Nashville: Vanderbilt University Press, 2005.

Schama, Simon. *Landscape and Memory*. London: Harper Collins, 1995.

Sheldrake, Philip. *Spaces for the Sacred: Place, Memory, and Identity*. Baltimore: Johns Hopkins University Press, 2001.

Tuan, Yi-Fu. *Topophilia: A Study of Environmental Perception, Attitudes, and Values*. New York: Columbia University Press, 1990.

Vilas, Manuel. "Lorca Reloaded." *ABCD*. January 2, 2010.

Wilson, Diana de Armas. *Allegories of Love: Cervantes's* "Persiles and Sigismunda." Princeton: Princeton University Press, 1991.

Žižek, Slavoj. *The Sublime Object of Ideology*. London: Verso, 1989.

◆ 2

"Granada": Race and Place
in Early Modern Spain

William Childers

For María Soledad Carrasco Urgoiti, *in memoriam.*

On January 1, 1492, Fernando and Isabel, the "Catholic Monarchs," took possession of the Kingdom of Granada, until then a Muslim country, the last remnant of Al-Andalus. In 1610, their great-grandson Philip III expelled the descendants of its inhabitants, the Granadine Moriscos. Thus the full integration of this physical space as part of Spain and, parallel to it, the exclusion of its autochthonous population as emphatically *not* Spaniards took a little over one hundred years. This chapter analyzes the process whereby this double outcome was obtained. In the cultural sphere, I argue that the literary trend known as *maurophilia*, though often viewed as a failed defense of the Moriscos, can be seen in large part as an effort to give the newly acquired territory a glorious past that would incorporate it fully into the emerging Spanish nation. The connection of this positive image with their Moorish ancestors to the average Morisco was tenuous at best, as numerous archival documents demonstrate. After the invasion, the native population lived the contradictory situation of all colonized subjects: on the one hand, as a vanquished enemy, viewed with suspicion and kept under vigilance and control; on the other, as an economic resource, in demand by the owners of the means of production. Their place of origin served as a guarantee of the quality of their workmanship at the same time as it stigmatized them as "disloyal." In the legal arena, a considerable number of individuals and families fought successfully to differentiate themselves from the Moriscos *of Granada*, marked for their low status. In some cases, however, they simultaneously claimed that their ancestors were noble Moors of the Nasrid kingdom. This participation in the semi-mythical past by means of which Granada was being integrated into Spain allowed this minority-within-a-minority to remain as a vestige of former glories when the rest of their community was expelled.

The place name "Granada," then, had different meanings and different values, depending on whether it referred to territory or people and, in the latter case, depending on whether these were people of legend or flesh and blood. But these variations are far from arbitrary; they are instead signposts of a colonizing process that was already imaginatively underway in the early fifteenth century, as the *romances fronterizos* attest, and that reached its zenith with the 1610 expulsion. The territory, retroactively celebrated as the missing piece that, once conquered, made the entire peninsula Christian, thereby became metonymic for the nation as a whole. It stood for victory. But the "race" of people born there before 1492, though emblematic of the struggle to win that place, was only a historical remainder. They stood for defeat. In the century-long process whereby the defeated were expunged and the spoils converted to a national treasure house of memory, numerous players had their role, including the state, the former population of Granada, its new population, and members of the Church hierarchy. In this complex process of negotiation, certain people and things associated with the place name "Granada" were preserved as part of "Spain" and others were cut off, lost, or destroyed.

In the axiology of place, the history of "Granada" is special, though not unique. It is the nature of colonies to be simultaneously loved and resented by those who have taken them by force and who have imposed their own political, social, and cultural order on a population that inevitably includes many who resist and many who collaborate (and some who do both, one openly, the other secretly). We love that which we learn to think of as "ours," that which legitimizes our claim, while our resentment is reserved for the irreducibly "foreign" element, which reminds us that we are usurpers. But however tempting it may be to think of this as a simple distinction between the place and its people, we must remember that people make places, differentiating the natural continuum of space and conferring proper names and histories on delimited segments of the earth's surface (Tuan 8–33, 161–78). So when we invade and take over a new territory, we also appropriate its past, and with that past a set of relations to its current population. The dividing line between what is theirs and what is ours can never simply reject the people as a whole and embrace the land that has been taken from them. It must, of necessity, traverse the population as well, separating them into the "good" colonized (sometimes termed "collaboration-ists") and the "bad" colonized (members of "the resistance," or "insurgents"). One thing the colonial process in Granada reveals particularly well is that the vestige among the colonized that will become part of the nation, in addition to making an overt display of loyalty to the new order, must establish an originary link to the place, must form a bridge between the mythologized past and the living present of this newly acquired territory. The Morisco elite who assimi-lated into Castilian society over the course of the sixteenth century succeeded in forming such a bridge.

A word about the relation among religion, ethnicity, and race is in order. Certainly religious difference played a prominent role in defining the border-line between those who belonged to, and those who were excluded from, the Spanish nation. The Christian-Muslim distinction was, quite simply, the clear-est available marker for distinguishing between the two communities. It there-fore became invested with tremendous significance, though the intensity of this investment is not a manifestation of profound spirituality or fervent conviction on either side, but rather part of a political process. Unlike indigenous peoples in European colonies in the Americas, Africa, and Asia, here the colonized did not display an immediately visible difference in physical appearance.[1] Eth-nicity set them apart in everyday life, and though the monarchy strove to elimi-nate such practices as veiling, bathing, and speaking Arabic, the entire set of practices differentiating the Moriscos was too all-encompassing to legislate out of existence. At the same time, however, as religious difference underwrote ethnicity through perceived vestiges of Islam in Morisco cultural practices, it also formed the basis of a "racial" distinction. Moriscos were subject to cer-tain specific restrictions and obligations, but the legal definition of Morisco depended on who one's parents were, and when they converted to Christianity. If they switched sides and sought baptism before the conquest of Granada, they could be declared *cristianos viejos de moros*, and their descendants in perpe-tuity would not legally be Moriscos at all. If they were baptized before the forced conversions of 1500, this also implied they had chosen allegiance to the Crown, and they could at least be declared exempt from some restrictions, even if they were still *cristianos nuevos*. Thus the religious difference served as a genealogical marker with legal implications for status. Unless we are will-ing to limit the use of the term "race" to differentiation by skin color alone, we must accept that the Morisco-Old Christian distinction was racial, even though ethno-religious background provided its original basis.[2]

Maurophilia and Territorialization

"Maurophilia," a term introduced by Georges Cirot in 1938, refers to the six-teenth-century literary idealization of Moorish nobles of the late medieval Nas-rid kingdom of Granada, usually in the period leading up to the conquest. In maurophile texts, the Moor is gallant and bold, with emphasis placed on the extravagant elegance of his adornments. His clothes are embroidered with silk and his weapons and accoutrements decorated with silver, gold, and jewels. When he rides out into the countryside he looks more like he is going to a gala at court than to do battle with Christians. He is sensual and passionate, as much a lover as a fighter, and he composes songs for his beloved that he sings as he rides along. Life at the Nasrid court is depicted as a continual contest in gallantry, with rivalry for women, or simply for the reputation for being the most elegant and admired, taking precedence over practical and military con-siderations. Similarly, though Moorish knights fight with Christians, these en-counters are invariably for honor, without strategic military value, and no loot or ransom is taken. They either duel in single combat or fight in small group skirmishes. The Moor's relations with his Christian enemies are respectful, even friendly. References to the Muslim faith are almost nonexistent, though place names of the Kingdom of Granada abound, including the names of far-flung towns and cities, as well as the streets, plazas, and gates of the capital it-self. The most vividly drawn settings are the Alhambra, seat of courtly intrigue, and the Vega of Granada, locale par excellence of the duels and skirmishes of Moors and Christians. In the end, the most admirable characters willingly sub-mit to Christian domination, either by freely chosen conversion or recognition of the moral superiority of their Christian rivals.[3]

At its height, from the 1580s through the first years of the seventeenth cen-tury, the maurophile trend became a craze, proliferating in three genres simul-taneously. The *Romancero nuevo* passed through a period in which most new ballads were of this type, including the lamentations *à clef* of the young Lope de Vega, banished to Valencia for his illicit affair with Elena Osorio, and for libeling her family. During the same period, several prose romances appeared, beginning with the anonymous *El Abencerraje* (earliest known version, 1561), continuing with Ginés Pérez de Hita's *Guerras civiles de Granada* (1595), and including Mateo Alemán's tale *Ozmín y Daraja*, incorporated in the first part of *Guzmán de Alfarache* (1599). Considering that a version of *El Abencerraje* was included in editions of *La Diana* after 1561, this means that maurophile texts were present in three of the top five best-selling works of prose fiction of the Golden Age, as Keith Whinnom has observed. Finally, maurophile works also enjoyed success in the theater, with Lope de Vega alone contributing at least eight plays in the genre, the most successful of which was *El remedio en la desdicha* (circa 1602).

All the major texts of the maurophile cannon were written in the second half of the sixteenth century or the first years of the seventeenth, coinciding with the period of the Morisco crisis. But rather than focusing on the Moriscos, maurophile texts are about the Moors of Granada a century before. In the period immediately preceding the beginning of the trend, emerging historical narratives of the Spanish nation began to define Granada as the last territory that had to be recovered for the "Reconquest" to be complete (Bernabé Pons).[4] When the maurophile craze reached its peak, Granada was still a relatively new territory, without a Christian past. That a body of literature should emerge toward the end of the century celebrating Granada and congratulating the Spanish Crown on its capture ought not to surprise us. That the status of the Moriscos and their integration into Spanish society continued to be a problem was not necessarily related to the maurophile texts in the minds of many who wrote or enjoyed them, though obviously in historical terms they are at least parallel phenomena, two ongoing consequences of the invasion and occupation of Granada.

The maurophile genre has its roots in the medieval *romances fronterizos*, frontier ballads, which narrated events in the ongoing, low-level conflict along the Christian-Moorish border: skirmishes, sieges, and so forth. In fact, Pérez de Hita's great historical novel, the first part of the *Guerras civiles de Granada*, uses a prose narrative to frame a collection of old frontier ballads along with new so-called Morisco ballads composed by Lope and others, including Pérez de Hita himself. Indeed, there is significant continuity between the frontier ballads and maurophile literature, such that the latter can be called to some degree a nostalgic recreation of the former. Interestingly, though, the element of nostalgia was always already present in the frontier ballads, taking the form of a particular theme to which these poems return repeatedly: the sadness of a Moorish ruler who receives the news that a city or fortress has been taken by the Christians. Several of the best-known frontier ballads take this as their theme, among them two concerning the siege and conquest of Antequera; another, the most famous of this type, on the taking of Alhama; another on Boabdil's reaction to the news that Fernando and Isabel had arrived in the Vega of Granada, swearing to remain camped there until they conquered the kingdom; and a final, poignant ballad in which Boabdil sorrowfully contemplates Granada from the Sierra Nevada as he withdraws into exile in the Alpujarras. The trajectory of these five poems re-creates the gradual conquest of the Kingdom of Granada, a process of territorialization in stages, in which the Muslim-dominated area gets smaller and smaller.[5]

These scenes deserve our attention, as they are the earliest examples of the sympathetic identification with the last Moors of Granada, the affective foundation of all maurophile texts. In them, the Christian audience paradoxically enjoys its victory by imagining how terrible it must have felt to lose what they have won. With the Christian gaze turned around and the landscape contemplated through the eyes of the Moorish king, the newly acquired places are bathed in an atmosphere of anticipatory nostalgia. Already the ballads on the loss of Alhama and the arrival of the Christian army in the Vega de Granada look forward to the final outcome of the war. Through the tragic figure of Boabdil, the last Moorish king of Spain, the Christian audience vicariously identifies with the past of these new possessions, but that identification is concentrated in a single individual, and the loss suffered at the hands of the Christian invaders is reduced to the personal emotion of the ruler.

In the justly celebrated "Romance de la pérdida de Alhama" the Moorish king is a fairy-tale figure, who, upon receiving the news of the loss of this key fortress, burns the letters and has the messenger killed: "Cartas le fueron venidas que Alhama era ganada. / Las cartas echó en el fuego, y al mensajero matara. / *¡Ay de mi Alhama!*" (lines 3–4, qtd. in Martínez Inhiesta, translations are my own unless otherwise noted) (Letters arrived saying Alhama was won. / He threw the letters in the fire, and killed the messenger. / *Oh, my Alhama!*). His dramatized emotional outcry, "*¡Ay de mi Alhama!*" echoes throughout the poem as if floating in some timeless, disembodied evocation of anguish. Moreover, although the poem purports to narrate from the Muslim point of view, the news he receives is that "Alhama era *ganada*,"—that is, Alhama has been *won* (i.e. by the Christians). This seemingly insignificant lapse, in which the outcome is conceived from the Christian point of view, confirms that the king is a mere puppet, a mask the audience puts on to imaginatively recreate the feeling of what it might have been like to be present at the moment of conquest, when *we* arrived and took this land.

In what can be described as both conceptually and chronologically the last frontier ballad, Boabdil's gaze serves to memorialize the topography of his loss:

Desde una cuesta muy alta Granada se parecía;
volvió a mirar a Granada, desta manera decía:
"¡Oh Granada la famosa, mi consuelo y alegría!
¡oh mi alto *Albaicín* y mi rica *Alcaicería*!,

¡oh mi *Alhambra* y *Alijares* y *mezquita* de valía!,
¡mis *baños*, *huertas* y *ríos*, donde holgar me solía!;
¿quién os ha de mí apartado que jamás yo os vería?
Ahora te estoy mirando desde lejos, ciudad mía;
mas presto no te veré, pues ya de ti me partía.
¡Oh rueda de la fortuna, loco es quien en ti fía,
que ayer era rey famoso y hoy no tengo cosa mía!"
("Romance del Rey Chico que perdió a Granada," lines 10–20, qtd. in Martínez
Iniesta, emphasis added)

(From a high hill he could see Granada; / he looked once more upon Granada,
and spoke thus: / "Oh, Granada the famous, my comfort and joy! / Oh, my high
Albaicín and my rich Alcaicería! / Oh, my Alhambra and Alijares and the priceless
Mosque! / My public baths, gardens, and rivers, where I used to take my rest! / Who
has taken you from me so I might never see you again? / Now I contemplate you
from afar, my city; / but soon I will see you no more, since I am departing from you.
/ Oh, wheel of fortune, he who trusts in you is mad, / for yesterday I was a famous
king, and today I have nothing of my own!")

Here Boabdil is already absent—"te estoy mirando desde lejos," (I am
looking at you from afar)—so his gaze records only the moment of his own
disappearance, leaving behind, like an invisible film overlaid onto the landscape, the memory trace of his having been its ruler in a now legendary past to
which he is consigned. His sorrowful "last sigh" makes that past permanently
available to the new Christian inhabitants of the land.

The other side of the coin to the anguish at the loss of territory expressed in
these ballads is the well-known dialogue between the Christian king Don Juan
and a Muslim informant, Abenámar. Don Juan is fascinated by the beauty of
the Alhambra, Torres Bermejas, and the Generalife, and asks Abenámar about
them. Along with the place names, he supplies detailed information about the
extravagant cost of the workmanship. The Christian king then offers to marry
a Granada suddenly personified as a woman, expressing the territorial impulse
as erotic desire. Granada's response makes clear that the king's desire is inspired by his rivalry with the Moorish ruler: "Casada soy, rey don Juan, casada
soy, que no viuda; / el moro que a mí me tiene muy grande bien me quería"
("Abenámar, Abenámar," lines 22–23) (I am married, King Don Juan, married,
not a widow; / the Moor who has me, loved me very much).[6] In the frontier
ballads, then, the invasion of Granada is imagined as a process of one man, the
Christian king, conquering beautiful places belonging to his male rival as one
might take a beautiful woman, producing in the process an erotic play of desire

and nostalgia. Indeed, the longing for Granada is a classic instance of Girardian triangular desire, in which the existence of the rival is what gives the object of desire its heightened value.[7]

The entire maurophile genre can be read as an *amplification* of a single, poignant moment of desire and loss preserved in the frontier ballads. Thus in *El Abencerraje*, Abendarráez, defeated in battle, sighs so despondently that Narváez, the victor, entreats him to tell his story. When he admits that being taken captive means he will lose his beautiful Moorish lover Jarifa, Narváez magnanimously grants him his freedom so he can return to her. From this moment forward, as Israel Burshatin brilliantly pointed out, Narváez controls the destinies of the other characters, acting as a kind of author within the story. Over the objections of Jarifa's father he brokers their marriage, thereby consigning the couple definitively to the innocent past of their youthful passion. This story functions as an allegorization of the frontier ballads, with the lost world of pre-1492 Granada nostalgically evoked for the reader and then permanently preserved as the image of a passionate adolescence to which mature Christian moral control and sense of duty become the continuation. The first part of *Guerras civiles de Granada* is an expanded, novelized version of the world of the *romances fronterizos*, but with the erotic element of the Christian conquerors' desire for Granada literalized in the courtly *galanteos* of the Moorish knights. At the end of Pérez de Hita's novel, in fact, the entire world of Nasrid Granada is transformed into a Christian Granada in which continuity with the Hispano-Arabic past is guaranteed through the religious conversion of all the most admirable Moorish knights.

Through these narratives, then, the geography of the Kingdom of Granada is imbued with an affective sense, a set of deep emotions, imaginatively attributed to those who lived there before the Christian conquest, to which they give Spaniards vicarious access. Through maurophile texts Granada's Moorish past is made available to them as part of their own past; it becomes possible to emotionally inhabit it just as they already could do with the Castilian past of Conde Fernán González and El Cid Ruy Díaz de Vivar. It is crucial to recall that the sixteenth century is a period in which both general and local histories proliferated in Spain, combining archival evidence with legend and pure invention, and that regions and towns strove to outdo one another in fanciful tales of past glories. Granada, to become fully part of Spain, needed such tales of its glories of days gone by, and the maurophile trend fulfilled that function beautifully.[8]

The setting par excellence for these vicarious emotions is the Alhambra, which is thus constituted, as Barbara Fuchs points out in *Exotic Nation*, as a *lieu de mémoire* (site of memory), referring to the concept developed by the

French historian Pierre Nora to discuss the process of memorialization through which national history is constructed (47–51). Certainly the Alhambra satisfies Nora's basic criterion that "they are *lieux* in three senses of the word—material, symbolic, and functional" (18–19). Its material reality is a powerful physical presence in Granada to this day, and the chief tourist attraction of Spain. Though tourists perhaps visit the site more for its symbolic value, were it not for its sheer material beauty they would not do so. Its functionality as a fortress in sixteenth-century Spain was crucial. Indeed, it was to the fact that the insurgents were unable to take the Alhambra that many attributed the failure of the 1568 rebellion. And its symbolic resonances, concentrated in the image of Boabdil's surrender of the keys to the red fortress as the moment in which Granada became part of the Crown of Castile, are many. Above all, they point, Janus-like, to both the Moorish past and the Christian future. As Fuchs persuasively shows, the meaning of the Alhambra was contested between seeing it as a reminder of the glorious past of Nasrid rule, and as a symbol of the triumph of the Catholic Monarchs, though some, such as Francisco Núñez Muley, argued it could be both (47–50). This understanding of the hybrid nature of the *lieux de mémoire* is very much in keeping with Nora's formulation of the concept as a site of multiple meanings:

> If we accept that the most fundamental purpose of the *lieu de mémoire* is to stop time, to block the work of forgetting, to establish a state of things, to immortalize death, to materialize the immaterial . . . all of this in order to capture a maximum of meaning in the fewest of signs, it is also clear that *lieux de mémoire* only exist because of their capacity for metamorphosis, an endless recycling of their meaning and an unpredictable proliferation of their ramifications. (19)

But when Fuchs goes on to argue that maurophile literature in general is constituted as such a *lieu de mémoire*, her use of the term is comparatively flattened, since she repeatedly insists these texts be understood as advocating the integration of the Moriscos as a whole into Spanish society, in contrast to the polemical anti-Morisco texts also circulating at the time, which she terms "maurophobic." To some extent, this overlooks their materiality as texts that circulated among readers or were recited or performed in a range of settings before many types of audiences. And it is also to prematurely foreclose on the discussion of their functionality, since to call the Alhambra or maurophile literature *lieux de mémoire* does not in itself clarify their relationship to the Moriscos who remained on the Iberian Peninsula throughout the long sixteenth century. Rather, the use of this concept only *opens* the question of what was being memorialized there, by whom, and for what purpose. While some descendants of Granadine Moors were able to claim status as a result, the Moriscos of Granada were for the most part constituted as a *catégorie maudite*.

Though Fuchs views maurophile literature as a defense of the Moriscos, her most important contribution in *Exotic Nation* lies elsewhere. She places maurophilia in a broad cultural context, examining the underlying set of cultural practices, dating from the thirteenth century, that make a positive representation of Moorishness possible. Drawing mainly on three specific aspects of material culture—architecture, fashion, and horsemanship—she argues for the existence of what she terms a Moorish *habitus*: a set of customs historically derived from Hispano-Arabic culture, but which had become so widespread by the sixteenth century that they were no longer consciously marked as alien. She takes the term "habitus" from Pierre Bourdieu, who posited it as a way of accounting for the fact that social behavior follows rules of which individuals are not necessarily conscious. Analogous to the competence of a native speaker (especially as that concept was employed by Chomsky), the habitus is "the durably installed generative principle of regulated improvisations" (Bourdieu 78), that is, a capacity members of a given society have to respond appropriately in situations they have not previously experienced. Bourdieu's habitus is thus a dynamic concept, useful for analyzing social interaction and behavior (72–95). Fuchs's Moorish habitus needs to be viewed as it functioned for those who were actually engaged in the construction of Spanish identities, not as a pure, fixed abstraction. Only then we will see how subtly maurophilia and islamophobia interacted and interpenetrated, and how the literary inventions she so insightfully interprets functioned as strategic interventions, both in their production and their reception. Yes, appreciation of *mudéjar* craftsmanship and enthusiasm for love poems about gallant Moors and their ladies belonged to the habitus of sixteenth-century Spaniards. But the ability to deny that these attitudes had any bearing whatsoever on the status of flesh-and-blood Moriscos was part of that habitus, too.

Consider the case of three nuns in a convent in Huete (Cuenca) entertaining themselves one afternoon in 1584 by singing a Morisco ballad about Jarifa (ADC, Inquisición, Libro 325, folios 351r–353v). Suddenly, "Hernandico," a Morisco from Granada who is working, unnoticed, in a corner, chimes in, declaring his enthusiasm for such songs: "se holgaba mucho de oír aquel nombre porque era su parienta" (he always enjoyed hearing that name since she was his relation). He is claiming, in effect, that the maurophile element of what Fuchs refers to as a "Moorish habitus" confers status on him. Not so, insist the nuns, putting him in his place: "que no se preciase de tan mala parienta pues estaba en el infierno" (he should not take pride in having such a bad relation since she was in hell), whereas "tú si te quieres salvar puedes y ella no" (you can be saved if you wish, but she can't be). By which last comment the nuns meant, I take it, he can be saved if he accepts his social inferiority and their tutelage. Echoing a widespread medieval belief that each of the three religions could lead to salvation, Hernandico answers that whether Jarifa is in hell or not depends on her works ("según sus obras"). The nuns denounce him to the Inquisition, an act that, to be sure, is also a part of the habitus of sixteenth-century Spain.

During the same period in which the attractive, idealized image of the Moors of Granada reached the height of its popularity, facilitating Spaniards' identification with the new territory as part of their nation, the descendants of those Moors were stripped of their homes and property, forced into exile, and constituted as the lowest rung of society. Admittedly, the most extreme mani-festations of this repression came after the armed rebellion known as the War of the Alpujarras, instigated by a group of Moriscos in December 1568. To a significant extent, however, this rebellion was provoked by pressures emanat-ing from above. On the one hand, the all-important silk industry was being taxed out of existence by Philip II. On the other, the newly empowered civil administration, under its president Pedro de Deza, brought increased pressure on the Moriscos to assimilate.[9] Ironically, the same mentality that produced the prototypical maurophilia of the frontier ballads awakened a desire for plunder in the ancestral memories of all able-bodied men who could afford a horse and arms, and thousands descended on the Kingdom of Granada, sacking its towns, including those that had not rebelled, for anything of value. An initially small, contained insurrection thereby spread throughout the region, which encom-passed present-day Granada, Almería, and Málaga. Deza used the rebellion as a pretext for a hard-line policy that led to the full-scale deportation of the Moriscos in the winter of 1570–71. Those accused of participating in the rebel-lion, along with thousands who had not rebelled, especially women and chil-dren, were literally enslaved, and sold in marketplaces all over Andalusia and Castile, generally ending up as household servants. The rest were herded off to Andalusia, La Mancha and points farther north to be exploited by local authori-ties and nobles. Since more Moriscos remained behind than the Crown initially believed, additional deportations were organized in 1573–74 and 1584.[10] Yet a Morisco middle class would soon reconstitute itself, both in Granada and in other parts of Andalusia and Castile, and within that middle class a significant number of families successfully integrated into Castilian society. Because of the racial stigma attached to the category "Morisco del Reino de Granada," those members of the Morisco elite and middle class who could do so used every legal resource at their command to distance themselves from that status.

The *Pleitos de Cristiano Viejo*

Because members of their group had participated in an armed rebellion against the Crown, the Granadine Moriscos were singled out for a series of especially harsh restrictions. They could not carry arms and were forced to live in the towns where they were registered. They were not allowed even to set foot outside the town limits without written authorization in the form of a "passport." They could not live more than one family to a house or gather publicly in groups of more than three. Every Sunday they were required to attend a special Mass in which roll would be called, and they were periodically lined up by local authorities, who made sure none were absent. These measures created a perception of them as a wretched group, suspected of plotting against the king, and the controls were considered necessary security measures as well as punishment for their transgressions.

In general, the arrival of Moriscos from the Kingdom of Granada in cities and towns that had significant *mudéjar* communities was not greeted with enthusiasm by their former coreligionists (Tapia Sánchez 310–25). Under these circumstances, established *mudéjar* communities who were not Moriscos from the Kingdom of Granada jealously guarded privileges that had been granted to them by the Catholic Monarchs, including the right to bear arms, to move from one place to another without passport or special authorization, and exemption from the *farda*, a tax dating back to the Nasrid kingdom, to which only Granadine Moriscos were subject. Among the specific groups that had won from the Crown the privileges of *cristianos viejos* were the Moriscos of the Cinco Villas (Five Towns) of Calatrava (Villarubia de los Ojos, Almagro, Aldea del Rey, Bolaños, and Daimiel) and those of Hornachos.[11] They strenuously objected to being lumped together with the newcomers, as this clearly resulted in a reduction in their status. The most frequent type of incident that dramatized this situation was their being arrested for wearing a sword in public. Such arrests led to full-scale lawsuits in which the *mudéjares* defended their status against the public perception of them as belonging in the same category as the newcomers from Granada.

The difference in legal status between Moriscos from the Kingdom of Granada and those who could claim to belong to other groups led to numerous legal challenges, many of which are preserved in Spanish archives to this day. When the Crown attempted a "definitive" deportation of all remaining Moriscos from Granada in 1584, an elevated number of such challenges originated from those who simply said that "the decree does not apply to me" (el bando no va conmigo). As the scope of the issues surrounding the application of the category became apparent, the Crown created a unique jurisdiction just for those who, despite being classified as Moriscos at some point by some authority, claimed the rights and privileges of *cristianos viejos*. From September 1585 until January 1596, all such cases had to be reviewed by the Consejo de Población in Madrid, including cases already resolved in favor of the plaintiff. Hundreds of cases poured in from all over the Crown of Castile, not just the Kingdom of Granada, and more than three hundred are still preserved, in whole or in part, along with all the documentation concerning the administration of this issue, in the papers of the Consejo de Población in the Archivo General de Simancas (AGS). Most often, the explicit motivation for the legal defense was to be able to bear arms in public—carrying a sword had become the degree zero of masculinity in early modern Spain. The next most frequent reason was the right to remain in Granada or to have freedom of movement in general. Some wanted to avoid paying the *farda*, or simply insisted that their names be stricken from the rolls of Moriscos kept by the town hall or the parish church. In one sense or another, whether out of a practical motive such as having freedom of movement or not paying a tax, or for purely symbolic reasons, all of these lawsuits had as their overarching goal the enhancement of the individual's status and that of his family, including his extended family. When one individual successfully defended his privileges, his cousins would often initiate proceedings based on his favorable verdict. For all concerned, it was first and foremost a matter of slipping out of the category of the wretched, of avoiding the place-and-race-based label "Morisco from the Kingdom of Granada."[12]

The justifications invoked can be conveniently divided into the four main types: (1) those who acknowledged that they descended from Muslims from Granada, but who claimed the privileges of old Christians based on loyalty and service to the Crown, usually demonstrated by the date of their ancestors' conversion (before the conquest of 1492 or before the general conversion of 1500–1501); (2) those who claimed to be descended from Muslims from somewhere else, including Berbería (Morocco), Tunisia, Algiers, Sub-Saharan Africa, or Turkey, or from *mudéjares antiguos* of Castile, especially Hornachos or the Cinco Villas of Calatrava; (3) those who claimed to be descended from old Christians (at least on their fathers' side), most of whom were the product of mixed marriages, though a significant number claimed to be *illegitimate* sons of old Christians with Moriscas, including a handful who said their fathers were priests, and some who insisted both their parents were old Christians and the whole thing was a mistake; (4) orphans who claimed not to know who their biological parents were, but who had been raised as Christians. In reading over this list of justifications for claiming non-Morisco-from-Granada status, we may well smile at some of them. To publicly proclaim oneself the bastard son of a Morisca and an old Christian who seduced (or raped) her before (or after) she was married, apparently just to be allowed to carry a sword! But we should keep in mind that almost all the lawsuits preserved in the papers of the Consejo de Población in the Archivo General de Simancas are there because the "Morisco" plaintiff had them sent in order to justify his claim, and most include favorable judgments from local officials. These were considered entirely legitimate reasons to declare a person, even one who had been raised in a Morisco household and displayed all the characteristics of the ethnoreligious minority, to be *cristiano viejo*, or at least to have the equivalent "rights and privileges."

For legal purposes, then, the Moriscos of Granada constituted a race. It appears from this example that the primitive racial categories of early modern Europe (before the establishment of biologically based racial theory) were hybrids of religious distinction and place of origin. One of the interesting things that this corpus demonstrates is that racial categories come to be established as much in terms of who is excluded from them as in terms of who is included, and especially in terms of who successfully claims *not* to belong to the category. The purpose of these lawsuits was to demonstrate that one was *not* a member of the despised, marginalized race, "Morisco from the Kingdom of Granada." Any other racial or genealogical category would do, as is demonstrated by the cases of those who claimed to be descended from black slaves, illicit relations with priests, or Muslim converts from North Africa. The point was to disassociate oneself from the *catégorie maudite*. Most, though themselves born in Granada, claimed to be autochthonous from somewhere else because their parents and grandparents were from there. These other places ranged from the *España profunda* of blood purity, such as the Montaña de León, Salamanca, Medina del Campo, Vizcaya, Zaragoza, or Galicia, to the most absolutely and unambiguously Muslim locales, including Turkey and Morocco. In a few cases, young men were classed by local officials as Moriscos from Granada simply because their old Christian parents had lived for a few years in Granada and then returned to Murcia, Toledo, or Córdoba, but *they* had been born in the place of suspicious alterity. The problematic nature of being from Granada stems from colonial ambiguity: neither Muslim enough for one's presence in Spain and conversion to Christianity to stand as proof of one's loyalty, nor Christian enough to constitute a guarantee of never having been tainted by contact with the undesirable.

One important group in particular, however, did claim to be fully entitled to old Christian status, and yet at the same time proclaimed themselves autochthonous descendants of the Granadine Moors: the *cristianos viejos de moros*, grandchildren and great-grandchildren of those who voluntarily converted to Christianity before January 1, 1492 (several of these conversions literally took place in the last week of December, 1491). To a much greater extent than has heretofore been understood, this group is at the center of the *maurophile* trend, and their legitimacy as old Christians forms the slender bridge uniting the Moorish past with the living present of early modern Spain. They alone fully unite the territory of Granada, understood as a *Spanish* territory, with the Granadine Moors of literary fame. Their exact number cannot be calculated, though it would appear to be in the hundreds. This is so in part because several generations have passed, and with each generation the number of descendants grows. Undoubtedly some of these cases are fraudulent, though my view is that most are not. The lawsuits preserved in Simancas often contain transcriptions of previous lawsuits won by their parents and grandparents, sometimes as far back as 1518. Each generation successfully defended its rights before various tribunals. Often there are eyewitness reports of those who say they remember seeing the ancestor in question arrive in the Catholic Monarchs' camp at Santa Fe to request baptism. Occasionally there are transcriptions of documents from 1491 or before, in which Fernando and Isabel grant the status of *cristiano viejo* to a specific individual and his descendants in perpetuity, in recognition of his having converted to Christianity and served them in the Conquest of Granada. At least fifteen of the plaintiffs chose to request transcripts of such documents directly from the Archivo General de Simancas in order to accredit their claims.[13] Beginning in 1610, when the expulsion of the Moriscos from Granada was decreed, the Count of Salazar, who was charged with carrying out the expulsion, tried, for the most part in vain, to expel these families. In 1614, the Consejo de Estado finally gave up on pursuing them, and declared that those whose lawsuits were still pending should not be disturbed any longer.[14] Their descendants, presumably, remain in Spain to this day.

Maurophile Literature and the Negotiation of Identity

Two of the most important maurophile texts, Pérez de Hita's *Guerras civiles de Granada* (1595) and Mateo Alemán's *Ozmín y Daraja*, an interpolated story in the first part of his *Guzmán de Alfarache* (1599), include accounts of Muslims who convert to Christianity during the final stages of the Catholic Monarchs' conquest of the Kingdom of Granada. Indeed, Alemán's novella ends with Fernando and Isabel themselves serving as godparents at the protagonists' baptism, while the entire outcome of the internecine strife depicted in Pérez de Hita's historical novel has its denouement in the decision of all the most admirable Moorish knights to become Christians and join the fight on the Catholic Monarchs' side:

> Todos éstos llevaban intención de ser Christianos, como lo fueron, porque siendo llegados adonde estaba el Rey Don Fernando, fueron dél y de su Corte muy bien recibidos. Y tornados todos Christianos, con gran plazer del Rey y de sus grandes, les fueron assentadas plaças de grandes y aventajados sueldos. Las damas moras, siendo Christianas, la Reyna Doña Isabel las hizo damas de su estrado.[15] Los Christianos cavalleros fueron puestos en la lista de la milicia y dadas muchas pagas adelantadas. (209)

> (All these intended to become Christians, as they did in fact, for when they arrived where King Fernando was, they were very well received by him and by his Court. And once they had all become Christians, to the King's great pleasure and that of his grandees, they were granted important positions with excellent salaries. Queen Isabel made the Moorish ladies, having become Christians, maids of her dais. The Christian knights were added to the ranks of the militia and given many advances of their pay.)

Though it has long been understood that these conversion stories had some basis in historical fact, it is only now coming to light how immediately relevant they were to the legal status of hundreds of people who claimed to be the descendants of those who converted, and whose ongoing legal battles to prove it were the object of the monarchy's attention precisely from late 1585 through 1595. It certainly appears that the authors of *Guerras civiles de Granada* and *Ozmín y Daraja* were aware of the legal battles taking place concerning the very subject about which they were writing: the dates of conversion of specific lineages and the relative status those dates conferred. In all likelihood, many of their readers were familiar with this context as well. As we will see, some of these readers were evidently inspired by Pérez de Hita's historical fiction to try their own hand at inventing stories about the past, though for more than just their value as entertainment.

Among the lawsuits brought by those who claimed to be descendants of *cristianos viejos de moros*, the reader familiar with Pérez de Hita, *Ozmín y Da-*

raja, or *El Abencerraje* is occasionally startled to find names and descriptions that sound as if they could have come directly from the pages of a maurophile novel. Thus Pedro el Jaení and his brothers, who won their suit in Valladolid in 1590, only to be told they had to argue it again before the Consejo de Población, claimed to be great-grandchildren of Pedro de Mendoza el Jaení and María Abencerraje, his wife (AGS, CdC leg 2202). Alonso el Gací sent the Consejo the transcript of a lawsuit his brother Diego el Gací won in Granada in 1550, in which he claimed to be the grandson of Fernando el Gací, about whom Diego told the following story:

> Puede haber sesenta años poco más o menos que siendo el dicho Fernando el Gací moro en esta ciudad de Granada en una escaramuza que hubo entre los cristianos que estaban en el Real de Santa Fe y los moros de esta ciudad de Granada, el dicho Fernando el Gací se fue y probó la parte de los cristianos en un caballo morcillo y de allí se fue al dicho Real donde los señores Reyes Católicos de gloriosa memoria estaban y se bautizó y tomó el nombre de Hernando. (AGS, CdC leg 2203)

> (It could have been sixty years ago, more or less, that the said Fernando el Gací, a Moor [i.e. a Muslim] in this city of Granada, being in a skirmish between the Christians of the Camp of Santa Fe and the Moors of the city of Granada, the said Fernando el Gací went out and put the Christian side to the test, mounted on a black stallion, and from there he went on to the said Camp where their majesties the Catholic Monarchs, of glorious memory, were, and he was baptized and took the name Hernando.)

These cases appear prior to the publication of Pérez de Hita's novel, but there are other suits that were only brought several years later, and that may well be fraudulent claims inspired by the novel. Although it is perhaps impossible to know for certain, I have found at least one that I believe was invented out of whole cloth, based on the plaintiff's reading of *Guerras civiles de Granada*.

In 1589, Alonso de la Fuente, registered as a Morisco from Granada in the village of Borox (in Las Sagras de Toledo), was the subject of a lawsuit, which he appealed to the Consejo de Órdenes and lost (AHN, OO MM, AHT 38.151). He was accused of trying to maintain two residences (*mantener dos alojamientos*), one in Borox and the other in Toledo, in spite of the rules governing Moriscos, which required them to be registered in one place and stay there. He alleges that he had legally sought permission to live temporarily in Toledo for business purposes (he is a merchant) and had never really changed his residence. He is found to be in violation and fined, though by appealing his case he at least managed to escape the public whipping local authorities had included in his original sentence. There is no mention in the 1589 lawsuit of his claiming the rights of *cristiano viejo* or proclaiming himself to be descended from someone who converted before 1492. In 1595, the first edition of Part One of the *Guerras civiles de Granada* was published in Zaragoza. Among its minor characters are a number of *alcaides* named Alavéz, and one in particular is praised as a *caballero valiente*: Alavéz, alcaide de Vera. This character greets the Catholic Monarchs on their arrival in Vera:

> Y assí, en llegando el Rey a una fuente que le llaman de Pulpí, fué del buen Alabez recebido con mucha alegría y le entregó las llaves de la ciudad de Vera y de su fuerça. . . . Los tres Alabezes luego suplicaron al Rey que los mandasse hazer Christianos; conviene a saber: Alabez, Alcayde de Vera; Alabez, Alcayde de Vélez el Rubio; Alabez, Alcayde de Vélez el Blanco. (XVI, 273–74)

> (And thus, as the King arrived at a spring they call Pulpí, he was greeted by good Alabez with great joy, and he relinquised the keys of the city of Vera and its fortress to him. And the three Alabezes then entreated the King to arrange for them to be made Christians; to wit, Alabez, the commander of Vera; Alabez, the commander of Vélez Rubio; and Alabez, the commander of Vélez Blanco.)

In 1599, Alonso de la Fuente, still living in Borox, is again the plaintiff in a lawsuit, but this time he claims to be the grandson of Luis Aben Muza Alabéz, *alcaide* de Vera and resident of Alfacar, who converted to Christianity long before Granada was conquered, "at the time of the famous conversion of the Abencerrajes and Alabeses":

> Mucho tiempo antes que la dicha ciudad de Granada se ganase de los moros, estando los señores Reyes Católicos de gloriosa memoria sobre ella con su Real y gente de guerra en la ciudad de Santa Fe se vino, siendo moro al dicho real con otros moros cuando la famosa conversión de los Abencerrajes y Alabeses y se presentó ante los dichos señores Reyes y se volvió cristiano y recibió agua de baptismo y le pusieron por nombre Luis Aben Muza Alabés, llamándose antes Mahomat Aben Muza Alabés; y siendo cristiano fue capitán de una compañía de sesenta hombres de a caballo. (AHN, Consejos leg 27.842)

> (Long before the aforesaid city of Granada was won from the Moors, while their majesties the Catholic Monarchs of glorious memory were camped nearby with their army in the city of Santa Fe, he came as a Moor [i.e. Muslim] to the said camp with other Moors when the famous conversion of the Abencerrajes and Alabezes took place, and he presented himself before the said Monarchs and became Christian and received the water of baptism, and they gave him the name Luis Aben

Muza Alabez, his having been called prior to that Mohammed Aben Muza Alabez. And as a Christian he was the captain of a company of sixty men on horseback.)

The fact that in defending himself against the charge of moving from place to place illegally a few years *before* Pérez de Hita's novel appeared Alonso de la Fuente made no mention of this ancestry, but that now, a few years *after* its appearance he claims to be the grandson of a character who figures prominently the book, and therefore demands to be allowed to carry arms, makes it seem almost undeniable that he must have invented the genealogy he here presents.

Assuming Alonso de la Fuente's pretension to be fraudulent establishes a clear and specific function for at least some maurophile literature, insofar as it could be used as a tool in the defense, not of all Moriscos generally, but of *certain* Moriscos whose level of assimilation and socioeconomic class allowed them to hope that they could successfully overcome the stigma and marginalization to which they had been subject and become, for all intents and purposes, old Christians. In the most direct sense, literary texts could thus supply the material for fictional selves to be adopted and passed off as real identities. But in a more general way, maurophile representations may well have facilitated the process of integration for those Moriscos (or *cristianos viejos de moros*) who sought full acceptance in Castilian society.

For those who argue that maurophilia aimed at the defense of the Moriscos *in general*, the expulsions of 1609–1614 are an indication of its failure. In that case, it represents a beautiful illusion, an oppositional perspective that was out of step with the society of its time, but that preserved for future generations the image of a Spain that "might have been" but never was. One discrepancy faced by this interpretation, however, is the extraordinary popularity maurophilia enjoyed, precisely in the years we now see, after the fact, as leading up to the expulsion. If we agree with Fuchs that maurophilia is a *lieu de mémoire*, it is perhaps best to think of it as that cultural space in which producers and audiences *negotiated* what could and what could not be salvaged from the Moorish past. Such an approach may be the only one that truly does justice to both the popularity and the obvious critical engagement of the genre. Among the former native population of Granada, there were some with enough economic and social capital to negotiate successfully their inclusion in the nation, without denying their Moorish heritage. In this regard it is interesting to note that many of the litigants claiming to be *cristianos viejos de moros* kept some version of their Arabic surnames, though generally in combination with a Castilian one: Hernández Aduladín, Enríquez Ozaízan, Fernández Abenzulema, Pedro el Jaení, García el Madravi, and so forth. For this group of perhaps a thousand or so descendants of Granadine Muslims, maurophile literature may well have contributed to the cultural and social climate that permitted them to save themselves. In that sense, at least, it could reasonably be seen as a *successful* defense of at least some Moriscos.

In fact, if we think of maurophilia in these terms, as a space in which to negotiate the place of Granada, its past, its natives and its former natives within the Spanish nation, it may well be that it successfully contributed to all three of the outcomes of the Morisco crisis, namely, the consolidation of the Kingdom of Granada as an integral part of modern Spain; the permanent adherence to the nation of a certain minority within the (formerly) Morisco population; and the final expulsion of those Moriscos who, like Hernandico, were unable to persuasively lay claim to the maurophile legacy. To delegitimize the right to remain in their ancestral homeland of an entire population of hundreds of thousands, many of whom have lived in a place for eight centuries, is not a simple task. It is a long, complex process, and the expulsion of 1610 could not have taken place if the conditions of possibility had not been fulfilled beforehand. Perhaps Pérez de Hita, Miguel de Luna, and all those whom we have become accustomed to think of as tragically failing to prevent the inevitable should, rather, be thought of as succeeding in what they were attempting: namely, to save themselves, although they thereby participated, however reluctantly, in the process whereby others were cut off.

Notes

1.   This was argued decades ago by Vincent in an article based on documents containing physical description of Moriscos, "¿Cuál era el aspecto físico de los moriscos?" (303–13). More recently Harvey has succinctly stated that " if there *were* differences of skin pigmentation, they were not so marked that one could tell at a glance to which community a person belonged" (9).

2.   The best introductions are still Caro Baroja's *Los moriscos del Reino de Granada* and Domínguez Ortiz and Vincent's general introduction. Very little is yet known about the *cristianos viejos de moros* (see below). Fredrickson discusses the Morisco question as an early manifestation of racism (34–36).

3.   A complete review of criticism on maurophile literature is beyond the scope of this discussion; the seminal studies mainly concern *El Abencerraje*, which thereby serves as a paradigmatic case. Since Cirot, the studies that have done the most to shape debate are those by Carrasco Urgoiti, Guillén, Shipley, Burshatin, Márquez Villanueva, Bass, Liu, and Fuchs.

4. See also García Cárcel's introduction to *La construcción de las historias de España*, as well as Cuart Moner's contribution to that collection.

5. For a useful discussion and helpful anthology of frontier ballads, see Martínez Inhiesta's online article in the electronic journal *Lemir.* The most complete current anthology is Pedro Correa's two-volume study and collection, *Los romances fronterizos.*

6. According to Pedro Correa, this version of the ballad, whose superiority he acknowledges, has been modified by Ginés Pérez de Hita. He specifically mentions the references to place names such as Generalife and Torres Bermejas, which were not in use in the fifteenth century (XLVIII–LI).

7. I refer, of course, to René Girard's influential account of novelistic desire in *Deceit, Desire, and the Novel.*

8. On the general subject of the fad of intentional falsifications of history in this period, see Godoy Alcántara's 1868 study, reissued in 1981, and Julio Caro Baroja's *Las falsificaciones de la historia.* Though beyond the scope of this discussion, both the *libros plúmbeos* hoax and Miguel de Luna's *Historia verdadera del Rey Rodrigo* are relevant to the process of incorporation of Granada into the Spanish nation that I explore here. On the *libros plúmbeos*, see, most recently, Harvey (264–90) and especially Harris's *From Muslim to Christian Granada.* On Luna's *Historia verdadera*, see Márquez Villanueva (45–97), Bernabé Pons, and García Arenal and Rodríguez Mediano.

9. Concerning the role of taxes on silk production in provoking the rebellion, see Garrad's seminal article. On the origins of the war, all three chroniclers of the time, Diego Hurtado de Mendoza, Luis Mármol Carvajal, and Pérez de Hita (*Segunda parte de las Guerras Civiles*) demonstrate more or less clearly that the Moriscos were provoked into rebellion by Pedro de Deza, the new president of the Real Chancillería and Audiencia of Granada.

10. The most thorough account remains Bernard Vincent's "La expulsión de los moriscos del Reino de Granada y su reparto en Castilla" (215–66).

11. Trevor Dadson reproduces the text of this *privilegio* and its 1577 reconfirmation in an appendix to his vast study of the Moriscos of Villarrubia de los Ojos (839–42).

12. There is no published study of the *pleitos de cristiano viejo* as such. This section is based on my own ongoing research in the Archivo General de Simancas, the subject of a monograph to be entitled *Los moriscos que no lo eran: Pleitos de cristiano viejo en el Archivo General de Simancas.*

13. Rodríguez de Diego analyzes the use of documentation from the royal archive in Simancas to support private lawsuits during the reign of Philip II. Of course, the fact that the plaintiffs in some of these cases participated in such a use of documentation from Simancas demonstrates their exceptional command of the legal system. I thank Isabel Aguirre for referring me to this fascinating article.

14. AGS Estado 252 and AGS Estado 2644. In these two sets of documents there are reports from the Count of Salazar confirming that the plaintiffs won some eight

hundred such cases, and that the central authority finally grew tired of fighting to expel such individuals, conceding that the rest who had suits pending should not be harassed over it.

15. The term "damas de su estrado," which I have translated literally "maids of her dais," refers to the use by Castilian noblewomen of a raised platform on which they sat, Moorish style, and is thus an important instance of the Moorish habitus, here invoked somewhat ironically at the precise moment of their conversion, and as a sign of the high status conferred upon them. Fuchs discusses the exotic impression the *estrado* made on foreign visitors (14–15).

Abbreviations

ADC	Archivo Diocesano de Cuenca, Cuenca
AGS	Archivo General de Simancas, Simancas
AHN	Archivo Histórico Nacional, Madrid
CdC	Cámara de Castilla
OO MM, AHT	Órdenes Militares, Archivo Histórico de Toledo

Works Cited

Alemán, Mateo. *Guzmán de Alfarache.* 2 vols. Ed. José María Micó. Madrid: Cátedra, 1987.

Bass, Laura. "Homosocial Bonds and Desire in the Abencerraje." *Revista Canadiense de Estudios Hispánicos* 24.3 (2000): 453–71.

Bernabé Pons, Luis. "Miguel de Luna, pasado de Granada, presente morisco." *Studi Ispanici* 32 (2007). 37–71.

Bourdieu, Pierre. *Outline of a Theory of Practice.* Cambridge, UK: Cambridge University Press, 1977.

Burshatin, Israel. "Power, Discourse, and Metaphor in the Abencerraje." *MLN* 99.2 (1984): 195–213.

Caro Baroja, Julio. *Los moriscos del Reino de Granada.* Madrid: Istmo, 1991.

———. *Las falsificaciones de la historia (en relación con la de España).* Barcelona: Seix Barral, 1992.

Carrasco Urgoiti, María Soledad. *El moro de Granada en la literatura.* Madrid: Revista de Occidente, 1956.

Cirot, Georges. "La maurophilie littéraire en Espagne au XVIe siècle." *Bulletin Hispanique* (1938-1944): 40–46.

Correa, Pedro, ed. *Los romances fronterizos. (Tradición crítica).* 2 vols. Granada: Universidad de Granada, 1999.

————. "Estudio preliminar." Pérez de Hita, Ginés. *Historia de los bandos de Zegríes y Abencerrajes (Primera parte de las Guerras civiles de Granada).* Ed. Paula Blanchard-Demouge. Madrid: Bailly-Baillière, 1913; Ed. facsimile. Granada: Universidad de Granada, 1999.

Cuart Moner, Baltasar. "La larga marcha de las historias de España en el siglo XVI." *La construcción de las historias de España.* Ed. Ricardo García Cárcel. Madrid: Marcial Pons, 2004.

Dadson, Trevor J. *Los moriscos de Villarrubia de los Ojos (siglos XV–XVIII): Historia de una minoría asimilada, expulsada y reintegrada.* Madrid: Iberoamericana; Frankfurt: Vervuert, 2007.

Domínguez Ortiz, Antonio, and Bernard Vincent. *Historia de los moriscos: Vida y tragedia de una minoría.* Madrid: Alianza, 1978.

Fredrickson, George M. *Racism: A Short History.* Princeton: Princeton University Press, 2002.

Fuchs, Barbara. *Exotic Nation: Maurophilia and the Construction of Early Modern Spain.* Philadelphia: University of Pennsylvania Press, 2009.

García-Arenal, Mercedes, and F. Rodríguez Mediano. "Médico, traductor, inventor: Miguel de Luna, cristiano arábigo de Granada." *Chronica Nova* 36 (2006): 187–231.

García Cárcel, Ricardo. "Introducción." *La construcción de las historias de España.* Ed. Ricardo García Cárcel. Madrid: Marcial Pons, 2004.

Garrad, Keith. "La industria sedera en el siglo XVI y su conexión con el levantamiento de las Alpujarras (1568–1571)." *Miscelánea de Estudios Árabes y Hebraicos* 5 (1956): 73–104.

Girard, Réne. *Deceit, Desire, and the Novel.* Trans. Yvonne Freccero. Baltimore: The Johns Hopkins University Press, 1988.

Godoy Alcántara, José. *Historia crítica de los falsos cronicones.* (1868). Madrid: Alatar, 1981.

Guillén, Claudio. "Literature as Historical Contradiction: *El Abencerraje,* the Moorish Novel, and the Ecologue." *Literature as System: Essays toward the Theory of Literary History.* Princeton: Princeton University Press, 1971.

Harris, A. Katie. *From Muslim to Christian Granada: Inventing a City's Past in Early Modern Spain.* Baltimore: The Johns Hopkins University Press, 2007.

Harvey, L. P. *Muslims in Spain, 1500–1614.* Chicago: University of Chicago Press, 2005.

Hurtado de Mendoza, Diego. *Guerra de Granada.* Ed. Bernardo Blanco-González. Madrid: Castilia, 1970.

Liu, Benjamin. "Ransom, Gifts, and Interfaith Fraternization in *El Abencerraje.*" *Bulletin of Hispanic Studies* 80.3 (2003): 307–17.

Mármol Carvajal, Luis. *Historia del* [sic] *rebelión y castigo de los moriscos del reino de Granada.* Biblioteca de Autores Españoles, Vol. 21. Madrid: Rivadeneyra, 1946.

Marquez-Villanueva, Francisco. *El problema morisco (Desde otras laderas).* Madrid: Libertarias, 1998.

Martínez Iniesta, Bautista. "Los romances fronterizos: Crónica poética de la reconquista granadina y antología del romancero fronterizo." *Lemir* 7 (2003): no pagination. Accessed 05/03/2010. http://parnaseo.uv.es/lemir/Revista/Revista7/Romances.htm

Nora, Pierre. "Between Memory and History: *Les Lieux de Mémoire*." *Representations* 26 (1989): 7–24.

Pérez de Hita, Ginés. *Historia de los bandos de Zegríes y Abencerrajes.(Primera parte de las guerras civiles de Granada)*. Ed. Paula Blanchard-Demouge. Madrid: Bailly-Baillière, 1913; Ed. facsimile and "Estudio preliminar" Pedro Correa. Granada, Universidad de Granada, 1999.

———. *La guerra de los moriscos. (Segunda parte de las guerras civiles de Granada)*. Ed. Paula Blanchard-Demouge. Madrid: Bailly-Baillière, 1915. Ed. facsimile and "Estudio preliminar" Joaquín Gil Sanjuán. Granada: Universidad de Granada, 1998.

Rodríguez de Diego, José Luis. "Un archivo no sólo para el rey: Significado social del proyecto simanquino en el siglo XVI." *Felipe II (1527–1598): Europa y la monarquía católica*. Vol. 4. Ed. J. Martínez Millán. Madrid: Parteluz, 1998.

Shipley, George. "La obra literaria como monumento histórico: El caso de *El Abencerraje*." *Journal of Hispanic Philology* 2 (1977): 103–20.

Tapia Sánchez, Serafín de. *La comunidad morisca de Ávila*. Salamanca: Universidad de Salamanca, 1991.

Tuan, Yi-Fu. *Space and Place. The Perspective of Experience*. Minneapolis: University of Minnesota Press, 1977.

Vincent, Bernard. *Andalucía en la Edad Moderna: Economía y sociedad*. Granada: Excma. Diputación Provincial de Granada, 1985.

Whinnom, Keith. "The Problem of the 'Best-Seller' in Spanish Golden-Age Literature." *Bulletin of Hispanic Studies* 57 (1980): 189–98.

◆ 3

Agi Morato's Garden as Heterotopian Place in Cervantes's *Los baños de Argel*

Moisés R. Castillo

Human places are sites of competing memories linked to physical and symbolic systems of spatialization. Even the most intimately familiar sense of the *here* and *there* is dependent on a complex network of symbolic recognition that cannot be divorced from the dynamics of power (Lefebvre). I take these notions as my starting point as I examine Cervantes's countercultural (re)construction of the Algerian landscape as heterotopian place in *Los baños de Argel* (*The Bagnios of Algiers/The Dungeons of Algiers*). I focus on the symbolic value of the theatrical space of Agi Morato's garden as an alternative space of human interaction that stands beyond the familiar distinctions between *self* and *other*, *us* and *them*. Positioning himself against the exclusionary logic of the official ideology of religious and cultural purity (la ideología de la sangre), Miguel de Cervantes projects in *Los baños de Argel* a syncretic ideal of freedom, compassion and human brotherhood over the landscape of the African Other.

There are not many studies that inquire into the significance of landscape in the theater of Cervantes, and even fewer researching the role of Agi Morato's garden in *Los baños de Argel*.[1] Among them, there is the essay by Maryrica Ortiz Lottman, titled "The Call of the Natural World in *Los baños de Argel*." She notes that in this work "Cervantes explores the city's landscape, and especially its gardens, in order to present nature as a beneficent force that offers the possibility of freedom" (363). Following in the wake of Ortiz Lottman's work, this essay will examine the symbolic function of Agi Morato's garden in light of the theory of heterotopian spaces developed by Foucault in his 1967 talk "Des Espaces Autres."

Surprisingly, literary criticism has not paid much attention to the dramatic landscape of Agi Morato's garden, or has underplayed its importance, despite the garden's centrality during climactic moments of the second and third acts, and the emphatic reference to it that marks the end of the play. While the play does not include a physical description of the garden, there is little doubt that this "unseen space" is of enormous importance in terms of not just the play's actions but their symbolic significance. Whence, then, the emphasis that Cervantes puts on this garden? What does this site represent in *Los baños*? One might think that Agi Morato's garden is a utopia understood as "no place," that is, a truly non-existing place, an unreachable space, a longing of the captive protagonists of the *comedia*, rather than a concrete site—hence the muting of its physical details in favor of its symbolic meaning. However, it is obvious that the garden does exist in the context of the play insofar as the characters interact with it or "inhabit" it. Agi Morato's garden is the destination of the captives during the second and third acts of the play, appearing as a *locus amoenus*, an escapist site of sensorial enjoyment that can be connected with the captives' dreams of liberation, as Ortiz Lottman and Edward Friedman ("Introducción") have recently suggested. This is why it seems useful to think of this utopian space not in the most common or better-known meaning of the term "utopia" (no-place) but in the sense of a "place without limits." This variant is also suggested by the etymology of the word *outopos*. As I will try to show in the following pages, the notion of the *place without limits*, as incorporated and reworked by Cervantes, comes remarkably close to the Foucauldian concept of *heterotopia*.[2]

Foucault speaks of different heterotopian models, including heterotopias of crisis, deviation, illusion and compensation. What interests me here, beyond classificatory tags that might prove problematic in practice, is the critical potential of heterotopian symbols, their demystifying power. Hence, I propose a reworking of the notion of heterotopian space for literary analysis distinguishing it not only from escapist and compensatory utopias (such as those of chivalric and pastoral romances) but also from literary dystopias. In the sense I use it here, the concept of *heterotopia* has something in common with Maravall's understanding of *Don Quixote* as "counter-utopian" writing

(*Utopía y contrautopía en "El Quijote"*), and especially with Castillo and Spadaccini's interpretation of Cervantes's *Los trabajos de Persiles y Sigismunda* as an experimental narrative that exposes the contingency and arbitrariness of Counter-Reformation utopias ("El antiutopismo en *Los trabajos de Persiles y Sigismunda*"). Yet, in its applicability to Cervantes's plays of captivity, the Foucauldian concept of heterotopia adds an important dimension to our understanding of the Cervantine construction of alternative spaces by underscoring their *Otherness*, specifically in terms of their locality. Thus, I argue that Agi Morato's garden may be thought of as a fully developed *heterotopian space* within the dramatic context of *Los baños de Argel*, that is, a place imagined as *Other* in reference to, or more precisely, in contrast with, the symbolic and physical spaces that structure the ideological field of Imperial and Counter-Reformation Spain. While the established social and cultural order rests on exclusionary notions of cultural centrality and religious integrity, the heterotopian space of Agi Morato's garden may be said to model alternative forms of human interaction outside the limits of the dominant or official ideology.[3]

Recent contributions to the study of Cervantes's theater have tended to focus on the theme of captivity. These critical works have pointed out a series of potential connections between the dramatic situations developed in these plays and Cervantes's experience of captivity at the hands of Algerian pirates. In *The Unifying Concept*, Edward Friedman notes that the captivity theme is the central leitmotiv of *El trato de Argel* (70) and *Los baños de Argel* (71). Louise Fothergill-Payne underscores the suffering and human degradation evident in *El trato*'s scenes of captivity (177) as well as Cervantes's appeals for sympathy and charity in *Los baños*, which she says, has a marked "carácter de documental" (182). The "documentary character" of *Los baños* would extend to the staging of the journey undertaken by several captives to the garden of Agi Morato during acts II and III and the events that take place during their crossing. This would be the context in which the symbolic meaning of this *locus amoenus* would have to be examined.[4] In her book *Cervantes in Algiers* (2002), María Antonia Garcés systematically explores "the dynamic borderline between 'the life' and 'the work' in Cervantes" (4). Her approach is informed by historical and biographical studies as well as "literary testimonies" (4) and psychoanalytic theories, especially trauma theory. Garcés attributes to Cervantes's writings on the subject a *testimonial* and cathartic function. Through his fictional and dramatic treatment of his own experience of captivity, Cervantes would "reclaim his own history and . . . break out of his emotional imprisonment to start a new life in Spain" (11).

Scholars continue to puzzle over the fact that Cervantes's life was spared in Algiers despite his numerous escape attempts even as his accomplices were reportedly tortured and in many cases executed.[5] Hasán may have been expecting to get a large sum of money for Cervantes's ransom, or perhaps he respected his daring and intelligence. Rosa Rossi, in her work *Escuchar a Cervantes*, speculates that Hasán may have had homosexual relations with Cervantes, or that at the very least he may have been in love with the Spanish soldier.[6] Garcés, on the other hand, entertains "the possibility that Cervantes was an unofficial informer to Hajji Murad [Agi Morato], who maintained ambiguous relations with the Spaniards" (208), and presumably intervened before Hasán to spare the life of a captive who had friends in Oran and supposedly connections with the Spanish powers (208).

McGaha's explanation springs from his critical research—based on Oliver Asín's findings—with regards to the possible identity of the two Zaharas in the *comedias* and the Zoraida of "The Captive's Tale" in *Don Quixote*. All three characters would represent, according to this view, Agi Morato's daughter, the wife of Muley Maluco and (through a second marriage) of Hasán Bajá, granddaughter of Christians on both sides, and possibly a secret lover of Cervantes who would have pleaded for his life before the king of Algiers. McGaha contends that there is no other explanation for the fact that Cervantes's life was spared after four escape attempts, and even as he tried to free other Christian captives. Agi Morato's daughter would have inspired the character of Zahara in *El trato*, the married princess who tries to seduce her slave Aurelio—a theatrical representation of Cervantes—as well as the bride of Muley Maluco who frees don Lope in *Los baños* and flees to Spain in order to convert to Christianity, and even the maiden Zoraida who frees the captive in *Don Quixote*.[7] McGaha's conclusion is that Cervantes may have revealed in his theatrical and literary elaborations of the theme of captivity his own frustrated plans to turn his Moorish lover into his Christian bride and escape with her to Spain. Don Lope says in Act II:

> En fe de lo que en ti [Zahara] he visto,
> del deseo que te doma,
> de adorarte no resisto,
> no por prenda de Mahoma,
> sino por prenda de Cristo.
> Yo te llevaré a do seas
> todo aquello que deseas,
> aunque mil vidas me cueste. (vv. 781–88)

(From what I've seen of you [Zahara],
of the desire that subdues you,
I cannot help but adore you,
as a treasure not of Mohamed,
but rather as one of Christ.
I'll take you where you can be
everything that you desire,
even if it costs me a thousand lives.)

The plot of *Los baños* would thus contain key aspects of Cervantes's own biography of captivity while expressing his veiled desire to rescue for Christendom the woman who had saved him from certain death and possibly help him liberate other Christian captives.[8] Indeed, for Don Lope, Zahara represents *freedom* from prison and renewed life: "de mi prisión libertad, / de mi muerte alegre vida, / crédito de mi verdad" (III, vv. 646–48) (liberty from my prison, / life of happiness from my death, / pledge of my being).

The Zahara of *Los baños* and the Zoraida of "The Captive's Tale" are both virgins who free captives (Moner 53–54). They have in fact been associated with the Virgin Mary (Garcés 214–15). Significantly, Mary is iconographically represented in *Los baños* as *stella maris*, a religious guide in a journey of personal and spiritual salvation: "Francisquito: Tengo yo el *Ave María* / clavada en el corazón, / y es la estrella que me guía / en este mar de aflicción / al puerto de la alegría" (II, vv. 1041–45) (Francisquito: I have the *Hail Mary* / attached to my heart, / and she is the star that guides me / in this sea of affliction / toward the port of joy). Zahara is also called "otro nuevo Moisén" (III, v. 590) (a new Moses) in this Egypt of captives that is Algiers.

These passages would seem to add verisimilitude to McGaha's speculations on the subject of Cervantes's survival while possibly providing context to understand the events that take place in Agi Morato's garden. From this perspective the garden would emerge as the site of liberation on which Cervantes may have projected his own dreams of shared freedom. We could even say that the "freedom boat" the captives await in the garden is ultimately an extension of this utopian paradise that enables the "felice fin" (happy ending): "D. Lope: También escribió en el fin / que sepamos el jardín / de su padre, Agimorato, / do a nuestra comedia y trato / se ha de dar felice fin" (II, vv. 646–50) (D. Lope: She also wrote in the end / that we should know the garden / of her father, Agi Morato, / in which our drama and dealings / a happy ending shall come).

Agi Morato's garden is the site that makes the happy ending possible at the conclusion of both *El trato* and *Los baños*. As D. Lope says in *Los baños*, "Y aún hoy se hallarán en él [Argel/cuento] / la ventana y el jardín. / Y aquí da este *trato* fin, / que no le tiene el de Argel" (III, vv. 1069–72) (D. Lope: And to this day you can find in it [Algiers/the tale] / the window and the garden. / And here this *trato* comes to an end, / although that of Algiers has none). Don Lope's climactic mention of the garden follows his remarkable pronouncement that the events dramatized in the play are grounded in factual truth:

> No de la imaginación
> este *trato* se sacó,
> que la verdad lo fraguó
> bien lejos de la ficción.
> Dura en Argel este cuento
> de amor y dulce memoria,
> y es bien que verdad y historia
> alegre al entendimiento. (III, vv. 1061–68)

> (This *trato* was not taken
> from the imagination,
> for truth molded it
> quite far from fiction.
> This tale of love and sweet memory
> still lingers in Algiers,
> and it is good that truth and story
> should delight the mind.)

Is this a Cervantine wink to the reader? Are we to read this text as a confession of sorts, a Cervantine suggestion that although the work is obviously fiction (tale/story), the staged events are based on real experiences (possibly personal experiences) of captivity? If we were to follow Garcés's line of argumentation we would say that Cervantes's dramatic revisiting of his own experiences of captivity would allow the author to overcome traumatic memories by transforming them into "cuento de amor y dulce memoria." This view would seem to explain the microcosms of the garden as "compensatory space," in line with the traditional notion of utopia in the Maravallian sense.[9] For my part, I propose a different reading of this space as *humanist heterotopia*.

To be sure, there is little doubt that the works of McGaha, Garcés, and others provide important information on the subject of Cervantes's captivity and the potential impact that these biographical facts may have had on his work, yet what interests me here is not the possible correspondence between the dramatic situations of Cervantes's play and his own experience of captivity.

Rather, I propose an interpretation of the theatrical space of Agi Morato's garden as a symbolic manifestation of Cervantes's humanist principles and ideals. As Ortiz Lottman has noted, the play does not contain significant information about the garden, which means that the "reader" is implicitly asked to imagine its physical details using his/her own expectations and knowledge of Islamic gardens: "We never actually see this garden or hear it described. On a practical level, Cervantes knew his readers were familiar with the Islamic gardens of Spain. On a symbolic level, the absence of description compares this garden to Paradise, a place that can only be imagined, while simultaneously leaving its meaning wide open" (355).

I would suggest that Agi Morato's garden functions as a liminal space on which historical memories can be re-articulated in connection with humanist ideals of brotherhood and solidarity that transcend racial, cultural, and religious divides.[10] It is thus significant that this place of humanist hope is explicitly linked to the cultural tradition of the Islamic garden, a terrestrial version of the Koranic paradise (Clark; Khansari), which is strictly separated from other natural or urban spaces by barriers that prevent the external world from penetrating this much-valued refuge. Researchers have identified two main functions of the Islamic garden—one sacred, the other hedonistic in accordance with a perceived dualism that arguably originates in the Koran. Yet it is also true that gardens of similar appearance may be designed for very different types of activities in the Islamic world, as Wescoat has pointed out in his illuminating essay "The Islamic Garden: Issues for Landscape Research" (1986). According to Wescoat, Islamic gardens become more specialized as the urban and architectural structures with which they are associated evolve—tombs, mosques, areas of palace recreation or courtly retreats, fortifications, madrasahs—and as the garden complexes begin to replace individual palace gardens (12). However, there are common attributes shared by Islamic gardens that are based on the imagery of the Koranic paradise: axial symmetry, trees, and running water. Its rectangular shape puts the four parts of the world in communication with the pool, and the fountain at the center, the most sacred place. In the Maghreb, and more specifically in the Algerian garden of the sixteenth century, fruit trees, flowers, and aromatic plants become essential elements of these exuberant places located on the outskirts of the walled city and, occasionally, near the sea. These gardens are often used as second homes during the summer months and as places of recreation. We can say that the sacred meaning of the garden does not exclude hedonistic considerations as well as horticultural uses and notions of aesthetic value. Cresti mentions the studies of George Marçais, who traces the Oriental and pre-Islamic origins of the koranic garden to Iran, where most of our fruit trees came from (59). Cresti observes that these gardens typically maintain a harmonious relationship with the topography of their surroundings "and in some way appear determined by a juxtaposition of elements which did not necessarily require a precise overall view" (63).

The Algerian garden is neither an *agdal* nor a *riyad* in the proper sense; i.e., it is neither a complex of large, walled-in palace gardens, nor the miniatures that can be found in the interior yards of buildings, but rather a *villa rustica* that includes an orchard and probably a vineyard where one can enjoy the sensual pleasures provided by exuberant nature, the sound of running water traveling down the irrigation channels, and the scent of aromatic herbs and flowers in an environment meant to promote spiritual contemplation and carnal pleasures in keeping with the Koranic notion of "a *sensual* Paradise, a garden (*janna*) of moisture and shade" (Dickie 1017). The cemeteries and *rawdas* or mausoleums were built side by side (albeit properly identified by their architecture) with spaces meant for strolling, praying, writing poetry or enjoying the harem. As Canavaggio notes in his book *Cervantes*, it is clear that the Spanish author knew the Islamic culture well and was acquainted with these types of gardens, their recreational uses, and also their symbolic meaning.

In his elaboration on the subject of heterotopias, Foucault mentions the Persian garden as a distinctive place, a radically *Other* space, that symbolically contains "the totality of the world" (26). In keeping with the Foucauldian notion, we could link Agi Morato's garden to the classic *heterotopia of crisis*, i.e., a microcosmic space radically separated and hidden from the rest of the world (in this case between the city walls of Algiers and the Mediterranean Sea) in which everything is literally possible; a *multilocality* that contains seemingly incompatible sites. To this sacred place, access is by permission only, and in this case the captives have the explicit authorization of the qadi: "Osorio: Pidióle Agimorato / al cadí que nos fuésemos / a su jardín por tres o cuatro días" (III, vv. 848–50) (Osorio: Agi Morato asked / the qadi to let us come / to his garden for three or four days).

The symbolic work of this heterotopian space is first signaled in the *comedia* by a break in time and space that coincides with the captives' journey to the garden. Significantly this journey begins on Good Friday (Act II) and continues through Resurrection Sunday (Act III). The arrival of Cauralí and the Qadi introduces the scene of Francisco's martyrdom, the *figura Christi* who—as Ortiz Lotmann has noted—will be buried in the garden as an illustrious Muslim. This is one of the most dramatic illustrations of the dissolution of cultural and religious barriers inside the confines of the heterotopian space of the garden.

The radical juxtaposition of Muslim and Christian symbolism paves the way for a series of dramatic situations that elude interpretation in terms of traditional religious and cultural demarcations. We can say that religious dogma (whether Christian or Muslim) has no (privileged) place in this sacred multilocality. Instead, the sacred space of the garden seems to inspire feelings of solidarity and a sense of shared destiny among its dwellers. In retrospect one can see that the journey to the *garden of liberation* is not a Christian or a Muslim pilgrimage but a journey of collective self-discovery. In the end, what the travelers discover in this sacred space is their common humanity, which they express in images of their individual and collective hopes and dreams.

While there may be discernible connections between the experiences of the captives in *Los baños* and certain aspects of Cervantes's own captivity in Algiers (as Garcés, McGaha and others have argued), and while the setting of the garden must be inspired in Cervantes's familiarity with Islamic gardens— including Hajji Murad's—I would argue that in the context of the play Agi Morato's garden functions as a heterotopian space on which the Spanish author projects his own ideals of freedom, tolerance, human integrity, virtue, charity, and solidarity.[11] There is of course little doubt that Cervantes's captivity and, generally speaking, his experiences in Algiers must have inspired many of the dramatic motifs and situations of *Los baños*, yet we must also recognize that the rich image of humanity that emerges within the confines of Agi Morato's garden is ultimately rooted in humanist values and ideals. As Alberto Sánchez put it:

Es evidente que los cinco años de Argel han inspirado a Cervantes en su creación literaria. Lances, percances y motivos de sus comedias de cautivos y de varias novelas ejemplares se han nutrido de aquella triste experiencia. Pero si hubiera que determinar concretamente la motivación suprema inspirada por el cautiverio, yo me inclinaría por la exaltación de la *libertad* a lo largo de toda su obra y su condenación a todo género de exclavitud y servidumbre. La libertad como corolario indispensable de la dignidad humana y la tolerancia religiosa e ideológica son conceptos básicos del humanismo renacentista plenamente sentidos y divulgados por Cervantes. (23)

(It is evident that the five years that he spent in Algiers inspired Cervantes's literary creations. The incidents, mishaps, and motifs of his plays of captivity and several of his exemplary novels were grounded in his sad experiences. But if I had to determine specifically the highest motivation inspired by his captivity, I would be inclined to point out his defense of freedom and his condemnation of slavery and servitude throughout his work. Liberty, as a necessary corollary of human dignity, and religious and ideological tolerance are the basic concepts of Renaissance humanism, which Cervantes embraced and propagated.)

We must note that Cervantes's humanist vision has very little to do with the regressive utopianism that drives much Renaissance literature and Siglo de Oro theater, including pastoral narratives and poetry, chivalric novels, Christian romances, and Lopean comedias. The "multicultural space" of Agi Morato's garden is the virtual antithesis of the ideology of racial purity that permeates the Lopean-style "alabanza de aldea" or praise of the countryside. We can say that Agi Morato's garden is a heterotopia not because it is irretrievable or irrevocably lost (like the quixotic golden age invoked in *Don Quixote* I, XI) but because it is not yet realized, because it can only be imagined as a future possibility and not as a present reality in the context of Counter-Reformation Spain. Insofar as the garden may be viewed as an inverted mirror-image of the Spanish society of the early 1600s, which is plagued by religious and cultural fundamentalism, the promise of the captives' liberation can only be realized in liminal spaces outside the confines of ordinary time and space: the Islamic garden and its extension, the freedom boat.

It is remarkable that in his short elaboration on the subject of heterotopias, Foucault mentions the Islamic garden as an example of a fully developed heterotopian place. Even more significant, he notes that the boat is "the heterotopia *par excellence*" and "the greatest reserve of the imagination" (27). His description of the boat as the quintessential heterotopia is certainly evocative of the freedom boat in which the shared dreams of the captives are finally realized in *Los baños*: "a floating piece of space, a place without a place, that exists by itself, that is closed in on itself and at the same time is given over to the infinity of the sea" (Foucault 27). The captives speak longingly of Spain. "*¡Cuán cara e[re] s de haber, oh dulce España!*" (II, v. 526; v. 539) (*How dear and difficult you are to be had, oh sweet Spain!*). Yet it would be difficult to imagine that Counter-Reformation Spain (the country that expelled hundreds of thousands of its own citizens in 1609–1614 in the name of cultural and religious purity) would be the beacon of freedom and tolerance the captives long for. Thus, Agi Morato's garden and its symbolic extension—the boat, the place without a place given over to the infinity of the sea—is arguably the true "promised land" of *Los baños*.

Willard King may be right when he claims that, after his experience of captivity, Cervantes had the perception that "las religiones nos dividen, mientras que la conducta moral generosa une a todos los hombres civilizados" (290–91) (religions divide us, while a generous moral conduct unites all civilized people). Throughout Acts II and III, we witness humanitarian actions and expressions of solidarity that transcend cultural and religious barriers. In the following passage Zahara (a Moorish woman) compassionately laments the death of a Christian:

Zahara: Dicen que guardó un decoro
que entre cristianos se advierte,
que es el morir confesando
al Cristo que ellos adoran.
Y estúvemele mirando,
y, entre otros muchos que lloran,
también estuve llorando,
porque soy naturalmente
de pecho humano y clemente. (II, vv. 114–22)

(Zahara: They say he kept a decorum
commendable among Christians,
which is confessing, at death,
to the Christ they all worship.
And I watched him very closely,
and among many who wept,
I myself was also weeping,
for I hold in my bosom
a human and clement nature.)

Vivanco shows his amazement ("admiración") about the fact that their Muslim masters allow the captives to practice their religion ("guardar nuestra religión") and even celebrate mass on Resurrection Sunday (III, vv. 48–54). Act III includes a wealth of amorous scenes involving Zahara and the Spanish captive don Lope. Their love, which transcends religious and cultural borders, will prove instrumental (we could even say providential) in the unfolding of the *felice fin* or happy ending. In another passage, a Christian (Sacristán) tries to force a Jew to carry a barrel to his master's house, and another Christian (Viejo) takes pity on him despite his own allusions to derogatory stereotypes of the Jewish people:

Sacristán: ¡Vive Dios, perro, que os arranque el hígado!
Judío: ¡Ay, ay, mísero y triste!
Por el Dío bendito,
que si hoy no fuera sábado,

	que lo llevara. ¡Buen cristiano, basta!
Viejo:	A compasión me mueve.
	¡Oh gente afeminada,
	infame y para poco!
	Por esta vez te ruego que le dejes.
	Sacristán: Por ti le dejo; vaya. (II vv. 404–13)

(Sacristán:	By God, dog, I will rip out your liver!
Jew:	Ah, ah, woe is me!
	By our blessed God I swear
	that if today were not Saturday
	I would carry it. Good Christian, enough!
Viejo:	I am moved to compassion.
	Oh, effeminate people,
	infamous and good for nothing!
	Just this once, I beseech you, let him be.
Sacristán:	For you I will do it; go on.)

Just as the mirror is a heterotopia for Foucault, that is, a real object that shapes our relationship with our own image reflected in it,[12] so too is the garden inasmuch as it is a place that allows us to interact, without fissures or contradictions, with a diversity of spaces that represent different human categories ("calidades") and different aspects of humanity. And therein lies the equalizing character of the space represented by the garden in *Los baños de Argel*. Osorio exclaims: "Argel es, según barrunto, / arca de Noé abreviada: / aquí están de todas suertes, / oficios y habilidades, / disfrazadas calidades" (III, vv. 43–47) (Algiers is, as I conjecture, / a Noah's ark abbreviated: / here you find men of all kinds, / trades and skills, / disguised categories).

The garden is also a mythical space in the precise sense of Yi-Fu Tuan's definition: "Mythical space is an intellectual construct . . . a response of feeling and imagination to fundamental human needs. It differs from pragmatic and scientifically conceived spaces in that it ignores the logic of exclusion and contradiction" (99). In their inclusiveness Agi Morato's garden and the freedom boat become the dramatic settings on which Cervantes projects his humanist ideals of liberty, justice, and solidarity. They simultaneously displace and interconnect different cultural spaces and different human aspirations. In this sense, these all-inclusive spaces can be conceived as heterotopic mirrors, which show an alternative cultural geography of the Mediterranean world. We could say that Cervantes's humanist heterotopia encourages spectators/readers to think of the Mediterranean world as a synchretic *multilocality* with many stories/histories to tell. From this perspective the Cervantine text seems to be doing what Philip Sheldrake calls for in his book on place, memory and identity:

> We need to become aware of what might be called 'a longer narrative' in which 'the others' who have been made absent by those who control public and institutional histories are now being restored as people who are fully present. . . . The notion that place relates to issues of empowerment and disempowerment forces us to think of multilocalities (that actual locations are many different 'places' at the same time) and multivocalities (that there are a variety of different voices to be heard in a place). (21)

The syncretic space of the boat, *a place without a place given to the infinity of the sea*, represents a clear alternative to the racially and culturally purified Spain of Philip III. As heterotopian symbols, Agi Morato's garden and the freedom boat signal a radically different notion of human community which would stand in opposition to the fundamentalist worldview that had led to the expulsion of the *moriscos*.[13]

Thus, what I am suggesting here is that in reexamining the cultural significance of Cervantes's captivity plays we may need to open the critical lens to incorporate not only the traumatic memories of a Spanish soldier but the collective trauma of a deeply scarred nation.[14] The "therapeutic" aspect of these plays could be read at several levels as readers/spectators are invited to reflect on cultural, religious, political and philosophical conflicts from a humanist (profoundly anti-dogmatic) perspective.[15] As I have argued elsewhere, Cervantes's captivity plays question official orthodoxy relocating the spectator/reader in hybrid spaces in which inclusive notions of shared human integrity and cultural tolerance can be tested against racialized images of otherness. As is the case in *Don Quijote*, *Los trabajos de Persiles y Sigismunda*, and his *Exemplary Novels*, Cervantes's plays of captivity bring his "lector avisado" or prudent reader into the realm of a literary imagination in which absolute certainties are often short-lived. As alternative spaces of human interaction Agi Morato's garden and the providential boat that enables the *felice fin* at the conclusion of *Los baños de Argel* are reservoirs of the Cervantine imagination that "transgress, undermine and question the alleged coherence or totality of self-contained systems" (Sheldrake 100).[16] As Foucault would put it, these heterotopian spaces are microcosmic mirrors of illusion that reflect all the sites of human experience—among them: death, life, captivity, suffering, charity, desire, love, hope and freedom—while exposing all other ordinary spaces as even more illusory.

Notes

1. Citations from this play are from Florencio Sevilla Arroyo's edition.
2. The concept of heterotopia or heterotopian place was developed by Michel Foucault for a talk he delivered in March 1967. Based on this talk, in October 1984 the French periodical *Architecture Mouvement Continuité* published a text titled "Des Espaces Autres." Even though this text was never reviewed by Foucault for publication, and therefore cannot be officially considered part of his work, it was presented to the public in Berlin as a Foucauldian text shortly after Foucault's death. I use an English translation from the French by Jay Miskowiec, published by the journal *Diacritics* in 1986. Foucault distinguishes between two distinct types of sites: utopias and heterotopias, both of which are connected with other types of spaces, with which they may also at times conflict. Fundamentally, a utopia is a thoroughly *unreal* space, while a heterotopia is simultaneously *mythical and real*, as H. Nasstrom Evans has pointed out.
3. In his elaboration on Foucault's concepts of heterotopia Edward W. Soja establishes conections with Lefebvre's thinking on spatiality and also with Homi Bhabha's notion of hybridity in order to underscore the critical potential of this type of alternative space. As he writes in *Third Space*: "*the assertion of an alternative envisioning of spatiality (as illustrated in the heterotopologies of Foucault, the trialectics and thirdings of Lefebvre [. . .], the hybridities of Hommi Bhabha) directly challenges (and is intended to challengingly deconstruct) all conventional modes of spatial thinking.* They are not just 'other spaces' to be added on to the geographical imagination, they are also 'other than' the established ways of thinking spatially. They are meant to detonate, to deconstruct, not to be comfortably poured back into old containers" (his emphasis, 163).
4. Stephen Rupp analyzes the spiritual concern of the captives in *Los baños* and concludes that: "Taken in sequence, these plays affirm the importance of religious constancy, but they subject martial heroism to a marked shift in value. In *El trato* Saavedra evokes the memory of the 1541 armada to maintain a hope (however limited) for rescue by force of arms; in *Los baños* such a hope is not present, and the captives turn to spiritual remedies alone. This separation of spiritual and martial heroism coincides with the gradual abandonment of large-scale warfare among the Mediterranean powers and suggests a keen awareness in Cervantes' mind of the conditions that compromised the objectives and the ethos of crusade in his time" (330). Among the many critics who have studied the theme of captivity in Cervantes's texts, looking to establish connections with his own captivity in Algiers, one must mention the works by Haedo, Zamora Vicente, Astrana Marín, Eisenberg ("Cervantes"), Canavaggio, Zmantar, Rossi, Percas de Ponseti, McGaha, and Garcés.
5. With regard to the period of captivity in Algiers, we know that Cervantes's first escape attempt occurred early, at the beginning of 1576, only four or five months after being captured, and was quickly thwarted when the Moor whom a group of

Christians had paid to bring them by land to Oran abandoned them to their own resources after a few days on the road, so they had to return to Algiers. Cervantes was punished. As a result of the evidence in the book *Topografía e historia general de Argel* (1612) generally attributed to Brother Diego de Haedo, but also to the cleric Antonio de Sosa—although Daniel Eisenberg in "Cervantes" attributes it to Cervantes himself—and in the legal document *Información de Argel* (compiled in Astrana Marín), collected and produced by Cervantes in 1580 to counteract common suspicions that arose from the time he spent with the *Other*, many are aware that Cervantes, risking his own life, hid, sheltered, and provided food for fourteen Christian captives ('cristianos principales') in a cave later known as "cueva de Cervantes" in the garden of the renegade Hasán, on the outskirts of Algiers.

In this environment he conceived his second escape plan, which consisted of waiting for the arrival of a Spanish frigate sent by his brother Rodrigo, already freed, and whom Cervantes had previously paid for his rescue. He had to plan a new escape because the money sent by his family in 1577 through the Mercedarian friars Jorge de Olivar and Jorge de Ongay, rescuers of captives, proved insufficient to satisfy the greed of Dalí Mamí, his captor and master, who demanded 500 golden escudos for his freedom. Betrayed at the last minute by "el Dorador," nickname of a renegade who had rejoined Christianity but then reneged again, Cervantes ended up being bought as a slave by the Venetian renegade Hasán Bajá, new king of Algiers, after his second escape attempt. In order to prevent another escape attempt, Hasán Bajá had Cervantes locked up for five months in the baths of his palace, and executed the gardener, Juan, who had helped him. The third evasion attempt in 1578 consisted of sending a Moor, with whom Cervantes had supposedly gotten along well while he was locked up, to Oran with some letters addressed to the enclave's general, Martín de Córdoba, asking him to send someone to help Cervantes and three other captive gentlemen escape. The Moor was caught, and thus the letters were intercepted. Through the intercession of a third party, Cervantes was spared the punishment of two thousand lashes, and the Moor was impaled.

After this incident, Hasán Bajá returned Cervantes to his master Dalí Mamí. Finally, in the autumn of 1579, Cervantes attempted his fourth escape, and as McGaha puts it, the account of this escape attempt is "quizá el más inverosímil de todos" (543) (perhaps the most implausible of all). First, Cervantes convinced the renegade Girón to rejoin Christianity, and then he convinced the Valencian merchant Onofre Ejarque to give Girón 1,300 doblas in order to buy an armed frigate with which to free more than sixty Christian captives, along with Cervantes himself. The plan was thwarted because, according to Cervantes, a slave of Hasán Bajá, the Dominican Juan Blanco de Paz, revealed it to his master. Not even after planning the escape attempt of so many Christians was Cervantes condemned to death; he was merely locked up for five months in Hasán's prison, under his home. Finally, Cervantes's captivity ended in September 1580 when the Trinitarian friars Juan Gil and Antonio de la Bella—according to Cortines Murube—ransomers of captives, paid the escudos that were being asked in exchange for his freedom.

6. To trace and study the evolution of this conjecture see *Cervantes y la Berbería* by historians Sola and de la Peña, and Garcés (110–15).

7. McGaha claims that "así, en las tres versiones, la heroína va idealizándose progresivamente, transformándose de mujer adúltera [*El trato*] en novia [*Los baños*], y luego en doncella ["Historia del cautivo"]; y el amor entre ella y el cautivo cristiano también va depurándose cada vez más, hasta que en la 'Historia del cautivo' aparecen ambos con una iconografía que nos recuerda inmediatamente a la Virgen y S. José" (545). (In this way, in the three versions, the heroine is being progressively idealized, changing from an adulterous woman [*El trato*], to a bride [*Los baños*], and then to a maiden ["The Captive's Tale"]; and the love between her and the Christian captive is also purified more and more, to the point that in "The Captive's Tale" both characters appear with an iconography that inmediately reminds us of the Virgin Mary and Saint Joseph). To study in detail this iconography and simbolism, see Camamis. One might think that this progressive idealization of Zahara, to which McGaha is referring, assumes that *Los baños* was written before the episode of "The Captive's Tale," a fact still surrounded by controversy. In any case, the argument is still sound if we assume that *Los baños* came at a later date, and consecuently the idealization of Zahara would progress from adulterous, to maiden, to bride.

8. This episode might represent what for Alda Tesán would be "un ejemplo magnífico de la poetización de episodios autobiográficos mezclados con elementos imaginados y resueltos como en su caso hubiera deseado Cervantes" (159) (a superb example of the poetization of autobiographical episodes intertwined with imagined elements and settled the way Cervantes would have wished). Likewise, Percas de Ponseti's thesis is that the episode of the cave of Montesinos in *Don Quixote* embodies a whole series of semantic, symbolic, and character double meanings, which apparently point to various autobiographical episodes of Cervantes's Algerian captivity. Cervantes supposedly wanted to use his literary skills cathartically to tell the wise reader many details of what he went through in Algiers. What happened in the cave of Montesinos will thus become a documentary allegory and will connect perfectly with the experiences of *El trato* and *Los baños*. Oliver Asín underlines the fact that in *Los baños* Cervantes always subordinates historical elements to legendary and autobiographical content (291).

9. Julia Domínguez proposes a similar reading of the Cervantine dramatization of captivity as a form of compensatory catharsis in her treatment of the "psicodrama" that represents *El trato de Argel*.

10. Menéndez Pelayo, Castro, Bataillon, and Vilanova are also among the scholars who have suggested connections between Cervantes's narrative and theatrical production and some of the foundational texts of European humanism, especially those of Erasmus.

11. For an analysis of how Cervantes defends, in *El trato*, *Los baños* and *La gran sultana*, a kind of humanism that criticizes dogmas and absolute truths by revealing the nonsense of social fantasies that separate us from the Other, see my essay "¿Ortodoxia cervantina?: Un análisis de *La gran sultana*, *El trato de Argel* y *Los baños de Argel.*"

12. As Foucault says about the mirror: "In the mirror, I see myself there where I am not, in an unreal, virtual space that opens up behind the surface. . . . [The mirror] makes this place that I occupy at the moment when I look at myself in the glass at once absolutely real, connected with all the space that surrounds it, and absolutely unreal, since in order to be perceived it has to pass through this virtual point which is over there" (24).

13. Barbara Fuchs and Aaron J. Ilika express a similar idea in their discussion of Ottoman themes in Cervantes's theater, specifically in *La gran sultana* (*The Great Sultana*): "Cervantes's texts on the Ottomans—both the play included here and the novella 'El amante liberal' (The Generous Lover)—share with the *Viaje* [referring to the anonymous *El viaje de Turquía*] a distinctly humanist and cosmopolitan sensibility, in which the depiction of otherness obliquely reflects Spain's limitations" (xix).

14. In his review of Garcés's book, Bradley Nelson offers a similar view calling for the incorporation of Spain's traumatic history in our reexamination of Cervantine allusions to racial tensions and racist politics in the context of the *culture of crisis* of the seventeeth century: "What is missing from this study . . . is Cervantes's answer to the traumatic historicization of his texts. Why not, for example, take Zoraida not as the representation of Cervantes's utopian dream but as the recognition of the violently divided, i.e., traumatized, nature of Cervantes's life and, by extension, Spain itself? If Cervantes was indeed tempted by the other, haunted by the *other*, even loved by the *other*, does not the terrible scene in which Zoraida takes leave of her father become all the more pathetic, all the more indicative of the cut introduced by politically driven discourses of racial and ethnic superiority?" (549). For more on the culture of crisis of seventeenth-century Spain from the perspective of racial politics and the wide spread obsession with the preservation of Christian blood lines (pureza de sangre), see Americo Castro's *De la edad conflictiva: Crisis de la cultura española en el Siglo XVII.*

15. I agree with Enrique Fernández when he claims: "Lo que Cervantes nos ofrece en esta [*El trato de Argel*] y otras obras de cautiverio es una instancia de lo que se denomina la 'memoria heroica,' una forma de recordar que busca en los hechos una visión moral, un principio que muestre a los individuos como responsables de sus acciones incluso en las circunstancias más adversas" (21). (What Cervantes offers in *El trato de Argel* and other captivity plays is an instance of what has been called "heroic memory," a form of recalling that seeks to find a moral view, a principle that would make individuals responsible for their actions even in the most adverse of circumstances).

16. Several critics have associated the Cervantine dramatization of captivity in *El trato*, *Los baños*, and "The Captive's Tale" with the opening of spaces of poetic creativity. Ortiz Lottman focuses on the figures of Zahara and Zoraida as emblems of freedom for Cervantes: "Zara and Zoraida are emblems of freedom for Cervantes the captive and writer, representing not only his physical liberation from the chains of slavery but also his mental breakthrough into a world of creativity" (359). For Garcés "The apparition of Zoraida [in "The Captive's Tale," and her double Zahara in *Los baños*], then, speaks not only to the reenactment and reelaboration of the traumatic experiences in Cervantes's fiction but also to fantastic and salvific images that open the window of creation" (218). In addition, Ortiz Lottman points out that: "Cervantes would have automatically associated gardens with creative activity, for Spanish literary academies often met in gardens and he attended the Academia Imitativa, the first to be founded in Madrid. Gardens were associated with writing poetry in both the Christian and Islamic traditions" (358). Finally, Daniel Eisenberg ("¿Por qué?") maintains that, given the presumably easy life that Cervantes could have lived had he become a renegade, as many others did—half the population of Algiers were renegades, according to Haedo—what made him return from Algiers were his desire to write and his love of the language, poetry and books.

Works Cited

Alda Tesán, J. M. "Los cautivos de Cervantes." *Boletín de la Biblioteca Menéndez Pelayo* 23.2–3 (1947): 150–62.

Astrana Marín, Luis. *Vida ejemplar y heroica de Miguel de Cervantes Saavedra.* 7 vols. Madrid: Instituto Editorial Reus, 1948–58.

Bataillon, Marcel. *Erasmo y España: Estudios sobre la historia espiritual del siglo XVI.* Trans. Antonio Alatorre. México: Fondo de Cultura Económica, 1950.

Camamis, George. "El hondo simbolismo de 'La hija de Agi Morato.'" *Cuadernos Hispanoamericanos* 319 (1977): 71–102.

Canavaggio, Jean. *Cervantes.* Trans. Mauro Armiño. Madrid: Espasa-Calpe, 1987.

Castillo, David R., and Nicholas Spadaccini. "El antiutopismo en *Los trabajos de Persiles y Sigismunda*: Cervantes y el cervantismo actual." *Cervantes* 20.1 (2000): 115–31.

Castillo, Moisés R. "¿Ortodoxia cervantina?: Un análisis de *La gran sultana*, *El trato de Argel* y *Los baños de Argel*." *Bulletin of the Comediantes* 56. 2 (2004): 219–40.

Castro, Américo. *De la edad conflictiva: Crisis de la cultura española en el siglo XVII.* Madrid: Taurus, 1972.

———. *El pensamiento de Cervantes.* Madrid: Imprenta Hernando, 1925.

Cervantes, Miguel de, *El ingenioso hidalgo don Quijote de la Mancha.* 2 vols. Ed. John Jay Allen. Madrid: Cátedra, 1998.

————. *El trato de Argel. Comedias y entremeses*. Vol. 5. Ed. Rudolph Schevill and Adolfo Bonilla. 6 vols. Madrid: Bernardo Rodríguez, 1915–22.

————. *Los baños de Argel*. Ed. Florencio Sevilla Arroyo. Biblioteca Virtual Miguel de Cervantes. Accessed 13 July 2009. *www.cervantesvirtual.com/servlet/ SirveObras/46850574656352274754491/index.htm*

Clark, Emma. *Underneath Which Rivers Flow: The Symbolism of the Islamic Garden*. London: Prince of Wales's Institute of Architecture, 1996.

Cortines Murube, Felipe. "Cervantes en Argel y sus libertadores trinitarios." *Boletín de la Biblioteca Menéndez Pelayo* 23. 2–3 (1947): 87–100.

Cresti, Federico. "Agdal, Jenan and Riyad in the African Maghreb." *The Garden as City, The City as Garden*. Ed. Attilio Petruccioli. Spec. Issue of *Environmental Design: Journal of the Islamic Environmental Design Centre* 2 (1986): 58–64.

Dickie, James. "The Hispano-Arab Garden: Notes towards a Tipology." *The Legacy of Muslim Spain*. Ed. Salma Khadra Jayyusi. Leiden, New York, Koln: Brill, 1992. 1016–35.

Domínguez, Julia. "Los escenarios de la memoria: Psicodrama en *El trato de Argel* de Cervantes." *Bulletin of the Comediantes* 61.1 (2009): 1–23.

Eisenberg, Daniel. "Cervantes, autor de la *Topografía e historia general de Argel* publicada por Diego de Haedo." *Cervantes* 16 (1996): 32–53.

————. "¿Por qué volvió Cervantes de Argel?" *Ingeniosa Invención: Essays on Golden Age Spanish Literature for Geoffrey L. Stagg in Honor of His Eighty-Fifth Birthday*. Eds. Ellen M. Anderson and Amy R. Williamsen. Newark, DE: Juan de la Cuesta, 1999.

Fernández, Enrique. "*Los tratos de Argel*: Obra testimonial, denuncia política y literatura terapéutica." *Cervantes* 20.1 (2000): 7–26.

Fothergill-Payne, Louise. "*Los tratos de Argel, Los cautivos de Argel* y *Los baños de Argel*: Tres 'trasuntos' de un 'asunto.'" *El mundo del teatro español en su Siglo de Oro: Ensayos dedicados a John E. Varey*. Ed. J. M. Ruano de la Haza. Ottawa: Dovehouse, 1989.

Foucault, Michel. "Of Other Spaces." Trans. Jay Miskowiec. *Diacritics* 16 (Spring 1986): 22–27.

Friedman, Edward H. "Introducción." *Bulletin of the Comediantes* 56.2 (2004): 187–92.

————. *The Unifying Concept: Approaches to the Structure of Cervantes' Comedias*. York, SC: Spanish Literature Publications Company, 1981.

Fuchs, Barbara, and Aaron J. Ilika, eds. and trans. *The Bagnios of Algiers and The Great Sultana: Two Plays of Captivity*. Miguel de Cervantes. Philadelphia: University of Pennsylvania Press, 2010.

Garcés, María Antonia. *Cervantes in Algiers: A Captive's Tale*. Nashville: Vanderbilt University Press, 2002.

Haedo, Diego de. *Topografía e historia general de Argel*. Madrid: Sociedad de Bibliófilos

Españoles, Vols. II y III, 1929. (El volumen I pertenece a la edición de Valladolid: 1612).

Khansari, Mehdi, M. Reza Moghtader, and Minouch Yavari. *The Persian Garden: Echoes of Paradise*. Washington, DC: Mage, 1998.

King, Willard F. "Cervantes, el cautiverio y los renegados." *Nueva Revista de Filología Hispánica* 40.1 (1992): 279–91.

Lefebvre, Henri. *The Production of Space*. Oxford: Blackwell, 1991.

Maravall, José Antonio. *Utopía y contrautopía en el Quijote*. Santiago de Compostela: Pico Sacro, 1976.

McGaha, Michael. "Hacia la verdadera historia del cautivo Miguel de Cervantes." *Revista Canadiense de Estudios Hispánicos* 20 (1996): 540–46.

Menéndez Pelayo, Marcelino. *Erasmo y Cervantes*. Instituto Miguel de Cervantes de Filología Hispánica, Delegación de Barcelona. Barcelona: CSIC, 1949.

Moner, Michel. "Moros y cristianos en el *Quijote*: El caso de Zoraida, la mora cristiana (*Don Quijote* I, 37–42)." *¿ "¡Bon compaño, jura Di!"?: El encuentro de moros, judíos y cristianos en la obra cervantina*. Ed. Caroline Schmauser and Monika Walter. Frankfurt am Main: Vervuert; Madrid: Iberoamericana, 1998.

Nasstrom Evans, H. "About Heterotopia." Accessed 13 Jul. 2009. *www.flickr.com/groups/heterotopia/*.

Nelson, Bradley J. Review of *Cervantes in Algiers: A Captive's Tale*, by María Antonia Garcés. *Comparative Literature Studies* 43.4 (2006): 544–49.

Oliver Asín, Jaime. "La hija de Agi Morato en la obra de Cervantes." *Boletín de la Real Academia Española* 27 (1947–48): 245–339.

Ortiz Lottman, Maryrica. "The Call of the Natural World in *Los baños de Argel*." *Bulletin of the Comediantes* 56.2 (2004): 345–66.

Percas de Ponseti, Helena. "¿Quién era Belerma?" *Revista Hispánica Moderna* 49 (1996) [1997]: 375–92.

Rossi, Rosa. *Escuchar a Cervantes: Un ensayo biográfico*. Valladolid: Ámbito, 1988.

Rupp, Stephen. "Remembering 1541: Crusade and Captivity in the Algiers Plays of Cervantes." *Revista de Estudios Hispánicos* 32 (1998): 313–35.

Sánchez, Alberto. "Revisión del cautiverio cervantino en Argel." *Cervantes* 17.1 (1997): 7–24.

Sheldrake, Philip. *Spaces for the Sacred: Place, Memory, and Identity*. Baltimore: The Johns Hopkins University Press, 2001.

Soja, Edward W. *Thirdspace: Journeys to Los Angeles and Other Real-and-Imagined Places*. Oxford: Blackwell, 1996.

Sola, Emilio, and José F. de la Peña. *Cervantes y la Berbería: Cervantes, mundo turco-berberisco y servicios secretos en la época de Felipe II*. México: Fondo de Cultura Económica, 1995.

Tuan, Yi-Fu. *Space and Place: The Perspective of Experience*. Minneapolis: University of Minnesota Press, 1977.

Vilanova, Antonio. *Erasmo y Cervantes*. Barcelona: Lumen, 1989.

Wescoat, Jim, Jr. "The Islamic Garden: Issues for Landscape Research." *The Garden as City, The City as Garden.* Ed. Attilio Petruccioli. Special issue of *Environmental Design: Journal of the Islamic Environmental Design Centre* 2 (1986): 10–19.

Zamora Vicente, Alonso. "El cautiverio en la obra cervantina." *Homenaje a Cervantes.* Ed. Francisco Sánchez-Castañer. Valencia: Mediterráneo, 1950.

Zmantar, Françoise. "Miguel de Cervantes y sus fantasmas de Argel." *Quimera* 2 (1980): 31–37.

4

Signs of the Times:
Emblems of Baroque Science Fiction

Bradley J. Nelson

> Semantic Faculties: Factions within the mathic world, in the years following the Reconstitution, generally claiming descent from Halikaarn. So named because they believed that symbols could bear actual semantic content. The idea is traceable to Protas and to Hylea before him. Compare Syntactic Faculties.
> (THE DICTIONARY, 4th edition, A. R. 3000)[1]

In his 2002 tour de force essay on the Hispanic baroque *Barroco*, Fernando R. de la Flor introduces Juan de Borja's emblem, *Hominem te esse cogita* (think that you are [only] a man), as evidence of a Hispanic counter-proposal to the Cartesian revolution, signaled by Descartes's emblematic motto *Cogito ergo sum* (Fig. 1). The Spanish scholar's lengthy dissertation on Spain's contestatory relationship with European modernity deploys Borja's emblem as a prolepsis for his hypothesis concerning a specifically Hispanic strategy for negotiating the modern marriage of (proto-)capitalism and political absolutism. The essay goes to great lengths to excavate what the author identifies as the subversive nihilism at the heart of Counter-Reformation efforts to close off the Spanish empire from the progressive and instrumentalist thrust behind Descartes's attempt to define and legitimize the individual subject's encounter with, and analysis of, the real physical causes of the universe.

R. de la Flor's argument is dialectically anchored in his rejection of José Antonio Maravall's more instrumentalist (Cartesian) definition of the Spanish baroque: "I believe that the peculiarity of this hispanic baroque culture resides, precisely, in what Maravall denies from the beginning: that is, in the manifest capacity of its expressive system to move in the opposite direction to any established ends" (*Barroco* 19).

R. de la Flor's face-to-the-wind navigation of Spanish mysticism and skeptical philosophy frames its anti-Cartesian characterization of the Spanish baroque within Borja's emblem of *desengaño*:

> [Borja] manages to give a precise body to a Counter-Reformation ethos, profoundly contrary to what is revealed to be the growing substance and process of self-sufficient individuation, attached to the expansive logic of capitalism. An axiom, of course, which we could certainly not call foundational, rather, to the contrary, profoundly delegitimizing, since above all it introduces the concept of contingency and decay, that which is precisely opposed to what, I'll say it once more, the proud Cartesian *cogito* and the *sum* and the *e[r]go* erect. (*Barroco* 50)

According to this stance, the quixotic yet still modern drive of the Spanish baroque is produced in the very effort to seal Spain off from modernity in order to override internal material and social decay through the erection of what R. de la Flor calls, in another place, the "metaphysical peninsula."[2] In essence, the insistent and cruel ironization of the real reduces social and political hierarchies to dust and thus open to derision. These "anarchical" tendencies of

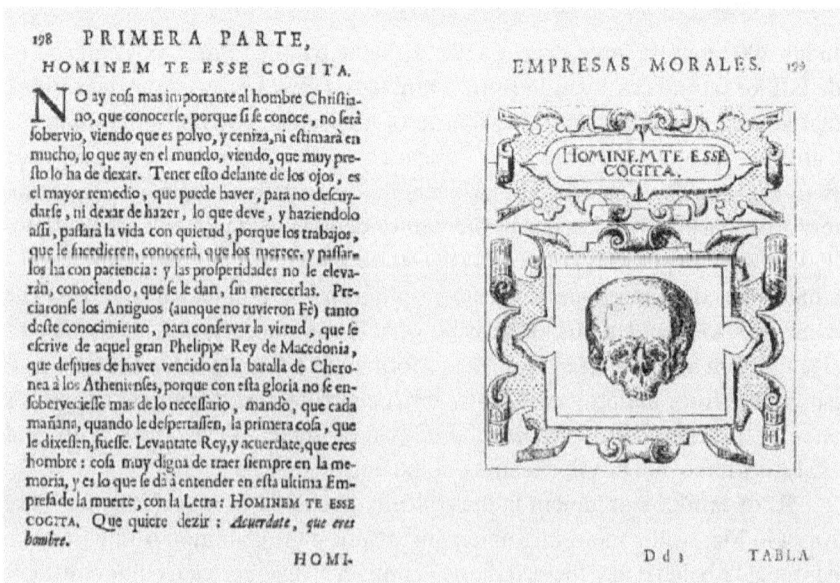

198   PRIMERA PARTE,
HOMINEM TE ESSE COGITA.

NO ay cosa mas importante al hombre Christiano, que conocerse, porque si se conoce, no será soberuio, viendo que es polvo, y ceniza, ni estimará en mucho, lo que ay en el mundo, viendo, que muy presto lo ha de dexar. Tener esto delante de los ojos, es el mayor remedio, que puede haver, para no descuydarse, ni dexar de hazer, lo que deve, y haziendolo assi, passará la vida con quietud, porque los trabajos, que le sucedieren, conocerá, que los merece, y passarlos ha con paciencia: y las prosperidades no le elevarán, conociendo, que se le dan, sin merecerlas. Preciaronse los Antiguos (aunque no tuvieron Fè) tanto deste conocimiento, para conservar la virtud, que se escrive de aquel gran Phelippe Rey de Macedonia, que despues de haver vencido en la batalla de Cheronea à los Athenienses, porque con esta gloria no se ensoberveciesse mas de lo necessario, mandò, que cada mañana, quando le despertassen, la primera cosa, que le dixessen, fuesse. Levantate Rey, y acuerdate, que eres hombre: cosa muy digna de traer siempre en la memoria, y es lo que se dà à entender en esta ultima Empresa de la muerte, con la Letra: HOMINEM TE ESSE COGITA, Que quiere dezir: *Acuerdate, que eres hombre.*

HOMI-

EMPRESAS MORALES.   199

HOMINEM TE ESSE COGITA.

D d 3   TABLA

Fig. 1. Hominem Te Esse Cogita, in Juan de Borja, *Empresas morales* (1680), (198–99)

Hispanic baroque nihilism are seen to offer a perverse reflection of Cartesian scientific rationalism: where Descartes's indicative *cogito* rejects the neoscholastic desubstantialization of the human subject, Borja's imperative *cogita* reduces all hierarchical structures, including Reason, to the same nothingness at the heart of the confessional subject, thus preparing the ground for the liberating drive of modernity. In scientific terms, the gradual displacement of neoscholastic dogma concerning physical causality by "hypothetical" mathematical theorems results in a nihilistic relativism, especially where political necessity is concerned.

There are several problems with this characterization of the Spanish baroque, the most intractable of which arises from what has become a commonplace: the oft-lamented and/or celebrated *difference* as regards Spain's relationship to Europe. Another arises from a similarly categorical understanding of Descartes's place in modernity. As Lyle Massey points out, Descartes's attempts to legitimize an empirical approach to the central questions of natural philosophy are plagued by the same Augustinian interdictions concerning the finitude and fallibility of human faculties and bodies that R. de la Flor associates with an exclusively Counter-Reformation understanding of human (un) reason. In this light, Descartes's attempt to plot a mathematical way out of the vacuum that begins to surround traditional Neoscholastic notions of physical causality is no more or less modern than attempts by political and social elites, in baroque Spain, to respond to an analogous power vacuum that accompanies the erosion of traditional doctrines concerning blood-based social hierarchies. Seemingly overlooked by R. de la Flor is the fact that Maravall's notion of "baroque guided culture" as a reactionary social mentality is dependent on the nihilistic potential—and concomitant melancholy, or terror—of this epochal change (*Culture of the Baroque*).

The struggle between an unbounded—in theory at least—will to knowledge and institutional attempts to control the scientist's curious desire can be approached from a number of perspectives. But the point of departure and central trope of this essay will be "the emblematic mode of representation" (Daly). My thesis is that the emblem and the images of knowledge that it configures function as a middle space or medium for the negotiation of a residual desire to identify a unified meaning in the cosmos, on the one hand, and a fragmented, hybrid, and contradictory search for knowledge symptomatic of the modern world, on the other. In opposition to a nihilistic reading of Borja's emblem, *Hominem te esse cogita*, my reading of this emblem—and the two I will interpret toward the end of this essay—will focus on how Borja's desire to rein in the desiring intellect can be seen as a conservative reaction to a modern intellectual program initiated within his own religious order, the Society of Jesus. More to the point, what is arguably culturally specific about Borja's emblem— although this is debatable as well—is the relationship between the desire for knowledge and the guilt produced by institutional attempts to lead the subject to reject his own desiring intellect. In the end, what is most evident in the emblem is not the actual existence of epochal change but rather the fear of change as it is represented in a literary expression emanating from one of the most powerful families in Europe. For this reason, I will take up R. de la Flor's linking of emblematics to science in a very literal sense.

Although he never produced an emblem book, no texts are more emblematic of the baroque, courtly subject of representation than Baltasar Gracián's. Alciato's emblems appear sixteen times in *Agudeza y arte de ingenio*; moreover, in Gracián's assemblage of a genealogy of writers of "philosophical truths," emblematics is situated at the center of the curious relationship between baroque science and aesthetics.[3]

> A un mismo blanco de la filosófica verdad, asestaron todos los sabios, aunque por diferentes rumbos de la invención y agudeza. Homero con sus Epopeyas, Esopo con sus Fábulas, Séneca con sus Sentencias, Ovidio con sus Metamorfosis, Juvenal con sus Sátiras, Alciato con sus Emblemas, Erasmo con sus Refranes, el Bocalino con sus Alegorías y el príncipe don Juan Manuel con sus Cuentos. La semejanza es el fundamento de toda la invención fingida, y la traslación de lo mentido a lo verdadero es el alma de esta agudeza. (Gracián 425)

> (All wise men took aim at the same target of philosophical truth, although by different paths of invention and wit. Homer with his Epics, Aesop with his Fables, Seneca with his Sentences, Ovid with his Metamorphosis, Juvenal with his Satires, Alciato with his Emblems, Erasmo with his Adages, Bocalino with his Allegories and the prince Don Juan Manuel with his Stories. Semblance is the foundation of all feigned invention, and the translation of falseness into truth is the soul of this wit.)[4]

One of the most interesting aspects of this philosophical canon is the assertive way in which aesthetics and philosophy are held to be inextricably related, an early modern commonplace that is often overlooked by modern critics, who tend to bracket off literary creation from more "scientific" fields of practice. However, as Thomas Kuhn argues in his study of the Copernican revolution, "the real appeal of sun-centered astronomy was aesthetic rather than pragmatic. To astronomers the initial choice between Copernicus' system and Ptolemy's could only be a matter of taste, and matters of taste are the most difficult of all to define or debate" (172). What unites Gracián's authors is the indirect or oblique manner in which they assemble and communicate their philosophical truths. All discourse falls under the rubric of what he terms *ficciones* in some places and *mentiras* in others, as aesthetic-philosophical practice becomes situated at the center of "a system of moral and epistemological rigor. . . . Truth, in short, becomes a function of learned judgment, not of the material itself, which in time seems to owe even its existence to the [literary subject]" (Said 67). Due to the self-conscious way in which they foreground their representational status, these allegorical genres both display and problematize the unstable and tenuous relationship between language, history, truth, and subjectivity. In Massey's words, "it is in the moment when skeptical doubt is strongest and most overwhelming that a glimpse of the truth or certainty of being is possible" (1163). Gracián foregrounds the fundamental cut between the desire for epistemological certitudes emanating from what R. de la Flor terms a medievalizing "organicist" ontology, based on Aristotle's metaphysics of substance and form, and the "fallacious" nature of man's epistemological faculties and instruments. If science, whether practiced by Aristotelian natural philosophers or Copernican astronomers, must rely on an inescapably fictitious terrestrial syntax, then what we find in Gracián's philosophical canon is the problematic and tension-filled space of science fiction.

Much can be learned about baroque representations of truth and the cosmos by relating early modern debates between mathematical astronomers and natural philosophers to the popular postmodern genre of science fiction: or as Neal Stephenson dubs it, "speculative fiction" ("Note" xiii). Science fiction deals primarily with hypothetical realities derived from theoretical speculation and technological projections, often based on actual scientific discoveries, which makes it an ideal sounding board for the complicated relation between science, fiction, and natural philosophy in early modernity. For example, Stephenson's *Snow Crash* (1992) is a sci-fi thriller whose most exciting action, both theoretical and "physical," takes place in the virtual space of the World Wide Web; and his bestseller *Cryptonomicon* (1999) is a mindbender that spans the years between WWII and the end of the twenty-first century, and whose plot is embedded in a complex history and performance of cryptography. In both novels, narrative space and storyline developments are formulated as binary mathematical duels and geometrical witticisms that have a direct bearing on the immediate or *real* circumstances of their metafictional worlds. Stephenson is probably best known for his trilogy *The Baroque Cycle* (2003–2004), which weaves a vast and compelling narrative from the philosophical, scientific, economic, and political currents that drive the West's transition to modernity. Whether set in the past or the future, what sets Stephenson's fiction apart are his approachable and witty explanations and performances of complex theoretical concepts and conundrums, such as the ingenious parallels he draws between Leibniz's invention of "the calculus" and major advances made in cryptography in the seventeenth century (*The System of the World*).

His latest work of speculative fiction *Anathem* (2008), whose emblematic name combines the seemingly antithetical notions of *anthem* and *anathema*, takes place on the fictional world of "Arbre," and appears to be set simultaneously several millennia in the future and the past. *Anathem*'s narrator and protagonist is named Fraa Erasmas, and the action follows his movement between the two main social and political spaces on Arbre (a clever and theoretically plausible ramification of Earth). In one space we find the "mathic universe," which is made up of diverse, enclosed *monastic* orders of "avouts," each with its own theoretical or dogmatic identity—think aristotelians, neoplatonists, cartesians, etc. On the other side of the wall, literally, is the "extramuros world," which sports the technologically based, sensory overload of our own postmodern cosmopolis, and whose leaders, although they draw on the expertise and advice of high ranking members of the maths, wield the real power on Arbre and are referred to as the "saeculars." At several points in Arbre's violent history, the extramuros populations have succumbed to their fear of the avouts' ability to translate their theoretical discoveries into various forms of alternately amazing and terrifying praxis. This saecular fear of the avout has resulted in the separation and isolation of the latter in the aforementioned maths, as well as a strict prohibition on almost all forms of praxis (enforced by *The Inquisition*), especially any new ones that could give the mathic world power over the Saeculum. There are, in other words, at least two alien "races" already occupying parallel universes in the Arborean microcosm.

Anathem's rather conventional plot is triggered by an astounding astronomical phenomenon: a massive spacecraft has been spotted orbiting the planet, and its discovery turns Arbre's society on its head, forcing the mathic and extramuros populations to work together to confront a possible common threat.[5] This is where the conventional part ends and Stephenson's particular genius for explaining and dramatizing ontological and epistemological conundrums begins to pull the phenomenological rug out from underneath his readers. For although the spacecraft displays a number of images (i.e., platonic forms) that are recognizable to avout and educated saeculars alike—such as triangles, circles, and, most importantly, a geometrical proof [Fig. 2]—Stephenson does not allow the reader to completely anthropomorphize the alien

"Geometers," a strategy which also effects a useful dehumanization of the Arboreans, lest we be lulled into forgetting that they also come from another time and space.[6]

The discovery that the aliens may deploy the same geometrical language as the Arboreans is the occasion for Stephenson to introduce a number of speculative thought experiments, which the avout use to explain the theoretical problems that arise from attempting to understand an alien linguistic system. One example features platonic models of a fly (all eyes), a bat (all ears), and a worm (all touch), and asks how three beings that rely on mutually exclusive perception faculties and linguistic systems might work together to solve a common problem. (We are not so far removed from the Augustinian denigration of the human senses that lies at the foundation of Counter-Reformation ontology

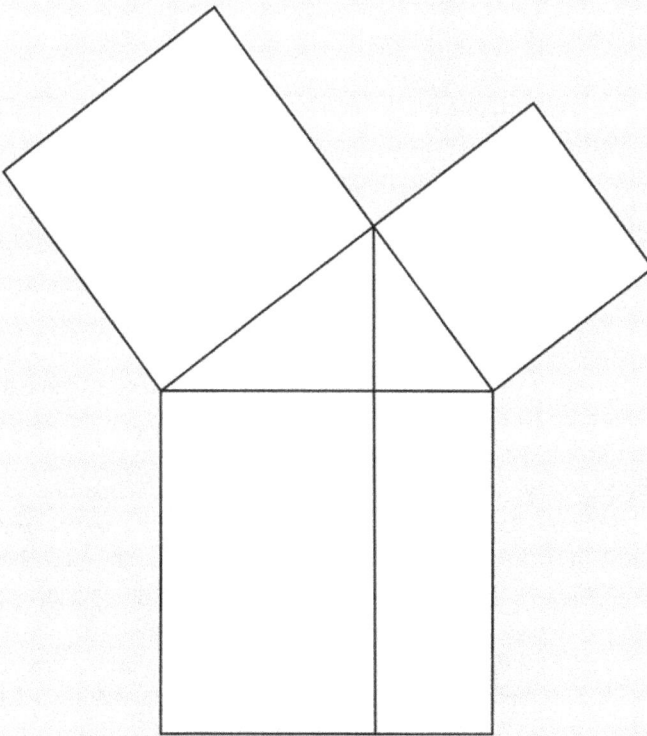

Fig. 2. Pythagorean theorem. (Courtesy Cilpart FCIT.)

and the nihilistic epistemology described by R. de la Flor.) The Geometers, it turns out, come from four different planets, each of whose evolutionary history has produced a type of matter that is literally impossible on any of the others, including Arbre. Each race is more different in nature from the others than is, say, a fly from a bat or a worm, all of which are carbon-based life forms and share fundamental molecular material. The theoretical problems produced by this situation are as numerous as they are profound, in that the same sensory faculties that allow a race to navigate and manipulate its reality turn out to be serious obstacles in encounters with competing realities: unless, of course, they can find a common syntax through which to communicate, such as geometry.

The plot line most germane to this essay concerns the decoding of the emblem engraved on the side of the ship, the aforementioned geometric proof, which introduces the opposed, linguistic orders mentioned in the epigraph at the beginning of this essay: the Syntacticians and the Semanticists. For the Syntactician, the emblematic riddle presents a series of challenges, the foremost of which is deciding which unique syntax, out of all imaginable syntaxes, might help identify the Geometers' intended meaning. This is complicated by the fact that each of the four races of Geometers communicates according to a different material and linguistic matrix. Since language is both made possible and absolutely limited by biological and chemical mechanisms embedded in corporeal matter, incompatible material matrices result in incompatible syntactic faculties. For the Semanticist, the problem may appear less difficult, since each linguistic sign harbors, a priori, a meaning unique to itself. The problem here would be to identify which of the inherited, or iconic, meanings the Geometers are deploying and whether this meaning would be unique to one of the four cosmologies, or common to all.

In Thomist terms, all of this speculation concerning the authorial intent of the Geometers is performed *ex suppositione*, or from effects to causes, which carries the potential of producing an infinite number of causal explanations in which the Geometers' arrival "makes sense." By bringing these competing cosmologies to bear on the scant physical evidence produced by the *starry messengers,*[7] Stephenson fashions a baroque space in which there are no stable foundations or boundaries, only increasingly complex folds of mathematical, philosophical, and religious matrices revolving around what is taken for a geometrical emblem, but which functions, in the end, as a limit or void; a veritable vacuum where reality and meaning are concerned.[8] Rather than stabilize the reality of the interstellar encounter, the emblem on the side of the ship functions as a medium in which distinct linguistic, scientific, and ideological orders are negotiated and questioned: in other words, a space where definitions and speculation concerning the self and the other are brought into contact and conflict. Much like Borja's emblem of the skull, the meaning of the Geometers' trademark is never satisfactorily established. Indeed, although *Anathem*'s plot ends with a conventional romantic liaison, the reader is left with the impression that this is only one of a large if not infinite number of actual, coexisting endings, all but one of which is absent. This last one, in which "boy gets girl," also happens to be the one most desired by the reader. Other endings suggested by the text include: the death of all the main characters and the destruction of Arbre; or the death of all the main characters and the destruction of the spaceship. There are, in other words, a significant number of simultaneously hypothetical and real universes produced by the syntactic arrangement of the semantic possibilities of the novel, reflected, once again, in the title of the book: *Anathem*.

We find an analogous situation in the baroque, where emblems serve as a theoretical space and strategic praxis for the negotiation of power and meaning in virtually every literary practice of early modernity.[9] Emblem scholars such as Daly, Russell, and R. de la Flor (*Emblemas*) have established the emblem's central role in the baroque culture of spectacle, but I would like to use Stephenson's speculative model as a guide for analyzing emblematics as a medium for the negotiation and problematization of dominant and emergent scientific paradigms of early modern Europe. We begin with the observation that the most important astronomical discovery of the seventeenth century is framed not as a scientific achievement but instead takes the form of an emblem, in which the discoverer Galileo exploits his discovery of the four moons of Jupiter (1609) in the celebration of the celestial legitimacy of the political dynasty of Cosimo II de Medici. Mario Biagioli writes:

> What he had observed, Galileo claimed, was not a discovery but a confirmation of the Medici's destiny, almost a scientific proof of their dynastic horoscope. . . . It was not by chance that the "bright stars offer[ed] themselves in the heavens" right after Cosimo II's enthronement. It was not by chance that such stars were circling around Jupiter (Cosimo's planet) like his offspring and that Jupiter was actually above the horizon at the time of Prince Cosimo's birth, thus passing on to him the virtues of the founder of the dynasty. (128)

Scientific achievement and emblematic wit are wedded in Galileo's device, and rather than framing the mathematical rigor of his method or the astronomical implications of such a discovery, the Medicean stars symbolize a political end: the destiny of the Medici dynasty. Nor is this Galileo's first attempt at emblematizing a scientific phenomenon in politico-mythological terms. It was, in fact, an emblem he assembled on the occasion of Cosimo's wedding (to Maria Maddalena of Austria), that paved the way for his self-transformation from a university mathematician into the preeminent court philosopher in Italy. On that occasion, he composed an emblem based on the image of a lodestone, "identifying in the sympathetic attraction between the lodestone and the small pieces of iron a fine metaphor for the Medici political agenda" (Biagioli 121). Far from an exception to the rule, Galileo's Medicean stars tell us much about the interpenetration of mathematical astronomy and more courtly social practices in the baroque. In order to understand why and how emblematics becomes such an important key to the struggle for legitimacy of mathematical astronomy (and heliocentric cosmology), it is necessary to take a more comprehensive look at the hierarchies internal to early modern intellectual institutions: specifically, the relationship between the alien paradigms of mathematically based astronomy and neoaristotelian natural philosophy.

Let us recall that Copernicus wrote his famous treatise advocating the shift to a heliocentric conception of the universe in 1543. Sixty-five years later, Copernican astronomy has still not become the dominant cosmological model, even though its mathematical innovations made a significant impact on both the calculation of the movement of the planets and related efforts to reform the calendar. As Kuhn explains, "Using Copernicus' mathematical system without advocating the physical motion of the earth provided a convenient escape from the dilemma posed by the contrasting celestial harmonies and terrestrial discord of the *De Revolutionibus*" (187). The reasons for this seeming contradiction are numerous and stem from technical problems internal to Copernicus's mathematical models, as well as from external resistance emanating from philosophical, theological, and sociopolitical traditions. As previously mentioned, Galileo's *Sidereus Nuncius* demonstrates how any boundaries between these domains cannot be maintained without serious bracketing operations coming into play. In the words of Biagioli, "patronage is the key to understanding processes of identity and status formation that are the keys to understanding both the scientists' cognitive attitudes and career strategies" (14). His landmark study *Galileo, Courtier* convincingly demonstrates that the conversion of mathematical realism into the dominant scientific paradigm of modernity is, in the main, a question of social prestige and intellectual legitimacy, rather than a case of an empirically-based science triumphing over myth. Although Galileo's astronomical discoveries would not have been possible without his training and expertise in mathematics and optics, it was thanks to his artistry and wit as an emblematist that his discoveries became spectacular marvels in the Court, thus launching him into his new identity as court philosopher.

The main challenge facing the inventor of the telescope, one which he never completely overcame, was the low scientific and social status given to mathematics and astronomy in Scholastic and Neoscholastic thought and academic institutions. Analogous to the artisan status of medieval painters and sculptors, mathematicians and astronomers were considered mere technicians who dealt with abstract, hypothetical, syntactic devices—"syn-dev" in Stephenson's vocabulary—unlike natural philosophers, who dealt with the real *necessary* causes and meanings of cosmological phenomena. According to Rivka Feldhay's analysis of the Jesuits' attempts to legitimize mathematics as a necessary part of natural philosophy, "astronomical theories had the status of probable, hypothetical truths . . . but could not become the basis of a new cosmological vision" (206). Although mathematical calculation was useful and necessary to the practical problems of mechanics, navigation, and optics—as well as military installations, weaponry, and strategizing—mathematical forms, signs, and syntax were considered hypothetical rather than real. Furthermore, since mathematical proofs proceed from effects to causes (*ex suppositione*) rather than from universal causes to material effects, "mathematics could never secure the absolute necessity of a physical cause" (Feldhay 206). According to Gracián's view, its philosophical truths were communicated through fictional means.

In this light, one of the most surprising alliances of the Counter-Reformation was that between Galileo and Jesuit mathematicians and scholars at the Collegio Romano. A. C. Crombie and A. Carugo have demonstrated that "two autograph treatises on natural philosophy which [Galileo] published as juvenilia were based on textbooks, sometimes copied word for word, by three well-known Jesuit philosophers at the Collegio Romano" (167). Biagioli notes that, "without being Copernicans, the Jesuits eventually gave a very strong endorsement of Galileo's telescopic observations" (93). This relationship becomes less of a mystery once we recognize that the Jesuits, behind the forceful writings of Christopher Clavius, initiated an ingenious program to legitimize mathematics as both necessary and useful to the search for absolute causes at the heart of Thomist natural philosophy. As detailed above, the motivations for this tentative and incomplete rapprochement were as social and political in nature as they were philosophical and theological. But the kernel of discord in this modern struggle—essentially between the Dominicans and the Jesuits—is emblematic of the shift from the essentializing dogmas of Scholastic theology, wedded to the Ptolemaic cosmological system, toward the decentered scientific realism of the Copernican revolution.

At once theological and scientific, ontological and epistemological, the main bone of contention at the heart of Neoscholastic thought, according to Feldhay, is man's free will: specifically, what God knows absolutely and/or hypothetically about man's future actions. Contrary to what is generally presupposed, "the Counter-Reformation gave birth to two different Thomist interpretations embedded in different institutional settings, with different problems and goals, different ideological frameworks, and different attitudes to knowledge" (Feldhay 197). In modern (fictional) scientific terms, we are looking at two distinct, if simultaneous, "Causal Domain[s]: A collection of things mutually linked in a web of cause-and-effect relationships—THE DICTIONARY, 4th edition, A.R. 3000" (Stephenson, *Anathem* 788). The "pure" Thomists were the Dominicans, who believed that God's foreknowledge of man's actions is absolute, because God's knowledge and will must remain inseparable if his omnipotence is to remain absolute: "The necessity of predestination derives from the absolute character of God's foreknowledge and will. Only by emphasizing the absolute necessity of predestination can God's omnipotence be satisfactorily vindicated" (Feldhay 205). Moreover, since *knowledge* and *will* only become knowable in God's willed *decree*, these three aspects constitute a closed triangle of simultaneous, atemporal acts, a formal structure that removes God's knowledge and actions from any temporal or spatial sense of progression. There is no room for hypothetical knowledge, which would arise only if there were to appear a space of indetermination, temporal in nature, between divine knowledge and the exercise of divine will, which would then resituate God's decree within a temporal framework and, in this way, allow for hypothetical knowledge.

This, however, is exactly what Clavius attempts to do by resituating God's knowledge and will according to a temporal relationship in which the exercise of his will in the realization of a divine decree is postponed, similar to the way a *deus ex machina* decrees the meaning and status of a dramatic representation after the action has come to a halt. Until such time as the decree is willed, God's foreknowledge remains hypothetical: "Separate and prior to the decree, the Jesuits contended, God has '*scientia media*' by which he knows with a certain and infallible knowledge man's future acts, although these are not yet predestined by his will. To some degree, God's voluntary decree is guided by his knowledge" (Felday 205). There is, of course, an irresolvable contradiction here, since if God's knowledge is infallible there is no logical reason for him to delay the exercise of his will and the pronouncement of his decree. Nevertheless, it is no more problematic than the Dominican concept of man's predestined free will. More importantly, it opens up a space for God's knowledge itself to become hypothetical in nature, which allows for the legitimation of hypothetical fields of human knowledge, such as mathematics.

The problem for Copernicus, Galileo, and now Clavius is that Thomism "appeared to have doubts about the real essence of mathematical entities (geometrical circles, for example), and probably accepted the opinion that they differed essentially from physical entities (material bodies in the form of a sphere)" (Feldhay 206). In other words, it is as much a question of ontology as epistemology; or, perhaps better stated, ontology and epistemology are welded together by the doctrine of free will, whichever doctrine one happens to ascribe to. As Robert Westman writes, "Copernicus has made a physical claim and . . . this claim has violated accepted divisions of knowledge" (108). Since astronomical theories were dependent on these hypothetical, mathematical entities to express their theses and proofs concerning the calculation, measurement, and causes of the movement of celestial bodies, "[they] had the status of probable, hypothetical truths" (Feldhay 207). In institutional terms, this doctrine produced a de facto intellectual hierarchy that placed mathematicians in a socially and intellectually subordinate position. Westman has determined that mathematics professors earned about one-fifth the salary of professors of more prestigious disciplines, such as philosophy and medicine. Moreover, "at none of these institutions was there provision for the doctorate in mathematics or astronomy, no licensing, that is, which recognized that symbol of full disciplinary autonomy" (117). It is for this reason that the Jesuits' prolonged effort to raise the profile and legitimacy of mathematics moves in two directions at once.

From the theologico-philosophical point of view, Clavius, professor of mathematics at the Collegio Romano from 1564 to 1612, assembles an innovative defense of mathematics by performing a dialectical turn on Thomism's attempts to yoke it to the concept of a "middle, or mixed, science": "It was Aquinas who developed the concept of the 'mixed science,' which implied the denial of any methodological autonomy to sciences applying mathematical methods to physical principles (optics, mechanics, and music were also included in this group)" (Feldhay 206). Clavius turns this relation around by emphasizing the mediatory and necessary position and function of mathematics where the study of real physical objects and the analysis and communication of their causes and effects are concerned, since the latter cannot be properly analyzed and understood without the logical syntaxes of mathematics and geometry. Crombie and Carugo note that this posture is neoplatonic in nature: "Mathematics was necessary to natural philosophy because it was concerned with 'middle essence' lying between the 'sensible essence' of things and the purely 'intelligible essence' of the divine" (195). In Clavius's own words: "[The mathematical sciences] are concerned with things that can be considered apart from sensible matter, although they themselves are immersed in matter, thus being like both metaphysics and physics, each of which shares one of these modes of consideration" (qtd. in Feldhay 207). In this way, he is able to destabilize the rigid dichotomy between the hypothetical and the real, the sensible and the intelligible, and the probable and the necessary. Clavius's next move extends his critique of these dichotomies to the marriage between ontological and epistemological necessity. Since mathematics can be considered separate from "sensible matter" according to its designation as a middle or mixed science, true and real knowledge can also be separated from real objects: "There is true knowledge of mathematical entities, whose ontological status is now redefined as a hybrid between the hypothetical and the real. This special intermediate status constitutes them as a nexus between the rational structure of the mind and the real structure of the physical world" (Feldhay 208). By making this cut between being and knowledge, Clavius is able to argue that epistemological necessity may be established in the relationship between hypothetical knowledge and observed effects, although "this necessity is not guaranteed by an (ontological) necessity of the relation between causes and effects" (Feldhay 210). Scientific knowledge, thus, functions in the same way that "God's knowledge of the future acts of men was considered true knowledge of hypothetical objects, neither speculative nor practical—infallible, but not entailing ontological necessity" (Feldhay 207). Although the Jesuits do not ascribe to Copernicus's neoplatonic elevation of mathematical and geometrical forms to the plane of intelligible reality, one can see an affinity between Clavius's statement and Galileo's assertion that "the book of philosophy is that which stands perpetually open before our eyes, but because it is written in characters different from those of our alphabet it cannot be read by everybody; and the characters of this book are triangles, squares, circles, spheres, cones, pyramids and other mathematical figures fittest for this sort of reading" (qtd. in Crombie and Carugo 217).

According to the Dominicans' orthodox stance, Galileo's statement is untenable due to the aforementioned problems that arise when working from effects to causes (*ex suppositione*). Since mathematical and geometrical figures and symbols carry no stable, i.e., necessary, semantic content, relying on them in the establishment of causes creates the potential for multiple, even contradictory, cosmological truths. As Andrea Battistini points out, the possibility of what Stephenson calls the "polycosmic universe" carries serious ontological and epistemological consequences: "Human minds were upset by the melancholic sensation that the Earth was deprived of its ancient centrality, lost in the infinite spaces that lacked secure points of reference as there no longer existed anything motionless in the universe" (22).

Fig. 3. O Quarto Dia, in Francisco de Holanda, *De Aetatibus Mundi Imagines* (1545?), folio 6r

If the Earth is just another planet orbiting the Sun, then it is but one of an infinite number of centers, which brings us close to Stephenson's speculative experiments with multiple causal domains.[10] It is precisely this type of instability, or freedom, that Galileo proposed when he began the process of self-transformation from university mathematician to court philosopher.

The subsequent history of the Jesuits tells us that, in political terms at least, their ingenious attempts to rewrite the Thomist doctrine of free will, as well as the philosophical program concerning hypothetical versus physical knowledge, were ultimately suppressed. Nevertheless, the drive to alter the hierarchical relation between mathematics and natural philosophy bore real fruit, in spite of the 1616 condemnation of Copernican astronomy and the censure of its most famous and accomplished proponent. Once again, the parallel movement of Galileo's career as courtly philosopher and Clavius's assertion of the legitimacy of mathematical-scientific knowledge provides a productive counterpoint. In opposition to the way in which philosophical disputations were traditionally organized in the university, Clavius argues that mathematics professors ought to be able to participate in these academic events. Following up on Westman's earlier comments, the Jesuits are in fact instrumental in creating many of the first mathematics professorships in Europe. That being said, it is ultimately in the absolutist court where mathematics first achieves the status desired by Clavius, through marvelous marriages of courtly spectacle and scientific achievements designed by figures like Galileo, Tycho Brahe, and Johannes Kepler. In the words of Biagioli, "in the same way artisans had become artists by representing the prince's mythologies of power in painting, sculpture, and architecture, Galileo turned himself into a philosopher by representing the satellites of Jupiter as Medici dynastic emblems" (156). Thus, even though the philosophical and scientific arguments and achievements would seem to be the substance of the transition to modern scientific realism, the material vehicle for this transition is the allegorical and iconological medium of the emblem. And although the emblem proved useful and effective for Galileo, its allegorical and philological machinery is not wedded to any one philosophical or ideological current of thought or institution in the baroque, especially in Spain. Like the geometrical figures it so often deploys for allegorical ends, its syntax carries no inherent semantic or ideological substance.

To this point, I have probably given the impression that the Jesuits were a progressive force in Counter-Reformation thought; and, by comparison with the Dominicans, they were, at least where scientific education is concerned. And it is in Jesuit emblematics, specifically the Hispanic emblem pioneered by Juan de Borja, where we once again find an alliance between scientific images and a Jesuit-inspired educational program.[11] Credited with the invention of the "empresa hispánica," Borja is the first Spanish author to write an original emblem book, and the changes he initiates in the genre are substantial enough to warrant his placement at the vanguard of Spanish emblematics.[12] It is noteworthy that during the years he was probably working on the book Borja is known to have brought into his diplomatic and social circles figures such as Francisco de Holanda, the painter and draftsman who composed the unpublished *De Aetatibus Mundi Imagines*, and Luis Jorge Barbuda, a well-known cartographer and draftsman. The influence of both *letrados* can be found in Borja's predilection for mathematical and geometrical images and metaphors.[13]

Francisco de Holanda was a court painter, architect, and sculptor for King John III of Portugal and, later, for the ill-fated Sebastian. Although he finds favor within the pro-Castilian reign of John III and his widowed daughter-in-law Doña Catarina of Hapsburg (sister to Felipe II), Holanda's dynastic connections will eventually contribute to his marginalization under the more independently minded Sebastian. But it is most likely the vast transformations in intellectual and artistic doctrine and practice ushered in by the Counter-Reformation that result in the condemnation of his work to the recondite shadows of the Iberian baroque. If we consider Holanda's first image of *The Creation*, the problems become immediately apparent in light of our previous discussion of sixteenth- and seventeenth-century Thomism: "Starting from a perfect circle, three triangles merge in the abyss, provoking a strange sensation as much of movement as of immobility. Alpha and Omega are inscribed on the first equilateral triangle, perfectly inscribed in the circle" (Deswarte 12) [Fig. 4].

Holanda represents the intelligible reality of the Holy Trinity through a "hypothetical" syntax of geometrical figures. Even though he will insist on the contrast between the plane of ideal, incorporeal forms and the "imperfect copy in the terrestrial zone," his visual language betrays its genealogical indebtedness to the mixed sciences of Neoplatonism, hermeticism, Christian cabala, and Lulism (Deswarte 22).[14] From 1545 to 1547, when Holanda begins working on his ambitious project, this is perhaps not so problematical; but his work on the cosmological history of the world is interrupted by the religious, aesthetic, and social reforms initiated at the Council of Trent. By the time he returns to *De Aetatibus*, Spain and Portugal have been colonized by Counter-Reformation artistic and philosophical theories and practices, which is where Juan de Borja enters the scene.

Borja comes to Portugal in 1570 as Felipe II's ambassador, with the assignment of arranging the forever-postponed marriage of Don Sebastian. Deswarte writes: "As the son of Francisco de Borja, he is particularly well received by the queen, who is very dedicated to his father [eventually canonized as San Francisco] who was her valet in his youth in Tordesillas and whose spiritual influence, since he was a Jesuit priest and general of the Society since 1565, had grown during his various sojourns in Portugal" (64). Borja, who will eventually publish the *Empresas morales* in Prague in 1581, meets Holanda and apparently counsels him on how to alter *De Aetatibus Mundi* so that it will

Fig. 4. O Primeiro Dia da Criacão, Francisco de Holanda, *De Aetatibus Mundi Imagines*, (1545?), folio 3r

be more attractive to potential patrons and publishers. Without going into detail, Holanda transforms his mystical and geometrical history of the world into a series of spiritual meditations more in line with Ignatius of Loyola's *Spiritual Exercises*: "It is, in truth, difficult to reconcile it with the spirit of the first images, that vast cosmogonic and neoplatonic poem" (Deswarte 62). Even though the work is never brought to press, Holanda's influence on Borja's book of emblems is undeniable, although the *Empresas morales* move in the opposite direction to Holanda's project, as well as to what we have seen with Galileo.

One of the most important aspects of the *Empresas morales* is the way in which Borja redefines his chosen emblematic vehicle, the *empresa*. According to its humanist theorists, the *empresa* differs from the emblem in that it contains and expresses a future, personal goal, often associated in the Renaissance and early baroque with feats of martial or amorous prowess.[15] In this light, Galileo's emblem of the Medicean stars is much closer to the Italian *impresa* than to the Spanish emblem. In the words of García Mahíques, "Juan de Borja formally composed in the Italian manner, adapting and inventing conceptual artifices according to the model provided by *empresas*, but he eliminated from these their particular character—associated with the knight's intention or the praise of his virtues—and makes them applicable to the moral universe" (Introducción 45). In essence, Borja converts a heretofore individualistic enterprise into what Maravall calls a "program of cultural guidance," as preexisting predispositions for allegorical play are set in motion around a newly articulated reading practice (*The Culture* 57). Instead of participating in an ingenious courtly joust, or penetrating the hieroglyphic sign in search of ideal and original knowledge, Borja's reader is guided toward a hermeneutical practice in which all signs point to the impossibility of illumination and transformation of the worldly self and, by extension, the world.

The sixth emblem of the first part of the *Empresas* is titled *In pusillo nemo magnus* (no one is great in small things). Its body is composed of what appears to be a representation of the world, with a cross on top and a tiny dot in the middle of the circle so small that it could almost be an ink stain produced in the printing of the book. The subscription reads: "Quan pequeño sea todo lo que en el Mundo, es tenido, y estimado por grande, se puede bien conocer, si se entiende primero, quan pequeño sea el mismo Mundo; el qual, segun los Astrologos lo prueban, es como un punto en comparación de la circumferencia de la ultima Esfera, y siendo tan pequeño, aunque señoreandole, y governandole todo?" (We can see how small everything in the world is, which is esteemed and taken for great, if we first understand how small the World actually is; which, as the Astrologers prove, is like a small point in comparison with the circumference of the last sphere, and being so small, what in it could be great, even mastering and governing it?) (14) [Fig. 5].

What appears to be the Earth is actually the entire cosmos, with the Earth reduced to a tiny point. The spiritual thrust of the emblem could not be any clearer: one should not worry about things as tiny and insignificant as the terrestrial world; rather, one should look to the next world. Thus, R. de la Flor is correct when he identifies the nihilistic drive of the emblem; on the other hand, this negative ontology extends its reach to encompass the desire of the reading subject to act in the world, which means that there is no way out of Borja's "desert."

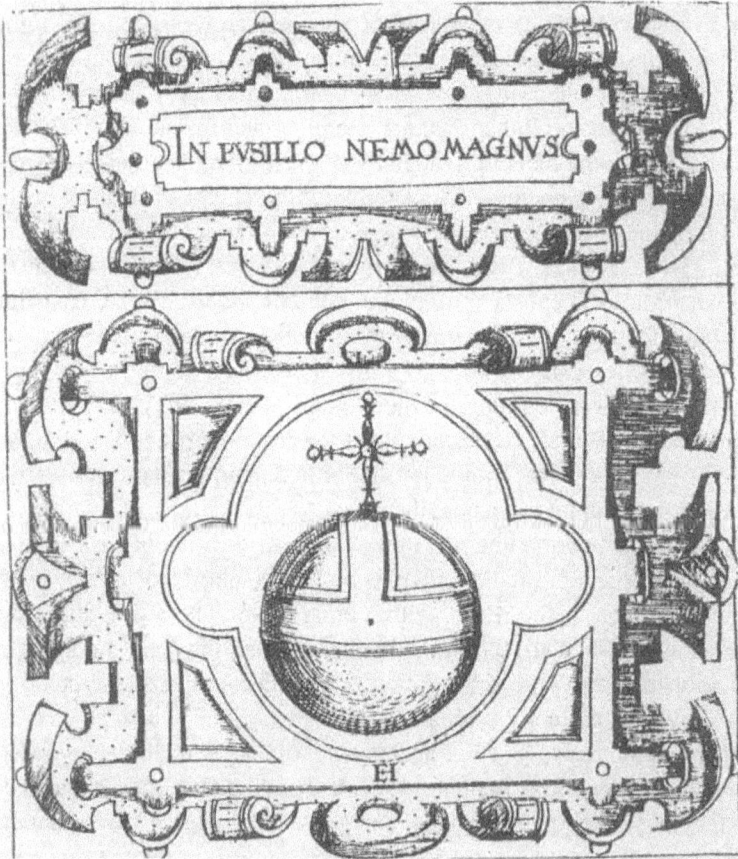

Fig. 5. In Pusillo, in Juan de Borja, *Empresas morales* (1680), 15[16]

Another emblem shows an elliptical space through which two lines pass horizontally: a solid line above, and a line of dots underneath. The inscription reads: "*Sic instantibus aeternitas*" (Thus does eternity depend on individual moments), and the commentary clarifies:

> Ninguna cosa es mas de estimar, ni verdaderamente es mas nuestra, que el tiempo . . . no el passado, ni el de por venir, sino tan solamente el presente . . . que es tan breve, que no se mide, sino con un instante; que es el mas corto espacio, que se puede imaginar (porque assi como un punto, que no se puede dividir, por no tener partes indivisibles, pero con todo esto de muchos puntos se forman las lineas) de la misma manera, aunque un instante no se puede dividir, se deve much estimar, pues de infinitos instantes consta la Eternidad. (140) [Fig. 6]

> (Nothing is more dear, nor more truly our own, than time . . . not the past, nor the future, but rather only the present . . . which is so brief, that it cannot be measured, but with an instant; which is the shortest space, that one can imagine (because like a point, it cannot be divided, since it has no divisible parts, but even so from many points lines are formed) in the same manner, although an instant cannot be divided, it should be held dear, as from infinite instants Eternity is composed.)

In both emblems, Borja performs the same dialectical turn with respect to neoplatonism and its influence on sixteenth-century mathematics and astronomy that R. de la Flor perceives in the Spanish diplomat's anticipatory transduction of Descartes's *cogito ergo sum*. In spite of Clavius's energetic and ingenious attempts to save mathematical realism from the charge of hypothetical fictions, Borja's conservative use of astrology and geometry ties the mathematical sciences to a program of spiritual introspection that explicitly rejects any attempt to find lasting truth and meaning on the terrestrial plane. The reduction of mathematics and geometry to terrestrial dust also acts as an inhibitor where the social aspirations of mathematical astronomers are concerned. If mathematical science merely serves to underline the impossibility of intellectual insight concerning physical objects and their causes, what aspirations can a practitioner of these mundane praxes dare hope to realize? The difference with respect to Galileo's and Copernicus's assertions to the contrary could not be greater.

So, what are we to do with these seemingly contradictory programs for deploying identical mathematical and geometrical syntaxes? Stephenson uses the sci-fi term "causal domain shear" to refer to the radical effects that occur when two completely distinct universes come together, even if it is only "a single photon that manage[s] to travel somehow between them" (*Anathem* 28). In the case I have just presented, the conflicting cosmologies that result from opposing syntactical arrangements of mathematico-geometrical figures share much more than a single particle of light; they are produced by the same religious order, or math. I would argue that in spite of, or even thanks to, the efforts of Jesuit emblematics to enclose the curious modern subject within a guilt-ridden ontological and epistemological vacuum, nevertheless, the theoretical substantiation of previously immaterial hypothetical truths charts an equivocal course toward the conflicting and multiple perspectives we associate with the more modern characteristics of the baroque. Once Clavius initiates his dialectical at-

Fig. 6. Sic Ex Instantibus, in Juan de Bora, *Empresas morales* (1681), 141

tack on the doctrine of free will, the cut is made, and there is no way to neatly contain the forces of hypothetical world-making unleashed by the legitimation of syntactical play that comes at the expense of semantic rigor. Similarly, the syntactical possibilities of Borja's circles, triangles, and lines cannot be completely contained by his allegorical program of spiritual guidance. This does not mean, however, that R. de la Flor is correct when he states that baroque aesthetics willingly moves to destroy the foundations of the monarchical-seigniorial metaphysics of presence; rather, in modernity, no organicist framework for meaning can avoid subverting its drive toward legitimacy, since the syntax on which it depends necessarily places its causal domain in contact with competing cosmologies. Its natural philosophy becomes one more expression of science fiction, a tiny speck in an infinite universe of other fictions.

Notes

1. Neal Stephenson, *Anathem* (511).
2. See R. de la Flor, *La península metafísica.*
3. Selig has compiled all of the references to Alciato's *Emblematum liber* in the *Agudeza* in his study of Gracián.
4. All translations from Spanish to English are my own.
5. The spaceship's form is that of an *icosohedron* (twenty sides), which is one of Plato's five basic solid forms, and is associated with the element of water.
6. The aliens' emblem turns out to be a representation of the Pythagorean theorem, which on Arbre is called the "Adrakhonian Theorem." Stephenson includes the image in the text. It seems that Arbre's Syntacticians base their thought on an ancient figure named Protas, who bears a striking resemblance to Plato: "Protas: A student of Thelenes during the Golden Age of Ethras, later the most important theor in Arbran history. Building on the foundation laid by Hylaea and later strengthened by the Orithenans, developed the notion that the object and ideas that humans perceive and think about are imperfect manifestations of pure, ideal forms that exist in another plane of existence" (Stephenson 905).
7. The title of Galileo's treatise announcing his discovery of Jupiter's four moons in 1609 is *Sidereus Nuncius* (Starry Messenger).
8. For a baroque reading of Leibniz through the extended metaphor of *the fold*, see Deleuze.
9. See my *The Persistence of Presence: Emblem and Ritual in Baroque Spain* (2010).
10. "CAUSAL DOMAIN: A collection of things mutually linked in a web of cause-and-effect relationships" (Stephenson, *Anathem* 893).

11. Juan de Borja is the third son of (San) Francisco de Borja, Captain General of the Jesuit Order in sixteenth-century Spain (see García Mahíques).

12. The first critic to note the Spanish turn toward a more religiously informed and institutionally framed theory and practice of the emblem is Giuseppina Ledda, *Contributto*. For a more complete picture of the Spanish emblem book scene, see Pedro F. Campa, *Emblemata Hispanica: An Annotated Bibliography of Spanish Emblem Literature to the Year 1700*.

13. García Mahíques (37).

14. As far as education is concerned, the privileged place Holanda gives to mathematics and geometry anticipates Clavius's reforms of the late 1500s: "Francisco de Holanda gives a privileged place to cosmography and astrology in the education of the painter. On par with geometry, mathematics and perspective, he recommends them . . . in order to reach the heavens in the hope of one day arriving to the Empyreum and realizing celestial works" (Deswarte 24).

15. Daly writes, "The *impresa* represents the 'principle of individuation' (Sulzer 35): it was used by one person only 'as the expression of a personal aim' (Schöne 45). The word itself comes from the Italian for 'undertaking,' which underlines the functional purpose of the *impresa*. The emblem, on the other hand, is addressed to a larger audience, its message is general, and it fulfills a didactic, decorative, or entertaining function, or any combination of these" (*Literature* 23).

16. Although Borja's collection was originally published in 1581, the more common edition to cite is the 1680 edition, due to its inclusion of a second century of emblems.

Works Cited

Battistini, Andrea. "The Telescope in the Baroque Imagination." *Reason and Its Others: Italy, Spain, and the New World*. Ed. David Castillo and Massimo Lollini. *Hispanic Issues* 32. Nashville: Vanderbilt University Press, 2006. 3–38.

Biagioli, Mario. *Galileo, Courtier: The Practice of Science in the Culture of Absolutism*. Chicago: University of Chicago Press, 1993.

Borja, Juan de. *Empresas Morales*. Brussels: F. Foppens, 1680.

Campa, Pedro F. *Emblemata Hispanica: An Annotated Bibliography of Spanish Emblem Literature to the Year 1700*. Durham: Duke University Press, 1990.

Crombie, A. C. "Mathematics and Platonism in the Sixteenth-Century Italian Universities and in Jesuit Educational Policy." *Science, Art, and Nature in Medieval and Modern Thought*. London: The Hambledon Press, 1996. 115–48.

———. and A. Carugo. "The Jesuits and Galileo's Ideas of Science and Nature." *Science, Art and Nature in Medieval and Modern Thought*. London: The Hambledon Press, 1996. 165–230.

Daly, Peter M. *Literature in Light of the Emblem: Structural Parallels between the*

Emblem and Literature in the Sixteenth and Seventeenth Centuries. Toronto: University of Toronto Press, 1979.

Deleuze, Gilles. *The Fold: Leibniz and the Baroque*. Trans. and foreword Tom Conley. Minneapolis: University of Minnesota Press, 1993.

Deswarte, Sylvie, ed. *As Imagens das Idades do Mundo de Francisco de Holanda.* Lisboa: Imprensa Nacional-Casa de Moeda, 1987.

Feldhay, Rivka. "Knowledge and Salvation in Jesuit Culture." *Science in Context* 1.2 (1987): 195–213.

García Mahíques, Rafael. "Introducción." *Empresas morales de Juan de Borja: Imagen y palabra para una iconología*. Ed. García Mahíques. Valencia: Ajuntament de Valencia, 1998. 17–51.

Gracián, Baltasar. *Agudeza y arte de ingenio.* Buenos Aires: Espasa-Calpe, 1942.

Holanda, Francisco de. *De Aetatibus Mundi Imagines: As Imagens das Idades do Mundo de Francisco de Holanda*. Ed. Sylvie Deswarte. Lisboa: Imprensa Nacional-Casa de Moeda, 1987.

Kuhn, Thomas S. *The Copernican Revolution: Planetary Astronomy in the Development of Western Thought*. Cambridge, MA: Harvard University Press, 1957.

Ledda, Giuseppina. *Contributo allo studio della letteratura emblematica in Spagna (1559–1613)*. Pisa: Pisa University Press, 1970.

Maravall, José Antonio. *The Culture of the Baroque. Analysis of a Historical Structure.* Trans. Terry Cochran. Minneapolis: University of Minnesota Press, 1986.

Massey, Lyle. "Anamorphosis through Descartes or Perspective Gone Awry." *Renaissance Quarterly* 50.4 (1997): 1148–89.

Nelson, Bradley J. *The Persistence of Presence: Emblem and Ritual in Baroque Spain.* Toronto: University of Toronto Press, 2010.

R. de la Flor, Fernando. *Barroco: Representación e ideología en el mundo hispánico (1580-1680)*. Madrid: Cátedra, 2002.

———. *Emblemas: Lecturas de la imagen simbólica.* Madrid: Alianza Editorial, 1995.

———. *La península metafísica: Arte, literatura y pensamiento en la España de la Contrarreforma.* Madrid: Biblioteca Nueva, 1999.

Rodríguez, Juan Carlos. *Theory and History of Ideological Production: The First Bourgeois Literatures (the Sixteenth Century)*. Trans. Malcolm K. Read. Newark, DE: University of Delaware Press, 2002.

Russell, Daniel. *Emblematic Structures in Renaissance French Culture.* Toronto: University of Toronto Press, 1995.

Said, Edward. *Orientalism.* New York: Random House, 1978.

Selig, Karl Ludwig. "Gracián and Alciato's *Emblemata.*" *Comparative Literature* 8 (1956): 1–11.

Stephenson, Neal. *Anathem.* New York: HarperCollins, 2008.

———. *The Confusion: Vol. 2 of The Baroque Trilogy.* New York: HarperCollins, 2004.

———. *Cryptonomicon.* New York: HarperCollins, 1999.

———. "Note to the Reader." *Anathem*. New York: HarperCollins, 2008. Xiii–xvii.

————. *Quicksilver: Vol. 1 of The Baroque Trilogy*. New York: HarperCollins, 2003.

————. *Snow Crash*. New York: Bantam Books, 1992.

————. *The System of the World: Vol. 3 of The Baroque Trilogy*. New York: HarperCollins, 2004.

Westman, Robert S. "The Astronomer's Role in the Sixteenth Century: A Preliminary Study." *History of Science* 18.2 (1980): 105–47.

Žižek, Slavoj. *Welcome to the Desert of the Real: Five Essays on September 11 and Related Dates*. New York: Verso, 2002.

5

"The Knowledge of This People": Mapping a Global Consciousness in Catalonia (1375–2009)

Colleen P. Culleton

There is a chronology to this project, although its final form more closely resembles a constellation. In 1375, a Jewish cartographer in Mallorca named Cresques Abraham composed a *mappamundi* at the request of his patron, King Pere III of Aragon. Shortly thereafter, it was sent to Paris as a gift to Charles V, and it can still be found there, in the Bibliothèque Nationale. In 1975, in honor of the six hundredth anniversary of what became known as the "Atles de Cresques," Editorial Diáfora, in Barcelona, produced a limited edition volume, which included a complete reproduction of the atlas, with a good deal of supplementary content, celebrating the atlas as a masterpiece of Catalan culture.[1] (In historical accounts, the 1375 work is sometimes called the "Atles de Cresques" and sometimes called the "Catalan Atlas." For the sake of clarity, I will refer to the 1375 atlas with the descriptor "Atles de Cresques" and the 1975 volume as the "Catalan Atlas.") In 1997, Catalan novelist and historian Alfred Bosch wrote a novel about the Atles de Cresques, relying on the Catalan Atlas for a good deal of historical material. In 2002, I read Bosch's novel, and in 2008, I went to Paris to see the 1375 atlas and to Barcelona to see the homage that had been paid to it in 1975. One year later, again in Barcelona, I visited an apparently unrelated exhibit at the Museu d'Història de Barcelona called "Barcelona Connectada," and everything fell into place.

Spatial Imaginations

Each of the texts presented here has something to say about space, but discovering the connections between them is an act of spatial imagination of a higher order. This essay briefly touches on several nodes in a network of cultural production, the navigation of which points to how spatial thought might open up a politics of inclusiveness that is portrayed as being rooted in a Catalan culture that predates the Spanish State, while at the same time, is projected as a model for the future.

My understanding of spatial thought relies heavily on the ideas that Doreen Massey presents in *For Space* (2005). Massey proposes that "space" is heterogeneous, processual, and relational, a dynamic of people and events that resists closure, fixture, or stability. In this reimagining of space, social forces and groups are seen as "stories-so-far," or "simultaneous trajectories" that should inform how we think about space, both as scholars and as global citizens. In sustaining its dynamic and changing nature, Massey refuses to allow space to be separated from time and, instead, adjusts her terminology for a treatment of "time-spaces," characterized by a sense of "throwntogetherness" that opposes the reductiveness of static accounts of space. Massey's theorization of space rescues it from a lifeless and staid way of thinking, and opens up academic and political discourses to heterogeneity and multiplicity: "Conceiving of space as a static slice through time, as representation, as a closed system and so forth are all ways of taming it. They enable us to ignore its real import: the coeval multiplicity of other trajectories and the necessary outward-lookingness of a spatialized subjectivity" (Massey 59). This proposal goes against common perceptions of space as fixed and transparent, and it also resists the project of cartography to pinpoint, locate, and *place*. Here, though, I propose to explore a network of cultural production that begins (in chronological terms) with an atlas, a text that seems to fix space in precisely the kind of representation that Massey wants to set aside. Reading this atlas through a novel, we will see the extent to which it is both the product and signifier of social, political, and cultural trajectories that can't be contained by plotted points on a map. The Atles de Cresques, in fact, is portrayed as the impetus for a continuing movement of peoples and narratives (Massey's "stories-so-far") into the twenty-first century.

The "stories-so-far" that characterize space for Massey find a graphic equivalent in the narrativity of some medieval and early modern maps. In a look at the location of Eden in early modern maps, Alessandro Scafi explains that "However picturesque *mappaemundi* may seem, they cannot be dismissed as devoid of scientific accuracy. On the contrary, the medieval map-maker seems to have been deeply aware of the fact that, if mapping is to express spatial relationships, geographical space cannot exist without time" (63–64). Likewise, while analyzing the role of cartography in Spain's colonization of the Americas, Ricardo Padrón draws out the polyvalence of maps. A map is a document that provides a "spatial understanding" for all kinds of events: "It thereby acknowledges, albeit implicitly, that 'space' is a plural, contingent concept that varies over time and across cultures, and that maps can differ in the sort of 'spatial understanding' they provide just as much as they can differ in the kinds of referents they represent" (58).

"Plurality," "multiplicity," "matrix," "network," "throwntogetherness": in every attempt to articulate a spatial imagination there is a struggle to find a language with which to represent it. In their own depiction of a centerless and nonlinear space, Deleuze and Guattari opt for the "rhizome" as a label. In their introduction to *A Thousand Plateaus*, they claim: "The ideal of a book would be to lay everything out on a plane of exteriority of this kind, on a single page, the same sheet: lived events, historical determinations, concepts, individuals, groups, social formations" (9). For Deleuze and Guattari, as well as for Massey, there is an urge toward spatialized narrative—a narrative that defies the linearity of language by appearing all at once, like the multiple points on a map. It might be argued that what Deleuze and Guattari hope for in a book Cresques accomplished in his atlas, which includes the expected shapes of the continents, locations of kingdoms, names of places. It is, however, also full of stories and explanations, colors, illustrations, and imaginings that act out trajectories and simultaneities. In *L'atles furtiu* Alfred Bosch takes on the Atles de Cresques as an image of a utopian multiculturalism, and a reminder of the value that the Other has had in the ongoing development of Catalonia. In so doing, Bosch implies that a solution for the problems of spatial politics that Massey looks for in some as yet unachieved articulation may well lie buried in a medieval garden in Mallorca.

L'atles furtiu: Introducing the Atles de Cresques

L'atles furtiu, by Alfred Bosch, received the Premi Sant Jordi in 1997. Part historical account and part fictional adventure, it is presented as the autobiography of Jafudà Cresques, the son of the Jewish cartographer Cresques Abraham, who lived in Mallorca from 1326 to 1387 and received special privileges and protection for being cartographer and instrument maker to the king of Aragon.

In its depiction of the political weight that maps carried, *L'atles furtiu* antici-pates by more than a century the social and economic function of maps and globes in early modern Europe as they have been understood by scholars like Tom Conley in *The Self-Made Map* (1996), Jerry Brotton in *Trading Territories* (1998), Denis Cosgrove and the contributors to his edited volume *Mappings* (1999), and Ricardo Padrón in *The Spacious Word* (2004), all of which begin their study of mapping some time after the transitional phase marked by the Atles de Cresques. In spite of the chronological disjuncture, their consider-ations play out quite neatly in *L'atles furtiu*, where Bosch portrays maps as both actors in and products of commercial, social, and political processes.

As the novel's narrator and protagonist, Jafudà begins the story with his birth in 1360. The novel ends thirty-one years later, shortly after the violent attacks on Jewish communities all over the peninsula that led to mass conver-sions to Christianity. Mallorcan cartographers were able to earn their reputa-tions as sought-after map-makers largely due to the Jewish community that mi-grated to the islands after fleeing the Almohed persecutions of the mainland. G. R. Crone explains that "these Jewish refugees also included scholars who could interpret the works of Arab scientists, and this contact between practical and skilled seamen and those versed in cosmography and astronomy was fruitful" (39). The Atles de Cresques is the product of a multicultural knowledge base and came into being thanks to the arrival of persecuted Jews from other parts of the peninsula, who brought with them a desirable set of skills. In *L'atles furtiu*, Bosch portrays the Atles de Cresques, a masterpiece produced on the cusp of modernity, as a map not of the world but of a potential Catalonia.

Early in the novel, Cresques receives an important commission from the king to produce a complete atlas of the known world. With this commission comes prestige, influence with the king, and notable economic advancement. Cresques decides to take advantage of the opportunity that the king's com-mission provides to produce a second, parallel atlas—the "furtive atlas" from which the novel takes its title. He describes his plan to Jafudà:

> A la primera obra li posarem les viles, serralades, rius i mars coneguts. Només hi anirà allò que sigui cert, que ens hagin relatat diversos viatgers i que haguem com-provat en ferm. A la segona parlarem de tot el que aprenguem, fals o vertader. Ens trobarem amb moltes llegendes i fantasies, i no cal dir que cometrem errors greus. Però deixarem una compilació única del saber humà. Els navegants i els mestres de demà ja s'encarregaran de separar les veritats de les illusions. (45–46)

(On the first work we'll place all the known towns, mountain ranges, rivers and seas. We'll only put there whatever is certain, whatever various travelers have told us about and what we've solidly confirmed. On the second we'll speak of everything that we learn, false or true. We'll find ourselves among many legends and fantasies, and it goes without saying that we'll commit grave errors. But we'll leave a unique compilation of human knowledge. The navigators and experts of tomorrow can take it upon themselves to separate the truths from the illusions.)[2]

For Bosch's readers, the idea that the commissioned atlas would include only that which was certain, as Cresques describes it in the novel and one of the characteristics for which the Atles de Cresques is celebrated, is confusing for two reasons. First, the commissioned atlas, lauded for what G. R. Crone has termed its "critical realism" (50), includes a great deal of what today would be considered religious ideology, or the stuff of legend. Second, in the novel, relatively little information is provided as to the content of the second, furtive atlas, which might otherwise clarify the difference between certainty and legend by way of a comparison. In the novel, the content of the furtive atlas is much less important than the concept. Once it is complete, the role that the atlas plays has little to do with this object as a source of information and everything to do with its symbolic potential.

The two atlases are rich terrain as metaphors for a changing worldview and literal "projections" of what their world was. The convergence of cartography and shifting worldviews that defined this moment in Catalan history means that in the novel, the signifying potential of cartography shines through and illustrates Denis Cosgrove's point that "[t]he central role that mapping practices have played in shaping and figuring Western modernity as a global encounter, their significance in collecting, collating, producing and mobilizing knowledge, make them a vital entry point into an appreciation of changing mentalities" (12–13). L'atles furtiu introduces its reader to a moment in Catalan history that was characterized by relative religious tolerance and intellectual exchange (idealized through the eyes of an intelligent and sensitive adolescent narrator), and to the moment when that way of life came to an end.

In terms of sources of information on which the cartographer relied, historians often focus on how Marco Polo's stories of trade routes to China are reproduced or revised in the Atles de Cresques. In the novel, however, the emphasis is placed on the narratives of two travelers who come to live with Jafudà and his family: one is an Armenian Christian named Betros, and the other is an African Muslim princess named Selima. The oral narratives of these two travelers form long segments of the novel in such a way that the same oral tradition that supplied the cartographer with his lines and images becomes the stuff of which the novel is made. Selima's narrative, for example, begins thus: "Quatre vegades va lluir esplèndid el Mali a la llum del jorn; quatre vegades es va perdre i es va enfosquir. Una vegada per avarícia, una per infidelitat, una per discòrdia i una per vanitat" (207) (Four times the Mali shines splendid in the light of day, four times he was lost and it got dark. Once for avarice, once for infidelity, once for discord, and once for vanity). The musicality of her story-telling contrasts with the novel's other narratives and manifests the exoticism that Selima brings to the household, which holds obvious attraction for the adolescent Jafudà.

When Selima comes to work for the family, Jafudà is immediately enamored of her, although it is quite some time before she allows him to act on his desires. She prolongs the courtship, telling Jafudà the story of her life and how she came to be a slave in his house. Selima's tale is a matchless source of information for the cartographer and his apprentice, and this character's presence in the novel offers a fictive explanation for the appearance, in the real atlas, of the Mali ruler Mansa Musa on a pilgrimage to Mecca. After a long separation (during which Jafudà travels to Barcelona to sell the commissioned atlas, loses the furtive atlas [which he eventually recovers], and grows from adolescent to adult as he navigates the treacherous streets of Barcelona and hallways of royal residences), he and Selima join in an unofficial marriage and have a baby—the son of a Catalan Jew and an African Muslim, to whom we will return later in this analysis.

The premium placed on first-person narratives as the best source of knowledge for cartographers highlights space as experiential and reveals the Atles de Cresques to be more complex than a tracing of points on a page. Maps are understood not simply as a translation of a physical reality. They are, rather, an image of an image or, better yet, an image of an imagining, especially if one considers that most medieval cartographers, themselves, rarely traveled. Ricardo Padrón wants us to understand the role that mapping plays in the construction and dissemination of a worldview, but also as an on-the-ground experience of space and what it means. Through mapping, space is narrativized: "They were only beginning to learn how to imagine their world, relate to it, and transform it in ways that depended upon the unique conceptualization of space that lay at the heart of the modern map" (12).

The Atles de Cresques is not a bound atlas, as we imagine them today. It was drawn on twelve wooden panels that can be folded up, but which allow the entire atlas to be laid out flat and viewed at once. It is visually striking, displaying a multitude of illustrations in ten colors, the artistry of which is difficult to capture in a few words. Every inch of seascape is covered in fine, wavy blue lines. All of the lands are filled with figures that illustrate the life that occupied the landscape: warring pygmies, the cremation of an Indian woman, the voyage of the three kings, and countless others, that give weight to Alessandro Scafi's contention that "place becomes bound to human experience because the map makes it visible" (53). Each town or city is shown as a collection of buildings, with a castle or a church or a mosque all with banners waving above them. Many illustrations are accompanied by written descriptions of peoples, kingdoms, or customs. In his study of the iconography of the atlas, Gabriell Llompart i Moragues explains that,

> El resultado de este mosaico de colores variadísimo, completado con los dibujos . . . es una sensación de alegría visual. Surge la curiosidad de adivinar el sentido de las escenas, de inquirir el porqué de la presencia de los personajes, de comprender, en una palabra, la *historia* que la pintura apunta pero sólo deja en evidencia a los espíritus que no tienen necesidad de entretenerse en la trabajosa lectura de los textos. (45, emphasis in original)

> (The result of this mosaic of varied colors, complete with pictures . . . is a sensation of visual joy. There emerges a curiosity to guess the meaning of the scenes, to inquire as to the whys and wherefores of the characters' presence, to comprehend, in a word, the *story* that the painting points to but only makes evident to those spirits who don't feel the need to entertain themselves in the laborious reading of the texts.)

In this way, Llompart i Moragues captures the narrativity of the atlas, which is not only contained in the verbal descriptions, but in the pictorial cues, as well. Cresques's composition makes explicit that space is both place and process. In practice, the representation of space takes shape in the multitude of figures that are illustrated onto the mapped places and the inscribed descriptions of the kinds of people, curious cultural practices, different kingdoms, the wealth and power of their monarchs, and events that took place there. For Cresques, space narrates, and the imperative to capture that is evident on his atlas.

In his literary treatment of the Atles de Cresques, Bosch focuses on elements of it that lead toward an imagination of Catalan cultural history that is both founded in and open to what Massey would call "contemporaneous plurality," cultural diversity that spreads across space and time. Drawn and written out on wooden panels, the places and events coexist on a single temporal plane even as the narrative elements lend dynamism and process to the mapping. A map acts out simultaneity in a way that a book, read word by word and page by page, simply cannot emulate.

Of special importance, from the point of view of this analysis, is the fact that the Atles de Cresques predates European cartographers' use of latitude and longitude in mapmaking. Instead, the Atles de Cresques maintains the characteristic of the Mallorcan School: it is crisscrossed not by a grid pattern, but by a network of "rumbos" (bearings), pointing out the routes travelers should follow (Sureda i Blanes 10). This, in combination with its vibrant iconography, lends to the atlas a sense of movement, of space as process, that coincides with the characterization that Massey asserts of space being inextricably wrapped up in time. To the eye of the reader, it is spatial practice, more than geometry, that rescues this round world from flatness.

Scholars of early modern cartography have pointed to the latitude/longitude grid system as offering not only a God's-eye view of the world but also an illusion of global homogeneity. Latitude and longitude transformed a round world into what Deleuze and Guattari have described as a *striated* space, available for the inscription of the values of Empire (370). Striated space, the space of the State, is opposed to *smooth* space, "the pure act of drawing a diagonal across the vertical and the horizontal" (Deleuze and Guattari 478). In a fascinating look at the "The Heritage of Ptolemaic Cartography in the Renaissance," Samuel Edgerton shows the cartographic grid to be a "talismanic symbol of Christian authority" during that period (11). Be that as it may, the ideological underpinnings that supported this way of representing space were easily obscured by an illusion of transparency and geometrical objectivity, which, in turn, bestowed a particular authority on maps that were drawn on a grid (Padrón 39–40). Alessandro Scafi points to the systematic exclusion of precisely the sort of narrative elements that lend richness to the Atles de Cresques, which was brought on by the regulating impulse of the grid pattern, wherein "no one point in the map was more important than any other" (67). And Ricardo Padrón observes that "The hegemony of the gridded map is something from which we are only beginning to liberate ourselves, as we gradually shed our old definitions of maps and mapping and look for more inclusive language with which to think about territorial representation" (71).

Cresques Abraham and his contemporaries were not yet taking Ptolemy's principles into account and did not map the world onto a grid. Rather than see that as antiquated and irrelevant, Bosch takes up the Atles de Cresques as a response to twentieth (and now twenty-first) century concerns about plurality and a politics of inclusiveness. The utopianism of this project is captured by the naiveté of the young protagonist/narrator, most especially by his musings in the concluding chapter, called "El Paradís furtiu" (Furtive Paradise), as well as by the idealism of Cresques Abraham himself, which inspired the drawing of a second, all-inclusive atlas.

Naming Places: From the Global to the Local

The atlas drawn by Cresques Abraham in 1375 did not immediately carry the title "The Catalan Atlas." Its complete title is "Mappamundi, that is to say, image of the world and of the regions which are on the earth and of the various kinds of peoples which inhabit it" (Crone 41, Crone's translation). In 1975, Editorial Diáfora published a complete reproduction of the Atles de Cresques, now in book form, with all of its inscriptions transcribed in Catalan and translated into Spanish. The atlas, itself, is preceded by an array of scholarly essays that explain its history and its content. Likewise, the collaboration of two great Catalan cultural figures was solicited: Salvador Espriu composed a poem, and Antoni Tàpies provided an etching. These two original works open the volume and announce the atlas as a predecessor in a long history of specifically Catalan cultural production: this document bears the title *El atlas catalán de Cresques Abraham* (*The Catalan Atlas of Cresques Abraham*).

In *A Thousand Plateaus*, Deleuze and Guattari express a preference for a map rather than a book as the most desirable format for their thinking:

> The map is open and connectable in all of its dimensions; it is detachable, reversible, and susceptible to constant modification. It can be torn, reversed, adapted to any kind of mounting, reworked by an individual, group, or social formation. It can be drawn on a wall, conceived of as a work of art, constructed as a political action or as a meditation. (12)

In a well-known opposition, Deleuze and Guattari contrast the *map*, as defined above, with the *tracing*, which is a mere repetition or reproduction (12–15). Borrowing from Deleuze and Guattari's terminology, I would argue that, in spite of its reproduction of the Atles de Cresques, the 1975 volume is not a tracing, since it speaks to Catalan cultural accomplishment in a way that the 1375 atlas does not manage (or even attempt) to do. It is a map in its own right, in which the Atles de Cresques (composed by a Mallorcan Jew, under the protection of the King of Aragon, a century before that kingdom would be bound to Castile) becomes a "Catalan" atlas in a contemporary sense of the term. My reading of *L'atles furtiu* departs from the conviction that it is informed by *this* map more than by the atlas of 1375. This perspective is sustained by Bosch's choice of verses from Espriu's poem, called "El passat i el pou, a trenc d'alba" (The Past and the Well, at the Break of Dawn), as an epigraph, which includes the following verses: "i vells mapes de terres, de mars, del firmament / ens diuen com va ser de profund el domini, / el saber d'aquest poble del qual nosaltres som / legítims fills, hereus i servidors alhora" (N. pag.) (and the old maps of lands, of seas, of the firmament / tell us how profound was the dominion, / the knowledge of this people of which we are / legitimate children, at once heirs and servants).

Evoking Espriu in this way renders this novel, which might otherwise be read as a popular romantic adventure, significantly more political. The evocation of a Catalan national poet at the opening of the novel places *L'atles furtiu* within the same cultural tradition that begins with the Atles de Cresques, as read through the Diáfora edition. What's more, through the epigraph, Bosch allies himself with Espriu's treatment of the Jewish cultural tradition as part of a Catalan historical identity. This is evident in Espriu's contribution to the Catalan Atlas and actually precedes that text, in his dramatic work *Primera història d'Esther* (*First Story of Esther*) (1948) and his extended poem *La pell de brau* (*The Bull-Hide*) (1960). The latter of these is especially fitting for its geographical resonances. The poem's title comes from the Greek geographer Strabo, who, in the first century A.D., compared the shape of the Iberian Peninsula to that of an ox's hide. The ox has changed to a bull, given that animal's significance in the Spanish cultural imaginary. Throughout the poem, Spain is referred to by its Hebrew name Sepharad, and a parallel is drawn between the historical persecution of the Jews and that of Catalonia during and after the Spanish Civil War.

In *L'atles furtiu*, Cresques meant the second, furtive atlas to be a compilation of all that was known and believed about the world, but it could not have been compiled just anywhere. Its composition was made possible by the geographic and commercial position of Mallorca in the fourteenth century, as well as by the expertise and reputation of Mallorcan cartographers. As the novel progresses and its protagonist grows older, the significance of the furtive atlas shifts. At first, as a depiction of the literally global, the furtive atlas represents to Cresques the locus of knowledge and to his son an instrument of power. Later, though, after Cresques has died and the violent persecution of Jews changes Jafudà's whole world, the atlas becomes, for the young cartographer, a profoundly personal symbol of the community to which he belonged, which has been lost.

Jafudà is born into a world fraught with superstition. Beginning with the first line of the novel and continuing throughout, he refers back to his inauspicious birth: "El meu naixement fa de mal parlar, així com tots els fets prodigiosos que, segons algunes veus, el van acompanyar" (Bosch 13) (My birth is the stuff of rumors, as are all of the prodigious events that, according to some voices, accompanied it). His birth came on the heels of famine and plague, for which the Jews were blamed, and the diminishing protection of the King toward the Jewish community, and, while Jafudà's mother was pregnant with him, their king confronted the Castilian king, which led to Andalusian forces attacking the Mallorcan coast (Bosch 13–14). The narrator-protagonist's obsession with origins leads to a certain sensation of destiny in the text. The midwife who assisted with Jafudà's birth swears that she saw lightning, in the shape of a Christian cross, over the Cresques family home upon the delivery of Jafudà, thereby anticipating the forced conversion of Jafudà, his family, and his neighbors, with which the novel concludes (Bosch 18).

This question of origins joins with the dominant theme of identity in Bosch's novel, which is made manifest by the significance of its most obvious coordinates: names. Each of the novel's first six chapters has as its title a character's name. The importance of narrating a person's life in order to understand who that person is comes out in the inserted stories of Betros and Selima, as well as in Jafudà's own story, that he so specifically begins with the night of his birth. Only the novel's last chapter--really more of an afterward--does not have a proper name for a title. Deleuze and Guattari open their introduction to *A Thousand Plateaus* with a resistance to one-dimensional, univocal identities, and they speculate about a moment wherein "it is no longer of any importance if one says I" (3). Jafudà Cresques has not reached this extreme, although his narrative points to an emergence of and existence within multiple identities, as he and his fellow converted Jews adopt new names and behaviors for the outside (Christian) world, and maintain traditional Jewish behaviors at home.

In the novel's brief conclusion, Jafudà describes his life since the riots in persecution of the Jews, the disappearance of Selima and his newborn son, and his family's subsequent conversion to Christianity, an event marked by their public baptism (Jafudà becomes Jaume Ribes). The protagonist reflects, "Jo sóc el mateix, i al mateix temps sóc tot un altre" (318–19) (I'm the same, and at the same time I'm entirely another). Jafudà contemplates the garden of his family home where now Betros and Cresques lie buried next to a memorial to Selima, and the furtive atlas is interred beside its author. He insists,

No tot ha finat, no tot ha mort. Hi ha tres recordatoris sota el taronger, sí, tres memòries d'un deixeble de Crist, un de Moisès i una de Mahoma, que evoquen una vida que ja no tornarà. Hi ha un llibre ple de prodigis que els pertany a tots tres. Però queda també una fina escletxa d'incertesa, per on s'escolen les llums del passat. (320–21)

(Not everything has ended, not everything has died. There are three reminders under the orange tree, yes, three memories of a disciple of Christ, one of Moses, and one of Mohammed, that evoke a life that won't return. There's a book full of marvels that belongs to all three. But there's also left a fine crack of uncertainty, where the lights of the past flow through.)

Jafudà refuses to accept the definitive death of Selima and his son, and is frustrated by the fact that, as the years pass, it will be possible for him to see his son and not recognize him. The lack of conclusiveness surrounding the fate of Jafudà's son, the offspring of a Catalan Jew and a Muslim Princess, is significant in the vague hopefulness that there remains some remnant of the disappeared community out of which the furtive atlas was born, which might return when least expected. In the end, Jafudà comes to understand the open-endedness of systems of meaning, which parallels what Denis Cosgrove points out about maps:

[Maps] are also troubling. Their apparent stability and their aesthetics of closure and finality dissolve with but a little reflection into recognition of their partiality and provisionality, their embodiment of intention, their imaginative and creative capacities, their mythical qualities, their appeal to reverie, their ability to record and stimulate anxiety, their silences and their powers of deception. (2)

The novel's end, with the now, dual identity of its protagonist, unresolved questions about Selima and her son, and the buried, furtive atlas, the content of which is never specified, bears out the open-endedness of politicized space. The furtive atlas that Bosch's readers are meant to imagine still lies buried somewhere in Mallorca, containing all of the iconographic motion of the Atles de Cresques, reflects the accumulated knowledge of a Christian, a Muslim, and a Jew, and offers an image/imagination of a Catalonia chronologically predating, and culturally independent of, an alliance with Castile, in a world that, likewise, predates the homogenizing impact of the cartographic grid. The furtive atlas, then, is a representation of space, and a space in its own right, that resists dominant narratives of modernity. This is why it matters that Bosch's readers don't know conclusively what's on it or where it is. It is suspended in a state of potentiality: "*For* the future to be open, space must be open too" (Massey 12, emphasis in original). Rather than overcoming the grid pattern in a projected future, we might, perhaps, return to a time before we had been over-come by it. A spatial mode of thought allows for this, by drawing relationships and finding meaning in juxtapositions that work outside the limits of linear time.

In the Network, but Not Off the Grid

Early in 2009, the Museu d'Història de Barcelona opened a temporary ex-hibit, accompanied by online content, called "Barcelona connectada, ciutadans transnacionals: Creixements migratoris i pràctiques urbanes" (Barcelona Con-nected, Transnational Citizens: Migratory Growth and Urban Practices). The project set out to increase sensitivity to immigrants in Barcelona by situating them in a historical tradition in which immigration forms an indispensable part of Barcelona's development. The reference to "connectedness" in the exhibit's title as well as the physical and visual layout of the exhibit call attention to the pivotal role that communications media, most notably the internet, play in defining the contemporary immigrant experience in Barcelona. As immigrants make use of communications media to remain "connected" to their homelands, they more fully integrate Barcelona into a global community. According to this logic, Barcelona is connected *because* it is a destination for immigrants and because those immigrants to maintain connections with their points of origin. The exhibit is equally attentive to economic, cultural, technological, and hu-man considerations. There are lines to be drawn between *L'atles furtiu* and "Barcelona connectada," if we understand the museum exhibit, Bosch's novel, and, through it, the Atles de Cresques, all to be arguing in favor of the inter-weaving of cultural difference into the social fabric as a necessary and produc-tive maneuver.

Both in the museum installation and online, the content is divided into five "àmbits" (spheres): "Imaginaris," "Connexions," "Intimitats," "Negocis," and "Asimetries" (Imaginaries, Connections, Intimacies, Business, and Asym-metries). Taking the five "àmbits" in order, we start with the assertion that the immigrant community in Barcelona, through its "connectedness," contributes to the city's continuing development and, by extension, to that of Catalonia and Europe. The remaining "àmbits" explore different aspects of immigrants' lives in Barcelona. Ending with the fifth "àmbit," "Asymmetries," the exhibit insists that the ability of immigrant communities to contribute to Barcelona and, in-deed, the global community is contingent upon the protection of their social and political rights. As the website puts it:

Si no ho impedeixen fractures socials profundes, una metrópoli com Barcelona constitueix, per la densitat i varietat dels contactes que s'hi produeixen, un catalitzador d'innovacions privilegiat. Però les noves aportacions, perque siguin tals, han de poder inserir-se d'una manera satisfactòria dins de la trajectória cultural pròpia de la ciutat .

(If it's not impeded by deep social fractures, a metropolis like Barcelona constitutes, by the density and variety of contacts that are produced there, a priviledged catalyst of innovation. But the new offerings, in order for them to be that, have to be able to insert themselves in a satisfactory way into the cultural trajectory that belongs to the city.)

The five "àmbits" are followed by a section with the notably spatial title "Trajectories," which provides a historical overview of immigration in Barcelona, pointing out that Barcelona's vibrance as a metropolis is due in large part to the arrival of immigrants to the city, who contribute to its growth in size and its economy at the same time.

While the network may provide the conceptual backbone of the project, the organizing principle of both the website and the installation is the grid pattern. When one enters the exhibit at the museum, one finds oneself in the cabin of an airplane, and while seated, instead of watching a video on aircraft safety, there is a video about immigration in Barcelona that provides an introduction to the main themes of the exhibit. After "exiting the aircraft," one finds oneself among large, illuminated cubes, several meters high, that portray a collage of urban images, texts, sounds—we have emerged into the city streets of Barcelona, the grid pattern of the Eixample neighborhood, and of urban life more generally, readily evoked by the rows and columns of illuminated blocks. The blocks are arranged thematically, following the five "àmbits" that structure the exhibit's content, but one can move through them freely and negotiate one's own geography of immigration in Barcelona. The opening page of the website shows a 6 x 3 grid of photographs, all portraying either Barcelona's street life or images of the installation, itself. Throughout, photographs show how immigrants are taking ownership of city spaces and leaving their own marks on them. The referencing of travel via the installation's airplane cabin and the use of the Internet in the dispersion of the exhibit content illustrate the ease, perhaps even the inevitability, of global connectedness.

In addition to the obviously spatial nature of its content and presentation, the exhibit, both in the museum and online, is peppered with cartographic language that is remarkably evocative of Massey's vocabulary of a politicized spatial imagination. "Barcelona connectada" projects Massey's "throwntogetherness" onto the streets of Barcelona, with an illuminated and digitized collage of urban sound and spectacle, and embodies Massey's contention that "Places pose in particular form the question of our living together" (151). Both the website and the installation allow for an infinite variety of inclusions, and exclusions, based on each visitor's navigation of their content. Further, "Barcelona connectada" captures Massey's "radical contemporaneity" in the visual and auditory cacophony of the museum exhibit. As one feels a certain sense of claustrophobia or overwhelmedness in the midst of the illuminated cubes, one's mind is pressed to move beyond the angular spaces to the more abstract and less easily plotted movements of people, commodities, and even sentiments, along the paths of the global network. So while one physically navigates the urban grid, the spatial complexity of the global community hovers in the air. As we exit the simulated airplane cabin we encounter the force of Massey's contention that "One cannot seriously posit space as the outside of place as lived, or simply equate 'the everyday' with the local. If we really think space relationally, then it is the sum of all our connections, and in that sense utterly grounded, and those connections may go round the world" (185).[3] Making a leap from the cusp of cartographic modernity to the postmodern communications network, there is a certain parallel process between the compilation of narratives from travelers who had access to the world through the technology of navigation, from which the Atles de Cresques of 1375 was elaborated, and the proposed remapping of contemporary Barcelona, constructed in the museum, which calls for the continued incorporation of Others into the cultural production and economic development of the city.

Open Ends

Both the museum exhibit and Bosch's novel point to a foundational narrative for Catalonia that rests on the valued contribution of Others. At the same time, their revisiting of Catalonia's past locates historical points of origin in instability and movement through space. In telling the story of the Atles de Cresques, Alfred Bosch recovers for the Catalan national imaginary a cultural artifact from a time before the political alliance of Aragon and Castile, a time in which Catalonia's political and cultural position was not overshadowed by the Spanish State. The specific choice of an atlas from this period is propitious for a number of reasons.[4] *L'atles furtiu* at once reveals a moment of exceptional cultural accomplishment for Catalonia, but also of social uncertainty, which Bosch captures in the tenuous position of the Jewish community within the kingdom of Aragon. The persecution of the Jews is rendered all the more incomprehensible precisely because of their contributions to culture and knowledge at the time. In *L'atles furtiu*, and in the Atles de Cresques, their respective creators capture moments of shifting world views, where the drive to name things and pin them down can be read as a reaction to radical instability. A similar argument might be made about the publication of the Catalan Atlas in 1975, another moment in which Spain and Catalonia, in relation to Spain, were in a moment of potential reimagining.

With eyes trained by the Museu d'Història de Barcelona, *L'atles furtiu*, and the Catalan Atlas, we might revisit Cresques Abraham's fourteenth-century masterpiece as an alternative exercise in globalization, in which the heavily weighted term takes on a different significance—one that would leave room for the coexistence of multiple spatial imaginaries. Tracing treatments of Otherness, of multiplicity, or of tolerance through the various texts in this "constellation," the high premium placed on Others can be understood in at least two ways. On the one hand, we are led to appreciate the extent to which cultural diversity has defined the historical development of Catalonia as well as to perceive this as a characteristic of Catalonia's cultural heritage that distinguishes it from the Spanish State. On another level, though, the call for tolerance emerges from Catalonia and is directed outward, from within a community that has, for some centuries, itself been depicted as the Other.

A spatial approach to this material allows for a juxtaposition of texts in simultaneous signification. *If* there is a history here, it is a resistant, retrospective one that moves from the present backward in search of a rootedness, an origin, a foundation that proves impossible to place. We move in reverse chronology from the grid pattern of Barcelona's streets in "Barcelona connectada" to the trajectories of the Atles de Cresques, the combined efforts of word and image that seem more adequately to capture the complexities of globalization (the early modern version of it, or the postmodern one) and representations of space, which in turn throw us back to the networked residents of contemporary Barcelona. Again, it proves impossible to draw a straight line, arrive at the end of a trajectory, or point to its origin.

It is easy to see why Deleuze and Guattari would prefer a map to a book, as they look for a way not to be linear but still work within the bounds of language. A map can be read in any order and with any level of simultaneity (as much as our imaginations can accommodate). Neither the signifier nor the signified can ever be pinned down or closed off. Still, a map is not enough; it should be a map that is not a *projection*, that does not rest upon the "pillars" of latitude and longitude. For Deleuze and Guattari, "the model is a *vortical* one; it operates in an open space throughout which things-flows are distributed [*smooth* space], rather than plotting out a closed space [or *striated* space] for linear and solid things" (361). For Deleuze and Guattari, *smooth* space is the locus of *nomadology*, wherein paths determine points rather than the other way around (380, 478). In this light, the *furtiveness* of Bosch's furtive atlas becomes crucial: it is not a stone in the foundation of contemporary Catalonia, nor is it a fixed starting point for an already determined destination. Better, it is an elusive gesture in the direction of a multiplicity of possible outcomes, an embodiment and celebration of multiplicity, itself.

Deleuze and Guattari cite the seas as a notable example of the striation of a smooth space, through the development of modern European cartography, in which the Atles de Cresques plays a pivotal role. They argue that "In striated space, one closes off a surface and 'allocates' it according to determinate intervals, assigned breaks; in the smooth, one 'distributes' oneself in an open space, according to frequencies and in the course of one's crossings" (481). If we imagine the global communications network the way "Barcelona connectada" wants us to, do we not witness a smoothing out of space that undermines, overrides, or circumvents the binding impulse of the State? This would be an inverse of the process of striation in which Jafudà de Cresques/Jaume Ribes finds himself at the end of Bosch's novel and which Cresques captures in the "bearings" of his atlas. The Atles de Cresques, *L'Atles furtiu*, and "Barcelona connectada" all meet, then, in the middle ground between striation and smoothness, alluding to a foundational myth and, in that very act, pointing to the myth of foundation itself.

Open-endedness is a notable characteristic that the texts in this study share. The Atles de Cresques, which relies on a multidirectional network of "bearings" instead of the parallels and perpendiculars of latitude and longitude, shows such a strong urge for signification that the storytelling of illustrations spills over into verbal description and, thus, seems a perfect performance of Massey's "stories-so-far." (It does not stretch the imagination to picture the medieval cartographer laying this atlas out and explaining, "[t]his is what we know . . . so far.") More than six centuries later the atlas continues to invite the question: Where do we go from here? Subsequent texts that have taken up the challenge offered by the Atles de Cresques deny a definitive answer to that question, almost compulsively returning to the past in search of a vision of the future, even as artifacts of the past point inexorably forward. This is certainly the case in Bosch's *L'atles furtiu*, which leaves its readers with the tantalizing suggestion that there's an atlas hidden in the earth of Mallorca, an ironic burying of the treasure map, itself. Meanwhile, within the novel, Jafudà repeatedly returns to the story of his birth in search of an explanation for why he is who he is, only to become someone else ("I'm the same, and at the same time I'm entirely another"). Ultimately Jafudà refuses to allow for the closing off either of his own definition of self, or of the story that started with the inception of the atlas, an effort that Bosch supports by not letting us know what happened to Selima and their son. Tracing a trajectory toward the future from the past, and the open-endedness of that gesture, is perhaps most explicitly addressed in the last verse from Espriu's poem for the Catalan Atlas: "del clos avui al lliure demà que guanyarem" (N. pag.) (from the closed off today to the far off tomorrow that we will win), which holds a privileged position in both the Catalan Atlas and Bosch's novel, thereby informing our reading of both.

"Barcelona connectada" is more prescriptive in its advocacy for openness, proposing an openness to diversity and difference, to immigrants as potential founders of the future city, and, if we accept this model, then we can imagine Barcelona in a constant process of refoundation. Of course, at the same time that the museum argues in favor of tolerance, it too easily sets aside the diversity of the immigrant communities that constitute the historical trajectory of the city by glossing over the fact that earlier immigrant groups came from within Spain and didn't confront linguistic, racial, and religious differences to the same degree that contemporary immigrants do. On the other hand, "Barcelona connectada" *is* sensitive to the dual identities that many immigrants adopt, an issue that is not the same as Jafudà's internal conflict, as he takes the Christian name of Jaume Ribes, but that does mirror that struggle in some respects. This simultaneous doubling and dividing of the subject is perhaps best explored in the museum's treatment of "Intimacies," wherein is noted the painful irony that (mostly) female immigrants who take domestic positions in Barcelona often leave behind their own children and households in order to do so.

Even as I round out this study, I resist the temptation to conclusively close off the network of spatial imaginations. More than a study of *L'atles furtiu* and the other texts to which it points, this is an exercise in the kind of thinking that is opened up through and by these texts. To borrow again from Massey's terminology, there is a "throwntogetherness" of the texts that has been touched upon here. The relations of meaning between the Atles de Cresques, *L'atles furtiu*, "Barcelona connectada," and the multitude of texts that surround them (the Catalan Atlas, Espriu's poetry, the museum website) are not defined chronologically. It is a spatial dynamic, not a temporal one, out of which emerges a certain articulation of Catalonia's cultural heritage that is open to alterity, and stubbornly points toward the future, while refusing to paint a picture of exactly what it will be.

Notes

1. My thanks to Alfred Bosch for taking an interest in this project and drawing my attention to this text.
2. All translations to English are mine, unless otherwise noted.
3. Massey acknowledges the connectedness that comes to European cities via immigration in analyses of Hamburg and London. About the latter, for example, she points out: "And this intrusion by those who service the City [in London] is linked into its own global relations—with family and friends, for instance, in Nigeria, Portugal, Colombia—other globalizations which highlight the particularities of, and the hiatuses and disconnections within, the City's own reach" (190).
4. Of late medieval Mallorcan Catalan cartography, Julio Sansó Moya and Juan Casanovas have said, "Es una época en que la cultura astronómica catalano-aragonesa ha llegado a su cenit y ha arrebatado, por un breve período de tiempo, la supremacía que en el siglo anterior había tenido la ciencia castellana" (1975, 23) (It is an epoch in which the Catalan-Aragonese astronomic culture has arrived at its zenith and has snatched away, for a brief period of time, the supremacy that Castilian science held in the previous century.)

Works Cited

Bosch, Alfred. *L'atles furtiu*. Barcelona: Columna, 1998.

Brotton, Jerry. *Trading Territories: Mapping the Early Modern World*. Ithaca, NY: Cornell University Press, 1998.

Conley, Tom. *The Self-Made Map: Cartographic Writing in Early Modern France*. Minneapolis: University of Minnesota Press, 1996.

Cosgrove, Denis. "Introduction." *Mappings*. Ed. Denis Cosgrove. London: Reaktion Books, 1999.

———. Ed. *Mappings*. London: Reaktion Books, 1999.

Crone, G. R. *Maps and Their Makers: An Introduction to the History of Cartography*. London: Hutchinson, 1968.

Deleuze, Gilles, and Félix Guattari. *A Thousand Plateaus: Capitalism and Schizophrenia*. Trans. Brian Massumi. Minneapolis: University of Minnesota Press, 1987.

Edgerton, Samuel Y., Jr. "From Mental Matrix to *Mappamundi* to Christian Empire: The Heritage of Ptolemaic Cartography in the Renaissance." *Art and Cartography: Six Historical Essays*. Eds. David Woodward. Chicago: University of Chicago Press, 1987.

Espriu, Salvador. "El passat i el pou, a trenc d'alba." *El atlas catalán de Cresques Abraham*. Barcelona: Diáfora, 1975. n. pag.

———. *La pell de brau/La piel de toro*. Trans. José Agustín Goytisolo. París: Ruedo Ibérico, 1963.

Llompart i Moragues, Gabriel. "Aspectos iconográficos." *El atlas catalán de Cresques Abraham*. Barcelona: Diáfora, 1975.

Massey, Doreen. *For Space*. London: Sage, 2005.

Padrón, Ricardo. *The Spacious Word: Cartography, Literature, and Empire in Early Modern Spain*. Chicago: University of Chicago Press, 2004.

Sansó Moya, Julio, and Juan Casanovas. "Cosmología, astrología, y calendario." *El atlas catalán de Cresques Abraham*. Barcelona: Diáfora, 1975.

Scafi, Alessandro. "Mapping Eden: Cartographies of the Earthly Paradise." *Mappings*. Ed. Dennis Cosgrove. London: Reaktion Books, 1999.

Sureda i Blanes, Josep. "Cresques Abraham y los descubrimientos geográficos de la Edad Media." *El atlas catalán de Cresques Abraham*. Barcelona: Diáfora, 1975.

"Web de l'exposició Barcelona Connectada." *Museu d'història de Barcelona*. Web. 30 September 2009. *www.barcelonaconnectada.cat/ca/*.

PART II
Modern(ist) Sceneries

◆ **6**

Topofilia Porteña: Imaging Buenos Aires and Modernity in (and around) the Journal *Sur*

Justin Read

Walter Gropius's "Total Theater" (ca. 1927) is one of the most perfect expressions of international modernist architecture. Although the project was never realized, Gropius envisioned his Total Theater, *avant la lettre* of Le Corbusier, as a "*machine à émouvoir.*" The Total Theater was not to be a mere monument, or merely a space in which to enact monumental theatrical representations. Rather, it was to be a "quite perfect theater-instrument" (Gropius 143) that would incorporate three distinct historical phases of theater-construction: (a) the classical Greek theater-in-the-round, a circular stage (circus) surrounded by the audience at 360 degrees; (b) the semicircular proscenium of imperial Rome, an amphitheater surrounding a "hemi-arena" at a 180-degree angle, backed by *scaenae frons* of columns from which to enter and exit the stage; and (c) the modern theater with an elevated stage set off from the seating area by a large archway, orchestra pit, and curtains. In this last theatrical design, known as the *Guckkastenbühne* in Gropius's native German, the spectator is completely removed from the "world of the farce" (Gropius 142–43).[1]

Gropius clearly saw this architectural-historical progression from ancient Greece to modern Germany as a change in spectatorship—in which audience members had been progressively removed from the time and space of the dramatic spectacle, and through which architectural design had spliced the chronotope of the play being acted away from the chronotope of the spectator.

The Total Theater would have surpassed all three historical phases of construction by uniting them. If spectators had entered the theater, they would have seen an enclosed amphitheater with seating areas arrayed 180 degrees around a modern elevated stage. Like most modern theaters, the seating area would have been divided in two general sections, with a walkway dividing an upper level from lower-level seating; this lower-level seating, in turn, would surround a separate oval platform situated directly in front of the elevated stage. This oval proscenium could have been raised or lowered mechanically, used either as an extension of the stage when raised, or an orchestra pit when lowered. However, the oval proscenium, along with the lower-level seating surrounding it, would also have been attached to a large disc on the floor of the theater building. This disc could have been rotated mechanically a full one hundred and eighty degrees, so that a small circular theater-in-the-round could be formed with lower-level seating now facing the stationary upper-level area. Moreover, the Total Theater was to be equipped not only with modern lighting, but also a battery of movie projectors. These would not only be able to project films "forward" to the stage area, but also to the walls behind the audience and the ceiling above them. Gropius writes, "spectators will find themselves, for example, in the middle of a waving sea, or will see great multitudes advancing over them from all directions. . . . We see, therefore, that instead of the projection system employed until now (cinematographic) with a simple screen, we enter into a *projector space*" (Gropius 147; my emphasis).

In our contemporary world we would recognize the elements of Gropius's Total Theater as commonplace in any major-city sporting arena, which might be used one night for a rock concert (elevated proscenium) and the next night for basketball (theater-in-the-round), with large monitors and display screens scattered throughout. But in the world of the 1920s and 1930s, Gropius's theoretical theater space was intended to be revolutionary rather than ordinary. Gropius conceived the Total Theater as a totalized machine, one replete with moving parts and special effects. Yet the impetus behind this machine was a certain form of humanism: the audience entering the Total Theater would not just sit within it, but would also learn how to see the world anew through the machine. The audience would no longer be directed to a moving image projected away from them, but rather, the movie would be projected back toward the audience so that the spectator might be able to enter the spectacle. By bringing the classical space of tragedy back into the modern theater, moreover, Gropius hoped to facilitate new modes of catharsis from which the audience might imagine

new social relations. In this way the Total Theater envisioned both the creation of multiple chronotopes and the *collapse* of distinct chronotopes into one
another: "The finality of this theater resides, therefore, not in the material accumulation of refined technical installations and tricks, but rather in that all
will be means and ends so that the spectator appears transported into scenic
movement, and enters completely into the environment of the stage" (Gropius
147–48). The architectural machine permits the mutation of real space, so that
one can *really* inhabit a virtual space. In effect, the Total Theater would have
opened multiple frames of time and space that could have been experienced
concurrently, and in so doing would have opened new ways for spectators to
share common realities. In short, the architect may lose his own unitary perspective to the impersonal machine of his architecture, but he does so in order
to unleash the personal potential, the human potential, of directors, actors, and
spectators alike.

The Total Theater was thus intended as a pedagogical instrument to be
utilized to teach spectators how to see a new world. Accordingly, the scope of
this new mode of vision was not merely spatial (to see the space of the theater in new ways), but also temporal-historical: spectators would come to see
historical development as such through a refined critical lens. In this Gropius
tacitly endorsed a particular view of history, progress, and development. The
Total Theater imagined a rather smooth historical progression of civilization
from ancient Greece northward to modern Germany, as if both societies were
parts of a singular historical and cultural whole. Gropius's work of the period
may therefore be seen as a continuation of a German-Romantic, and hence Eurocentric, world order: that there exists such a thing as "Western civilization"
in the first place, which began in Athens several centuries before the birth of
Christ, reached an apex in nineteenth-century Germany, and fell into decline
with the Great War of the twentieth century. Of course, Gropius produced his
plans for the Total Theater during the *entre guerre*, at a point in time (1927) in
which the Weimar Republic was increasingly unable to cope with economic,
political, and ethnic-cultural crises. Gropius's plans in this context operated in
the "negative space" of what is nevertheless perceived to be "Western" civilization. The operant historical purview of the Total Theater is one borne of civilizational decline: new ways of seeing—new modes for spectators to see themselves, others, and the space between themselves and others—were required
precisely because German society (and Western civilization more generally)
needed to be reconstructed from the ground up. Civilization—*all* civilization—
had come to an end, and so needed to be re-created.

As I mentioned, the Total Theater was never constructed, and thus no new civilization around it. Nevertheless, it did find a New World: I would argue that the Total Theater found its most perfect expression in Buenos Aires, Argentina shortly after Gropius proposed it. The purpose of the present essay is to trace how this paradox came to be: that by *not* being built, the Total Theater remained a modernist ideal that fed directly, in its way, into a concrete manifestation of Latin American idealism—the modernization of Argentina.

After traveling extensively through Western Europe in the latter half of the 1920s, Victoria Ocampo had become enamored of modernism. Once back in her hometown of Buenos Aires in 1928 and wishing to build a new townhouse there, she contacted none other than Le Corbusier, who indeed drew initial plans for the project in September of that year. By the time Le Corbusier traveled to the Argentinean capital in 1929, Ocampo would entertain the Swiss architect in her brand new, stark white Purist house in city's Palermo district. The modernism of the home, which still stands today, is immediately recognizable: both interior and exterior appear as stark repetitions of geometrical forms (cubes, straight lines, right angles). As Ernesto Katzenstein has written of the Ocampo house, "This effort to create a silent testimony of timeless architecture was materialized in the home's exterior through a relationship of volumes, solids and voids that gives a sensation of *gravitas* to the house, depriving it of any experimental characteristics" (Katzenstein 59). He goes on to relate Le Corbusier's impressions of the house in 1929: "the absolute consistency in treatment and, in every case, the total absence of decoration, the austerity of its light-colored walls, the striking presence of a constant lighting and, finally, the stark anonymity of its furniture made Le Corbusier admit, in *Precisions*, that 'he had seen Picassos and Légers framed by a seldom-to-be-found purity'" (Katzenstein 59).

In stating this Le Corbusier was not being self-aggrandizing however, since Ocampo decided *not* to use the plans Le Corbusier drew for her. Instead, she turned to the *porteño* architect Alejandro Bustillo an odd choice given that Bustillo openly detested modernism. Bustillo has been described as an "eclectic" designer, but in fact he was most widely known for buildings squarely in the Beaux-Arts or neo-classical styles—a traditionalist, in other words. Katzenstein argues convincingly that Ocampo sought a seasoned professional for her new abode, rather than a difficult artist or a youngster prone to wild experimentation. The Ocampo house was thus shaped as much by economic concerns as purely aesthetic ideals. On one hand, there can be no doubt that Ocampo had a keen sense of *modernist* style and its importance for Argentina. In building her house she attempted to promote the transformation of Buenos Aires into a *modernized* world city. By all accounts the Buenos Aires of 1929 was unbearably ugly: situated on a flat, muddy bank of the Río de la Plata, the urban core consisted of squat edifices (with a few new skyscrapers) in a hodgepodge of imported styles, while the sprawling suburbs (still growing at a rapid rate) were generally dirty and desperately poor. According to Adrian Gorelik's seminal history of the city (1998), *porteño* urban planners of the period could never quite decide whether to centralize the *urbs* in a downtown core, or incorporate suburban *arrabales* (*barrios*) into a comprehensive urban order. As Le Corbusier would state in 1930 after his South American sojourn, the result was chaos: "that gigantic city, one of the most inhuman imaginable, had crushed, compressed me enough that I reacted and imagined (quite humbly) something like a remedy" (Le Corbusier 2). Ocampo's architectural tastes favoring Purism, though not overtly political, were shaped by a desire to "cleanse" her city of its "distasteful" demeanor. On the other hand, the actual execution of the project she commissioned came down to pragmatic economic choices: wishing her house to be built as efficiently as possible, with (as one supposes) minimal cost overruns due to artistic flair or youthful inexperience, she sought out in Bustillo one of the most experienced architects available, who in turn must have been paid sufficiently to cast all of his aesthetic ideals aside in order to receive the commission.

Similar tensions between aesthetics and economics come through in the journal Ocampo began to plan some time in 1929. After the first issue emerged in 1931, Ocampo's quarterly review *Sur* arguably became the most important cultural institution in Argentina from the 1930s until well into the 1960s (Ocampo remained as editor-in-chief until the journal's demise in 1970). The first several years of the journal's existence were particularly remarkable, including a veritable constellation of national and international cultural luminaries. A glance at the journal's tables of contents in the first two years of its existence is striking: Waldo Frank, Alfonso Reyes, Ricardo Güiraldes, Hermann Graf Keyserling, Drieu la Rochelle, Jaime Torres Bodet, Ramón Gómez de la Serna, Eduardo Mallea, Guillermo de Torre, Alberto Prebisch, Pedro Henríquez Ureña, Lewis Mumford, Aldous Huxley, Edgar Lee Masters, Langston Hughes, Martin Heidegger, Jorge Luis Borges, and Walter Gropius.[2]

By including such luminaries, most of whom (including Borges and Reyes) were part of both American and European avant-garde movements, Ocampo unabashedly strove to locate Buenos Aires as a cultural center of Western civilization. With Ocampo at its helm, *Sur* would advocate for the necessity of aesthetic vision (and in particular literary/poetic judgment) in the (re)construction of society and civilization. Notably this was an argument quite similar to that espoused by both nineteenth-century liberals like Domingo Faustino

Sarmiento and, as we have just seen, by twentieth-century radicals like Walter Gropius. As John King writes, the journal's first issues claimed "to be above and beyond politics and to reconstitute liberalism in eternal terms and on a purely cultural level: literature demonstrated the superiority of art over life and set up an alternative tribunal against which events could be judged. New times called for a new tone: *Sur* would always be a mature text, conscious of literary decorum and the need to establish standards in years of discord" (43–44). Unlike Gropius, however, Ocampo would not position Buenos Aires as a cultural center amidst civilizational decay, thus offering modern aesthetics as the salvation of society as Gropius had proposed with his Total Theater. Rather, Ocampo's ideas emerged from a position of optimism, out of her love of place, her topophilia for Buenos Aires. Instead of decay, a modernized Buenos Aires had boundless potential for new growth to become a major center of the "West."

Of course, the city's potential as described in my last sentence could only be *doubly* potential: a "modernized" Buenos Aires could *potentially* lead the West, but when Ocampo started *Sur* the city only existed *in potentia* since it had not yet "modernized." Or more precisely, as we will soon see, the modernity Buenos Aires experienced did not correspond to some pure "city on the hill" envisioned by Ocampo's preferred strain of modernism. It is indubitable, furthermore, that Ocampo was highly Eurocentric in her general world-view: she proposed to modernize Buenos Aires and Argentina by bringing the Argentinean intellectual elite into contact with the cultural elite of the "developed" world. *Sur* was therefore designed as the conduit through which national and international orders would begin to circulate and merge. This would "lift" Argentina into modernity; and by the same token, Buenos Aires would also serve to lift the developed "West" out of its decadence.

Over time, Ocampo and *Sur* have been attacked for their elitism and snobbism—often deservedly so. Nonetheless, despite the overt Eurocentrism of the editor, the initial volumes of the journal are remarkable for their strident Americanism. In her "Carta a Waldo Frank," Ocampo describes her "Americanist" engagement with Europe as a quasi-dialectical relation: in order to truly see Western civilization, Ocampo feels compelled to turn away from Europe. Similarly, to lay claim to European modernity, Ocampo suggests that Americans must turn their gaze westward toward their own continent. As she states:

> Drieu [la Rochelle] quería decir que somos americanos, Waldo, y que en nosotros la inocencia es todavía auténtica. Que puede, por consiguiente, hacer milagros.
> Yo pensaba que si América es joven, el mundo no lo es y que nuestro continente se parece a esos niños cuya infancia se marchita de vivir siempre entre adultos.

América no cree ya en los cuentos de hadas, pero lleva en sí la eternal necesidad que los hizo nacer. Como necesita creer en ellos acabará por inventarlos de nuevo. Y ese será su milagro. (Ocampo 1931a, 12)[3]

(Drieu la Rochelle wanted to say that we are Americans, Waldo, and that for us innocence is still authentic. That miracles, therefore, can be made.
I thought that if America is young, the world is not and that our continent seems like one of those children whose childhood wastes away from always living among adults. America no longer believes in fairy tales, but it takes within itself the eternal need for them. As it needs to believe in them it will end up inventing them again. And this will be its miracle.)

Ultimately, Ocampo shows her Eurocentrism to be a negative aspect still integrated into her sense of topophilia for her homeland. In the final paragraphs of her "Carta" she writes: "Este amor se dirige a lo que está más allá de nosotros y parte de lo que está más allá de nosotros. Tener conciencia de ello, sufrir por ello es saludable. Así está usted, así estamos nosotros enamorados de América" (1931a, 18) (This love points to what is beyond ourselves and departs from what is beyond ourselves. To be conscious of it, to suffer for it is healthy. This is how you are, this is how we are enamored of America).

This dialectic of extending European civilization by "becoming" American comes through most viscerally in the configuration of writings in the first issue. The first issue of *Sur* consists primarily of critical considerations of art and poetry, interspersed with travel narratives in which the authors "discover" some aspect of South America. The essays are also punctuated by images— drawings by Picasso, for instance, next to exotic photographs of Brazil or the Iguazu Falls. In one article, Waldo Frank takes the reader through his journeys across Brazil; in another Eugenio d'Ors discusses the "architecture" of Picasso's sketches. Tellingly, in the "Notas" section at the back of the issue, there are two short articles on Le Corbusier—one on his furniture designs by Victoria Ocampo, and another a review by Alberto Prebisch of the recently published *Précisions*. These reviews, however, surround a local-color piece, "Séneca en las orillas," in which Jorge Luis Borges looks at local fruit carts in Buenos Aires and admires the rhetorical flourishes of their signage.

Perhaps a more direct index of Ocampo's Europe/America dialectic occurs in Borges's other contribution to the first volume, "El coronel Ascasubi." In his essay, Borges seeks to recover the *gauchesco* poet Hilario Ascasubi from literary-historical oblivion. Though seldom read, Ascasubi is typically thought of as a forerunner of José Hernández and his masterwork, *Martín Fierro*. Borges attempts to display Ascasubi as the superior poet, particularly in the way he captures a truly *criollo* voice and character. The actual merits of Borges's essay are debatable. The essay must be considered a minor piece in his canon, except in the way it portends, perhaps unwittingly, his later *faux* literary histories of "Pierre Ménard" or "Tlön, Uqbar, Orbis Tertius." That is, Borges plays the part of the dogged literary critic who, knowing his conclusions to be false in some way, nonetheless rewrites history based on a minor piece of archival evidence. Beyond the question of inherent literary value, however, "El coronel Ascasubi" gains interest contextually, given the physical, material location it occupies in *Sur*: Borges's article leads directly into the Spanish translation of Walter Gropius's "El teatro total"—perhaps the first appearance of Gropius's theoretical sketch for the project anywhere in the Americas.

The Total Theater was never realized, of course, and yet theoretically the Total Theater made one of its first appearances in the cultural sphere of Buenos Aires, in a journal that purported to be the guiding light of American culture. Let us recall that one of the aims of the Total Theater was a particular kind of modernist simultaneity—the past collapsed into the present, such that the time and space of aesthetic representation might cross into the time and space of modern reality. Borges's re-visioning of Ascasubi is intended to provide a classical, *criollo* tradition for Argentinean culture, to take an archaeological relic of the past (Ascasubi) and refashion it for the modern moment, in order to re-order future histories. This effort is entirely aesthetic and mythic. As Borges writes of Ascasubi, "Basta nombrarlo para estar en mitología de esta esquina de América" (Borges 1931a, 140) (It is enough to name him to be mythologized in this corner of America). Borges seeks to *collapse* the mythical time and space of *criollo* poetry into the real, concrete time-space of *porteño* modernity.

Has Borges's Ascasubi just entered Gropius's Total Theater? Or has Gropius entered the theatrical space of an imaginary *payada gauchesca*? When Jorge Luis Borges returned to Buenos Aires in the 1920s, he may have returned to a city from which he had never really left in the first place. Buenos Aires in 1921 (the date of Borges's return to Argentina) was arguably a different Buenos Aires than the one from which the fourteen year-old "Georgie" and his family had left to go to Geneva in 1914. The generations of *porteños* just prior to Borges—that of his father and grandfather—literally inhabited a different world. In 1870, just as Argentina emerged from a long period of political upheaval and the disastrous War of the Triple Alliance against Paraguay, the population of the capital was a relatively modest one hundred and eighty thousand. By the time the Borges family left in 1914, less than fifty years later, the population had grown to roughly one and a half million.

Whereas the city barely had indoor plumbing and sewage in 1870, by 1910 the city had become the major port of entry to South America, with modern shipping facilities, automated streetcars, metro, railroads, and electric light (Scobie 11). Wealthy residents had built up areas such as Palermo and La Recoleta north of the traditional *centro* around the Plaza de Mayo. Often they commissioned designs from French Beaux-Arts architects, many of whom never traveled to the city or saw their finished projects. But Buenos Aires's spectacular growth was not only fueled by the wealthy. Like São Paulo and New York City, Buenos Aires was a principal destination for European immigrants, primarily Italian, as well as "internal" migrants from the interior of the nation. These new immigrants were typically concentrated, first, into overcrowded *conventillos* (tenement houses), before resettling to sprawling suburbs such as La Boca, Barracas, Nueva Chicago, and Villa Urquiza to the south and west. A great deal of these suburbs consisted of *villas miserias*, desperately poor shantytowns akin to contemporary Brazilian *favelas*, which were among the first modern slums in Latin America. The pace of change in Buenos Aires would only accelerate into the 1920s and 1930s, with the construction of electrical, lighting, telephone, and radio networks. As Beatriz Sarlo notes: "The inhabitants of the city lived at an unprecedented pace: the experience of speed, the experience of artificial light—and of long-distance communications, which would soon give rise to a powerful cultural industry—provided a new set of images and perceptions. Those who, like Borges, were older than twenty in 1925 could remember with nostalgia the city at the turn of the century, and could confirm the difference" (11).

To what were all these grand changes due? In retrospect it is clear that between 1870 and 1930 Buenos Aires lived within a sustained economic bubble. Between 1880 and 1910, for instance, the total value of Argentinean exports leaving the Port of Buenos Aires grew 600 percent (King 8). This period was marked by periodic economic spikes and crises, of course, but all the hallmarks of a bubble economy remained in place for several generations. By the latter half of the nineteenth century, economic reformers like Domingo Sarmiento succeeded in "domesticating" rural populations (or eliminating them, as in Argentina's treatment of indigenous groups). Moreover, the federal government had developed transportation networks between the capital and the provinces, culminating in the construction of a national railroad system with Buenos Aires as its central hub. This had the effect, first, of consolidating Buenos Aires's federal control over the provinces, perhaps for the first time in Argentinean history. Rapid transport also permitted the expansion of agricultural activities, primarily beef production, also spurred by the development of refrigerated shipping. In short order Argentina became Europe's principle source of beef and other agricultural products, and in so doing became one of the richest countries on the planet. This made Buenos Aires an alluring destination for poor European migrants, who had been devastated by a series of economic crises in Europe in the late nineteenth century.

These transformations were brought about by what we could call the "internationalization" of Argentina. By 1920, the nation had become the second-largest exporter of grain in the world, behind the United States; it also became a leading importer of European technologies, capital, and manufactured good. At the same time, it became a primary destination for European migrants. José Moya writes that, "More Europeans arrived in Buenos Aires in just the three years preceding the outbreak of World War I (one point one million) than had arrived in all of Spanish America during more than three centuries of colonial rule" (185).

Yet internationalization also brought with it destabilization and dependency. Argentina's economic rise was spurred by waves of speculative investment, mainly from financial markets in London. In typical fashion, foreign investments would rush into the country relatively quickly, and then evacuate just as quickly at the first sign of danger. Tulio Halperín Donghi notes that after 1880, "British capital became so routine an element of administrative life that municipal and provincial governments vied with the national state for funds in the London stock exchange" (Halperín Donghi 189). By 1930 the bubble had completely burst. Halperín Donghi continues, "In 1928, the country's export earnings reached two hundred million pounds sterling in gold, twice the total of 1913, but in the next year the first shock waves of the global financial crisis began to devastate Argentina's economic structures, always so open to the international environment" (Halperín Donghi 191). Worse yet, throughout the "bubble" years of 1870 to 1930, the *porteño* elite utterly failed to diversify economic activities, which would have hedged against global economic decline during the Great Depression. As Scobie has written, "The very success of the city's dedication to commerce and bureaucracy discouraged any change in economic and financial arrangements, and no pressures emerged to stimulate industrialization, encourage import substitution, or prod merchants and landowners to invest in factories" (144).

Paradoxically, because Buenos Aires entered into the modern global market, it failed to modernize its own economy until it was too late to do so in a fiscally prudent, economical fashion. The world Borges re-encountered after 1921 was distinct from the world of the past that he would try to remember in his early writings of the 1920s and 1930s. Physically, Buenos Aires had lost most of its traditional *criollo* characteristics of a *gran aldea*. Gone were the low-lying Spanish-style homes of unadorned stucco and interior patios, largely replaced by, on one extreme, ostentatiously ornate structures designed by foreign architects, and on another extreme, slapdash hovels and shacks in the *villas miserias*. Demographically, migrant communities soon overwhelmed the city's traditional *mestizo* and *criollo* populations. By the early decades of the twentieth century, immigration had become both a cultural and political problem. Urban planners struggled to find ways to forge a modern city, so as to create a space for a "modernized" citizenry, while retaining the traditional scale of the *barrio* (Gorelik 309–15). Cultural elites—most notably Leopoldo Lugones—likewise struggled to re-define *criollismo* as the essential national character, with the clear nationalistic aim of consolidating "native" power by excluding immigrant groups. As Julio Ramos comments, "For many intellectuals, just as for Lugones, for example, immigration generated—according to the most widely circulated metaphors of the day—a crisis of the national 'soul'; a crisis crystallized in the 'contamination' of the tongue in the mouths of millions of proletarian immigrants" (Ramos 7–8).

Starting in the late 1920s, this new brand of cultural nationalism would negatively impact Argentinean politics for the rest of the century, culminating in the abuses of the nationalistic military governments of the 1970s and 1980s. In his biography of Borges, Edwin Williamson characterizes this form of nationalism against which Borges would ultimately come to position himself: "Their basic contention was that the Argentine republic was threatened by the demagoguery fostered by party politics and mass immigration. In the short term, they wanted to restrict voting rights to native-born Argentines and to control immigration, but their aim was to institute a corporate society led by a supreme caudillo whose guiding principles would be derived from Catholic social doctrine and traditional criollo values" (161).

It is within this cultural, historical, political, and urban context that we must situate Borges's writings in the period of his involvement with *Sur*. Although Borges carries a certain cachet as a "cosmopolitan" intellectual, his early writings (prior to 1940) show him to be a writer deeply concerned with the national character, if not outright nationalistic. With major works like *Fervor de Buenos Aires*, and minor ones like "El coronel Ascasubi" and "Séneca de las orillas," Borges sought not only to rediscover his *criollo* heritage, but to invent a mythology of *criollismo* as such. In doing so he attempted to carve out a middle ground between a decadent oligarchy beholden to crass commercial interests and an ascendant, proto-fascistic nationalism bent on inflaming the crude passions of the populace and military. As Sarlo states, "The avant-garde saw itself as embodying an aesthetic 'truth' which, in opposition to the 'truth' of commerce, revealed the real conditions of production for the market" (100).

Borges thus came to locate himself in a difficult predicament, caught between "universal cosmopolitan" truth and "local" *criollismo*. Sarlo characterizes Borges's involvement with the *Martín Fierro* group as an effort to produce "a body of work that might be defined as "avant-garde urban *criollismo*" (112). Borges's nominally "cosmpolitan" aesthetics were borne not merely from patriotism but a deep-seated love for his native city and its traditional culture. The biographer Williamson has best explained the subtle nuances of Borges's topophilia in the period: "There were few legends, few original creations, in Argentina; the 'living reality' of the country, of Buenos Aires itself, was far greater than 'the reality of our thinking,' and so this new *criollismo*, based as it would be in the urban realities of Buenos Aires, entailed a form nation building" (141).

Borges thus sought to mythologize Buenos Aires through writing as a means of creating a modern nation that could enter into a world order of other "civilized" nations. Stated another way, Borges's "avant-garde urban *criollismo*" was a linguistic project, insofar as he sought a metaphysical idiom capable of both elaborating the *criollo* spirit in its own terms and communicating that spirit to the world at large. This strain of *criollismo* comes through most forcefully in a short, relatively under-analyzed prose piece, "Dos esquinas," that appeared in the 1928 book *El idioma de los argentinos* (the two sections of "Dos esquinas" were, if I am not mistaken, originally published separately; they only appear united in the 1928 volume). As indicated by its title, the piece takes place on two street-corners in Buenos Aires. In the first section, "Sentirse en muerte," the contemporary Borges leaves his house to the north in Palermo one evening and walks down south to the *arrabales* of Barracas. Once there, he encounters a neighborhood that is both poor and pious, dignified in the humble mold of traditional *criollo porteño* society:

> La visión, nada complicada por cierto, parecía simplificada por mi cansancio. La irrealizaba su misma tipicidad. La calle era de casas bajas, y aunque su primera significación fuera de pobreza, la segunda era ciertamente de dicha. Era de lo más pobre y de lo más lindo. Ninguna casa se animaba a la calle; la higuera oscurecía sobre la ochava; los portoncitos—más altos que las líneas estiradas de las paredes—parecían obrados en la misma sustancia infinita de la noche. La vereda

era escarpada sobre la calle; la calle era de barro elemental, barro de América no conquistado aún. (Borges 1928, 148–49)

(The vision, certainly nothing complicated, seemed simplified by my sleepiness. Its very typicality was irrealized in it. It was a street of low houses, and although its first signification was that of poverty, the second was certainly that of good fortune. It was among the poorest and most beautiful. None of the houses brightened the street; the fig tree shaded over the corner; the little gates—taller than the stretched lines of the walls—seemed to be built from the same infinite substance of the night. The sidewalk was cragged over the street; it was a street of elemental mud, mud of still unconquered America.)

Borges quickly realizes that this neighborhood is *exactly* the same as it was twenty years earlier, "época reciente en otros países, pero ya remota en este cambiadizo lado del mundo" (Borges 1928, 149) (recent times in other countries, but already remote in this utterly changed side of the world). The rate of urban change in Buenos Aires appears so rapid and hectic, that Borges stands amazed by the fact that a "traditional" part of the city still exists. But once he arrives to this realization, he also realizes that he has just encountered a form of *eternity*, that the space of the *esquina* is absolutely constant against the perceived flow of time:

La escribo, ahora, así: Esa pura representación de hechos homogéneos—noche en serenidad, parecita límpida, olor provinciano de la madreselva, barro fundamen-tal—no es meramente idéntica a la que hubo en esa esquina hace tantos años; es, sin parecidos ni repeticiones, la misma. El tiempo, si podemos intuir francamente esa identidad, es una delusión: la indisolubilidad de un momento de su aparente ayer y otro de su aparente hoy, basta para desordenarlo. (Borges 1928, 150)

(I write it, now, like this: That pure representation of homogeneous facts—night in serenity, limpid walls, provincial smell of honeysuckle, fundamental mud—is not merely identical to what there was on that corner so many years ago; it is, with neither semblances nor repetitions, the same. Time, if we can intuit frankly such an identity, is a delusion: the indissolubility of a moment in its apparent yesterday and another in its apparent today, is sufficient to disorder it.)

Time is a delusion, because the space of the city is unmoving, eternal. In this moment of epiphany, Borges approaches a metaphysical moment of death. He does not die, of course, but feels as if he leaves his body and hovers over the city, gazing upon its true spiritual, eternal, and *criollo* essence: "Me sentí muerto, me sentí percibidor abstracto del mundo: indefinido temor imbuído de ciencia que es la mejor claridad de la metafísica" (150) (I felt dead, I felt like an abstract perceiver of the world: indefinite fear imbued by science that is the greatest clarity of metaphysics).

The *criollismo* of this metaphysical death becomes the central focus of the second section of "Dos esquinas," entitled "Hombres pelearon." Whereas Borges travels north-to-south in the first section, in the second he narrates a symmetrical movement south-to-north. "Hombres pelearon" takes place, one imagines, in the period between independence and the end of the Paraguayan war, when humble *criollos* fought in the street to preserve their honor: "Hablo de cuando el arrabal, rosado de tapias, era también relampagueado de acero; de cuando las provocatorias milongas levantaban en la punta el nombre de un barrio; de cuando las patrias chicas eran fervor" (Borges 1928, 151) (I speak of when the slum, with pink walls, was also shot with steel lightning; when the provocative milongas raised on their point the name of a neighborhood; of when the native regions were fervent). At this point, a *criollo* from the southern edge of the city, "El Chileno: peleador famoso de los Corrales" (famous fighter from Corrales), decides to walk to the north to fight: "Le noticiaron [a El Chileno] que en Palermo había *un hombre*, uno que le decían El Mentao, y decidió buscarlo y pelearlo" (Borges 1928, 152) (They told El Chileno that in Palermo there was *a man*, one named El Mentao, and he decided to find him and fight him). There is no apparent motivation for El Chileno's decision other than to preserve his own honor and that of the "patria chica" of his neighborhood. El Chileno does indeed go to Palermo, where he encounters El Mentao in a *boliche*. The two pull daggers and fight, and El Mentao kills El Chileno in a bloody battle. The story, and "Dos esquinas," thus ends: "Así fue el entrevero de un cuchillo del Norte y otro del Sur. Dios sabrá su justificación: cuando el Juicio retumbe en las trompetas, oiremos de él" (Borges 1928, 154) (This was the clash of a knife from the North and another from the South. God will know its justification: when Judgment resounds in the trumpets, we will hear of it).

Of course, Borges knows perfectly well the justification for El Chileno's death. The two street-corners are *physically* separated in time and space: one in contemporary Barracas (south Buenos Aires) and one in the Palermo (north Buenos Aires) of yesteryear. The passage of time has permitted the growth of a city that is fundamentally unrecognizable to Borges. His only means to understand the city is through *what is not there physically*, but only present metaphysically. Walking through a location of "death" (a metaphorical "not-there-physically"), Borges may encounter a civic "spirit" that is immutable. El Chileno's death, as recounted in a mythological fiction, instantiates a *criollo* spirit of honor that serves to re-ground Borges in his native Palermo, a space he had lost as an adolescent and regained as a grown adult. Just as the past and present street-corners of "Sentirse en muerte" remain *the same* street-corner throughout time, so too are the "dos esquinas" occupied by El Chileno and El Mentao—corners which initially appear physically distant—collapsed into a single, eternal street-corner uniting north and south, past and present, in Buenos Aires. El Chileno's death is both local and eternal, and thus expresses Borges's urban sensibility that "he poseído entero en palabras y poco en realidad, vecino y mitológico a un tiempo" (Borges 1928, 148) (I have possessed wholly in word and little in reality, nearby and mythological at the same time).

Notably this view of Buenos Aires in both its historicity and mythology fits perfectly with the views of modernity espoused by Ocampo's *Sur*. Writings like "El colonel Ascasubi" and "Séneca en las orillas" appear at first glance to be mere local color—they are highly localized and circumscribed renderings of *criollismo porteño*. They appear in *Sur*, however, juxtaposed against highly universalized cultural essays, such as Gropius's "El teatro total" and Heidegger's "¿Qué es la metafísica?" In this latter piece, Heidegger provides one of the clearest summaries of his early philosophy by contrasting the physical sciences with metaphysical inquiry. If "physics" seeks to uncover "what is essential in all things" (130) in a universally true way—to affirm the "*being in-itself*" in terms of what *it is*—metaphysics seeks to understand being in what *it is not*: "Pero he ahí—cosa notable—en el momento en que el hombre de ciencia se asegura de lo que le es *más propio*, menciona precisamente *lo otro*. Sólo debe investigarse el ente, y fuera de él, *nada*; exclusivamente el ente, y más allá de él, *nada*; únicamente el ente, y por encima de él, *nada*. ¿Y esta Nada?" (131) (But here—notable thing—in the moment in which the man of science assures himself of what is *most its own*, he mentions precisely *the other*. He should only investigate the being, and outside the being, *nothing*; exclusively the being, and beyond the being, *nothing*; only the being, and above the being, *nothing*. And what is this Nothing?). If science questions something, metaphysics interrogates Nothing. Borges's early writings in *Sur* are there to embody Nothing. They revive a mythical past that has already expired, if it existed at all; and the writings do so, I would argue, to present a *localism* that is the negation of *universality*, which, in being the Nothing of *lo universal*, permits true being in time and space. In this way, at least theoretically, Argentina could attain some stabilizing, universal truth.

Borges thus represents his topophilia through spectatorship, through the perspective of his gaze upon the city. In "Dos esquinas" his gaze is double: it moves to the south and then back to the north. But throughout his early writing, Borges's gaze is also duplicitous: rather than north-south, his *criollo* eyes move both eastward to the cultural centers of Europe from which his sense of philosophy, metaphysics, and language originate; and westward to the geographic source of all things *criollo*, the Argentine pampas (the "elemental mud of a still-unconquered America"). Buenos Aires is crucial for this double-gaze, since it is the meeting point, the liminal border between east and west, between the Argentine pampas and the Atlantic Ocean, the border-crossing from which Borges may think and write. Yet this topophilic spectatorship is also a monumental act of *misrecognition*: Borges at once *overlooks* the new, mechanized port of eastern Buenos Aires from which communication with Europe *physically* enters and exits Argentina; and he *overlooks* the *villas* of western Buenos Aires, populated by mass concentrations of poor working-class immigrants. As with all things Borges, it is as important to note what he does *not* say as much as what he does say: seeing *criollismo*, making *criollismo* true and affective even as a doubled metaphysical phenomenon, requires historical and topographical blindness.

When Raúl Prebisch needed a new house in 1930, he called on his brother Alberto. Both were prominent residents of Buenos Aires, but neither was *porteño* by birth. In fact they were *tucumanos*, provincial elites from the northwest city of Tucumán, the provincial capital from which Argentinean independence was declared in 1810 and which would be particularly brutalized among Argentinean cities by the military during the *guerra sucia* of 1976–83. Despite their "foreign" or "provincial" *criollismo*, starting in the 1930s, both Prebisch brothers would become central to the modernization of Buenos Aires and, indeed, the modernization of Argentina and Latin America in general.

Raúl Prebisch was arguably the most important Latin American economist of all time. He is best known for the Singer-Prebisch thesis (a hypothesis devised independently by Prebisch and the German economist Hans Singer), which called into question the central tenets of Ricardian comparative advantage. According to Prebisch, structural macroeconmic imbalances existed between "central" and "peripheral" economies such that "developed" industrialized countries were able to extract profit with increasing efficiency from the "underdeveloped" countries that supplied natural resources for industrial production. Under the Ricardian notion of comparative advantage, certain nations should have a particular market advantage for certain products—as was the case for Argentinean beef from 1870 to 1910, or for United States–American cars from 1945 to 1985. Thus, poor (non-industrialized) nations under such a theory are best served to adhere to what they do comparatively well—extract natural resources. Rich (industrialized) countries are likewise best served to do the same—manufacture industrial goods. Raúl Prebisch—incredibly—was among the first to notice the fatal flaw of comparative advantage: that rich countries were using their comparative advantage in industrial manufacturing to create products that they then exported back to poor countries. Such products imported from the external market would "naturally" be cheaper than those that could be made internally, yet the same products would also be "naturally" priced up from the value of the extracted natural resources used to make them. Thus, poor nations such as Argentina would always be condemned to run trade deficits, since the goods (primary resources) they exported to rich nations would always be worth less than the goods (secondary manufactured products) they imported from rich countries and consumed (R. Prebisch 1950). The difference between the value of imports and exports could only be made up by taking on debt, which banks in Britain and the United States were gracious enough to supply.

The Singer-Prebisch thesis formed the basis for dependency theory, without which the work of Fernando Henrique Cardoso, Enzo Faletto, Aníbal Quijano, Antonio Cornejo Polar, Angel Rama, and Walter Mignolo—all significant figures in Latin American sociological or cultural theory—would have been quite impossible. Prebisch developed his theories as the director, of the United Nations Economic Commission for Latin America (ECLA, or CEPAL in Spanish and Portuguese), which he founded in 1948 and led until 1964. (He would later continue as director of the UN Conference on Trade and Development from 1964 to 1969.) CEPAL became the spawning ground for Cardoso and Faletto's work on "historical-structural" dependency. In essence, Cardoso and Faletto's masterwork *Dependencia y desarrollo en América Latina* is a continuation of Prebisch's initial hypotheses, insofar as Cardoso and Faletto essentially extend the Singer-Prebisch thesis to industrial development. Raúl Prebisch was particularly concerned with Latin America as a zone of *rural-agrarian* production that could not compete with *urban-industrial* production abroad. Prebisch therefore supplied the economic theories supporting state-sponsored Import-Substitution Industrialization (ISI) in order to propel Latin America into modernity. Starting with the ISI initiatives in the 1940s, Latin American nations began to raise protectionist tariffs on foreign industrial goods in order to nurture and foster national industries, which would thus have a protected market space in which to substitute goods that would otherwise be imported.

Writing in the late 1960s, Cardoso and Faletto began to notice strange effects brought about by dependency and development in the context of ISI modernization. If there was a structural-functional split between "traditional" and "modern" societies, through rapid industrialization Latin America had developed into a society somewhere in between. Indeed, it could now be seen that this was *always* the case throughout Latin American history such that "modern/traditional" dependency was a chronic "historical-structural" condition. Latin America could *never* develop into a "modern" society, even less so through the use of "functional" means like ISI, because it had always been to some extent a "modern" group of societies co-existing (and hybridizing) with "traditional" ones. Dependency merely meant that there would never be an internal market for nationally produced goods large enough to sustain industrialization; nor would national industries be able to compete with rich countries that already dominated the world market. The attempt to "leverage" modernity instrumentally through industrialization was doomed to fail on multiple accounts. Thus, the goal of acquiring some universal state of "modernity" was definitively fallacious. The real goals should be justice and prosperity, which could only be achieved through objective historical analyses of the region's internal social dynamics nationally, and its external economic dynamics (dependency) internationally (Cardoso and Faletto 1979).

The emergence of dependency theory in the 1960s and 1970s would lead directly to socio-cultural theories, such as Aníbal Quijano's "coloniality of power" or Walter Mignolo's "modern/colonial order" and "colonial difference," after 1990 (Quijano 2000; Mignolo 2002). Dependency theory seemed to offer a distinctly Latin American (or "Third World") way to critique history and space: rather than viewing Latin America in terms of time-lag, as a region progressing to full modernity but not quite "up to the level" of Europe or North America, dependency theory suggested that Latin Americans might be able to turn the tables and critically unhinge key concepts like "progress," "development," "modernity" and, most of all, "Western civilization" as colonizing gestures. Just as world economic order had served to place Latin America in perpetual dependency, so too had the whole epistemological order of "Western civilization" served to colonize Latin American institutions, subjects, and thought itself. Quijano's "coloniality of power" does not refer to some overt colonization of the region in this sense, but rather to the episteme of domination that infiltrates all language, communication, and knowledge.

As a corrective to the coloniality of power, Mignolo has sought nothing short of the total overthrow of the "modern/colonial" order through what he calls "border thinking." In essence, "non-Western" thinkers operate in the exteriority of the modern/colonial world-system: they are not outside this system entirely, but operate instead from its edges and fissures. From this vantage, border thinking purports to provide new ways to see: a) how modernity has always been produced in tandem with coloniality (that colonialism is not some after-effect of modernity; rather, modernity and coloniality are co-dependent and co-ordinated); and b) how the modern/colonial world-system consistently misrecognizes itself as universal rather than historically contingent and limited. Those who think from within the world-system (in its interiority) may be useful, but they will never see the world as clearly as those who gaze from the exteriority. Or so Mignolo claims.

Each in their way, both Prebisch brothers may be seen as architects of the modern world. In the case of Raúl, we have a conceptual architect of *global* reality—if not of twentieth-century modernization itself, then an architect of a powerful critical framework through which modernity and modernization can be properly understood, constructed and deconstructed, both socio-economically and culturally. In Alberto, we have a concrete architect of a *local* reality—an architect who literally shaped modern Buenos Aires, primarily with important civic monuments still standing today such as the Obelisco de Buenos Aires and the Teatro Gran Rex (each marked by a "form-follows-function" use of unadorned geometric figures, concrete, and [in the case of Gran Rex] glass). Raúl Prebisch taught us how to *see* Buenos Aires and Argentina as positioned on the periphery of a modern world-system; Alberto Prebisch provided us the clean architectonic lines to *see* Buenos Aires as a modernized urban center in a peripheral or marginalized space of the modern world-system.

This latter mode of vision is particularly clear if we pay close attention to the house Alberto built for Raúl in 1930. The house that Alberto Prebisch built, now destroyed, strongly resembled the early functionalist work of Le Corbusier and Walter Gropius: made primarily of white reinforced concrete, the Raúl Prebisch house consisted of a four-story cube (marked on its façade by three parallel rectangular rows of windows), intersected by a rectangular archway composed of three concrete slabs extending over a driveway to the right of the main house to form a carport. The top of this carport could be accessed from the house as a second-floor balcony. On the top floor of the main "cube," the front third of the floor appeared to be "cut-out" to provide a balcony for the fourth-story terrace, without, however, interrupting the geometric proportions of the overall structure. Inside the house, floor plans were left fairly wide open so that they could be modified according to the needs of the occupants. The four floors of the house were connected by a curving spiral staircase, also made of white concrete (just as the interior walls of the house were) giving the impression of being integrated into the overall form and structure of the house.[4] In this sense, the Raúl Prebisch house owed much to Le Corbusier's Purism—and perhaps the Purism of the Victoria Ocampo house analyzed earlier in this essay.

In this sense, was Alberto Prebisch merely attempting to mimic his European "masters"? An answer can only be given in highly qualified ambivalence. And Prebisch's ambivalence would be qualified in a specific location, in the second issue of *Sur*, in a short article entitled "Una ciudad de América." In that piece, Prebisch advocates for architectural modernism in Buenos Aires, and he concludes: "A la espera de ese castigo providencial, es conveniente que los arquitectos de Buenos Aires se instruyan con amor en el antiguo arte de construir casas humanas" (A. Prebisch, 220) (In expectation of this providential punishment, it is necessary that the architects of Buenos Aires lovingly instruct themselves in the ancient art of constructing human houses). The "providential punishment" Prebisch envisions is the destruction of Buenos Aires, which he then hopes to revive by re-building on a (modernist) "human scale." We can thus see the Raúl Prebisch house as his attempt to concretize this human scale. Yet in using such terms he is unmistakably echoing the terms of Le Corbusier, terms explicitly laid out in a series of ten lectures Le Corbusier's delivered in Buenos Aires in 1929 that were published as *Précisions* in 1930. (As mentioned earlier, Alberto Prebisch wrote a review of this volume for the first issue of *Sur*.) In perhaps the most famous lecture of that series, "A Dwelling at Human Scale," Le Corbusier states bluntly: "What I call searching for the 'dwelling unit at human scale' means forgetting all existing houses, all existing building codes, all habits or traditions. It is to study pitilessly the new conditions in which our existence goes on" (Le Corbusier 103). Like Le Corbusier, Prebisch argues for the destruction of "all existing houses, all building codes, all habits or traditions" in Buenos Aires, in order to reconstruct a modernity that is "more intelligent" and humane.

All the same, Le Corbusier speaks in universal terms of forgetting "all" prior architecture and city planning so that "all" mankind might benefit from the modern order of things. But in "Una ciudad de América," Prebisch speaks to a specifically local environment out of a strange yet typically *porteña* form of *topofilia*. Prebisch begins his essay with an astounding statement:

> Si nos apartamos de la opinión más o menos interesada o deliberadamente amable del extranjero, si cerramos nuestro espíritu a cualquier insinuación de nuestro muy loable optimismo patriótico, nos veremos forzados a reconocer la verdad dolorosa de esta afirmación: vivimos en la ciudad más fea del mundo. (A. Prebisch 216)

> (If we disregard the more or less interested or deliberately amiable opinion of the foreigner, if we close our spirit from whatever insinuation of our most laudable patriotic optimism, we will see ourselves forced to recognize the painful truth of this affirmation: we live in the ugliest city in the world.)

The ugliness of the capital is not an essential trait, but a historical contingency that has emerged from *modernity* as it was known in the early twentieth century. Prebisch's advocacy of *modernism* stemmed from a desire to correct *modernity* as he had experienced it up to 1931. Prebisch recalls that the city's original planners constructed Buenos Aires according a reduced yet highly organized geometry of straight lines (an urban grid typical of colonial Latin American urbanism). This caused the city to grow on a "humble" scale: "Una ciudad humilde, sin diagonales, subterráneos ni pretensiones; pero, con la belleza de las cosas que son exactamente lo que parecen" (A. Prebisch 218) (A humble city, without diagonals, subways, or pretensions; but, with the beauty of things that are exactly as they seem to be). The small-scale honesty of the original *criollo* city, however, had been overrun by the *nouveau riche* excesses of the city's initial modernization after 1870, and the bourgeois desire for whatever aesthetic whim of the day. Hence Prebisch's appetite for destruction:

> Eso es lo que hoy ocurre en Buenos Aires. El rumboso capricho personal del "parvenu" ha extendido a lo largo de nuestras calles las más absurdas variedades de disparate arquitectónico. Para este caos—que no tiene la grandeza ni el interés del neoyorquino—queda una sola posibilidad de orden: un terremoto diligente y circunspecto que pulverice con sumas precauciones la chuchería de los frontispicios. (A. Prebisch 220)

> (This is what happens today in Buenos Aires. The rambling personal caprice of the "parvenu" has extended throughout our streets in the most absurd varieties of architectonic disparity. For this chaos—that has neither the grandeur nor the interest of New York—there is only one possibility left for order: a diligent and circumspect earthquake that will pulverize, with supreme caution, the silliness of the frontispieces.)

Prebisch wants modernism, but only in order to see a "diligent and circumspect" dismantling of *modern* Buenos Aires so as to uncover the "human scale" of the original, *traditional* Buenos Aires. Nevertheless, anticipating his brother's work in economics by some two decades, Alberto Prebisch recognizes the urban problem of Buenos Aires as an intractable contradiction of *development*:

> Esa desavenencia denuncia en forma categórica la incapacidad de perfección de Buenos Aires: el exceso de vida material no le permite evolucionar en el sentido impuesto por sus fundadores. Y, a menos que se la rehaga, tampoco podrá *desarrollarse* en el sentido de una gran ciudad moderna, por impedírselo la irremediable característica de su planta urbana. (A. Prebisch 217; my emphasis)

(This discord denounces categorically the incapacity for perfection in Buenos Aires: the excess of material life does not allow it to evolve in the sense imposed by its founders. And, unless it remakes itself, neither will be able to develop itself in the sense of a great modern city, being impeded by the irreparable character of its urban plan.)

Here, then, is the crux of the problem: modernity had overloaded the original (*criollo*) configuration of Buenos Aires with "excessive material life," by which we may suppose Prebisch means both excessive buildings and excessive immigrants; but conversely, the original *criollo* character of the city irremediably impeded the proper *development* of Buenos Aires into a "great *modern* city," retarding its evolution until such point as the city could be "remade" by modernist aesthetes. Not for nothing, then, has Gorelik astutely labeled Alberto Presbish a kind of "Catholic modernizer" or "classicist vanguardist" (Gorelik 408–26). Perhaps more significantly, however, we may come to see that Alberto Prebisch in 1931 provides a physical, architectonic portrait of the political-economic theory of dependency that Raúl Prebisch would publish in 1950.

We cannot read of Alberto Prebisch's peculiar *topofilia porteña* without also thinking of Jorge Luis Borges's "double-spectatorship." Let us recall that Borges located his *criollismo* by locating Buenos Aires as a border-zone between east and west. Borges *looks* eastward to Argentina's entrance into the modern cosmopolitan order of Europe and its putative "Western civilization," and he *looks* westward to the irrepressible, mythological *criollo* spirit that arrives to Buenos Aires from the pampas. Yet Borges also *overlooks* the material site (the Port of Buenos Aires) connecting Buenos Aires to the North Atlantic, and *overlooks* all the people that actually lived and migrated to Buenos Aires (*villas miserias*). His overlooking of physical spaces seems purposeful, since it would have disrupted the recovery of his metaphysical *criollismo*. By the same token, Prebisch looks eastward to the "human scale" of Le Corbusier's pure, radiant modernist city; and he looks westward to the "re-making" of Buenos Aires by means of the modernist "love for the ancient art of building human houses." Prebisch does not overlook the "presently existing" Buenos Aires—he merely wants erase it altogether.

This erasure is directly tied to a critique of dependency and development, which in turn raises a provocative question: What was overlooked in the theorization of Latin American dependency? I am not doubting the value, validity, or importance of dependency theory, but I am asking for some clarification: was Raúl Prebisch seeking to dismantle modernity, but only to return to some idealized *criollista* order of things, unconsciously overlooking one sense of modernity in order to "modernize" another? If so, is the elaboration of dependency theory by Cardoso and Faletto subject to the same modes of "double" spectatorship? And much more problematically, is (what one might call) "border thinking along the exteriority of the colonial difference to the coloniality of power" yet another expression of some deep-seated and long-lost *criollismo*?

Nothing will answer these questions, at least in form of a logical argument. All we have are parts and fragments, marks of history, handed down to us through the *teatro total porteño* of Victoria Ocampo's *Sur* circa 1931.

Notes

1. All translations in this essay are my own.
2. I realize that, in addition to the fact that all the names on this list are famous, a few have become quite infamous—most notably Heidegger and Drieu la Rochelle, both of whom would be full-fledged Nazis by the end of the decade. (One cannot mention the latter without also recognizing him as one of the most detestable literary opportunists of the twentieth century.) Furthermore, the political sympathies of Victoria Ocampo (and others in proximity to her, like Borges) have been subject to vociferous debate: certainly the silence of both Ocampo and Borges in the face of abuses committed by various military regimes in Argentina proved deafening. Nevertheless, in all fairness I must state also that the exact political inclinations of *Sur*, particularly in the first years of its existence, are not at all clear. Or rather, the relations of the journal's brand of modernist/modernizing aesthetics with fascism and political violence are matters that still need to be ascertained critically. I hope that this present essay provides a basis for that critical discussion to occur.
3. Remarkably, Ocampo unself-consciously fuses two meanings of "development" in this passage without even mentioning the word: the political-economic development of modern nation-states and childhood development. The infantilization of Latin America, although commonplace among intellectuals of the time, would later be attacked (if only tacitly) by *dependentistas* and other subsequent critical movements.
4. Critical discussions focusing specifically on the 1930 Raúl Prebisch house are relatively few. Images and descriptions of the project may be accessed online at: *1en100.blogspot.com/2008/02/casa-ral-prebisch-en-belgrano-1930.html* and *www.arquitectura.com/historia/protag/prebisch/prebisch.asp*.

Works Cited

Borges, Jorge Luis. "El coronel Ascasubi." *Sur* 1.1 (1931): 129–40.

———. "Dos esquinas." *El idioma de los argentinos*. Buenos Aires: Colección Índice, 1928.

————. "Séneca en las orillas." *Sur* 1.1 (1931): 174–79.

Cardoso, Fernando Henrique, and Enzo Faletto. *Dependency and Development in Latin America*. Trans. Marjory Mattingly Urquidi. Berkeley: University of California Press, 1979 (1971).

Gorelik, Adrian. *La grilla y el parque: Espacio público y cultura urbana en Buenos Aires, 1887–1936*. Buenos Aires: Universidad Nacional de Quilmes, 1998.

Gropius, Walter. "El teatro total." *Sur* 1.1 (1931): 141–48.

Halperín Donghi, Tulio. *The Contemporary History of Latin America*. Trans. John Charles Chasteen. Durham, NC: Duke University Press, 1993 (1967).

Heidegger, Martin. "¿Qué es la metafísica?" Trans. Raimundo Lida. *Sur* 2.5 (1932): 128–50.

Katzenstein, Ernesto. "Argentine Architecture of the Thirties." Trans. Edward Shaw. *DAPA: The Journal of Decorative and Propaganda Arts* 18 (1992): 55–75.

King, John. *Sur: A Study of the Argentine Literary Journal and its Role in the Development of Culture, 1931–1970*. Cambridge, UK: Cambridge University Press, 1986.

Le Corbusier. *Precisions on the Present State of Architecture and City Planning, with an American Prologue, a Brazilian Corollary, Followed by the Temperature of Paris and the Atmosphere of Moscow*. Trans. Edith Schreiber Aujame. Cambridge, MA: MIT Press, 1991 (1930).

Mignolo, Walter. "The Geopolitics of Knowledge and the Colonial Difference." *The South Atlantic Quarterly* 101.1 (Winter 2002): 57–96.

Moya, José C. "Modernization, Modernity, and the Trans/formation of the Atlantic World in the Nineteenth Century." *The Atlantic in Global History, 1500–2000*. Ed. Jorge Cañizares-Esguerra and Erik R. Seeman. Upper Saddle River, NJ: Pearson Prentice Hall, 2007.

Ocampo, Victoria. "La aventura del mueble." *Sur* 1.1 (1931): 166–74.

————. "Carta a Waldo Frank." *Sur* 1.1 (1931): 7–18.

Prebisch, Alberto. "Precisiones de Le Corbusier." *Sur* 1.1 (1931): 179–82.

————. "Una ciudad de América." *Sur* 1.2 (1931): 216–18.

Prebisch, Raúl. *The Economic Development of Latin America and Its Principal Problems*. New York: United Nations, 1950.

Quijano, Aníbal. "Coloniality of Power: Eurocentrism and Latin America." *Nepantla: Views from South* 1.3 (2000): 533–80.

Ramos, Julio. "El don de la lengua." *Paradojas de la letra*. Caracas: Ediciones eXcultura, 1996. 3–22.

Sarlo, Beatriz. *Jorge Luis Borges: A Writer on the Edge*. Ed. John King. London: Verso, 1993.

Scobie, James R. *Buenos Aires: Plaza to Suburb, 1870–1910*. New York: Oxford University Press, 1974.

Williamson, Edwin. *Borges: A Life*. London: Penguin Books, 2004.

Horacio Coppola: The Photographer's Urban Fervor

David William Foster

> Mi primera aventura fue descubrir las perspectivas geométricas [de Buenos Aires], las simetrías y sombras que dibujaban las siluetas negras de hombres de espaldas, aferrados a sus periódicos."("Horacio Coppola")

> (My first adventure was to discover [Buenos Aires's] geometric perspectives, symmetries and shadows that drew the black silhouettes of men on their backs, clinging to their newspapers.)

Horacio Coppola (Buenos Aires, 1906–) is the first major photographer of the city of Buenos Aires. His first project *Buenos Aires: Visión fotográfica* (1936) was executed in the context of the fourth centennial of the original (but ultimately unsuccessful) founding of the city in 1536 by Pedro de Mendoza. After important artistic experiences in Europe, especially in the Photographic Division of the Bauhaus, Coppola returned to photograph the city. There he met Grete Stern, who would return to Buenos Aires with him, become his wife, and establish with him in 1937 a joint photographic studio.[1] Although Coppola and Stern ultimately separated, Stern (1904–1999) went on to become an important Argentine photographer and was, unquestionably, a significant feminist voice in a field that in Argentina has had numerous important female practitioners (Foster, "Dreaming in Feminine"; Foster, "Sara Facio"; Foster "Annemarie Heinrich"). Coppola's work has received extensive attention in recent years, including a major 2006 exhibit at the Museo de Arte Latinoamericano de Buenos Aires (MALBA), as well as the publication of images of a 2005 exhibition by the Buenos Aires Galería Jorge Mara-La Ruche. Additionally, a dossier of Coppola's photography has been published by São Paulo's Instituto Moreira Salles, on the occasion of the acquisition of a portion of his archives; this publication included, as is the custom of the Instituto when it publishes a photographer's work, an exhibit at the Instituto. Although Coppola has had an extensive career in photography (as well as experimental filmmaking, including the six minute documentary, also from 1936, *Así nació el Obelisco*), it is his early work on Buenos Aires for which he is most remembered. In fact, in 2003 he was named "Ciudadano ilustre de la Ciudad de Buenos Aires."

As with any great city, there is a long history of photography relating to Buenos Aires. Although Buenos Aires has only sporadically been a tourist destination (Argentina did deserve its own Baedeker [Martínez] in the early twentieth century, with an emphasis on Buenos Aires), the only abiding images that have circulated internationally that index the culture of the city are those having to do with the tango. A bibliography of tango books would now be quite extensive. Films, as well, have also dealt with, or referenced, the Argentine tango; perhaps the best, recent one would be Carlos Saura's *Tango* (1998).[2] There has been, in the context of international tourist interest in the city, a recent surge of guidebooks relating to Buenos Aires. These guidebooks carry the usual raft of illustrative photos, although few of them can be artistic in any meaningful way. They are competent representations, but do not involve gestures at anything like a complex interpretation of urban phenomena. There are, to be sure, important photographers currently examining the city interpretively, and my own *Urban Photography in Argentina* examines the production of Marcelo Brodsky, Gabriela Liffschitz, Eduardo Gil, Adriana Lestido (a Guggenheim fellow), Marcos López, Gabriel Díaz, Gabriel Valansi, Gabriela Messina, and Silvio Fabrykant. Sara Facio, the dean of Argentine photographers, remains active, although her most important urban work (with Alicia D'Amico) was conducted several decades ago.

It is easy to understand the celebratory reception of Coppola's photography of Buenos Aires in the mid-1930s. Buenos Aires did not escape the international financial crisis and attendant social debacle of the 1929 stock market crash (indeed, the first military government came to power in Argentina in September 1930). The objects of Coppola's photographic gaze in 1936 were more like a reflex of the more halcyon period of the 1920s (the so called "años de las vacas gordas"), and what he set out to record was the level of urban development that Buenos Aires had attained, a level unmatched by any other city in Latin America. Although, in the 1920s, São Paulo had began to surge forward toward its eventual status as the financial center of Latin America, and was, in its own self-description, "O maior centro industrial de América Latina," Buenos Aires was, nevertheless, the undisputed giant of Latin American cities. São Paulo had a skyscraper by 1929, the Edifício Martinelli, which is still standing.

Buenos Aires's Edifício Kavanagh was not far behind; it was inaugurated in 1936 and is still standing. (By contrast, Mexico City had to wait until 1956 for the Torre Latino Americana, its first skyscraper.)

Buenos Aires had certainly been pretty much of a backwater during its first centuries of existence, and the fact that it had to be founded twice—first by Mendoza in 1536 and then, finally for good, in 1580, by Juan de Garay)—has often been cited as iconic of its initial, precarious nature. With nothing in the way of the precious goods and materials the Spanish Crown sought in the Americas, it was only with the development of the cattle industry (in the nineteenth century) that Buenos Aires had anything to sell the world and, in return, gained the monetary wherewithal to purchase European goods and, by then, international modernism. But Buenos Aires leapt forward with unstoppable dynamism. If Charles Darwin could describe Buenos Aires as an unimpressive backwater during his visit there on the occasion of the voyage of the Beagle (1831–1836; he seems to have been in Buenos Aires in late 1833, where he did find the beauty of the Porteño women worth commenting on; Moorehead 127–40), beginning early in the second half of the nineteenth century, Argentina embarked on a period of material growth. This growth so favored the city of Buenos Aires that there has been, ever since, an enormous national controversy over the proper relationship between Buenos Aires and the rest of the República. But, as anyone who has taught the survey of Latin American literature knows, there is no Argentine literature included until the nineteenth century, and then it becomes difficult not to talk about that country's sustained significance for the history of modern Latin American literature. Indeed, in the two decades spanning the turn of the century, Buenos Aires was the most important center of the important movement known as Modernismo.

The reader will excuse the extent of this information about the historical growth of Buenos Aires, which also included its conversion into the major immigrant society of Latin America and its current status as the second major demographic area in South America after São Paulo, because it is precisely this explosive transformation of the city in approximately fifty years, from the time of the so-called Generation of 1880 (see Foster, *The Argentine Generation of 1880*), that was there for Coppola to photograph on his return from Europe in 1935. Indeed, after five years spent mostly in Berlin, one can speculate that Coppola was overwhelmed in the presence of the city. Since Buenos Aires has little to show of its architectural history before the end of the nineteenth century (a few churches, the [nevertheless, mutilated] Cabildo, a few residences), the built environment of the early decades of the twentieth century constitutes nothing less than an uninterrupted display of what had been accomplished, in all order of social and cultural developments, in only a handful of decades. To put it differently, unlike the major European cities, where the projects of modernity stood side-by-side with other historical layers of urban development, and unlike the major, Latin American cities, where (as is the case of Mexico City to the present day) a fragmented project of modernity stands alongside the remnants of the Baroque colonial past (the sixteenth-century Zócalo is just down the street from the Torre Latinoamericana), Coppola's gaze in the mid-1930s was unbroken by little else than the absolute modernity, "toujours à la page," of Buenos Aires.[3]

To be sure, Coppola's gaze—at least as it becomes permanently recorded by his camera, and in contrast to subsequent urban photography of the city—is relatively circumscribed, and one can take a map of Buenos Aires, already quite widespread by the 1930s, and demonstrate how his vision was focused so intently on what is, in realty, a very narrow, downtown core. Buenos Aires architecture outside that core is still only about a hundred years old, and, in this sense, it is quite modern: what is often considered the most historically quaint, tourist area of the city is La Boca, where the gaily painted edifices, with their characteristic *ochava* corners and raised sidewalks, go no further back than the early twentieth century. Thus, what Coppola focuses on is not a modern core versus a pre-modern periphery, but rather a modern core in which the greatest projects of modernity are concentrated, both in terms of the skyscrapers and other large buildings, and also in an enormously variegated infrastructure of commerce and culture, manifestations of which exist elsewhere in the city, but which reach their greatest concentrated display in the central core. One could say the that display of modernity, in the case of Mexico City, is metonymic, while that of Buenos Aires, especially in the version provided by Horacio Coppola, is synecdochal.

In my analysis of Coppola's images, I will be making use of Yi-Fu Tuan's concept of "topophilia," the enthusiasm for—indeed, love of, to parse the word literally—place. As Tuan states with regard to great cities:

> In great metropolises, no man can know well more than a small fragment of the total urban scene; nor is it necessary for him to have a mental map or imagery of the entire city in order to prosper in his corner of the world. Yet the city dweller seems to have a psychological need to possess an image of the total environment in order to place his own neighborhood. Knowledge of a city varies enormously from person to person. Most people are able to designate by name the two extremes of the urban scale, the city as a whole and the street they live on. Intermediate divisions are, by contrast, vaguely conceived to the extent that few people can readily recall the

name of their district or neighborhood. The two ends of the scale appear to express a common human propensity to dwell on two widely disparate levels of thought: high abstraction and specific responses. (192)

In my view, the role of urban photography is to enable the bridging of Tuan's two extremes, the abstract and the specific. Photography, as we have come to agree, is not a record of reality but, rather, a personal interpretation—as is all art—undertaken by the photographer. The urban fragment captured by the photograph may place itself along a continuum of the specific, but it also implies the vast whole of the cityscape that extends beyond the fringes of the photograph, something like what one might see if the photograph could be superimposed on a fragment of the in-and-out zoom of Google Earth, for example.[4]

Coppola, therefore, can best be approached in terms of a photographic semiosis in which awe, admiration, enthusiasm, and even a certain degree of amorous reverence underlie his gaze of fragments of the city of Buenos Aires.[5] In fewer than fifty key images, Coppola rapidly captures the intensity of life in the city, whether perceived in terms of the movement—one might say, the rhythm—of public spaces, as seen in the presence in the spaces of the city of individuals and the trappings of their lives, or even in the density of examples of the built environment where, even though individuals might not be present, one understands that these are the instruments of a particularly dynamic urban life. Coppola never engages in portraiture, much less in the quaint or the curious, nor in vistas of landscapes. Rather, his narrative of the city is that of intense modernity, where there is an integral, correlated relationship between the individuals and the built environment through which they move and, evidently, on which they depend for the particular texture and quality of their life. If Coppola's images were less studied and more of the moment, one might be tempted to view them as propaganda for the quality of life in Buenos Aires— indeed, perhaps even for the legitimacy of the September 1930, fascist-inspired coup of General José Félix Uriburu (1930–1932).[6] The period following the 1930 coup was known as the Década Infame (Torres) in Argentine history (a subsequent Argentine film noir tradition will provide one artistic representation of the decade), and lasted until the triumphalism of the first presidency of Juan Domingo Perón [1946–1952].[7] Meanwhile, no artist undertakes to celebrate that period or the quality of public life. As I have stated previously, Coppola's photographic work in 1936, as part of the fourth centennial memorial to the city, is already historic, looking back to the development of the city during the previous half-century. In this sense, there is a certain nostalgic dimension to Coppola's images, because, at the time, it must have been very much an open question as to how Argentina was to fare under the consequences of the Great Depression.[8] If the 1930 coup was one effect of the depression, the emergence, fifteen years after the coup, of Peronism, and its profound restructuring of Argentine society, was yet another. By 1950, the cityscape of Buenos Aires was much changed from what Coppola contemplated upon his return to the city in 1935, and part of those changes included the architecture of fascism, of which many examples still remain (e.g., the Facultad de Medicina, where fascist imposition is complemented by unaddressed decay). I would venture to say that much of the current enthusiasm for Coppola's 1936 images of Buenos Aires has as much to do with the interest in recognizing and preserving great urban photography as it does with the fact that the Buenos Aires recorded in these images is—as we can register in retrospect—on the verge of enormous sociohistoric change. Moreover, the renewed political stability and economic prosperity in Argentina (admittedly, the record is not unmixed) can lead Argentines to have an substantial interest in a singular period of urban greatness.

I would like now to turn to the actual photographic record of Coppola's 1936 *dérive* through the streets of Buenos Aires, and there is no better place to begin than with the signature photograph that appears on the cover of the Galería Jorge Mara-La Ruche publication. "Avenida Presidente Roque Sáenz Peña" bears as its title one of the two ten block diagonals that angle off from Plaza de Mayo, the base of the city's street system. Mayo is where the Casa Rosada (government house) is located, and it anchors all maps of the city as the bottom center of its graphic representation. Sáenz Peña angles off northwest, while Presidente Julio Roca angles off southwest. As in the case of surrounding streets, the diagonals are the site of many government agencies and major business. Diagonal Norte (as Sáenz Peña is customarily called) runs one block beyond the Avenida Nueve de Julio (the anchor north-south boulevard of the city), where it passes through the site of the Obelisco (the major symbol of the city—and the butt of off-color jokes) and ends at Plaza Lavalle, the site of the nation's central court system. The Diagonal Sur (as Julio Roca is customarily called) ends two blocks short of the Avenida Nueve de Julio. Sáenz Peña is much more the major arterial because it traverses the north edge of the central core, wherein, and beyond, lie the most prestigious sectors of the city. Kittycorner from Plaza Lavalle is the Colón, which, since 1908, has been the artistic ground zero of the city (the Colón is considered the third most important opera house in the world). The Diagonal Norte also fans out from Calle (Avenida) Corrientes, the city's principal theater and entertainment district.[9] I have entered into so much detail here because it is crucial to understanding Coppola's choice for an urban cut of the city, in that it references the government center, a major commercial zone, a cultural arena, and a historically privileged residential area.[10]

I don't think Le Corbusier had anything to do with the layout of Buenos Aires (his one major claim to fame in South America is the 1954 Casa Curutchet in La Plata, the provincial capital of Buenos Aires). However, aside from modifications imposed by geographic features, Buenos Aires is reminiscent of Washington, D.C., in the rational checkerboard layout of the streets of the city, with Avenida Rivadavia (a continuation of the Avenida de Mayo, which connects Plaza de Mayo with the national Congress) running the entire length of the city, and bisecting it into the historically prestigious north side, and the historically disadvantaged south side. All streets change names at Rivadavia, and Coppola's 1936 photography moves back and forth from one side of Rivadavia to the other, but never straying far from the major anchor points. Even the old colonial area of San Telmo is laid out in strict geometric fashion.

With his modernist—and Bauhaus-trained—eye, Coppola seems to have been particularly entranced by the geometric possibilities of the views of Buenos Aires,[11] not only through the street layout as such, but through the symmetry of the successive examples of Belle Époque, Art Deco, and rationalist/modernist edifices. Because Buenos Aires has so many open public spaces (characteristically treed and grassed), buildings have little need for creating their own botanical buffers, and, thus, their lines are generally perfectly aligned with the street.[12] The geometry of the city is very much in evidence in the photography in question. Organized in terms of a vanishing point in the direction of Plaza de Mayo (an orientation to the photograph is provided by the subway station in the lower left-hand corner), the image is dominated by a building that is still standing at the intersection of Suipacha, Sarmiento, and Diagonal Norte. Because an angle is created by the diagonal, the building is reminiscent of the famous Flatiron Building in New York (situated at the intersections of Fifth Avenue, 23rd Street, and Broadway). This building is followed along the Diagonal by a series of other buildings that stand flush with the one in the foreground, and flush with the straight, inner line of a broad sidewalk. The street is equally broad. (This was before the widening of Corrientes in 1938, which made it the broadest street in the central core. It is bounded on the west by the Avenida Nueve de Julio, which, at the time, still did not run the north-south length of the city.) The sidewalk we see (due to the camera's position, we cannot see the opposing sidewalk) is dotted with pedestrians. Their physical presence is enhanced by the long shadows cast by the late afternoon sun, as are other details, such as the arch of the subway entrance.

What is most striking in the photograph are the cars, which, at the time, would have been mostly European imports. Not only do we see a mass of cars moving in the left-hand lane (at the time, drivers followed the British custom of the right-side driver), but we can also see cars moving in the right-hand lane, although less so, because of the aforementioned architectural overhang. It is important to note that the Diagonal is characterized by a parking strip down the center of the street, and we can see that most of the space is fully occupied. Thus, this image provides an immediate sense of urban hustle-and-bustle against the backdrop of an imposing array of architecture: one can count at least a dozen facades along the north side of the street. Their angle of repose looks as though it had been drawn with a T-square, which is surely the visual sensation of this fragment of the city Coppola was most interested in capturing. Moreover, the building that grounds Coppola's image is thoroughly modern and constructed strictly along the lines of geometric patterns, including the service installations on the roof (which, in turn, includes the chimney pots typical of the waste incineration systems prevalent in buildings of the day). As one examines this image closely, it is possible to discern a marquee, which displays the name "Metropolis," on the building's ground floor; "Metropolis" is quite possibly the name of the building.

One final note: if this scene is crucial to Coppola's interest in the extensive urban development of Buenos Aires, which was in evidence by the middle of the 1930s, there is a crucial affective dimension provided by the shadows of day's end, as though the poetic nature of impending sunset mellowed the stark lines of the built environment.[13]

It has become important to speak of the gendered city, and not just in terms of how different genders move in the city and make use of it (and understanding that gender here cannot any longer mean a strict male/female binary). Gender is also important in evoking the concept of the hegemonic, masculine city (and a corresponding hegemonic, masculine architecture) to understand how some cities in Latin America were much more strictly domains that systematically excluded most women from them.[14] In my study, I examined the urban photography project of the Swiss-German Hildegard Rosenthal in São Paulo. Also working in the mid-1930s, she dealt with an exclusively masculine city (as far as the public sector was concerned). She must have made a striking presence: a woman manipulating a camera, accompanied by a female assistant, who she often included in her images for contrast. Yet if São Paulo, at the time, remained resolutely male-dominated, Coppola would have been reminded, after his return from a much more cosmopolitan Europe (Rosenthal's own origins: she arrived in Brazil from Germany), how freely women moved in public space.

The public presence of women in Buenos Aires is apparent when we turn to an image like "Calle Florida." Intersecting the Diagonal Norte at one point, Florida was in the heart of the central core. This core, with its dominant commercial, financial, and administrative operations, was very much an island of the luxuries afforded by the surplus value of Argentine prosperity. Although Florida today is decidedly ratty (real elegance has moved to shopping malls and tourist hotel enclaves), until the 1960s, and even the early 1970s, it was an important venue of style. Harrods of Buenos Aires (its only foreign branch) opened in 1912 and gave a defining glamour to the street, which extends for ten blocks from "la City" (the financial district) to Plaza San Martín, the most elegant plaza in all Buenos Aires. During its heyday, not only did Florida house the best department stores and specialty shops but also the best cafes and restaurants, including the Sociedad Rural (the Cattlemen's Exchange) and the ultra-snobbish Jockey Club, which, as a symbol of the oligarchy, was burned to the ground in 1953 by Peronista sympathizers.

Coppola's photograph reminds us that Florida has long been a pedestrian mall, making it not only the site of some of the fanciest shops in the city, but also, historically, a promenade for people to see and be seen. If the street is much more proletarian today, it would have been, seven decades ago, much more the public sphere of a certain class of Porteños, those who knew full well that exclusionary police practices would ensure the haughty elegance of their most valued public site. The uniformity of style and dress in Coppola's photography is, therefore, immediately apparent as a mark of the authenticity of his gaze. The men's straw hats, and some of the sleeveless dresses worn by women (many of whom are also bareheaded), would indicate that it is late spring or summer. Although there is one man, a bit to the left of dead center, who appears to be inappropriately dressed, suits and ties were de rigueur for Argentine men of the dominant social classes until well into the last quarter of the twentieth century. The impression of the photograph is one of almost unanimity in the level of dress, and the dense pedestrian presence signals both the attraction of the street, as well as, behind that attraction, the level of prosperity that enables it. It is superfluous to insist that only a few blocks away from this street, most immediately beyond the southern terminus of Florida, one could find considerable evidence of modest living standards and even poverty. Coppola's vision of Buenos Aires, however, is imperiously that of the sophisticated modern city.

In terms of the question of gender, it is important to observe how there is a fairly even division of men and women on the street (unlike the considerable gender disparity I underscore in Rosenthal's contemporary photographs of downtown São Paulo). Moreover, in addition to women in each other's company, it is also apparent that women are traversing this very public place on their own, involved in what would have been the affairs of women of the day, to which Florida would certainly have catered. In this regard, one notes that Coppola captures accurately the hastened gait of the pedestrians, most especially of the women. One woman's right shoe is blurred: if the previous image is static in its geometric composition, this image shows how the photographer's camera captures rapid movement in a blur.

There is yet another gender note in the image, and that is the man in the lower right-hand corner who is studying the street intently. Buenos Aires has long been a city of *flâneurs*, men who roam the city (mostly in its socially prestigious realms) with the superior attitude of the *rigisseur*. This masculinist gaze, which Walter Benjamin has described so eloquently as the privileged commentator on the urban landscape, is still very much what one might describe as an example of the sexist dimension of the city. In Coppola's image, the man in question stands with his left arm akimbo, staring intently across the street. There is no way of ascertaining what the object of his gaze might be, but there is every reason to believe that it is a woman, or a group of women, displaying their feminine finery, sans overcoat.

Finally, although Coppola focuses in this image on the activity of a particular privileged social space in Buenos Aires, his photograph also captures the architectural modernity of that space, with a dominant modernist building (again, geometric lines prevail) and, off to the right, other imposing structures. A particularly modern detail is to be discerned in the upwardly directed facade lighting of the building in the foreground: it displays no fewer than four clusters, of two lights each. Public lighting, beyond the barest illumination against the night, is very much of a modern phenomenon, and to find it as part of the Calle Florida setting is not at all unexpected.

It would be impossible for Coppola to fully fulfill the goal of executing a benevolent and exuberant gaze of Buenos Aires, in the mid-1930s, without turning to the marvels of Avenida Corrientes, to the bright lights, and, if I may be allowed a cliche, the roar of the audiences of what had become the epicenter of the Buenos Aires theater scene.[15] Buenos Aires remains to this day the theater capital of Argentina and, indeed, of Latin America. Corrientes, itself, remains the principal venue of the dramatic arts for the city, even though there are now major theater installations elsewhere in Buenos Aires. In this vein, I

would like to discuss the image identified as "Teatro Nacional."[16] One immediate response to Coppola's image, one that connects Coppola's adulatory gaze
of the Buenos Aires of 1936 with subsequent historical events, is the fact that
the Teatro Nacional, which opened in 1906, was destroyed by fire in 1982, a
victim of the persecution by the de facto military regime (which was to be su-
perseded by a new democratic government in 1983).[17] The theater was totally
rebuilt in 2000 and re-opened under the name of Teatro El Nacional. Historically, the Teatro Nacional (I will revert to using its historical name) was one
of the first major theatrical installations in Buenos Aires, which is borne out
by the fact that it is located on Corrientes east of the Avenida Nueve de Julio.
As the importance of the theater grew, later installations were constructed on
Corrientes, the western side of the Nueve de Julio.[18]

In addition to the evident details of the Nacional that mark it as a combination of the architecture both of the Belle Époque (the general concrete mass
of the building and its decorative details, including the stylized porthole) and
Art Deco (the geometric design of the marquee, clearly affixed over the original facade), one is struck by the plethora of details regarding performances.
Once again, there is a mixture of styles: the principal playbill announces the
performance of the main star, Eduardo Parravicini (1876–1941), in a play
called *Cristóbal Colón en la Facultad de Medicina* (a comedy,[19] and one of
his greatest successes [Foppa 508]); Parravicini's co-star, Mecha Ortiz (1900–
1987), who was about to begin her career as one of the great female stars of the
Golden Age of Argentine filmmaking, deserves a separate poster, also displaying turn-of-the-century lettering (although part of the poster is torn away). To
the left of the traditionally designed posters, the doors of the theater carry the
main actor's name and the name of the play in the more geometric lettering of
the 1930s. The title and the star's name are also repeated in the same lettering
on the base of the aforementioned added Art Deco marquee. Most noticeable,
to the right of the playbill, is an enormous artist's rendition of Parravicini's vis-
age, a rendition that seems almost grotesque in the shadowed coloration of his
face. (The juxtaposition of this image and Ortiz's photograph, in her smaller
and inferiorly placed billing, clearly shows the relative market importance of
the two stars.)

The human faces of the theater billing contrast with the people moving
around the theater. Again, there are individuals walking by so fast that the
camera can only record a blur. The importance of the theater, however, is demonstrated by the fact that a man is walking up the steps of the front entrance
(to purchase tickets, one would like to imagine), while we see, vaguely in the
background, three well-dressed individuals on the other side of the entrance

doors. Of particular importance, however, is the reappearance of women in this very public space. A young and very stylishly dressed woman is conversing with an older woman, whose clothes and posture (which contrast vividly with that of the young woman on the left), including an overcoat, mark her, if not of a lesser social class, certainly as subscribing to a different fashion code. The most evident detail may lie in the clash between the styles of their hats. In terms of Coppola's vision of the modernity of the city, the younger woman echoes the carefree image of Mecha Ortiz, whose full head of wavy hair, open face, and laughing, lipsticked mouth echo the traits of the most advanced women of the day.[20]

This is one of the "busiest" of Coppola's images, in part because it focuses-in on a major public venue, one of the most congested streets of Buenos Aires, from long before the photograph was taken.[21] Indeed, the older character of the street, by contrast to what we can see in the paving characteristics of the Diagonal Norte, is definitely dated: the pre-modern blocks of stone pavement (overlain by the semi-modern feature of the trolley line; by 1930, Corrientes already had the city's second subway train line) and the narrow, yet nicely designed, pedestrian sidewalk. Viewed in these terms, the apparent importance of the Teatro Nacional, as judged by the people in and around it, and the importance of its two lead actors, is juxtaposed to the rather antiquated nature of the street space in front of it. Once again, Coppola has chosen to direct his camera at a street scene that emphasizes the modernity of Buenos Aires, this time in terms of the vitality of its cultural life.[22] Such an enthusiasm for an icon of the Porteño theater world is not without its dimension of metacommentary, because the companion visual art of photography had already been widely developed in Argentina, since at least the late 1860s (*Fotografías de Buenos Aires*), and Coppola will go on, with his then-wife Grete Stern and others, to make photography a very visible component of Argentine cultural life. (It is Stern's fellow German, Annemarie Heinrich, though, who will specialize in publicity shots of actors, including the young ingenue Eva Duarte; Heinrich's principal photograph of Mecha Ortiz is one of her most famous.)

In conclusion, Horacio Coppola's photographic gaze of Buenos Aires in 1936, on the occasion of the four hundredth anniversary of the original founding of the city, is marked by an intense enthusiasm and exuberance for the visual display of the city. Historically, Buenos Aires had a very difficult time moving beyond the failed founding in 1536, and by 1936, if Buenos Aires had become the most prosperous city in Latin America, as well as its undisputed cultural center, it could count on barely fifty years of spectacular development. It is that spectacular development, made photographic spectacle by the *dérive* of Coppola's camera, that has left one of the most outstanding founding photographic records of urban Buenos Aires.

Notes

1. Together with Fernando Márquez Miranda, in the early forties, they photographed indigenous cultural sites in Peru, *Huacos, cultura chancay* (1943).
2. On the urban importance of the tango, see Betancour and Hasdell.
3. São Paulo also attracted some important gazes, both in terms of its modernity and in terms of the juxtaposition between the modern and the premodern. Two foreign observers stand out, the Swiss-German Hildegard Rosenthal and the French Claude Lévi-Strauss, who subsequently used Brazil as the basis for his groundbreaking anthropological theories (see, respectively, Foster, "Downtown São Paulo" and Foster, "Saudades do Brasil").
4. Coppola's photography, at least with images such as the one being described here, involves the sort of hyper-reality that Rodaway describes, in the sense that the visual element of photography responds well to his proposition that "The 'hyper-realisation' of sense and the senses might be defined as the separation out of individual sense modes, the reduction or simplification of these sense modes to specific features or roles, the organization of the senses hierarchically, and the assignment of lesser senses, thus defined, under the hegemony of one re-defined sense" (172–73). Bachelard also speaks of an "*inner immensity* that gives their real meaning to certain expressions concerning the visible world" (185). I would argue that Coppola's photography of Buenos Aires insistently contributes to this sense of inner immensity; he would have his spectator experience this sense with regard to Buenos Aires.
5. Coppola surely must have known Carlos Gardel's signature tango, "Mi Buenos Aires querido" (lyrics by Alfred de la Pera), which was released in 1934 and was used as the soundtrack music of Julio Irigoyen's 1936 film of the same name.
6. Gorelik speaks of the importance, for the military coup, of promoting a "program to reestablish the meaning of urban modernization," one aspect of which was expanding the avenues of the city core, as well as the construction of the Obelisk that is now the signature monument of the city. I will discuss (below) two of Coppola's images relating to the city core, those tied to the diagonal Roque Sáenz Peña and Corrientes.
7. For a chronology of the period, see Acuña.
8. According to Rapoport and Seoane, by 1935, the economy had begun to improve in Buenos Aires, although it would not be until 1941 that wages returned to their 1929 levels (1.557).
9. For the history (and a rich array of anecdotes) about this most Buenos Aires of urban streets, see studies by Casella de Calderón *et al.* and Marechal; Marechal is one

of the city's most important urban novelists. See also the historic commentary on Corrientes before its widening, in Rapoport and Seoane (1.443–46).

10. Historically, it was also the first Jewish quarter of Buenos Aires, centered around Plaza Lavalle, where La Sinagoga Libertad, the principal Jewish institution of the city, is located. It was only in the late nineteenth century that the El Once neighborhood began to become the seat of Jewish life. El Once is still identified with the Jews of Buenos Aires, although few wonder why the major synagogue is some distance away (Foster, "Para ver").

11. When one examines the original publication of his photographs, one is struck by the aerial views he was able to accomplish in 1936, many of which look very much like fragments today as viewed from Google Earth.

12. Unlike São Paulo, where the lack of public spaces (aside from some major parks) has led architects in recent years to create botanical buffers around the base of their buildings (this is also true in Mexico City), some architecture in Buenos Aires is now beginning to display this characteristic. Such buffers are also a security enhancement.

13. See also the image "Avenida Presidente Roque Sáenz Peña and Suipacha," which brings Coppola's camera down to the street level of the photograph I have been commenting on. The concentration of male pedestrians is to be explained, most likely, by the fact that this is an administrative and business district. The density of automobiles is even more evident in this image.

14. There is now a well-established critique of the masculine nature of architecture (see Agrest *et al.* for one sample of the issue), as well as proposals for a feminist architecture (see Rendell et al.).

15. Bergero comments on the expansion of the Corrientes theater scene, beginning in the 1920s, as part of the cultural flowering of the period (300).

16. Actually, it is now identified as the Teatro El Nacional, to distinguish it from other installations with the generic designation of Teatro Nacional, such as the Teatro Nacional Cervantes or the Teatro Nacional Colón. As one can note by viewing the image, the 1936 playbill clearly says "Teatro Nacional." Martínez includes the Nacional in his listing of important theater venues in Buenos Aires in the early twentieth century; there are twenty-two institutions listed (124–25).

17. The most notorious torching of a theater attributed to the regime was that of El Picadero, early in the morning, following the opening, in March 1981, of a cycle of twenty-one plays critical of the dictatorship. Teatro Abierto, in 1981, went on to become one of the historically most important phenomena in Argentine theater. The torching of theaters is thematized in *La fabulosa historia de los inolvidables Marrapodi* (1998) of Los Macocos, Banda de Teatro. See Graham-Jones on the importance of Teatro Abierto.

18. The north side of Corrientes is dominated, in the 1500 block, by the Teatro Municipal General San Martín, a major performing arts complex, which was inaugurated by the city of Buenos Aires in 1960.

19. Written by the French playwrights Robert Frenchville and André Mouëzy-Eon, and made into a film by the same name in 1962, directed by Julio Saraceni.

20. A fascinating Argentine text, through which to study the play between different feminine conventions of the period, is the anarchist-follower, Salvadora Medina Onrubia's *Las descentradas* (1928).

21. The intense pedestrian and vehicular traffic on Corrientes will lead to a major widening of the street in 1938.

22. Significantly, the Argentine theater will be particularly enhanced by the arrival in the city, with the Spanish Civil War (1936–1939), of a major segment of the Spanish theatrical community, which will go on to make major contributions to the vitality of the Argentine theater. Federico García Lorca, by then doing important work in theater, visited the city between October 1933 and April 1934; his key play *La casa de Bernarda Alba* premiered posthumously in Buenos Aires in 1945, with the exiled grande dame of the Spanish theater Margarita Xirgu in the lead role; her company staged the play.

Works Cited

Acuña, Julia Elena. "Guía cronológica." *Argentina 1930–1960*. Buenos Aires: Editorial Sur, 1961.

Agrest, Diana, Patricia Conway, and Leslie Kanes Weisman, eds. *The Sex of Architecture*. New York: Harry N. Abrams, 1996.

Bachelard, Gaston. *The Poetics of Space*. Trans. Maria Jolas. Boston: Beacon Press, 1994.

Bergero, Adriana J. *Intersecting Tango: Cultural Geographies of Buenos Aires, 1900–1930*. Pittsburgh: University of Pittsburgh Press, 2008.

Betancour, Ana, and Peter Hasdell. "Tango: A Choreography of Urban Displacement." *The City Cultures Reader*. Ed. Malcolm Miles and Tim Hall, with Iain Borden. London: Routledge, 2003.

Casella de Calderón, Elisa, Elvira Grandinetti de Firpi, and Myrtha Laguzzi de Larcher. *Calle Corrientes: Su historia en cinco barrios*. Buenos Aires, 1984–1988.

Coppola, Horacio. *Buenos Aires: Visión fotográfica*. 2nd ed. Textos de Alberto Prebisch and Ignacio B. Anzoátegui. Buenos Aires: Municipalidad, 1937. Added title: *Buenos Aires 1936: Cuarto Centenario de su Fundación*.

———. *Buenos Aires años treinta*. Buenos Aires: Galería Jorge Mara-La Ruche, 2005.

———. *Imagema: Antología fotográfica 1927–1994*. Buenos Aires: Fondo Nacional de las Artes, Ediciones de la Llanura, 1994.

———. *Viejo Buenos Aires adiós*. Texeto de Juan Francisco Giacobbe. 1980. Buenos Aires: Ediciones de la Llanura, 1990.

———. *Visões de Buenos Aires*. São Paulo: Instituto Moreira Salles, 2007.

Facundo de Zuviría, and Adrián Gorelik. *Buenos Aires*. Buenos Aires: Ediciones Lariviere, 2006.

————. Dir. *Así nació el Obelisco*. 1936.

Foppa, Tito Livio. "Florencio Parravicini." *Diccionario teatral del Río de la Plata*. Buenos Aires: Argentores, Ediciones del Carro de Tespis, 1961.

Foster, David William. "Annemarie Heinrich: Photography, Women's Bodies, and Semiotic Excess." *Journal of Latin American Popular Culture* 25 (2006): 253–70.

————. "Downtown in São Paulo with Hildegard Rosenthal's Camera." *Luso-Brazilian Review* 42.1 (2005): 118–35.

————. "Downtown in São Paulo with Hildegard Rosenthal's Camera." *Revista tecnología e sociedade* 1 (2005): 41–58.

————. "Dreaming in Feminine: Grete Stern's Photomontages and the Parody of Psychoanalysis." *Ciberletras* 10 (2003): 10 pages. *www.lehman.cuny.edu/ciberletras/v.10/foster.html*.

————. *Fotografías de Buenos Aires 1860–1900: Vistas y costumbres*. Buenos Aires: Casa Figueroa Ediciones, 1997.

————. "Para ver el Once, el Abasto y sus alrededores." *Dale nomás! Dale que va! Ensayos testimoniales para la Argentina del siglo XXI; Voces, ciudades y lenguajes*. Ed. Christián Ricci y Gustavo Geirola. Buenos Aires: Editorial Nueva Generación, 2006.

————. "Sara Facio as Urban Photographer." *Buenos Aires: Perspectives on the City and Cultural Production*. Gainesville: University Press of Florida, 1998.

————. "*Saudades do Brasil*: Claude Lévi-Strauss's Photographic Gaze of the City of São Paulo." *Chasqui* 3 (2006): 98–125.

————. *Urban Photography in Argentina: Nine Artists of the Post-Dictatorship Era*. Jefferson, N.C.: McFarland Publishers, 2007.

Gorelick, Adrian. "A Metropolis in the Pampas: Buenos Aires, 1890–1940." *Cruelty and Utopia: Cities and Landscapes of Latin America*. New York: Princeton Architectural Press, 2005.

Graham-Jones, Jean. "Vigilant, Vigilante Theater: Teatro Abierto (1981–1985)." *Exorcising History: Argentine Theater under Dictatorship*. Lewisburg: Bucknell University Press, 2000.

"Horacio Coppola." *La nación. Revista* (23 de julio, 2006). *www.lanacion.com.ar/nota.asp?_id=825116>*. Accessed July 12, 2008.

Los Macocos, Banda de Teatro. "La fabulosa historia de los inolvidables Marrapodi." *Teatro deshecho I: Flora y fauna de la creación macocal*. Buenos Aires: ATUEL, 2002.

Marechal, Leopoldo. *Historia de la calle Corrientes*. Buenos Aires: Paidós, 1967.

Márquez Miranda, Fernando, Grete Stern, and Horacio Coppola. *Huacos, cutlura chancay*. Buenos Aires: Ediciones de la Llanura, 1943.

Martínez, Albert B. *Baedeker of the Argentine Republic*. 1900. Barcelona: R. Sopena, 1914.

Moorehead, Alan. *Darwin and the Beagle*. New York: Harper and Row, 1969.

Rapoport, Mario, and María Seoane. *Buenos Aires: Historia de una ciudad.* Buenos
    Aires: Planeta, 2007.
Rendell, Jane, Barbara Penner, and Iain Borden, eds. *Gender Space Architecture: An
    Interdisciplinary Introduction.* London: E and FN Spon, 2000.
Rodaway, Paul. *Sensuous Geographies: Body, Sense, and Place.* London: Routledge,
    1994.
Torres, José Luis. *La década infame 1930–1940: Apuntes históricos para el estudio del
    presente político.* Buenos Aires: Editorial Freeland, 1973.
Tuan, Yi-Fu. *Topofilia: A Study of Environmental Perception, Attitudes, and Values.* New
    York: Columbia University Press, 1990.

◆ **8**

Seeing "Spain" at the 1893 Chicago World (Columbian) Exhibition

Catherine Vallejo

World Exhibitions integrate characteristics of the spectacle and the museum display, the tourist attraction and the didactic opportunity, the advertisement and the amusement park.[1] They offer an opportunity for countries to exhibit themselves by making grand ideological and commercial statements ands are often publicized as cultural events with all the characteristics of participatory spectacle. They are frequently held to coincide with some important national commemoration—the American independence (Philadelphia, 1876), the French Revolution (Paris, 1889), the completion of the Panama Canal (San Francisco, 1915), the hundredth anniversary of the end of Canada's colonial status (Montreal, 1967). The Chicago World Exhibition (1893)[2] had as its theme the celebration of the four hundredth anniversary of Columbus's discovery of America, supposedly highlighting the relationship between Spain and America. But it was also, more importantly, a demonstration of how the United States had progressed in those four hundred years.[3]

A World Exhibition, though integrating exhibits from many different places, is not a neutral space, since it inevitably carries large quantities of cultural and ideological baggage pertaining to the site of origin. Chicago's Exhibition was a very North American spectacle. This factor influenced the perspective shown toward Spain by different participating and spectator groups, not in the least because of the incipient imperial aspirations on the part of the United States toward Latin America.

Politically and culturally, the late 1880s and early 1890s were crucial years for the relationship between Spain and the United States, and Cuba was its strategic axis, just prior to its second war of independence and the subsequent U.S. political intervention on the island. Throughout Latin America there was great ambivalence toward the economic, political, and cultural power of the United States and its intentions. Thus, the way Spain was perceived is complicated by the situation of Cuba, which was both politically and commercially part of the Spanish colonial system, yet culturally and geographically part of Latin America.

This chapter examines how Spain was perceived at the Chicago World Exhibition of 1893 based on reports describing the exhibits and the spectacles shown there, which reveal at least two separate but related transformations: that of the visual spectator turned narrator-producer of the texts to be published; and the transformations that take place in Spain's symbolic space, which I understand here to mean a "mental space" that mediates between external political reality, on the one hand, and historical actors, with their historically and culturally predetermined notions, on the other (Tuan 13). Perception, attitude, value, and world-view are the overlapping qualities (Tuan 4) that enter into this "seeing" of Spain. I will focus on the examination of four related issues: the impact of the princess Infanta Eulalia's visit to Havana and to the Chicago World Exhibition as the official representative of the Spanish nation; the definition of "home" and its concomitant metaphoric spheres in relation to a World Exhibition and the context of colonization; the significance of Columbus at the Exhibition; and conflicting views of U.S.–Spanish relations, all as presented by a number of correspondents and publications in the three countries. Correspondents to the Exhibition—simultaneously spectators and spokesmen of the symbolic (written) culture, who provided the larger public with their interpretation of the place and its exhibits—included the Cubans Manuel Serafín Pichardo, Raimundo Cabrera, and Aurelia Castillo de González and the Spaniards Rafael Puig y Valls, Eva Canel, and the Infanta Eulalia.[4] In the reports from the Chicago Exhibition, national pride was evident, and communicated through what today would be called an agenda. These texts, taken together, exhibit a complex and often contradictory web of perspectives at the cultural and political levels. In their creation and dissemination, the transformation from spectator to narrator will be eclipsed by the creation of Spain as a mental space with newly defined characteristics.

World Exhibition narratives tend to engender a certain sameness in style that reflects the observations of the spectator-turned-narrator. Overwhelmed by the multitude of objects and events that become representations—metonyms, synecdoches, metaphors—of their culture, industries, and ideologies, writers compile catalogues *of representative* samples presented in the exhibit, often without descriptive adjectives except for the superlative. The chronology of the visit tends to be replaced by repetitions—of countries, objects seen, artists, verbs of observation, movement, and information (we saw, we read, we learned, we visited, we walked). The several discursive strategies focus on the descriptions of places, buildings, objects, and other elements of the exposition, without the dynamic of movement, displacement, or the passing of time. Often the description is that of an image rather than a spectacle, in that the text is spatialized akin to an archive, becoming a collection of descriptive labels of objects, a list of nouns without narration.[5] The creation of "Spain" as a mental space, on the other hand, becomes more rhetorical and argumentative, drawing comparisons and evaluative statements of a nationalistic nature, rather than reflecting the encyclopedism and comprehensiveness typical of the *topos* of exhibition, which tends toward the nineteenth century's perspective on knowledge.

The reconstruction of Spain as a particular mental space was, of course, already evident prior to the Chicago Exhibition. In 1892, the actual four hundredth anniversary of Columbus's historic achievement, Spain had itself celebrated a year-long commemoration, the focus of which had been ambiguous (commemorate the Italian-born man Columbus, or the nation Spain's role in the discovery?), and whose events turned controversial (too many official functions, too much culture, and too little offered for the people).[6] The nation had celebrated an International Exhibition in Barcelona in 1888 and was going through a difficult economic and political period, the newspapers full of morbid headlines, such as "agitation in the provinces," "crisis in the financial sector," "tumults in the cities," "unrest in the colonies," and, particularly, what was called "the Cuban problem." Many government and cultural institutions in Spain had pondered the nation's status, those four hundred years after, in the course of attempting to forge closer ties to and acquire better knowledge about the former colonies, now established republics in South America (Bernabeu Albert). Invitations were extended to a number of well-known Spanish-American writers to speak at the many congresses held on a wide variety of topics, such as pedagogy, literature, art, geography, law, and commerce, all with the sub-title "Hispano-Americano."

During these events, the Spanish government sponsored the publication of a lavishly illustrated monthly magazine—that often appeared after lengthy delays—called *El Centenario*, which presented the views of well-known Spanish thinkers. In a lengthy article, rich in dense figurative language, José Alcalá Galiano, a regular contributor who would travel to Chicago himself in 1893, summed up the general sentiment regarding the role Spain was to have in the Columbian World Exhibition: a role that was, in the first place, seen as "natural," and which, as a result, justified the use of the paternalistic (and patriarchal) metaphors common to the relationship between the metropolis and its colonies:

> Natural es que la hija celebre la glorificación del padre; que la joven llena de vigor y entusiasmo ofrezca a su europea maestra el espectáculo de sus maravillas, progresos y grandezas, la visión deslumbradora de su porvenir. . . . Por eso la Exposición Universal de Chicago . . . viene a ser un duelo, no a muerte, sino a vida, entre dos Continentes; duelo santo ante el altar del que los unió, duelo . . . ante la sombra de Colón . . . España ha de tener en ella [la Exhibición] una representación ideal más que material, un puesto honorífico. . . . Pueblo soñador, artístico, romántico, aventurero, pero perezoso, inerte e inadecuado a la vida moderna, a Chicago . . . debemos sólo llevar para hacer buen papel, la representación, no de nuestro momento histórico, pues hoy no tenemos historia, sino de nuestro momento artístico, pues hoy tenemos arte vivo. . . . Debemos llevar la representación retrospectiva, arqueológica, típica, novelesca de nuestro pasado . . . el nombre, la grandeza y el prestigio de España obtendrán en América, si no el premio de su pobre industria, la medalla de honor por la magna obra de su pasado. . . . [La carabela,] esa minúscula *Santa María* . . . es la más simbólica representación, la vera efigie, la imagen de España. (*El Centenario* II 354, 366, 367)

(It is natural for the daughter to celebrate the glorification of the father; for the young woman full of energy and enthusiasm to offer her European mistress the spectacle of her wonders, progress and greatness, the dazzling vision of her future. . . . For that reason the World Exhibition of Chicago . . . is like a duel, not to the death but to life, between two continents; a holy duel before the altar of he who united them, a duel . . . before Columbus's shadow. . . . [In the Exhibition] Spain should have an ideal representation more than a material one, a place of honor. . . . [We are] a people that are dreamers, artistic, romantic, adventurous, but [also] lazy, inert and inadequate to modern life; in order to take an appropriate role we . . . should only take to Chicago the representation not of our historic time—because today we have no history—but [the representation] of our artistic high points—because today we [do] have live arts. . . . We must take the retrospective, archeological, typical, novelistic representation of our past . . . the name, greatness and prestige of Spain will obtain in America, if not the prize for its poor industry, [then] the medal of honor for its great work of the past. . . . [The caravel], this minuscule *Santa María* . . . is the most symbolic representation, the very image of Spain).

The evident hispanophilia in Galiano's perspective uncritically emphasizes the glories of the past and declares the present to be, artistically, in that glorious condition, all of which reveals an entrenched belief in Spain's colonial power and status in contradiction with the unreality of its dreaming, artistic, but lazy, people—that is, the backwardness of its present. Thus, Spain's imagined role in this spectacle takes place in the shadow of Columbus. Alcalá Galiano uses words that refer to both weapons and religion in a reflection of the cross and the sword *topos* emblematic of the Spanish conquest of America. The repetition of the term *representación* is also noteworthy; Spain will be represented—that is, not present, but presented by others who will act for her "again"—much like Columbus did, in fact. The writer feels that Spain has nothing to prove. Its name, prestige, and greatness speak for themselves, and his closing remarks argue that a very small token (the replica of Columbus's small ship the *Santa María)* is sufficient to constitute a true symbolic image of its magnificence. As a historic narrative, this self-reflection constitutes a self-fulfilling prophecy of what others would see as the negative qualities of Spain.

Spain sent two delegates to the Chicago Exhibition to embody this representation of historical presence, the Duke of Veragua, Columbus's direct descendant, and the Princess Eulalia, the youngest aunt of the child-king-to-be Alfonso XIII. Eulalia's live appearance at the Exhibition would give rise to spectacles in two different "colonial" spaces. According to her *Memorias*, her visit to Chicago, in June 1893, would "necessarily" imply a diplomatic stop in Havana first, which was seen as the more important destination: "Cuba . . . agitada por ideas liberales, conmovida por ansias de independencia y lista ya a emprender la Guerra contra su Metrópoli . . . era el punto árido y difícil del viaje." (83-84) (Cuba . . . disturbed by liberal ideas, excited by cravings for independence and now ready to undertake War against its Metropolis . . . was the sticking point of the voyage). She thus reiterates the mental image of Spain as the possessor-colonizer of Cuba. Yet even before her departure, she came to realize that "después de todo, sobraba razón a los cubanos en sus deseos de libertarse" (84) (after all, Cubans more than had right on their side in their desire to liberate themselves). During her visit to Havana, she speaks with a number of people, including several with an interest in changing Cuba's status, and as she leaves, she confirms her earlier premonition in a letter to her mother, foreseeing, regretfully, the end of Spanish rule in Cuba: "Si como presiento, ¡ay de mí!, la Isla de Cuba se separa de España, mi recuerdo permanecerá vivo" (*Cartas* 61) (If, as I have the feeling—alas!—the Island of Cuba will separate from Spain, my memory will remain alive). In this formulation, Cuba attains status as the agent of the separating action, and the possessive is limited to her own memories of "the island of Cuba," the latter on quite equal footing with Spain, which is no longer the "metropolis."

The success of Eulalia's Havana visit was perhaps due to her having sought consultations with people of different political views in Cuba, and, having listened sympathetically, the political and the personal become conjoined in a movement she very acutely understands: "Mi éxito 'personal' es de una naturaleza tan especial, que oculta, sin duda alguna, una intención política. . . . Todos los gritos que oigo se dirigen a *mí* y más aún a la 'mujer' que a la 'Infanta'" (*Cartas* 39) (My personal success has such a special character, that without any doubt it conceals a political intent. . . . All the shouts I hear are directed to *me*, and even more to the 'woman' than to the 'princess'). Not surprisingly, in the Havana of 1893 she is more appreciated for her personality as a woman than as a representative of royalty, an issue that comes to the fore again when she decides how to act in the United States. She first differentiates between her relationship to Cuba—to whose citizens she represents the *patria*—and the United States, once again emphasizing her status as a woman: "Naturalmente, no puede existir en este país [the US], por lo que a mí se refiere, el mismo sentimiento que une la Patria a la personalidad que la representa. Por eso voy a esforzarme por añadir a la dignidad de mi categoría la sencillez de la mujer" (*Memorias* 71) (Naturally, as far as it pertains to me, in this country [the US] the feeling that unites the Fatherland to the personality that represents it cannot exist. Therefore I will make an effort to add the simplicity of a woman to the dignity of my class), an effort she believed was successfully completed.

Eulalia's official visit to the Chicago Exhibition ran from June 6 to June 9, the 8th being designated *Infanta Eulalia Day*, when 170,000 people were reportedly present on the Exhibition site, marking a new attendance record (Howe Bancroft 971). Havana's Manuel Pichardo clearly realized Eulalia's role as "standing for" Spain, when he called Princess Eulalia Day also Spain's National Day (61). Eulalia's experiences in Chicago, however, present a dichotomy. Rafael Puig y Valls—an official Spanish government delegate—lauds Eulalia's "nobles cualidades," the adjective being both literal (Eulalia as royalty) and abstract (her moral qualities), as she was able to protect "los prestigios del trono, los intereses patrios y las susceptibilidades de las democracias con un tacto propio de la augusta dama a la cual se ha confiado una misión delicadísima" (I, 158) (the prestige of the throne, national interests and democratic susceptibilities with a tact appropriate to the august lady to whom this delicate mission was entrusted). His judgment is clearly within the view of Spain as a monarchy and a colonizing nation, and both Cuban and Spanish press agree as well as, superficially, the Chicago press (which Eulalia herself quotes in her

Memorias, having slipped out incognito on June 7 to buy local newspapers and enjoy the Midway Pleasance).

However, in spite of her charm and youth (the reasons Cánovas had chosen her to represent Spain, rather than her older sister Isabel), she does act like a typical princess, and her conduct was seen as arrogant, offending a number of exhibit organizers, especially Mrs. Bertha Potter Palmer, the director of the Board of Lady Managers of the Woman's Building, who had prepared a reception and banquet for her. Eulalia arrived late to the reception, snubbed the hostess, and was generally felt to have been rude, uninterested, and sulky. One State Department official responded to Mrs. Potter Palmer's complaints afterwards as follows: "While she is rather handsome, graceful and bright, she is effusive and insincere. . . . The Infanta treated you and the other Chicago people with gross impoliteness" (qtd. in Weimann 560). Eulalia, on the other hand, sums up her evaluation of the Chicago visit in terms of a personal triumph: "Para mí el viaje había sido un recorrido triunfal lleno de revelaciones en un mundo nuevo y democrático, libre, sobre todo, y que, por eso, me parecía feliz" (*Memorias* 91) (To me, the voyage had been a triumphant tour, filled with revelations in a world that was new and democratic and especially free, and which therefore seemed happy to me). In light of the earlier critique, this formulation may have implied the opposite about Spain: that it was *not* new, democratic, free, or happy. We can consider her visit to Chicago a spectacle, according to Guy Debord's notion, where the external world (the reality of Spain) is replaced by a selection of images (Eulalia's appearances as a "royal" and the popular frenzy that accompanied her) that mediate a social relation through its privileging of sight and the subsequent creation of superficial knowledge, which allows spectacle participants, including their main actors, to construct their own mental spaces (Debord 12, 26).

Madrid's *El Imparcial's* effusive praise of Spanish participation in the Exhibition— "Indubitablemente la sección española es una de las más brillantes de la Feria" (June 14) (undoubtedly the Spanish section is one of the most brilliant of the Fair)—was typical of Spanish evaluations of their nation's pavilion and exhibits in Chicago. But Rafael Puig y Valls details the struggles he had to overcome in the painful process to set up the Spanish exhibits (103). The Spanish pavilion itself, much admired in Spanish periodicals, was representative of the worldview, attitudes, and values perpetuated by the Spanish official perspective, being a replica of the Silk Exchange (Lonja de la Seda) in Valencia, a building constructed in 1442. Puig y Valls reports that all Spanish installations had been completed the day before Eulalia's visit (that is, five weeks after the Exhibition's inauguration), but even by July, Cuban Raimundo Cabrera reports that the pavilion was not fully functional. Many of its artifacts—old cannons, needlework, and paintings by members of the royal family—were explicit references to Spain's past glories and its monarchical status. The cannons—sent by Spain as her contribution to the Transportation Building(!)—caused Cabrera to cast a sad look at Spain's "bad taste" (66); but, more poignantly, this exhibit evokes an incident that occurred in New York Harbor, one in which Eulalia was implicated. On May 26, she had been taken on an American navy yacht to meet the incoming replicas of Columbus's ships, the *Niña, Pinta,* and *Santa María.* The captain of the latter wished to salute the royal princess with a salvo from the ship's cannon, but Eulalia insisted on removing herself from the area, as she did not trust the cannons. Indeed, there was an accident in which two sailors were wounded by shrapnel flying from the exploding gun-barrel (Borbón, *Cartas* 84; *El Imparcial* May 28). Both, the old cannons exhibited and the exploding gun barrel, would be emblematically prescient of the self-image Spanish ideologists constructed.

Yi-Fu Tuan proposes that an outsider's fresh perspective of a place allows for a perception of merits and defects that are no longer visible to a resident of an environment (65). Raimundo Cabrera's summary of his perspective on Spain, as seen through its exhibits in Chicago, curiously and quite closely reflects Alcalá Galiano's 1892 opinion quoted above, but it is quite different from the latter's insider view. In his negative evaluation, Cabrera implicates three perspectives: American, foreign, and an "us" whose only relation to Spain is the Spanish language and thus constitutes an outsider's view: "España, la nación que dio la América al Mundo, la más honrada y obsequiada en esta gran festividad . . . con la casa desamueblada aún . . . es un triste espectáculo para el forastero, una desilusión para el norteamericano, y para nosotros los que hablamos la lengua, una manifestación sumamente desconsoladora" (Cabrera 55, dated July 27) (Spain, the nation that gave America to the world, the most honored and lavished with gifts in this great festival, still with the house unfurnished . . . is a sad spectacle for the stranger, a disappointment for the North American, and for those of us who speak the language, an exceedingly heartbreaking manifestation). The house metaphor used by Cabrera is interesting, as many writers repeatedly intensify it to "home" and all it implies. Eva Canel, then living in Cuba, sees the Spanish Pavilion as her home: "Creo que debo comenzar por casa" (*Boletín* 101) (I feel I should start at home), she writes in her first report to the Havana Chamber of Commerce, referring to the Spanish pavilion and other things Spanish at the Exhibition. Her identification with the plants and flowers around the re-created *La Rábida* convent, where Columbus planned the voyage, allows her to synecdochically and metonymically claim the space as her own: "Tan españolas y tan bonitas me parecieron estas plantas y estas flores . . . que se me ensanchó el alma creyéndome transplantada a mi patria" (*Boletín* 153) (So Spanish and lovely these plants and flowers seemed to me . . . that my soul expanded, believing myself transplanted to my homeland).

Rafael Puig y Valls refers to the inauguration ceremonies as an "espectáculo sublime" for other people, but "para los españoles . . . [es] fiesta de familia" (81) (for the Spanish people . . . it's a family party), as he repeatedly appropriates the civilizing impulse attributed to Spain as a gift to the world: "una Gloria española que inició en el mundo la esplendorosa civilización moderna" (78) (a Spanish Glory that initiated the splendid modern civilization in the world). He is, however, ambivalent about the Spanish exhibit in the Agriculture Building, admiring Cuba's contribution as "ostentosa," which results in "un contraste desfavorable para España" (112) (an unfavorable contrast for Spain). Cuba, in fact, occupies fully one half of the "Hispanic" space in the Agriculture Building, as the exhibits of Puerto Rico, the Philippines, and "ya en tercer término . . . vaya la madre patria acompañando a sus hijas predilectas" (117) (then in third place . . . the mother country accompanying her favourite daughters) are relegated to the other half, which Puig y Valls nevertheless laments in patriarchal terms. Not surprisingly, Cuban Pichardo also feels the Hispanic section in the Agriculture Building to be home. It is the only place Cuba is present as such, and not as a Spanish dependency: "Me da salud respirar en nuestro pabellón [i.e. the section named 'Cuba' in Agriculture], donde acostumbro ir en busca de descanso, después de la fatiga que produce el andar" (111) (It is healthy for me to breathe in our pavilion, where I often go in search of rest after the fatigue produced by walking). He sees the Cuban installation in this section to be clearly superior: "¡Qué linda es la casa de Cuba! Vence a las demás instalaciones del Palacio de Agricultura" (113) (How pretty is Cuba's house! It is better than the other installations in the Agricultural Palace). He also constructs Cuba as a national space, more highly ranked than a simple home: "Escribo desde *Cuba*, desde el gallardo pabellón que luce nuestro país en el edificio de Agricultura. Y a fe que me siento orgulloso . . . porque la instalación cubana . . . supera a las de su categoría. . . . Parece . . . el recinto de una nación, no el de una colonia combatida, explotada y casi exangüe" (111) (I am writing from *Cuba*, from the dashing pavilion that our country shows off in the Agriculture Building. And truly I feel proud . . . because the Cuban installation . . . is superior to others in the same category. . . . It seems like . . . the site of a country, and not one of an embattled colony, exploited and almost bled dry).

The fact that Spain was well represented in the Agriculture Building by the Cuban production of tobacco marks a double irony: first, the anachronism of the continued dominance of agriculture in a late nineteenth-century European nation (a detail also noted by Pichardo [122], and so admitted by Alcalá Galiano); and then the reality that its best product did not originate on Spanish soil, nor was it manufactured in Spain. Here Spain is evidently shown to be commercially dependent on Cuba, yet without acknowledging this fact, one more confirmation—and at the same time a condemnation—of the process of colonization, as well as a reminder of Spain's status as a much reduced colonial power, with only Cuba (and to a lesser extent the Philippines) present as a token reminder of its glorious past.

The home metaphor is also exploited from a feminine perspective. In speaking of the library in the Woman's Building, Aurelia Castillo refers to the parent-child relationship. Using a figure from Greek mythology, she characterizes Cuba as "[l]a Niobe americana, castigada en toda su prole" (III, 114) (the American Niobe, chastised in all her offspring). Niobe, the wife of the king of Thebes, bragged to Leto of having seven sons and seven daughters, all of whom were then killed by Leto's two children in revenge for Niobe's remark. Her name is a symbol of mourning, and I take Castillo's qualification of the name as "castigada" as an infantalizing metaphor of the colony, who is punished for the mother country's sins (of arrogance and boastfulness). Eva Canel perorates extensively on women's role in society, especially Spanish women, in a long article titled "La mujer española," published in Madrid's *El Día* on September 20, 1893. There she explicitly states that the place for women, and their obligation to work, is in the home: "mientras el marido trabaja en la calle debemos *trabajar en casa*" (while the husband works outside, we have to *work in the home*) (emphasis in the original). She also positively relates this factor to progress for women: "¿Puede haber atraso intelectual para la mujer donde se publican diez o doce periódicos dedicados exclusivamente a las labores manuales de adorno?" (*Boletín* 193) (Can there be intellectual backwardness for the woman where there are ten or twelve newspapers dedicated exclusively to women's decorative arts?). An interesting comment in this respect, related to the colonial dimension, is added by Pichardo, who finds that the Spanish contribution to the Women's Building in Chicago is one of the few positive evaluations he can make of Spain, for which he significantly uses a term belonging to the colonial sphere: "es una de las pocas salientes con que figura la Metrópoli en este Certamen" (61) (it is one of the few outstanding things that the Metropolis presents in this contest). *Certamen* was a very common qualification of World Exhibitions, and of course among the meanings of the word is "competition" ("concurso abierto para estimular con premios determinadas actividades o competiciones") (RAE online dictionary) (a contest created to stimulate certain activities or competitions with awards). Spain was expected to be in competition with other nations regarding its place in late nineteenth-century modernity.[7]

Within Spain—the home country of Columbus the explorer, and of Cuba—there were great regional differences with respect to the nation's entry into modernity, some of which became evident at the Chicago Exhibition. Puig y Valls leaves no doubt that, because Spain had been late in accepting the invitation to participate in the event,[8] it was consequently assigned a not very propitious site for its pavilion, and, within the thematic buildings, its sites were away from the centers of activity and interest, in poorly lit corners (84). Puig y Valls was from Cataluña, and he also makes it clear that the participation by Spain was "tan menguada, que sin el esfuerzo de esas provincias, la sección de Manufacturas habría sido un fracaso tan manifiesto que, en mi concepto, deberíamos haber abandonado el local para no llenar de ridículo la consideración de España ante el mundo entero" (85) (so diminished that without the efforts of these provinces, the Manufacturing Section would have been such a rotund failure that, in my opinion, we should have abandoned the site so as not to expose Spain to ridicule before the entire world). He provides a long list of different Catalán industrial products and companies, and proudly quotes the Infanta Eulalia to the effect that she well knows that Cataluña "va a la cabeza de los adelantos industriales" (156) (is at the head of [Spain's] industrial advances). Here, together with his awareness of the importance of industry, technology, and commerce for nations toward the end of the nineteenth century, Puig y Valls still maintains the necessity for approval by royalty. These two elements clash in the contradictory mental space that is Spain, as constructed by the different narratives.

This contradiction is also evident in the mental space configured by Columbus, who was present in the Exhibition in different forms, each conceived by a different group—Americans, Spanish, and Cubans: every constituency reconstructed Columbus according to its particular stake in a historical competition. Among the official Spanish contributions was a very large painting (more than three meters high by four and a half wide) by Armando Menocal, a young artist from Havana. Set on the coast of Hispaniola, the painting shows a larger-than-life sized Christopher Columbus being led away to a small boat on the orders of the new Spanish governor Bobadilla, after his arrest at the conclusion of his third voyage in 1500. Columbus was to be returned to Spain and imprisoned for incompetence and abuses committed during his term as governor. Both Aurelia Castillo and Manuel S. Pichardo criticized the exhibition space the painting received, Pichardo recalling the metaphoric sphere of home—but negatively—by likening the light it receives to the opacity of a cave: "tiene por luz la opacidad de una cueva" (81). This painting—representation, image, constructed world—caused a furor between the Spanish exhibition organizers and Cuban intellectuals, as Menocal had been historically (or traditionally) correct in painting Columbus wearing handcuffs. Enrique Dupuy De Lôme, director of the Spanish exhibits, refused to allow the painting to be shown unless the handcuffs were removed—a request to which Menocal eventually and reluctantly consented (Pichardo 37). An intense discussion ensued among Cuban intellectuals in several Havana periodicals of the time. Raimundo Cabrera, propelled by "[u]n sentimiento de patriotismo local" (36) (a sentiment of local patriotism)—i.e., Cubanness—went to see the painting immediately upon his arrival at the Exhibition and voiced one of the strongest opinions of the controversy, including the use of the personal possessive for a Columbus enchained, to which one cannot help but make the connection to a colony enchained. "His" Columbus is not there (or this is not "his" Columbus); history has been hypocritically denied by a false sense of patriotism:

> Busco a mi Colón encadenado . . . quiero ver otra vez el hierro que sujeta al invicto descubridor y que en medio de este gran certamen, holocausto a su memoria imperecedera, recuerda la ingratitud de los que no tuvieron para él más que recelos y ultrajes. . . . Pero ¡ay! mi Colón no está allí; el pincel ha borrado del lienzo la cadena. . . . Que negar la historia, obscurecer la verdad . . . por un sentimiento apasionado e hipócrita de mal entendido patriotismo, es un acto punible. (37–38)

> (I search for my Columbus in chains . . . I want to see again the iron that fetters the undefeated discoverer, and who in the midst of this great competition, a holocaust to his undying memory, remembers the ingratitude of those who only had distrust and insults for him. . . . But, oh! My Columbus is not there; the brush has erased the chain from the canvas. . . . To deny history, to obscure the truth . . . by a passionate and hypocritical sentiment of a badly understood patriotism, is a punishable act.)

Cabrera makes two other interesting points in this lengthy text. He first interprets the painting as now showing Columbus as a sick man rather than a prisoner—which removes any indication of abuse of authority on the part of those having put on the handcuffs—and he looks for a suitable place or support ("una pierna") (a leg) to which the chain removed from Columbus can be attached in his desire to attribute this abuse to an agent (38). The painting, though its visual focal point is undoubtedly the figure of Columbus, created a mental world in which the handcuffs transgress the fixed iconography associated with Spain's Columbus and Columbus's Spain. This results in what Norman Bryson terms a *second space* (55) that is capable of subverting the *realism* of the received iconography of the handcuffs (127). Dupuy de Lôme's actions make it clear that the Spain constructed by Spaniards could not allow this type of questioning. And the correspondents make it clear that their interest lies not in making this painting real for their reading public in an ekphrastic exercise, but in the communication of their *own* mental construction of Spain.

With this large, strongly ideological painting, Cuba presented a vivid image of the discoverer and his history. Other expressions of Columbus at the Exhibition were not necessarily successful either, at least according to Pichardo: "En todas partes se ha pretendido interpretar alguna escena alusiva al Almirante; pero siempre con desgracia" (91) (Everywhere people have tried to interpret some scene allusive to the Admiral, but always with negative results). A portrait on the Exhibition admission ticket, a Columbus half-dollar (the first-ever commemorative coin struck in the United States [Bolotin and Laing 150]), as well as the Isabella quarter, both minted to raise funds for the Exhibition's costs, commercialized Columbus's image. The promotion of Columbus's image and representation—sponsored mostly by the American Exhibition organizers in Chicago—was, in fact, so pervasive on the Exhibition grounds as to be trivialized to the point of falsification.

On the day the replicas of Columbus's three small ships arrived in the Chicago lagoon, an impressive spectacle was staged representing Columbus's arrival in the New World, combining a Columbus stand-in, modern copies of old European ships, and descendants of America's original inhabitants in modern-made, "traditional" craft, savagely shouting in a make-believe celebration. Pichardo saw all of this as an event portending colonization and destruction: "El moderno Colón, cargado de cruces y charreteras . . . las tribus de indios que han venido a la Exposición, lanzáronse al encuentro de [las carabelas] en sus piraguas y canoas, celebrando con gritos salvajes de júbilo . . . el aniquilamiento de sus chozas y la destrucción de su raza, a expensas de la justicia egoísta y sangrienta que se llama civilización" (98–99) (The modern Columbus, weighed down with crosses and halberds . . . , the Indian tribes that have come to the Exhibition launched themselves to meet [the caravels] in their small boats and canoes, celebrating with savage jubilant cries . . . the annihilation of their huts and the destruction of their race, at the expense of the egotistical and bloody justice called civilization).

Spain's own contribution to the recreation and commemoration of Columbus was twofold, an exhibition and a delegation. However, the Columbus documents and memorabilia—detailed and greatly praised by a number of Madrid newspapers—were considered by some to be "of dubious authenticity" (Appelbaum 95).[9] Cristóbal Colón de Aguilera, a direct descendant of Christopher

Columbus and the fifteenth Duke of Veragua, was present as an official envoy of Spain, and was treated like royalty from the inauguration of the Exhibit on May 1. But his fame also had a negative aspect, as the letter from the State Department official to Mrs. Potter Palmer opines that he was "a common cheap fellow" (qtd. in Weimann 560). The "cheap" epithet is doubly interesting, as Madrid's *La Época* reports that in the United States there was a movement by some of those who had come to know the duke to take up a subscription to assist in the recuperation of his fortune, which was threatened by total loss because of bad investments and crushing debts (*La Época* July 8, 21, 30, August 3). This action on the part of American businessmen can be seen positively as a desire to help out a person who has fallen on hard times, or negatively as an imperialistic attempt to "take over" an important part of Spain's heritage.

This latter perspective was supported by Eva Canel, who, in an article published in *La Ilustración Artística* in Madrid, described the United States as a center of conspiracies to make Cuba independent of Spain, motivated by the zealous pursuit of Spanish-Cuban commercial products, and in whose cigarette factories "poco a poco se van formando colonias temibles de insurrectos cubanos y de peninsulares descontentos de su gobierno" (September 4, 1893) (little by little fearful colonies of rebellious Cubans and Spanish people unhappy with their government are being formed). Here she echoes the Spanish newspaper *El Correo*, which in May had accused the *New York Herald* of fomenting anti-Spanish propaganda concerning the "Cuban problem" ("Las mentiras del *Herald*," May 3).[10] And in fact they had it right: much of the planning on the Cuban independence project, launched by José Martí in 1895, was done from the United States, and much of it through Florida tobacco interests, staffed for the most part by Cubans. Pichardo would also tend to agree: "—¡Quiuba!— dicen [los americanos], y piensan en la anexión, solamente por fumarse los *imperiales*" (115) (—Quiuba!—say [the Americans], and think of annexation, if only in order to smoke [Cuban] cigars). U.S. interest in Cuba is thus seen as both political and commercial: the emphasized term *imperiales* clearly having a meaning beyond the name of a cigar brand. Spain, criticized or appropriated through its traditional noble and royal representatives, and disrespected because of the emphasis on tradition in all its exhibits, is disappearing from the picture (from the exhibition) altogether.

Although Pichardo, in his series of articles on the Exhibition, would claim that annexation or sale of Cuba to the United States is not an option, since Spain would not allow either (222ff), it is clear that the Exhibition viewers saw the United States as strongly implicated in Spain's Cuban problem, even during the 1893 Chicago World Exhibition, an event that would establish the United

States as a power in the world economy (Rosenblum, Stevens, and Dumas 64). Possibly spurred by the sensationalist and biased popular press, the perhaps reluctant admiration and respect felt for Spain and its history during the Chicago Exhibition would turn into confrontation and criticism of its colonial culture, by then seen as abusive. According to Eva Canel's summary judgment, Spain was relegated to a very minor role there and even suffered disrespect ("El poco respeto que indudablemente se nos ha tenido, culpa no sé de quién") (*Boletín* 101) (the little respect that people undoubtedly had for us here—I don't know through whose fault). This view was undoubtedly correct and curiously fomented by the official Spanish perspective itself—the creator, and original narrator, of the exhibit. The Spain created for the Exhibition, to be seen by visitors, was a mental space proposed for the nineteenth-century reality but situated completely in the past. The world constructed by much of Spain's contribution to the Chicago World's Fair emphasized the gap between the commercial power and the imperialistic tendencies of North America, on the one hand, and the old degenerate dynasty of the now moribund colonizing power, on the other. The Chicago Columbian Exhibition of 1893 redefined the symbolic world order: the New World "discovered" by Columbus was now represented by North America alone. Both South America and Spain were immersed in a dead past: the first, an erstwhile satellite territory of the metropolis and soon, imminently, of North America; and the second, the discoverer's sponsor, having become the place that stayed behind. Paternalistic metaphors of home and a parent-child relationship, still used confidently and lovingly to refer to a now almost extinct colonial connection, belied Spain's pretensions to remain, at least imaginatively, an imperial presence. What is more, the Exhibition displays of industrial regions, such as Cataluña, and cities such as Valencia and Barcelona were marginal and even contradictory to the official perspective into which they could not be successfully integrated. As Noel Valis has stated, the world exhibition is a public space that allows for the affirmation of national identity, in fact "stages" it (635–36), and confirms the dominant values of the participating nations. The Chicago World Exhibition was not a "duel to the death" between America and Spain, as Alcalá Galiano had quite correctly pointed out. Spain had already expired as a world power without realizing it, and did nothing in Chicago to change the world's opinion that it was an antiquated nation, filled with relics.

Notes

1.   Guy Debord considers a spectacle to be "a social relation mediated by images" (12); the reference to the exhibit as narrative is from Mieke Bal.

2·   The Illinois State Library—among many other sites—still maintains a website on the Chicago World Columbian Exhibition: see *www.columbus.gl.iit.edu/* (August 6, 2010).

3.   The venue of the exhibition had been hotly contested between Spain and the United States and, then, within the United States itself for several years (New York versus Chicago), a situation that caused this anniversary celebration event to be held one year late.

4.   Manuel Serafín Pichardo was the publisher of the prestigious art and culture magazine *El Fígaro* of Havana; Raimundo Cabrera was one of Cuba's most respected intellectuals of the times and contributed to several cultural periodicals: his Chicago reports were for the newspaper *El País*. Aurelia Castillo de González, the correspondent of the Havana *Revista de Cuba*, had already traveled to Paris for the 1889 World Exhibition, also as a reporter for *El País*. Puig y Valls, a forestry engineer, was an official Spanish government delegate to the Chicago Exhibition and a correspondent for the Catalán newspaper *La Vanguardia*, in charge of the Spanish section in the Manufacturing Building; his seven-month Chicago visit was to be followed by a two-month tour of Mexico and Cuba. Eva Canel was a Spanish woman who, after a very early marriage and widowhood, lived and worked in many Spanish American countries. She was appointed by the Chamber of Commerce of Havana, where she had lived since 1891, to be its official correspondent to the Chicago Exhibition. The Infanta Eulalia has left two records of her visit to Cuba and the United States: her public *Memorias* and the almost daily personal letters written to her mother during the voyage. All translations of the Spanish texts into English are mine.

5.   Eva Canel's collection of reports to the Havana Chamber of Commerce is an excellent example of this textual strategy, and can be seen as a textual representation of a commercial inventory, including prices for a number of items.

6.   In some areas of the country, people's discontent—already strong because of the difficult political and economic situation that obtained on a national level—led to riots (see Bernabeu Albert 59).

7.   Another meaning attributed by the RAE is "desafío, duelo, pelea o batalla entre dos o más personas," which makes the "competition" concept even stronger.

8.   Notable, and a concrete example of this slow movement through time in Spanish life, is the late arrival of extended reports on the Exhibition. While "los últimos telegramas" will offer very brief news items (often no more than three or four lines), the correspondents' articles arrive at least two weeks late. J. Vilardell's long and detailed report on the inauguration of the Chicago Exhibition, dated May 2, appears in the paper on May 17. *El Correo* of Madrid complained on June 29 that it had

received "escasas noticias" about the Infanta Eulalia's inauguration of the Spanish pavilion at the Chicago World Exhibit—which had taken place on June 8—and published details facilitated, ironically, by the American press. Puig y Valls's own volumes on his voyage to America were not published until 1894 and 1895.

9.   In addition, and among others, he appeared in the Court of Honor on a very large sculptured grouping, sitting on a throne on top of a barge "heralded by Fame at the prow and guided by Father Time at the helm, . . . propelled by eight maidens representing industry and the arts" (Bolotin and Laing 61). A statue of Columbus backed by a flag, surmounted by a cross, and holding a sword was a visible reminder of the emblems of the Spanish conquest at the eastern entrance to the Administration Building; there were several other statues of the discoverer in other areas.

10.   That newspaper, under the leadership of William Hearst, will, of course, play a major role in the 1895–1898 Spain-Cuba-United States conflict. One of the characteristics of the Spanish newspapers is their reliance on sources from other countries. Thus, news from the uprising taking place in Cuba in April 1893 is reported from three areas: a Spanish government spokesman (who plays down the gravity and extension of the rebellion) and news from France and the United States. The latter is again the *New York Herald*, and, again, the comments in *La Época* warn of the *Herald*'s exaggerations and falsifications ("hay que tener en cuenta la procedencia de la noticia," May 1).

Works Cited

Alcalá Galiano, José. "La Exposición universal colombina de Chicago." *El Centenario.* Tomo II, 1892.

Appelbaum, Stanley. *The Chicago World's Fair of 1893: A Photographic Record.* New York: Dover Publications, 1980.

Bal, Mieke. *Double Exposures: The Subject of Cultural Analysis.* New York: Routledge, 1996.

Bernabeu, Albert. *Salvador: 1892: El IV Centenario del Descubrimiento de América en España.* Madrid: CSIC, 1987.

Boletín de la Cámara Oficial de Comercio: Industria y Navegación de la Habana. Feb-Oct. 1893.

Bolotin, Norman, and Christine Laing. *The World's Columbian Exposition: The Chicago World's Fair of 1893.* Urbana IL: University of Illinois Press, 2002.

Borbón, Eulalia de. *Memorias de doña Eulalia de Borbón: Infanta de España (1864–1931).* 1935. Barcelona: Ed. Juventud, 3a ed. 1950.

———. *Cartas a Isabel II, 1893 (Mi viaje a Cuba y Estados Unidos).* Barcelona: Ed. Juventud, 1949.

Bryson, Norman. *Vision and Painting: The Logic of the Gaze.* New Haven CT: Yale University Press, 1983.

Cabrera, Raimundo. *Cartas a Govín sobre la Exposición de Chicago: Impresiones de viaje*. Habana: Tipografía de "Los Niños Huérfanos," 1893.

Canel, Eva. *Boletín Oficial de la Cámara de Comercio: Industria y Navegación de La Habana*, July-October 1893.

Castillo de González, Aurelia. *Escritos*. Tomo III. La Habana: Impr. "El Siglo XX" de Aurelio Miranda, 1913.

Debord, Guy. *Society of the Spectacle*. 1967. New York: Zone Books, 2006.

El Centenario. Revista Ilustrada (Madrid) 1892.

El Correo (Madrid), May-October 1893.

El Día (Madrid), July-October 1893.

El Imparcial (Madrid), May-October 1893.

Howe Bancroft, Hubert. *The Book of the Fair*. Chicago: Bancroft Publishing, 1893. Accessed August 6, 2010. *www.columbus.gl.iit.edu/*

La Época (Madrid), April-October. 1893.

La Ilustración Artística (Madrid), September-October. 1893.

La Ilustración Española y Americana. (Madrid)*, 1893–1894.*

Pichardo, Manuel S. *La ciudad blanca: Crónicas de la Exposición Colombina de Chicago*. Havana: Bibl. de "El Fígaro," 1894.

Puig y Valls, Rafael. *Viaje a América: Estados Unidos, Exposición Universal de Chicago, México, Cuba y Puerto Rico*. 2 vols. Barcelona: Tipolitografía de Luis Tasso, 1894–1895.

Rosenblum, Robert, Maryanne Stevens, and Ann Dumas, eds. *1900: Art at the Crossroads*. London: Royal Academy of the Arts, 2000.

Tuan, Yi-Fu. *Topophilia: A Study of Environmental Perception, Attitudes, and Values*. 1974. New York: Columbia University Press, 1990.

Valis, Noel. "Women's Culture in 1893: Spanish Nationalism and the Chicago World's Fair." *Letras Peninsulares* 13:2–3 (Winter 2000–2001): 633–64.

Vallejo, Catherine. "Writing the World and the Female Self: A Cuban Woman's Perspective of the Paris (1889) and Chicago (1893) World Expositions." *Decimonónica* I,1 (Otoño 2004): 113–27.

Weimann, Jeanne Madeline. *The Fair Women*. Chicago: Academy, 1981.

Exhausted Cosmopolitanism in Zamacois's
Memorias de un vagón de ferrocarril

Robert A. Davidson

Introduction

Eduardo Zamacois Quintana's 1922 novel *Memorias de un vagón de ferro-carril* (*Memoirs of a Railway Car*) is an intriguing, if at times long-winded and ultimately forgotten, example of the way in which avant-garde and mainstream artists confronted the challenges of Spanish modernity by exploring different categories of being within the context of the social changes of the early twentieth century. *Memorias* is remarkable, though, for its unusual choice of a luxury railcar as the story's narrator. In this essay I explore the ramifications of this narrative strategy by pushing further than a simple examination of the modernization of transport systems in Spain and the concomitant integration and disjunctures with northern Europe that this entailed at both the practical and metaphorical levels.[1] Instead, I propose that through a reading of both the machine narrator's unique birth and the role of the mechanical accident—modernity's unnatural catastrophe—in its maturation, one sees how the initial exaltation of cosmopolitanism and avant-gardism eventually becomes exhausted in the *thing-that-feels*.[2] In addition to offering a new version of the "Spanish" subject, I contend that Zamacois contributes to a growing reconsideration of modernist materialist aesthetics even as latent—yet explicit—Castilian Regenerationist concerns permeate his novel. And while the author may echo the work of the much-better-known Ramón Gómez de la Serna in his contemplation of inanimate objects, his is a different type of materialist history. Zamacois's novel is a materialist autobiography in which the day-to-day felt over a lifetime is perceived from a radically different, avant-garde angle: that of the living object. From its registration as a cognitive being—a moment that stands as an instance of the cosmopolitan avant-garde "appearing to itself"—to the quiescence of aftermath and the loss of use value, the trajectory of the existence of the railcar named Cabal informs a concurrent reading of the Spanish state.

Zamacois, who was born in Cuba and left Spain to go into exile in 1939, is somewhat of a forgotten figure in Spanish letters even though his literary production was prodigious and he can be credited for founding the influential journal *El Cuento Semanal* in 1907. Both this revue and another, *Los Contemporáneos*, provided an important forum for the publication of short novels in Spain.[3] In terms of his own literary production, Soler points out that "Zamacois brought the style and the philosophy of positivism into this century, incorporating it into more contemporary tendencies" (307). One of the most interesting ways that the author did this is evident precisely in *Memorias* through his inclusion of the inanimate world in his naturalistic and positivistic-inspired renderings of modern Spain. This strategy offers a novel take on how both the social and built environments in the country were changing and adapting to the pressures of modernity and modernization.

After a typical bourgeois sojourn in Paris, Zamacois led a bohemian life in Spain before he traveled to Latin America—later returning to Europe to work as a war correspondent during World War One. In 1916, he branched out to cinema and managed to secure financing for a silent film based on the daily life of great Spanish authors, *Escritores y artistas españoles*.[4] During the period leading up to the Civil War, Zamacois was strongly leftist even as the old bohemian streak persisted in his creative work. Regardless of his political orientation, he was a highly productive writer, authoring over the course of his career twenty novels, forty-six short novels, eleven collections of short stories, four autobiographical works, two books of war reports, nine theatrical pieces, five collections of essays, five travel books and countless newspaper articles. *Memorias* offers an incredibly detailed treatment of Spanish geography and makes clear Zamacois's keen enthusiasm for trains: indeed, by the end of his career he had traveled almost all of the railways in the country (Catena 264). Published first as a sixty-page *novela corta* that appeared in five chapters, it reappeared as a substantially larger, 379-page *gran novela* that makes use of intercalated stories and even employs a theatrical script form at one point in the narrative.

The novel's most attractive and interesting features remain, however, the intriguing introduction of the first-person narrator, the moments of mechanical catastrophe, and its eventual loss of use-value, all of which offer insights into the manner in which Zamacois's *thing-that-feels* elucidates the early twentieth-century period that it quite literally observes and describes.[5]

Zamacois's early novel engages and combines two interesting trends/tropes that had been on the European scene for some time. The first, the modern narrative use of inanimate objects as subjects, can be traced back to the beginning of the eighteenth century. As Christopher Flint points out, Charles Gildon's *The Golden Spy*, which was published in 1709, was the first novel to make the so-called speaking object popular in Britain (212). Flint goes on to contend that object narration in eighteenth-century British fiction is intimately connected to the circulation of books in the public sphere, and while that particular observation is more apropos of a specific cultural context, his earlier asseveration that object narratives are invariably picaresque on account of their shifts in plot and locale, which are linked to the indiscriminate ownership inherent to postindustrial commodities, is illuminating (212). So too, is Flint's argument that while "objects seek a unified national identity . . . they are subject to a variety of dislocations that not only disrupt their storytelling but also complicate the meaning of citizenship" (212). As I will show in my analysis of *Memorias*, this invocation of the notion of citizenship is a particularly suggestive point that takes on a new valence when considered through the lens of a country such as Spain, which, by the early 1920s had experienced a prolonged existential crisis after losing its overseas empire and was on the cusp of a period of exceptional avant-garde artistic creation that would be ostensibly apolitical in nature. That works by Zamacois and Gómez de la Serna in Spanish and Lluís Capdevila i Villalonga in Catalan tapped into the vogue for animate objects at different points at the beginning of the twentieth century—predictably later than in the rest of Europe given Spain's "lag"—is indicative of the growing convergence between these questions of "pertinence," the nature of being in a modernizing society, and how aesthetics could respond to new perspectives and perceptions that avant-garde approaches to art, changes to the built environment, and an increasingly decentralized sense of nationhood offered in a complex state such as Spain.[6]

The second important element—both physical and metaphorical—that *Memorias* engages is that of the railway. The idea of constructing a railway in Spain was conceived in 1825, but as Litvak points out, this "herald of modern civilization" and "most expressive symbol of the change in the landscape of the nineteenth century" was not actually begun until 1835, first with the Barcelona–Mataró line and then with the linking of Madrid and Aranjuez (Litvak 239).[7] While its incarnation as a marker of modernity and enterprise was a significant feature of Victorian literature in an England that experienced the full force of industrialization early on in its modern period, the railway's central appearances in Spanish or Catalan fiction are less numerous. That said, they are still notable, and the locomotive also figures in works by influential authors such as Mesonero Romanos, Modesto Lafuente, Pedro Antoni de Alarcón, Clarín, Pardo Bazán, and Blasco Ibáñez. The train is particularly memorable in Pérez Galdós's *Doña Perfecta* and Narcís Oller's *La febre d'or*, in which the separate dynamics of Castile and Catalonia are apparent. As Resina observes, the train's "civilizing mission to the slumbering provinces" in the former contrasts with the latter's treatment of it as central to "the great transformations brought by the industrial revolution" (13).[8] *Memorias*, though, appeared much later than these two emblematic novels and, as a result, subscribes fully to neither of their approaches. Nor, it must be said, is it a work that employs the train simply as a "mobile setting and conflict space [to] generate certain traditional mobile plot features"—a strategy that Van Baak considers one of the machine's characteristics in the wake of its initial shocking impact on society (47). While the train in *Memorias* does "motivate movement and the accidental meeting between people" (47), the novel's peculiar narrative stance gives these characteristics a bridging quality between the social mechanics of the space of the train and its materialist dimension, which is patent in the very animation of the object itself. That the object narrator undergoes a class-based transformation from upper to lower over the course of its own life is noteworthy in that it points to both the natural exhaustion of any avant-garde object or movement and Spain's own gradual modernization and gentrification.

Before proceeding to a close reading of the novel, it is necessary to locate the notion of cosmopolitanism in its Spanish context. In his book on *novecentismo*, Guillermo Díaz-Plaja offers an excellent overview of the way in which the concept of cosmopolitanism entered Spanish letters and then found its way into the work of various Spanish intellectuals at the beginning of the twentieth century. He begins by observing the influence of Rubén Darío and French novelists Paul Morand and Maurice Dekobra on Spanish literature before noting that the *novela corta* also played an important role in the reception of this new phenomenon, which was linked to both urban modernization and a concomitant internationalism. While Díaz-Plaja identifies specific spatial and cultural changes such as chaotic streets, new hotels, and the arrival of the tango and jazz (38) that mark what one might call a "classic" cosmopolitanism, he also acknowledges a more transcendent dimension to the concept by pointing to the way that the dynamic comes into tension with a nationalism "confined by borders" (43).[9] This more expansive experience of space, locality, and identity formation is the type of burgeoning modern (and supermodern) cosmopolitanism that I see at play in *Memorias*—one that is ultimately defeated.

Birth

Memorias begins with a description of the narrator train car's birth and an exclamation at its good fortune to have come into existence as a member of the first class variety. This upper class or aristocratic fact is important in that it corresponds to and informs the type of cosmopolitanism that the author will articulate throughout his novel and adds an extra charge to the object's eventual consignment to third class status before its use value is totally lost. That is to say, in keeping with Timothy Brennan's understanding of the cosmopolitan subject as a "non-exilic aesthete" (37), the material and spatial luxury afforded by the protagonist, as well as the effect that its presence has vis-à-vis the other animate train cars, creates a dynamic in which class difference is brought into relief while firmly placing the experience of internationalism in a sphere that is defined by material production and capitalism. This condition stands opposed to a conception of travel as displacement and of the "international" as a collective sense of solidarity—such as was the case with the anarchist and socialist groups that were growing in strength in Spain during the pre-Primo de Rivera period.[10]

Memorias's pragmatic approach to nationalism, which at first seems to inoculate the work against its own strong "Regenerationist" characteristics that are patent in the text's obsession with the land, comes to the fore immediately.[11] In the words of the animate train car named Cabal:

> Procedo de Francia, de los famosos talleres de Saint-Denis, pero fui construido con materiales oriundos de diferentes países, y esta especie de "protoplasma internacional"—llamémoslo así—que me integra, unido a mi vivir errático, me vedan sentir fuertemente ese "amor a la patria," en cuyo nombre la ciega humanidad se ha despedazado tantas veces. (5–6)

> (I hail from France, from the famous workshops of Saint-Denis, but I was constructed with materials hailing from different countries and this along with a species of "international protoplasm"—let's call it that—that holds me together, united to my erratic living, prohibits me from feeling strongly that "love of country" in whose name blind humanity has torn itself apart so many times.)

Inherent in this self-analysis is an awareness not only of the international-ization of manufacturing—especially luxury manufacturing—vis-à-vis the nar-rator's own subjectivity—literally, its base materiality—but also a moralizing perspective that stems supposedly from the "protoplasm" and errancy that lift it above the blinding effects of patriotic love.

This notion of universal "protoplasm" is highly suggestive not only on ac-count of the growing influence in Spain of the international avant-gardes at the time of the publication of *Memorias* but also because the specific context of its invocation in the novel revolves around the extraordinary animation of the in-animate. The common definition of protoplasm as a "primitive or primary form of something; a primordial substance" is germane to this extraordinary situa-tion in the sense that, in the beginning, the train car narrator represents a new, cosmopolitan Spanish subject, an avant-garde being that is intrinsically *supra-national* and intimately aware of its own materialism ("Protoplasm"). Cabal's existence—and more importantly, its own take on being—not only stand as an innovative contribution to the new aesthetics of representation but also ratify in a fresh way one of the key ideas promoted by the more progressive Regenera-tionist intellectuals: the need to "Europeanize" Spain.

What is more, as part of a train that embodies coordinated motion and interconnectivity *on the move*, the railcar points to a link between this inter-national "protoplasm" and what French anthropologist and critic Marc Augé has identified as the concept of the non-place. That is, as opposed to relational spaces—places that may be considered "historical and concerned with iden-tity" (Augé 77–78)—the train-in-motion corresponds to a fledgling new space of supermodern pertinence, one that in the early part of the twentieth century was beginning to expose the individual's consciousness to "new experiences and ordeals of solitude" (93) as a measure of "social trajectories" (94). The fact that in the end, the object narrator comes to accept its quiescence as a rail-car-turned-house at the intersection of the main lines to Barcelona, Sevilla and Valencia demonstrates how the avant-garde and supermodern impulse literally become exhausted—with the consequence being a plain and metaphoric root-edness in which dwelling trumps any emptying of (local/national) conscious-ness inherent in the non-place, thus ultimately undermining the cosmopolitan promise of the early part of the book.

Total consciousness and a sense of identity are not immediate for the nascent machine at the beginning of the novel, though, and in the prolonged "birthing/becoming" phase in which the reader learns that the car had to be transported from France to Irún because of the countries' differing rail gauges, Zamacois points to material hybridity as a metaphor for a practical cosmopolitanism that is both patently physical due to the machine's varied components and essential as regards the sense of pertinence that one instinctively feels. As the railcar explains: "Soy, de consiguiente español, puesto que 'nací' en España, pero de origen francés" (9) (I am, as a result, Spanish, since I "was born" in Spain, but of French origin). Only later, though, when the box had been mounted on the wheels and axels, does the "I" of being finally truly manifest. Note, especially, how the narrator highlights the finitude of the individual vis-à-vis the collective: "Lentamente, con la suavidad de un lento despertar, fui comprendiéndome separado de los cuerpos que me rodeaban y distinto a ellos" (9) (Slowly, with the smoothness of a slow awakening, I came to see myself as separate from the bodies that surrounded me and distinct from them).

Cabal undergoes various transformations during the course of its life, but its birth is particularly difficult. The narrator likens the workmen who construct it to executioners and torturers. Growing pains here, though, contribute to a greater awareness of the world—innate experience through the accumulation of material presence and diversification. Parts are added, and the nascent being's cognition improves. Obviously, this uncomfortable process stands as a none-too-subtle simile for the growing pains of the Spanish state, and the debt owed to Northern European influences for the country's own enlightenment. The reference to ideas is explicit: "Yo era como un cerebro que va llenándose de ideas" (11) (I was like a brain that was filling itself up with ideas). While acknowledging this intellectual element, Cabal's descriptions of its birth also invoke the scientific discourse that was in vogue in the early 1920s. Take, for instance this recognition of the contribution of the workers themselves: "Cada uno de aquellos obreros me daba—sin él saberlo—una partícula de su alma; estos elementos inteligentes y vibrantes, llenos de radioactividad, se acoplaban unos a otros y así mi espíritu, en estado de nebulosa todavía, iba surgiendo de la síntesis de todos ellos" (11) (Each one of those workers was giving me—unbeknownst to him—a particulate of his soul; these intelligent and vibrant elements, full of radioactivity, joined themselves together and thus my spirit, still in a nebulous state, began to emerge from the synthesis of all of them). In this way, one sees how Cabal is the sum of both the high-end components that comprise its physicality and the daily practice and specialized skills of the workers who construct it.

When finally complete and self-aware in the sense that all of its constituent parts are actuated, the railcar *feels*. At first the sensation is happiness, but it quickly changes to fear, which manifests in the eternal inquiries "Why?" and "What for?" (13). The answers to these existential questions come from the simple act of rudimentary locomotion. With its assembly complete, the workers push Cabal out of the shed. The act of moving has a tremendous effect, for not only does it realize that it will serve as the basis for its future mission in life—to transport people—but it provides the moment of differentiation that solidifies the essence of the cosmopolitan existence that the first class railcar embodies:

> La sensación de moverme, que todavía ignoraba, me produjo pasmo y regocijo delirantes. Hasta entonces yo había estado quieto, y ahora me movía. Aprecié mi fuerza. El movimiento! . . . ¿Qué es el movimiento? . . . Yo era, en aquellos instantes, el mismo que había sido; y, sin embargo, era "otro." Sin cambiar, tenía lo que nunca había tenido, y "siendo" con todo el imperio de un presente de indicativo, "me iba." (13)

> (The sensation of moving, which was still unknown to me, produced in me a delirious state of surprise and exhilaration. Until then I had been still, and now I was moving. I revelled in my strength. Movement! What is movement? I was, in those moments, the same as I had been; and yet, I was "another." Without changing, I had what I had never had before and "being" with all the imperiousness of a present of the indicative, "I was on my way.")

The movement that it will be afforded, though, is not unlimited, and therein lies the catch and the key to what will ultimately defeat the cosmopolitan impulse in this instance: the railcar is connected to a radial network that, while permitting travel within the Spanish state, reinforces Madrid's centrality, in turn ensuring an experience of the Spanish landscape that continually passes through Castilian lands. Thus, the cosmopolitanism inherent in the individual difference that Cabal displays exists in perpetual tension to a very precise national/collective referent, binding the errant nature of the subject in motion to a fixed set of possible trajectories—all while enabling it to see the landscape and populace through "new" eyes.

Life

The beginning of chapter 2 of *Memorias* addresses the inquiry—common to stories involving animate objects—that would have been on the lips of many a reader: "¿Cómo?—exclamarán los hombres—¿Es posible que los objetos que estimamos inanimados gocen de una vida consciente y razonadora, análoga a la nuestra?" (15) (How—men will exclaim—is it possible that objects that we adjudge to be inanimate enjoy a conscious and reasoning life analogous to our own?). The train car's answer invokes initially a "one energy" type of force similar—one assumes—to the protoplasm from which it sprang and that evidently encompasses all things: animate or not. This is merely a prelude, though, to a much more intriguing explanation. The railcar goes on to invoke the wonders of modern technology, such as the phonograph and the projector camera, as it reveals that the lives of its passengers have rubbed off on it. Just as a glove takes on human traits from being in such intimate contact with the hand, the car has retained sensibilities from those who constructed it as well as the emotions and ideas that spring forth from its sensory perceptions. In short, the train car is now describing itself as a *thing-that-feels*, a move that brings to bear an affective element even as it purports to deny adherence to any form of national soul searching. In this way, the chauvinism of the national, which is unambiguous in the irregularly gauged rail system that delimits its trajectory, is at least partly drained and replaced by the greater good of a cosmopolitanism that respects origins but leaves the door open to experience as a modifier. Zamacois's pragmatic use of a living object rather than a conventional subject as a narrative "vehicle" affords him a unique avenue not only for his observations on Spain but on the nature and nurture debates inherent to positivism and naturalism that informed Spanish thought in the second half of the nineteenth century and the first decades of the twentieth.

That said, however, Zamacois partly undoes this framework later in the novel in a way that I see as reinforcing my argument regarding the exhaustion of the avant-garde nature of the animate object in *Memorias*. When, in the later stages of the diegesis (and its own life), Cabal returns to its notion that humans transmit or communicate intelligence, will, memory, and physical sensation to the objects that accompany them, the effect is damaging to the earlier idealism regarding a supra-national cosmopolitan subjectivity. In explaining that a sculptor cannot help but transmit the "heat of his soul" to a piece of marble, the narrator valorizes the passing of time and the power of the continual effects of the everyday above the inaugural moment of creation or hybridity (300). The invocation of "alma" or "soul" is both redolent of the same rootedness that the Castilian intelligentsia sought in the wake of the Disaster of 1898 and, when connected to human "warmth," points to the passage of time and accumulation as key elements:

> El hombre divide su tesoro vital en dos partes, de las cuales se reserva la mayor, y la otra, que se le escapa por los ojos y por la punta de los dedos y con el calor de su propio cuerpo, es la que reparte y difunde alrededor suyo y queda adherida a las cosas. He ahí el por qué los trajes recién salidos de las sastrerías son "fríos," por

bien confeccionados que estén; y por qué las novellas autobiográficas, por sencillo que sea su argumento, apasionan más. (300)

(Man divides his vital treasure in two parts, of which he keeps the main one while the other, which escapes from the eyes and fingertips and the heat of his own body, is what imbues and infuses his surroundings and stays stuck to things. This is why suits that have just left the tailor shop are "cold" no matter how well made they are, and why autobiographic novels, no matter how simple their plot, inspire much more passion.)

The inclusion of autobiography in this soul-imbuing process further trumps the moments of invention or inspiration that come out of the avant-garde protoplasm by privileging the accumulation of experience within a recognized and codified continuum—the opposite of the avant-garde need to break with established parameters and to live or exist in a perpetual present.

Death

Intriguingly, it is the crash (or accident) that breaks the cosmopolitan ideal in the novel in that through demolition and reconstruction the object's awareness of itself leads to resignation as it tries to come to terms with its eventual "death." So, even if the birth of the object in the rail yards of France and Spain imbues it with subjectivity, thus bringing it into a continuum of life similar to that of humans, the accidents that occur to it later in the book cannot help but reveal its materiality in a way that exposes the object's finitude as a thing, thus propelling it towards obsolescence: the moment when use value is drained and base form of the material is exposed. The narrator understands death in both the human and mechanical contexts given that on one occasion it had split the skull of a suicide victim with its wheels and, at various points throughout its life, observed the old, dead train cars shunted off on railway sidings—still intact formally but consigned to the part of the circuit where distribution and movement had been curtailed. The exact terms of demise, though, are still couched in a way that is easily interpreted as pertaining to the newly emerging cosmopolitan worldview: "Morir es no moverse más" (141) (To die is to no longer move). Movement, in these more expansive terms, must refer to international travel, technology-fed progress through industry, and even to the foot-tapping and dancing inspired by the rhythms of the jazz bands that had stormed Europe during the First World War and which, by the early 1920s in Spain, were becoming increasingly popular in both Barcelona and Madrid. With social codes changing in response to the transculturation of the Roaring Twenties, movement and movements were indeed markers of "life" and action: to cease to travel, to stop an assembly line or to refuse to dance would be to metaphorically expire before exploiting one's potential. And while the concept of "the crash" may be seen as inherently avant-garde in and of itself—as the momentum of the new overtaking the stagnant body ahead of it, or as something different hurtling headlong from another direction—I propose that the anxiety it produces here is such that it places the cosmopolitan dynamic in stasis, precipitating in this case a return to the safety of the known by both providing perspective on mortality and contributing to the accumulation of experience in a familiar context.

There are two principal train wrecks that happen over the course of the narrator's service, and in the aftermath of both, changes occur that add to one's understanding of cosmopolitanism in the novel. I suggest that the release of the narrative, vital, and metaphoric tensions patent in the impacts and their consequences represent the key moment in the exhaustion of the cosmopolitan in the novel. The momentum of the new literally slows under the weight of Regenerationist aesthetics. For example, in the first case, the damage the railcar sustains leads to the break-up of its original train and the placing of the narrator in a much slower one: a mail route to Galicia during the long hours of which it does not speak but rather observes the geographic space around it, thus providing an opportunity to comment on disparities in urban and rural Spain. As part of the convalescence leading up to this important change of pace and function, the narrator becomes more aware of the influence of its organic parts: like someone with arthritic joints, the wood pieces that make up its luxurious interior have started to warp and expand, and this, combined with a new anxiety of aging, changes the narrator's outlook on life.

The second wreck is the one that brings about the car's ultimate removal from service. Condemned to the "incurable" yard, the long wait begins for rust and the elements to consume it and its forlorn colleagues. At this point, when weeds and plants start to invade and claim the car as its own, the door opens to a potential alternative: that this moment stands as the integration of the land and the cosmopolitan that the narrator initially represented. However, this possibility is undone by the fact that by this point in the narrative, the car is no longer what it once was. Earlier in the text, economic pressures and the basic passing of time and its own degradation had led to Cabal's downgrading and transformation into a third class railcar: "Yo era como un prócer arruinado, como un 'gran señor' que, ganado por el ambiente democrático de su época y para seguir viviendo, hubiese aceptado un empleo" (387) (I was like a magnate, like a "great man" who, defeated by the democratic nature of his time and in order to keep living, had accepted a job). In this way, deterioration is shown to be inevitable in this environment, and the reading that presents itself is that the cosmopolitan avant-garde object is not sustainable within this particular context. Of course, the counter-argument would be that this is part of the economy of all things and that Cabal would simply have been replaced by a newer luxury car. This line of thinking is valid but would obviate the important fact that the being in question here is an animate object, a new subject in the Spanish state that incarnated the cosmopolitan and then lost that charge through its acquired experience as a *thing-that-feels*. Put simply, even as a witness to life from a radically new perspective, ultimately, it could not resist the centrifugal pull of the local.

Simmel's work on the ruin is helpful to explain the exhaustion of cosmopolitanism here. As Karen Lang astutely points out, in his short essay on the subject in *Philosophische Kultur* (1911), Simmel notes how the aesthetic experience of ruins leads to an imaginative overcoming of the alienation of modern life (423). For Simmel, the ruin rests on the opposition between human *Geist* and the processes of *Natur*. While architecture represents "the most sublime victory of the human spirit over nature," in the ruin this relationship is reversed, thereby demonstrating that the "legitimate claim" of *Natur* over *Geist* was "never entirely extinguished" (qtd. in Lang 423). In this sense, a work of architecture destroyed by humankind "lacks the specific charm of the ruin," for only the latter yields the "opposition between human labor and the effects of nature" that is the ruin's defining feature (423). In *Memorias* Cabal's passing into ruin is a product of the modern mechanical catastrophe—the arbitrary event that belies modernity's penchant for control—combined with the power of Nature to claim that which is static. When animals invade the abandoned car and plants begin to incorporate it into the landscape, the lack of momentum signals the death knell for what was once a vital machine. That its post-accident trajectory was already leading it closer and closer to the "local" only reinforces how the cosmopolitan element is emptied out of it and makes what happens next in the story all the more predictable and symbolic.

Cabal does not disappear into the natural landscape. As per Simmel, the aesthetic appreciation of ruin saves the car from an eventual capitulation to *Natur*. Bought by a retired railway director who recognizes its potential as a dwelling, it is converted into a house that then can resist the pull of decay even as it gives itself fully to obsolescence vis-a-vis its original use value. Although it no longer moves and is thus "dead," it lives on in its situatedness neverthe-less and in this way presents a novel twist to Heidegger's key precepts in *Poetry, Language, Thought*: "1. What is it to dwell? 2. How does building belong to dwelling?" (qtd in Leach 100). As a train car-turned-abode the structure/subject now "gathers" to itself the so-called "fourfold" (earth, sky, divinities and mortals) in the Heideggerean sense and, in so doing, creates a *site*. This gathering—which makes for a location—is the exact opposite of the type of literal gathering that the train car participated in as part of the cosmopolitan social apparatus—that is, as a nascent non-place that collects and transports Brennan's non-exilic aesthetes. The intriguing twist in this specific case is, of course, the fact that the building itself is the sentient subject of the experience of dwelling; in its last incarnation it both provides for the "letting dwell" that Heidegger sees at the heart of the nature of building and, as a result of its own consciousness, it dwells as well (108).

The site that is created for the train car's dwelling is intensely symbolic given its physical location at the axis of the radial system that governs Spain's rail network. As a result, the formerly cosmopolitan subject is now embedded at the literal and metaphoric center of the state that it had once traversed. The rootedness in this dwelling is appealing to it: "El hallarme no suspendido en el aire, como antes, sino bien pegado a la tierra, me infundía una ignorada y confortadora impresión de quietud, de estabilidad: me sentía más a plomo y dueño de mí mismo, cual si mi personalidad hubiese crecido" (419) (Finding myself not suspended in the air like before but rather stuck to the ground infused me with a hitherto unknown and comforting sense of tranquility, of stability: I felt more like lead and master of myself, as if my personality had grown). Had Cabal been allowed to die its "natural" death—even after having passed through the reduction in class and status that came with decay—the initial avant-garde coding of the subject would still have kept some of its charge. To rescue it from obsolescence and ruin and deliver it once again to use value as a bourgeois object redolent of central Castilian *Geist* and symbolic dwelling, though, gentrifies the material and social difference that it had previously represented in a way that exhausts completely its former cosmopolitan ideal.

While Zamacois's *gran novela* may have had relative success at the time of its appearance, it has since vanished into the critical ether. This is a pity because his treatment of the material world and his contribution to the compelling phenomenon of granting subjectivity to objects in Spanish letters make him a prime candidate for reappraisal in the context of contemporary cultural studies. That he manages to straddle the aesthetic and sociological concerns of two very different generations, not so much in form but in content, is further reason to rescue him from the archive.

Notes

1. The different rail gauge used in Spain as compared to that of France is the most striking example of this disconnect.
2. Given that no mention of gender is made in the novel and that an important part of my analysis revolves around the animation of an inanimate object, I use the personal pronoun "it" throughout.
3. For more on collections of short novels and the diffusion of literature in the early 1920s in Spain, see Mainer (71–76).
4. For more on this film, see Jiménez León. Additional information regarding Zamacois's life can be found in Catena (260–63).
5. I borrow the term *thing-that-feels* from Mario Perniola. Early on in his extraordinary work *The Sex Appeal of the Inorganic*, Perniola describes it this way: "Feeling implies the union between body and spirit, mind and machine. A thinking thing can also not have a body, but a sentient thing has to have it. Who feels therefore is not God but the I, it feels because it thinks, because feeling, understood in its self-evident subjectivity, is none other than thinking" (7). The railcar's body, initially instilled by the spirit of cosmopolitanism and avant-garde potential, transforms as it acquires experience and deteriorates.
6. Gómez de la Serna's *El Rastro*, *El novelista*, and the short story *Las dramáticas chimeneas* offer examples of the author's fascination for objects and his predilection for animating them. For an analysis of these works as regards Nancy's concept of *being-in-common*, see Davidson, "Animate Objects." Capdevila i Villalonga's Catalan-language *Memòries de un llit de matrimoni* is another example of a book that is narrated by an animate object (in this case, a double bed). For an examination of this narrative strategy in the Catalan context and as regards the bourgeoisie's relationship with the countryside and the experience of the Miguel Primo de Rivera dictatorship, see Davidson, "The De-Natured Object."
7. For more on the history of railway development in Spain see Litvak (239). While much has been written on the way that railways changed people's concepts of space and time, Litvak's observations in relation to the station are insightful: "La estación interesa además como espacio *per se*, en primer lugar por ser el primer espacio de la nueva civilización, y, sobre todo, porque por sus materiales cuestionó a la arquitectura tradicional y sus inevitables contrastes de luz y sombra" (239) (The station is interesting also as a space *per se*, in the first place for being the first space of the new civilization and, above all, because it put into question traditional architecture and its inevitable contrasts of light and dark).
8. See also *Fortunata y Jacinta* and *Rosalía* by Pérez Galdós.

9. As regards the major thinkers of the time, the critic interprets d'Ors's rejection of the sentimental *nación* in favor of the intellectual idea of *imperio* to be related to a larger idea of cosmopolitanism—even though d'Ors rejected the word on account of its invocation of Europeanism. Ortega y Gasset, according to Díaz-Plaja, sees *internacionalismo* and *cosmopolitismo* as two separate phenomena, with the first relating to the political sphere (the League of Nations) and the second pertaining to the select intellectual minority. Importantly, the nature of cosmopolitanism at the time does not preclude politicization; the "national" or "local" is part of the cosmopolitan equation. Miguel de Unamuno's interpretation of the term as the ultra-local touches on this facet but is at once resistant to syncretism and seemingly rooted in the rural; according to Díaz-Plaja, Unamuno saw "the cosmopolitan" as a surreptitious way of introducing French culture, something the philosopher rejected at that point.

10. Miguel Primo de Rivera was the military dictator of Spain from 1923 to January of 1930, when he fled the country in the face of growing opposition.

11. "Regeneracionismo" is the term used to describe the trend in Castilian letters of the late nineteenth and early twentieth centuries of looking inwards towards Spain's geographic and metaphoric heartland for a sense of Spanishness and national identity in the wake of the loss of the Spanish empire's few remaining colonies and the imperial identity/history that they both represented and fuelled.

Works Cited

Augé, Marc. *Non-places: Introduction to an Anthropology of Supermodernity.* Trans. John Howe. London: Verso, 1995.

Brennan, Timothy. *At Home in the World: Cosmopolitanism Now.* Cambridge, MA: Harvard University Press, 1997.

Capdevila, Lluís. *Memòries d'un llit de matrimoni.* Barcelona: Collecció Balagué, 1930.

Catena, Elena. "Memorias de un vagón de ferrocarril, de Eduardo Zamacois." *Compás de Letras.* 7 (1995): 255–64.

Davidson, Robert. "Animate Objects: Being, Obsolescence and the Limits of Citizenship in Ramón Gómez de la Serna." *MLN.* 123 (2008): 274–93.

———. "The De-Natured Object in Lluís Capdevila's *Memòries d'un llit de matrimoni.*" *Anales de Literatura Contempóranea Española.* 35.1 (2010): 177–95.

Díaz-Plaja, Guillem. *Estructura y sentido del Novecentismo español.* Madrid: Alianza, 1975.

Flint, Christopher. "Speaking Objects: The Circulation of Stories in Eighteenth-Century Prose Fiction." *PMLA* 113.2 (1998): 212–26.

Gómez de la Serna, Ramón. "Las dramáticas chimeneas." *Obras completas.* Ed. Ioana Zlotescu and Juan Pedro Gabino. Vol. IV. Barcelona: Galaxia Gutenberg, 1997.

———. *El novelista.* Madrid: Espasa Calpe, 2005.

————. *El Rastro*. Madrid: Espasa Calpe, 1998.

Heidegger, Martin. "Building, Dwelling, Thinking." *Rethinking Architecture: A Reader in Cultural Theory*. Ed. Neil Leach. London and New York: Routledge, 1997. 100–109.

Jiménez León, Marcelino. "Las primeras aventura cinematográfica de Eduardo Zamacois." *Actas del XIII Congreso de la Asociación Internacional de Hispanistas. Vol. IV: Historia y sociedad comparada y otros studios*. Ed. Florencio Sevilla and Carlos Alvar. Madrid: Castalia, 2000. 373–82.

Lang, Karen. "The Dialectics of Decay: Rereading the Kantian Subject." *The Art Bulletin*. 79.3 (1997): 413–39.

Litvak, Lily. "'Abolición del tiempo y el espacio.' El viaje en tren a fines del siglo XIX." *Compás de Letras* 7 (1995): 239–53.

Mainer, José-Carlos. *La edad de plata (1902–1939): Ensayo de interpretación de un proceso cultural*. Madrid: Cátedra, 1983.

Perniola, Mario. *The Sex Appeal of the Inorganic*. Trans. Massimo Verdicchio. London and New York: Continuum, 2004.

"Protoplasm." *Oxford English Dictionary*. *www.dictionary.oed.com/* Accessed 14 October 2009.

Resina, Joan Ramon. *Barcelona's Vocation of Modernity*. Stanford: Stanford University Press, 2008.

Soler, Janice J. "Eduardo Zamacois, a Forgotten Novelist." *Kentucky Romance Quarterly* 29.3 (1982): 307–22.

Van Baak, Joost. "Where did Venička Live? Some Observations on the World of V. Erofeev's Poema Moskva-Petuški." *Russian Literature* LIV (2003): 43–65.

Zamacois, Eduardo. *Memorias de un vagón de ferrocarril*. Madrid: Ediciones del Viento, 2008.

PART III
National Panoramas

◆ 10

Cultural Landscapes:
Luis Cernuda's Exiled Poetry

Goretti Ramírez

(Translated by María José Giménez)

The culture of the Spanish Republican exile during Franco's dictatorship (1939–1975) is still far from being clearly understood. Although advances in archival research already enable a description of its *fields of cultural production*, its ideological processes remain obscure. The culture of the Republican exile encompasses a geographically dispersed community of intellectuals with divergent positions, who were representatives of all the movements that had converged during the Republic (1931–1936). Despite such a varied orography, the critical avenues explored thus far have been rather uniform. In particular, exile cultural production has been understood as a discourse on identity: that is, as a manifestation or construction of one of the multiple modalities of the Republican identity, such as woman, Catalan, Basque, or participant in a political or philosophical movement, among others.

In this study, I have gathered critical findings of the existing bibliography to propose another perspective, starting from two interrelated hermeneutic considerations. First, although culture is a concept of elusive definition, it can generally be considered as an "active construction of meaning, or the processes and codes through which meanings are constructed, negotiated, conveyed, and understood" (King 138). A fruitful way to approach culture in the Spanish Republican exile would be not as a product, but rather as a process characterized by irreducible ideological aporias and contradictions derived mainly from the constant appropriation and redefinition of cultural signs of the Franco period into a divided, conflictive modernity. Rather than defining modernity, we can describe the tension among various ideologies within modernity itself. Secondly, rather than interpreting it only as a discourse on identity, the Spanish Republican exile can be placed within the framework of representations of space in modernity and interpreted as a spatial category. In this context, the representation of natural and architectural space becomes the sphere in which the Republican exile complicates (affirms and negates at the same time) the cultural and political hegemony of Franco's Spain.

Luis Cernuda's poetry of exile offers representations of three types of landscapes in nature and the architectural world: urban landscapes, mostly in Anglo-Saxon settings (parks, cemeteries, and city ruins); Edenic landscapes, mostly in Hispanic settings (gardens, other cemeteries, and other ruins); and Spanish historic landscapes (Castile and the Escorial palace complex). Although the existing bibliography emerges from a variety of approaches, his poems have been interpreted largely as the tension Cernuda (1902–1963) felt between the Edenic spaces of his memories of Spain and the spaces of exile. However, if these same poems are inscribed within the theoretical framework of cultural landscape studies, it can be argued that the representation of landscape in Cernuda's poetry of exile shows a paradoxical coincidence with the ideological principles used by the culture of Franco's Spain (for example, José Ortiz Echagüe's photographic pictorialism), specifically in the attempt to restore the Spanish imperial and spiritual past in reaction to the cultural processes of Anglo-Saxon capitalism. From this perspective, the representation of the landscape of the Republican exile provides a foundation for considering the ideological framework of Spanish modernity as a struggle for the definition of cultural signs.

Landscape and Ideology

Beginning with the publication of *The Country and The City* (1973) by Raymond Williams and John B. Jackson's proposal of the term "cultural landscape," and continuing with the conception of landscape not as a static text but as a process in the formation of identities (Mitchell 1), the field of cultural landscape studies has developed revealing tools for the study of both rural and urban spaces. According to these conceptual parameters, landscape is a sign drawn by man in nature and, as such, a cultural product subject to readings and interpretations. Of particular interest is the dialectical relationship between landscape and history as described by Fred Inglis, among others: landscape is "the most solid appearance in which a history can declare itself" (489). Alan R. H. Baker elucidates the relationships between landscape and ideology:

> Ideologies, moreover, contain within themselves a contradiction: they seek permanence and continuity but argue for change. . . . "Actual" landscapes are constructions, 'ideal' landscapes are conceptualizations. At the same time, "actual" landscapes are moulded by ideologies and ideologies are themselves fashioned by "actual" landscapes: the relationship is reciprocal, the product is a dialectical landscape which is a resolution of nature and culture, of practice and philosophy, of reason and imagination, or "real" and "symbolic." (6–7)

From this perspective, landscape and ideology are interdependent factors in the study of culture. The term "dialectical landscape" (Baker 7) enables us to introduce historical, political, and cultural processes into the interpretation of landscape beyond its aesthetic disposition: that is, it enables us to introduce time into space. It is, thus, possible to discover and enunciate the systems of signification and domination that are hidden in a landscape (Baker 4). According to Baker, there are three characteristics of ideology that are relevant in landscape creation and interpretation: "the connections of an ideology to a quest for *order*, to an assertion of *authority*, and to a project of *totalisation*" (4). He describes them as follows:

> The function of ideology in this regard is to furnish assurance; it does so, paradoxically, either by highlighting perfect patterns in the present or by promising utopian forms in the future. . . . Ideologies compete with each other, so a given society and landscape may have several different systems of symbolic representations existing within it simultaneously and antagonistically. . . . Ideologies create, unintentionally as well as deliberately, a landscape as a system of signification, expressive of authority. . . . One way in which an ideology seeks to achieve its hegemony is through total conquest, be it of the physical and/or the human environment; another way is through total withdrawal, so that the ideology's essence can be isolated from the polluting influences of its existing environment. (4–6)

The interdependence between landscape and ideology can exist in any period (for instance, it has been applied repeatedly to the Renaissance Anglo-Saxon landscape) and in any political regime (whether governed by democratic codes or not). In any case, Baker's proposal can be especially fruitful in the critical consideration of the harsh dictatorial regimes that marked the twentieth century in Europe. In this light, the struggle for ideological hegemony during the Franco years can also be seen as a struggle for order, authority, and a totalitarian meaning of landscape:

> Spanish nationalism, as an expression of the ideology of the Spanish political right, was deeply rooted in a specifically agrarian notion of Spain. However . . . a state holding company, the Instituto Nacional de Industria (INI), was created with public funds, with the specific task of initiating industrial projects to boost national production in strategic sectors alongside the action of private capital. . . . According to a future INI president . . . "Traditional juridical relations between the elements of production have not been altered." (Richards 175)

Reading the landscape of the Franco years as a cultural product offers a privileged portrait of the dialectic described by Baker through which the effect of ideology on the landscape always uncovers a tension between change and permanence (Baker 6). This tension was particularly intense in the transition between autocracy and capitalism. The *desarrollista* (developmentalist) effort appears as a frustrated, paradoxical project of making landscape and ideology coincide, since a transformation of the landscape to its fullest extent would have entailed, as well, the dissolution of Franco's economy into democracy and the much-feared capitalist system. Indeed, the gap between landscape and ideology was largely due to the fact that an economic shift toward modern capitalism was initiated within the non-modern political structures of a dictatorship. A great number of landscape representations during these years reflect these unresolved ideological tensions. For example, the defense of Spain's spiritual and rural values against European and North American materialism contrasted with images in the NODO of dams and agricultural works inaugurated by Franco, the new profile being adopted by the urban and industrial periphery to accommodate the peasant exodus and rapid changes in coastal landscapes to accommodate tourism.

In the twentieth century, the history of cultural landscape evolved in close connection with the development of new technologies of perception, such as photography (Cosgrove 2003: 250–57), an art form that was linked to the representation of national landscape from its very beginnings. As Taylor highlights for the case of England, although by the late 1800s photography had already ceased to be considered a medium that faithfully reproduced the world, there were still groups of photographers eager to document all landscapes as a way to preserve national treasures (185–88). The turn of the century gave rise to photographic pictorialism, probably the last connection to Romantic landscape paintings.

In Spain, this type of landscape documentation emerged in parallel with patriotism, which arose in reaction to the fall of the Spanish empire (López Mondéjar 31). Spanish photographic pictorialism in landscape representation developed from the 1920s to the 1950s. Although it coincided for a few years with the historical avant-garde and the Republic, it soon evolved into a Romantic photography of national landscapes and became the most native Spanish medium of the Franco years (Fontanella 171). Its most representative figure was José Ortiz Echagüe (1886–1980), who published four volumes of photography with several re-prints and editions: *España: tipos y trajes* (Spain: Types and Costumes) (1933), *España: Pueblos y paisajes* (Spain: Villages and Landscapes) (1938), *España mística* (Mystical Spain) (1943), and *España: Castillos y alcázares* (Spain: Castles and Citadels) (1956). Reviews of his work were connected to his nationalist project (Mendelson 119), and prologues were signed by key figures of the time.

In parallel with Franco's Spain, the Spain of the Republican exile was producing its own cultural representations of landscape. In this context, Luis Cernuda's poetry during his years of exile (1937–1963) stands out, contemporaneous with José Ortiz Echagüe's books of photography (1933–1956, with repeated editions until 1971). As is characteristic of exiled culture, this poetic corpus of seven books was dislocated due to its creator's biographical circumstances: *Las nubes* (The Clouds) (England and Scotland, 1937–1940), *Como quien espera el alba* (Like Someone Waiting for the Dawn) (England and Scotland, 1941–1944), *Vivir sin estar viviendo* (Living Without Being Alive) (England and United States, 1944–1949), *Variaciones sobre un tema mexicano* (Variations on a Mexican Theme) (Mexico, 1952), *Con las horas contadas* (With Time Running Out) (United States and Mexico, 1950–1956), *Desolación de la Quimera* (The Disconsolate Chimera) (Mexico, 1956–1962), and *Ocnos* (Ocnos) (England, Scotland, United States and Mexico, 1940–1963). The entire collection offers an important casuistry of representations of spaces found in the natural and the architectural worlds: cemeteries, gardens, cathedrals, parks, El Escorial, ruins, northern lands, streets, coasts, trees by the river, roads, Sansueña, backyards, orchards, greenhouses, churches, and houses, among others. Its geographic referents are located in Spain and the three countries where Cernuda spent the exile: the United Kingdom, the United States, and Mexico.

In spite of their variety, the landscapes he represented during thirty years of poetry can be understood as three interwoven groups that present a cross-section of the entire trajectory of Cernuda's exile: urban landscapes mostly in Anglo-Saxon settings, Edenic landscapes mostly in Hispanic settings, and

Spanish historic landscapes. Although based on a variety of critical approaches, the existing bibliography interprets the landscapes in these poems mainly as the unresolved tension Luis Cernuda suffered between the desolation of his present in exile and the Edenic spaces of his memory in Spain. As such, the cultural production of Cernuda's exile is analyzed as a problem of discourse on identity; that is, how the historic, exiled character of Cernuda countered his nostalgia for Spain through memory and poetry. Other studies have striven to discern its relationship with the classical world and English Romantic tradition (vividly read by Cernuda in his book *Pensamiento poético en la lírica inglesa: Siglo XIX* (1958) (Poetic Thought in English Lyrical Poetry: Nineteenth Century), thus converting the analysis into a problem of literary reception.

It is worth noting, however, that criticism has not inscribed these poems within cultural landscape studies: expatriation is, after all, the loss of territory, of landscape. From such a theoretical framework, which enables an analysis of Cernuda's exiled poems as representations of cultural landscapes, the core of the problem would be neither discourse on identity nor literary reception, but a conflict of ideologies. Applying Baker's terminology, we can speak of *dialectical landscapes* that reflect the same ideological conflicts that mark the landscape of Franco's Spain as it is portrayed, for instance, in José Ortiz Echagüe's photographs. It may be impossible (and irrelevant to my objectives) to establish a connection of influences or genealogies between Cernuda and Ortiz Echagüe. Instead, I consider their works to be products of the same ideological period in the fragmented Spanish cultural history of the twentieth century. In this vein, the object of my study is not the dialectic between photography and poetry, but the dialectic between different ideologies of Spanish modernity within the representation of landscape. With this in mind, I will focus on Cernuda's poetry of exile, referring to Ortiz Echagüe's photography only at the end of my study as an illustration of the dialogue one might establish between landscapes represented in this poetry and landscapes represented in the culture of the Franco period.

Urban Landscapes: Parks, Cemeteries, and Ruins

Starting with their titles, the poems "Gaviotas en los parques" (Gulls in the Parks) and "Cementerio en la ciudad" (Urban Cemetery) announce that the landscapes represented are located in the urban world and in spaces where nature and culture overlap. Both spaces are intended for moments of private contemplation in a public space, for personal history within the framework of national history.

The cultural history of the park breaks off directly from that of the *hortus conclusus* or enclosed garden. Like the landscape, the enclosed garden and its derivations are interventions of man in nature that result in cultural productions that are subject to interpretation: "Each garden is an interpretation and reworking of nature and consequently a reflection of culture" (Aben and Wit 35). Starting from a medieval *hortus conclusus* closed to the outside, and defined by a vertical axis that unites the ground to the sky, the garden in the industrial city gradually broadens along a horizontal axis that joins it to the outside favoring a dialogue with the natural landscape. When nature is too far from the city, such a dialogue with the natural landscape disappears and the urban park emerges: "all that was left was a stereotyped landscape image, such as one sees in front gardens and public urban greenspace. Ultimately parks, parkways and swimming pool complexes would take over the role of the garden as a landscape reference" (Aben and Wit 120). The urban cemetery, a space in which nature and culture also dialogue, has at its origin the nineteenth-century dialectic between private space in the *hortus conclusus* and public space in the urban park (Upton 114).

Both "Gaviotas en los parques" (Gulls in the Parks) and "Cementerio en la ciudad" (Urban Cemetery) represent natural landscape as a dull vestige of nature within the urban landscape.[1] The first describes a "naturaleza sin encanto, entre la lluvia" (309) (disenchanted scenery and rain; Edkins 87), a "verde turbio" (309) (muddy green; Edkins 87) among "edificios uniformes" (309) (regimented buildings; Edkins 87). They are parks set in an interior city where seagulls—marine birds—are disoriented and exiled. Industrial activity and ecclesiastical activity are simply two phases that constantly follow one another, forming an urban cycle that is more important in measuring the passing of days than the cycles of nature.

Albeit indirectly, these verses reflect the change in temporal awareness imposed by capitalism through "the imposition of factory discipline as part of the process of rationalizing production and social relations" (Graham and Labanyi 12). This is also suggested by the fact that the setting of "Cementerio en la ciudad" (Urban Cemetery) is a "barrio pobre" (296) (poor district; Edkins 65) of an equally rainy industrial landscape of "ruido y miseria, frío largo y sin esperanza" (296) (with noise and poverty, long hopeless cold; Edkins 65). Like the park, it is far from being a desirable place to rest. It is contained within a landscape that is furthermore characterized by a human activity ruled by industrial rhythms. The activity of the cemetery is constant not only as industrial space, but also explicitly as economic space. It is surrounded by a "taberna" (296) (public house; Edkins 65) and "tiendas" (296) (shops; Edkins 65), and it is a place for the commerce of the body carried on by prostitutes.

The park and the cemetery are thus located within urban, industrial, and economic landscapes, that is, in landscapes where activities characteristic of capitalism take place. It is particularly meaningful that the poems focus on processes and not only on effects, thus emphasizing the dynamic, constant growth that David Harvey has pointed to as a defining clue in the historic-geographical change produced by capitalism (*Spaces* 121). In the same sense, the poem "Propiedades" (Property) condemns the voracity for accumulating capital that Harvey also identifies as a defining fact of the processes of capitalism (*Spaces* 121). In essence, this is the dialectic between continuity and change noted by Baker in the processes that encompass a relationship between landscape and ideology (6).

The city, damaged by capitalist processes, can only be described as British based on indirect cues (rain, cold, Cernuda's biography) in "Gaviotas en los parques" (Gulls in the Parks) and "Cementerio en la ciudad" (Urban Cemetery), but it seems unmistakably linked to the Anglo-Saxon world from the reference to Scotland in the title of the prose poem "Ciudad caledonia" (Caledonian City).[2] This city of "fachadas rojas manchadas de hollín" (594) (soot-stained red facades; Kessler 68) is not designed for life but for economic processes.

The same impulse to destroy the corrupted city and return it to nature unfolds in "Otras ruinas" (Other Ruins), in which the physical destruction of the city also destroys the notions of efficiency and productivity. This poem markedly criticizes capitalism. According to Cecilia Enjuto-Rangel, "Cernuda's critique of a capitalist society sustained by colonial products is intensified by the city's inability to produce food" (149). In addition, Harvey points out that within the processes of capitalism the construction of landscapes is quickly followed by their destruction (*Spaces* 247), which is linked more generally to the twentieth-century impulse to destroy everything that it constructed (*Condition* 18). Harvey also points out that the tension between building and destroying responds to the capitalist need to annihilate space by means of time (*Spaces* 83, 244). This dynamic is crucial when it comes to interpreting Cernuda's fixation on other Edenic spaces and landscapes that evoke the past, in the face of the acceleration of historic time in the cities.

Thus, several poems from Cernuda's exile both represent and condemn the landscape produced by capitalism. In particular, this landscape is characterized by the degradation of nature in parks and cemeteries set in industrial spaces, by the focus on economic processes instead of activities that do not produce capital, and by the impulse to destroy those very landscapes. Cernuda's poetry of exile here offers a first cross-sectional concurrence with the traditionalism that became so fiercely entrenched during Franco's regime. Apprehension about the erosion of relationships between urban-industrial communities and their natural surroundings was a characteristic source of concern throughout the twentieth century (Cosgrove 2003: 250). However, in several strata of Spanish thought during the Franco years, this idea of the landscape became interwoven with the exaltation of moral and national traditions in the face of the threat posed by the capitalist, Protestant world of Anglo-Saxon countries.

Edenic Landscapes: Gardens, Other Cemeteries, and Other Ruins

Parks and cemeteries in Anglo-Saxon cities appear in other poems that offer a representation of enclosed gardens, other cemeteries, and other ruins, but they are represented as landscapes connected to nature. In such poems, economic and industrial activity is absent, and, in fact, there is an attempt to stop or turn back time by means of space. In a similarly meaningful fashion, these are not Anglo-Saxon landscapes, in which history and capitalism advance at a dizzying speed, but Hispanic landscapes (mainly in Spain or Mexico) that lie outside the flow of time.

Representations of the enclosed garden in Cernuda's poetry are numerous. Almost every case suggests a space removed from both the urban and natural landscapes. One of the most revealing is "Jardín antiguo" (Ancient Garden),[3] because it contains all the elements that characterize this type of space in Cernuda's poetry: stillness, isolation from the outside world, nature in harmony with man, references to the light and geography of southern Spain, and the attempt to stop or turn back time by means of space. This space is also represented in other poems: it is able to separate itself from "La pisada ilusoria / Del tiempo" ("Jardín" [A Garden] 333) (The deceptive tread / Of time; Gibbons 133); it can contain a tree that can be "Ser de un mundo perfecto donde el hombre es extraño" ("El árbol" [The Tree] 394) (A being of a perfect world where man is strange); become a "paisaje de trasmundo" ("El parque" [The Park] 605) (otherworldly landscape; Kessler 84) thanks to its perfection; have the "luminosidad de un verano de San Martín ("El parque" [The Park] 605) (luminousness of a St. Martin's summer; Kessler 83) in mid-autumn; and can "si no luchar contra el tiempo, aplacarlo, demorarlo" ("Un jardín" [A Garden]

645) (if not fight against time, appease it, delay it). It is a luminous space with referents to southern Spain (Andalusia) or Mexico, set on the margins of the capitalist processes of acceleration of time and annihilation of space. Referring to Mexico as an imitation of Spain in Cernuda's poetry, Miguel García-Posada has spoken of a space as "yet unspoiled by capitalist productivity" (48–49).

The same can be said regarding the desolate cemetery in "Cementerio en la ciudad" (Urban Cemetery), which has its counterpoint in "El cementerio" (The Cemetery), "Otro cementerio" (Another Cemetery) and "Elegía antici-pada" (Foreseen Elegy). In contrast to the northern landscape of "Cementerio en la ciudad" (Urban Cemetery)—interior, industrial and fast-paced—the land-scape in "El cementerio" (The Cemetery) is "óleo de paz, luz, música y aroma" (374) (The music, light and scent sink in the grass, / A balm of peace; Gibbons 153). The landscape in "Otro cementerio" (Another Cemetery) is conceived as "descanso en las tareas" (407) (a rest from chores), where "El sol de mediodía, entre dos nubes, / Desciende para el hombre vivo o muerto" (406) (The mid-day sun, between two clouds, / Descends for man alive or dead); whereas in "Elegía anticipada" (Foreseen Elegy) it is set on a quiet coast in the south: "Por la costa del sur, sobre una roca / Alta junto al mar," (358) (Along the southern coast, on a high / Rock close to the sea).

This space of the enclosed garden is one of the motifs that have received the most critical attention in Cernuda's poetry. Although drawing on diverse critical approaches, practically all studies have interpreted it as a pristine space through which Cernuda returns to his childhood in Spain and recovers the land he has lost after exile. In every case it is understood as a textual appropria-tion of a motif in literary tradition: *locus amoenus* (Neira and Pérez Bazo 39), Sevillian *hortus conclusus* on the margin of temporality (Reyes Cano 34), Romantic Andalusia of nineteenth-century literary tradition (García-Posada 42–48); Garden of Eden (López Castro 262); hidden garden (Harris 62–95); Wordsworth's Childhood-Garden of Eden-Harmony with Nature-Paradise Lost (Silver 102); or mythical archetypical time (Sicot 25), among others.

Yet similarly to other motifs in Cernuda's poetry, one of the clues for in-terpretation lies in the introduction of space in cultural studies on landscape and its relationship with an ideological dialectics, namely, in its transformation into a *dialectical landscape*, in Baker's terminology. W. Scott Howard observes that Arcadia proposes, beyond its physical enclave, a mental space where man and nature can coexist in harmony (53). He points out two principles for the cultural interpretation of this landscape. First, there is the principle of "contra-distinction" or "dialectical temporality" (53):

Any utopian vision necessarily embodies some traces of an imperfect world—the "this place"—and then permits those touches of human complication and conflict to be present and active in the idealised landscape. The contradistinctions of Arcadia are not thus exclusionary and do not deny our entrance into that other world, but they are constructive and relational—that is, dialectical. . . . Representations of landscape in that more perfect realm therefore reveal much about not only our wishes to live in a more harmonious balance with nature, but also our eventual need to depart from that utopian space and return to a place or human time. (54)

In this context, Cernuda's garden of exile is not a space completely separate from the passing of time. On the contrary, the atemporality he seeks exists in dialectic with history. As Sophia McClennen points out, time in twentieth-century literature of exile is articulated in the dialectic with the time of dictatorial regimes. In the face of the attempt by these regimes to manipulate history by presenting themselves as the desirable consequence of a lineal evolution, exiles resort to the creation of other atemporal myths to connect their own existence to that of other exiles of history, and to consider time as a boundless notion in a lineal schema (222–23). Within these parameters, the landscape of Cernuda's Arcadia hints at a temporality in dialectic with the lineal, official history of Franco's Spain. However, it also proposes a return to a pre-industrial world, thus offering a paradoxical approach to the ideology of tradition of the Franco years.

The second characteristic of Howard's Arcadia is "sympathetic nature" (54–55). Given that the representation of Arcadia is in dialectic with temporal existence, it also contains traces of the imperfections that ought to be eliminated (54). As such, it results in a contradictory feeling of "tragic joy" (55), whose manifestations plunge man into an unstable equilibrium between loss and gain (55). This characteristic is also relevant for Cernuda's collections of poems, justly included under the title *La realidad y el deseo* (Reality and Desire). By favoring a return from exile to the past, the poem "Jardín antiguo" (Ancient Garden) recovers not only what is idyllic but also the suffering caused by all that could not be attained.

From similar parameters, Julio Neira and Javier Pérez Bazo observe that the landscape evoked in Cernuda's poem "Noche de luna" (Moon Night) has its referent in the lost past of the agrarian reform of the Republic (135). The representation of the Arcadia of his youth during Spain's Republic also brings the pain of war, which ends "El futuro que espera como página blanca" ("Tierra" [Earth] 330) (The future that waits as a blank page). This case is reflected in "Elegía española [I]" (Spanish Elegy [I]), in which an eternal, Arcadian landscape is later ruined by the intrusion of time and historical conflicts.

This second group of Cernuda's landscapes thus attempts to construct an Edenic space with the objective of shutting out the bustle of the external world by means of atemporality: enclosed gardens and other cemeteries and ruins, usually located not in the Anglo-Saxon world but in the Hispanic world. It is again a question of the desire to return to a pre-industrial, pre-capitalist world. In this sense, a reading of Cernuda's Eden as a cultural landscape shows that this exiled atemporality exists in dialectic with the passing history of the Franco years.

Historic Landscapes: Castile and El Escorial

Cernuda's poetry of exile represents a third cultural landscape. It is a landscape (natural or architectural) whose function is to evoke history directly; that is, a consideration of the landscape as a space in which history is manifest in the sense pointed out by Inglis (489), such as ruins or monumental buildings. Counter to the ruins of the industrial city in "Otras ruinas" (Other Ruins) or the understated dialectic with history in the landscapes of the *hortus conclusus*, the poems in this third group openly evoke and celebrate the Spanish past. In fact, as David Lowenthal points out, the memory of the past is more present in space than in time (180). The most representative of spaces in this group of poems is the Castilian landscape of Phillip II, in "El ruiseñor sobre la piedra" (The Nightingale on the Stone) and "Silla del rey" (The King's Chair). Next to "Águila y rosa" (Eagle and Rose) (which evokes the heirless marriage of the Spanish King with Mary Tudor, with only a brief description of the English landscape) these poems form a trilogy on Phillip II (Harris 102). The fact that some of the verses are enunciated by Phillip II himself entails a manifestation of "Cernuda's polyphonic richness " accentuated by irony and the presentation of "points of view that occasionally oppose each other" (Fuente García de la 246–48). Such strategies camouflage ideology and set it in a dialogue of different voices.

Beginning with the "Así, Escorial, te mira mi recuerdo" (313) (Thus, Escorial, my memory looks at you), from its first stanza, "El ruiseñor sobre la piedra" (The Nightingale on the Stone) announces that the motive of the poem is the desire to return from exile to this historic building and its surrounding landscape. As opposed to the Andalusian landscape evoked in other poems by Cernuda, this text is set in the interior landscape of Castile. With this turn of phrase, the context of the poem changes both geographically and historically:

it suggests that elapsed time lies in a space, in line with Lowenthal's observations (180).

Castile is a historic landscape recreated out of the same signs of austerity and inner strength that help endure exile in a northern land. This purity and austerity of the imperial Castilian landscape is also linked to the criticism of capitalism and materialism described as Anglo-Saxon in other poems (Harris 88; Neira 164). In this way, "Utilitarianism in the Anglo-Saxon north contrasts with the complete uselessness of El Escorial, the ultimate expression of Spanish character" (Faber 2000: 737).

In the poem "Silla del rey" (The King's Chair), the voice of Phillip II evokes a Castilian landscape and observes that visual control of a unified, centralized landscape is the equivalent of the centralist unity of the empire. The centralism of the landscape suggests the contingencies of order, authority, and totalization that Baker notes when describing the effect of ideology on the landscape (4). In particular, the landscape represented carries the ideological burden of perspective: "an important effect of linear perspective is to arrest the flow of history at a specific moment, freezing that moment as a universal reality" (Cosgrove 1984: 15). In this way, "Silla del rey" (The King's Chair) restores the Spanish empire as a historic moment worthy of being perpetuated. It is thus linked to other poems of Cernuda's exile in which the past is solidified and extolled by means of a landscape that combines architecture with nature. For example, the landscape of "Las ruinas" (The Ruins) has a therapeutic effect on the present, as pointed out by Rainey in his work on memorialistic landscapes (80).

The restored landscape in these poems of exile is thus not simply a space, but also a time: imperial Castile. Cernuda's homeland appears as "a combination of his native Andalusia, a certain cultural Spain and, above all, Phillip II's imperial Spain" (Faber 2000: 736). This singular combination is, in fact, a trait that continues throughout the entire length of his poetic and ideological trajectory in exile. For instance, "Ser de Sansueña" (Being of Sansueña) travels through a Spanish geography that contains these extreme elements of Spanish landscape.

In modern Spanish poetry, on the other hand, the landscapes of Andalusia and Castile are not simply geographic spaces but also historic and political ones. Cernuda is part of the group of poets from the 1920s and 1930s that restored "Andalusian geography as a field of lyrical energies and traditions" (García Montero 48) and as *hortus conclusus*. For instance, in "Divagación sobre la Andalucía romántica" (1935) (Digression on Romantic Andalusia),

Cernuda states that his ideal Edenic landscape "bien podría estar situado en Andalucía" (83) (could well be located in Andalusia). However, in exile he also emphasizes the Castilian landscape. That is how he expressed it in a radio program broadcast by the BBC in 1943 on the millennial celebration of Castile "as a counterpoint to the celebrations that took place in Franco's Spain" (Mayoral 62):

> nuestra nación no es obra del orgullo, sino de la humildad castellana. . . . De ahí ciertas cualidades típicas: la abnegación, la paciencia, el sacrificio, el respeto a la pobreza, el desprecio de los bienes materiales, el amor a no ser nada. . . . Y no se juzguen dichas cualidades como negativas y enemigas de toda manifestación externa de la grandeza temporal . . . allí [en El Escorial] está expresado en piedra, y con majestad sin par, un esquema político equivalente al esquema metafísico que sistematizan los escritores místicos, que así como hay una metafísica castellana, y una poética, brotadas del pensamiento mítico nacional, hay también una política en todo conforme a éste. ("Mito" 243–44)

> (our nation is not the daughter of pride, but of Castilian humility. . . . Thus certain typical attributes: abnegation, patience, sacrifice, respect for poverty, contempt for material goods, love of being nothing. . . . And may those attributes not be judged as negative and enemies of all external manifestation of temporal greatness. . . . it [El Escorial] expresses in stone, and with unparalleled majesty, a political schema equivalent to the metaphysical one systematized by the mystical writers, that—in addition to a Castilian metaphysics and poetics that arose from national mythical thought—there is also a politics to it.)

Therefore, although it is a cultural production of exile, the Castilian landscape of this group of poems invokes imperial and spiritual values that are similar to the ideology of Franco's Spain. This mythical Castilian nation "is better understood as part of a nationalist-cultural tradition that, emerging in the nineteenth century, is manifested with new strength in post-war Spain, both in the Peninsula and in exile" (Faber 2000: 735).

Landscapes of Exile, Landscapes of Franco's Spain

With different degrees of intensity, these three landscape representations in Cernuda's poetry of exile coincide with landscape representations in the ideology of Franco's Spain. An illustrative example is that of Ortiz Echagüe, who published four books of photographs of Spanish landscapes, whose tangible success is manifest in their numerous editions between 1933 and 1971. *España: Tipos y trajes* (1933) (Spain: Types and Costumes) offers a portrait of landscapes, history, traditionalism, and typical costumes of the Spanish regions that assuages the nationalist interest in those very regions, bringing it closer to Franco's Spain in its numerous editions even though it emerged in the context of the Republican Misiones Pedagógicas. *España: Pueblos y paisajes* (1938) (Spain: Villages and Landscapes) was mostly centered on the restoration of rural landscapes and non-industrial activities. *España mística* (1943) (Mystical Spain) gathers together Catholic rituals in rural or architectonic settings. Finally, *España: Castillos y alcázares* (1956) (Spain: Castles and Citadels) restores the glorious image of castles and Castilian landscapes (such as El Escorial).

In addition to the photographs, these books offer revealing commented indexes on the images and introductory texts. The texts included go beyond Spanish history as a framework, so that the landscape becomes imbued with history and embedded in time. The historic moment most vehemently connected to the photographs is the time between the Reconquest and the Spanish Empire, while the present is considered a degradation of the past ("España" 11). People appear engaged in rural and traditional activities, and José Ortega y Gasset questions the difficult interplay of the rural, industrial, and economic activities (7–8). Few urban landscapes are included, and a commentary on Madrid reflects the dialectic of a landscape trapped between tradition and industrial and economic capitalism: "En su recinto todo es desorden urbano: la inmensa y clásica mole de su regio Palacio junto a las más vulgares construcciones; las avenidas de pretenciosos rascacielos lindando con callejas de humildes casas dan la nota saliente en el desconcierto urbano" ("Índice" 12) (In its enclosure, everything is urban disorder: the vast classical massiveness of its royal palace alongside the most ordinary constructions; the avenues of presumptuous skyscrapers adjacent to narrow streets of humble houses set the salient tone in urban confusion).

The landscapes represented are *ideological interpellations* in the Althusserian sense. Lee Fontanella notes that Ortiz Echagüe's objective is to find the essence of Spain in the land (172): "In photographing his own country in a systematic way, and focusing on different categories of subjects—castles, towns, regional garb, and ritual customs—he grew in this 'Spanishness'" (173). Independent of Ortiz Echagüe's background of *franquista* principles "seguramente a su pesar" (López Mondéjar 34) (certainly to his regret), these photographs depict the juncture that the Spanish landscape was experiencing between tradition (associated with nature) and capitalism (associated with industrial development). In defending a particular type of Spanish landscape, Ortiz Echagüe's books take side with the moral and imperial values also being defended by Franco's regime in the face of Anglo-Saxon culture. It is no coincidence that Franco's foreign policy was also trapped between love and hate for Anglo-Saxon culture, which would bring the threat (and the promise) of capitalism and the loosening of Catholic morals. From this perspective, the Franco years constitute a tension between ideologies and, as the Republic, a period of cultural history that is impossible to map with a one-to-one equivalence.

From a different starting point, and aiming at a different target, the representation of landscape in Cernuda's poetry of exile shares the sense of *ideological interpellation* of landscapes represented during the Franco period. It is a nation struggling against the urban and moral degradation of capitalism, turned toward the past and proud of its imperial history. Specifically, three representations of the landscape are in dialectical tension within this poetry: urban landscapes mostly in Anglo-Saxon settings, Edenic landscapes mostly in Hispanic settings, and Spanish historic landscapes. The poems in the first group condemn capitalist economic processes in Anglo-Saxon cities: the degradation of nature in parks and cemeteries, the drive for economic productivity and efficiency in their inhabitants' activities, and the unstoppable destruction of the same constructed landscapes. All of them entail a destruction of space by means of time. As a way of counteracting these urban landscapes, the group of Edenic landscapes proposes gardens, other cemeteries, and other ruins in spaces with a geographical referent set in the Hispanic world. A focal point of this group of poems is the re-elaboration of the *hortus conclusus* motif as a Garden of Eden that aims to stop or turn back time, but in the end becomes embedded in historical events. In this case, there is an attempt to counteract time by means of space. Finally, the third group restores the Castilian landscapes of El Escorial and Phillip II's imperial Spain. These are spaces that are also historic moments, that is, a convergence of space and time.

Although it is not sensible to establish a direct link between Luis Cernuda and José Ortiz Echagüe, or between the civic and political aspirations of the exile and the Franco years, it can be claimed that the representations of landscape in the culture of exile and in the culture of Franco's Spain follow parallel, albeit separate, paths. An exhaustive interpretation of this disquieting ideological correspondence between exile and *franquismo* would surpass the objectives of my study, but the most efficient method to achieve it would be to consider that all culture is a process of struggle between different ideologies, rather than a homogeneous space. Cernuda's poetry of exile (like Ortiz Echagüe's photography), far from being only a discourse on identity, responds to a process of negotiation of the landscape as a sign of modern Spanish culture. As Sebastiaan Faber lucidly argues, supported by a Gramscian theoretical scaffolding, the cultural production of the Republican exile was in essence a struggle for the cultural hegemony that was lost to the Franco period: "This part of the political struggle for hegemony, over representation of and identification with the nation, is largely waged on the field of culture. Culture, moreover, is generally all that exiles have at their disposal" (2002: 35). Thus at the same time as Cernuda's poetry struggles to represent the Spanish landscape, the "purist adventure" (Palenzuela 98) of exiled literary critics recovers and redefines the same figures of San Juan de la Cruz and Calderón de la Barca that were celebrated in Franco's Spain; and *Pensamiento y poesía en la vida española* (1939) (Thought and Poetry in the Spanish Life), by María Zambrano, duplicates Ángel Ganivet's arguments on Spain's spiritual legacy to the Western World (Bundgård 197, 285).

The culture of the Republican exile can be better understood, in sum, not as a homogenous space but as a discourse engaged in a conflictive, oscillating relationship with the different ideologies of modernity that Franco's regime used and abused. From this perspective, the Spanish Republican exile proposes a foundation for considering the ideological framework of Spanish modernity in general as a struggle for the definition of cultural signs. With its questioning of capitalist urban and industrial processes set against Spain's imperial and spiritual history, Cernuda's poetry of exile does not deny modernity. It reveals that it was a process defined by multiple, unresolved internal dialectics that converged, in the end, on the representation of the landscape.

Notes

1. With the exception of the cases attributed to Edkins, Gibbons or Kessler, translation of all Spanish quotations are by María José Giménez in collaboration with Goretti Ramírez. Special thanks to Hugh Hazelton for his insights on the translation of some challenging words and lines.
2. Although his means and purposes differ from my approach, Kevin J. Bruton agrees with me on the Anglo-Saxon location of "Cementerio en la ciudad" (Urban Cemetery). He specifies it as the city of Glasgow (191), where Cernuda lived unwillingly between 1939 and 1943.
3. The title "Jardín antiguo" (Ancient Garden) is used for a prose poem in *Ocnos* (Ocnos) and for a versed poem in *Las nubes* (The Clouds).

Works Cited

Aben, Rob, and Saskia de Wit. *The Enclosed Garden: History and Development of the Hortus Conclusus and its Reintroduction into the Present-Day Urban Landscape.* Rotterdam: 010 Publishers, 1999.

Baker, Alan R. H. "Introduction: On Ideology and Landscape." *Ideology and Landscape in Historical Perspective: Essays on the Meaning of Some Places in the Past.* Ed. Alan R. H. Baker and Gideon Biger. Cambridge: Cambridge University Press, 1992.

Bruton, Kevin J. "The Cemetery Poems of Luis Cernuda." *Anales de la Literatura Española Contemporánea* 13:3 (1988): 189–208.

Bundgård, Ana. *Más allá de la filosofía: Sobre el pensamiento filosófico-místico de María Zambrano.* Madrid: Trotta, 2000.

Cernuda, Luis. "Águila y rosa." *Poesía* 441–45.

———. "Cementerio en la ciudad." *Poesía* 295–96.

———. "Ciudad caledonia." *Poesía* 594–95.

———. *Como quien espera el alba. Poesía* 319–798.

———. *Con las horas contadas. Poesía* 439–85.

———. *Desolación de la Quimera. Poesía* 487–54.

———. "Divagación sobre la Andalucía romántica." *Prosa II* 82–102.

———. "El árbol." *Poesía* 392–94.

———. "El cementerio." *Poesía* 374–75.

———. "Elegía anticipada." *Poesía* 358–60.

———. "Elegía española [I]." *Poesía* 258–61.

———. "El parque." *Poesía* 604–05.

———. "El ruiseñor sobre la piedra." *Poesía* 313–18.

———. "Gaviotas en los parques." *Poesía* 309–10.

———. "Jardín." *Poesía* 332–34.

———. "Jardín antiguo." *Poesía* 297.

———. "Jardín antiguo." *Poesía* 568.

———. *La Realidad y el Deseo. Poesía* 101–658.

———. *Las nubes. Poesía* 249–318.

———. "Las ruinas." *Poesía* 323–26.

———. "Mito poético de Castilla." *Prosa II* 241–45.

———. "Noche de luna." *Poesía* 251–54.

———. *Ocnos. Poesía* 549–615.

———. "Otras ruinas." *Poesía* 401–3.

———. "Otro cementerio." *Poesía* 406–7.

———. *Pensamiento poético en la lírica inglesa: Siglo XIX. Prosa I.* Ed. Derek Harris and Luis Maristany. Madrid: Siruela, 1994. 252–352.

———. *Poesía completa.* Ed. Derek Harris and Luis Maristany. Madrid: Siruela, 1993.

———. "Propiedades." *Poesía* 646–48.

———. *Prosa II.* Ed. Derek Harris and Luis Maristany. Madrid: Siruela, 1994.

———. "Ser de Sansueña." *Poesía* 417–19.

———. "Silla del rey." *Poesía* 419–23.

———. "Tierra nativa." *Poesía* 329–30.

———. "Un español habla de su tierra." *Poesía* 310–11.

———. "Un jardín." *Poesía* 644–45.

———. *Variaciones sobre tema mexicano. Poesía* 617–58.

———. *Vivir sin estar viviendo. Poesía* 381–437.

Cortines, Jacobo, ed. *Historial de una vida: Homenaje a Luis Cernuda en el centenario de su nacimiento (1902–2002).* Seville: Fundación José Manuel Lara, 2003.

Cosgrove, Denis. "Landscape and the European Sense of Sight—Eyeing Nature." *Handbook of Cultural Geography.* Ed. Kay Anderson, Mona Domosh, Steve Pile and Nigel Thrift. London: SAGE Publications, 2003.

———. *Social Formation and Historic Landscape.* Totowa, NJ: Barnes and Noble Books, 1984.

Edkins, Anthony, and Derek Harris. *The Poetry of Luis Cernuda.* New York: New York University Press, 1971.

Enjuto-Rangel, Cecilia. "Broken Presents: The Modern City in Ruins in Baudelaire, Cernuda, and Paz." *Comparative Literature* 59:2 (Spring 2007): 140–57.

"España: Pueblos y paisajes." In Ortiz Echagüe 1963: 11.

Faber, Sebastiaan. "'El norte nos devora': La construcción de un espacio hispánico en el exilio anglosajón de Luis Cernuda." *Hispania* 83:4 (diciembre 2000): 733–44.

———. *Exile and Cultural Hegemony: Spanish Intellectuals in Mexico, 1939–1975.* Nashville: Vanderbilt University Press, 2002.

Fontanella, Lee. "Landscape in the Photography of Spain." *Visualizing Spanish Modernity.* Ed. Susan Larson and Eva Woods. Oxford: Berg, 2005.

Fuente García, Mario A. de la. "Polifonía e ideología: diferentes voces en la poesía de Luis Cernuda." In Matas Caballero, Martínez Fernández, and Trabado Cabado, 241–52.

García Montero, Luis. "Luis Cernuda y Andalucía." In Matas Caballero, Martínez Fernández, and Trabado Cabado, 47–61.

García-Posada, Miguel. "Cernuda y las tradiciones andaluzas." In Cortines, 39–57.

Gibbons, Reginald, trans. *Selected Poems of Luis Cernuda.* Berkeley: University of California Press, 1977.

Graham, Helen, and Jo Labanyi, eds. *Spanish Cultural Studies: An Introduction: The Struggle for Modernity.* Oxford: Oxford University Press, 1995.

———. "Culture and Modernity: The Case of Spain." In Graham and Labanyi, 1–19.

Groth, Paul, and Todd W. Bressi, eds. *Understanding Ordinary Landscapes.* New Haven: Yale University Press, 1997.

Harris, Derek. *Luis Cernuda: A Study of the Poetry.* London: Tamesis Books Limited, 1973.

Harvey, David. *The Condition of Postmodernity: An Enquiry into the Origins of Cultural Change.* Oxford: Basil Blackwell, 1990.

————. *Spaces of Capital: Towards a Critical Geography.* New York: Routledge, 2001.
Howard, W. Scott. "Landscapes of memorialisation." *Studying Cultural Landscapes.* Ed.
    Iain Robertson and Penny Richards. London: Arnold, 2003.
"Índice comentado de las láminas." In Ortiz Echagüe 1963, 12–24.
Inglis, Fred. "Nation and Community: A Landscape and its Morality." *Sociological
    Review* 25 (1977): 489–514.
Kessler, Stephen, trans. *Written in Water: The Prose Poems of Luis Cernuda.* San
    Francisco: City Lights Books, 2004.
King, Anthony D. "The Politics of Vision." In Groth and Bressi, 134–44.
López Castro, Armando. *Luis Cernuda en su sombra.* Madrid: Verbum, 2003.
López Mondéjar, Publio. *Las fuentes de la memoria II: Fotografía y Sociedad en España,
    1900–1939.* Madrid: Ministerio de Cultura-Lunwerg, 1992.
Lowenthal, David. "European Landscape Transformations: The Rural Residue." In Groth
    and Bressi, 180–88.
Matas Caballero, Juan, José Enrique Martínez Fernández, and José Manuel Trabado
    Cabado, eds. *Nostalgia de una patria imposible: Estudios sobre la obra de Luis
    Cernuda.* Madrid: Akal, 2005.
Mayoral, Marina. "Cernuda y España." In Cortines, 59–77.
McClennen, Sophia A. *The Dialectics of Exile: Nation, Time, Language, and Space in
    Hispanic Literatures.* West Lafayette, IN: Purdue University Press, 2004.
Mendelson, Jordana. *Documenting Spain: Artists, Exhibition Culture, and the Modern
    Nation, 1929–1939.* University Park: Penn State University Press, 2005.
Mitchell, W.J.T. *Iconology: Image, Text, Ideology.* Chicago: University of Chicago Press,
    1986.
Neira, Julio, and Javier Pérez Bazo. *Luis Cernuda en el exilio: Lecturas de 'Las Nubes' y
    'Desolación de la Quimera.'* Toulouse: Presses Universitaires du Mirail, 2002.
Ortega y Gasset, José. "Para una ciencia del traje popular." In Ortiz Echagüe 1940, 7–10.
Ortiz Echagüe, José. *España: Castillos y alcázares.* Madrid: Publicaciones Ortiz-
    Echagüe, 1964.
————. *España: Pueblos y paisajes.* Eighth Edition. Vol. 1. Madrid: Publicaciones Ortiz-
    Echagüe, 1963
————. *España: Pueblos y paisajes.* Fourth Edition. Vol. 2. Madrid: Maife, 1950.
————. *España: Tipos y trajes.* Sixth Edition. Madrid: Bolaños y Aguilar, 1940.
————. *España mística.* Madrid: Mayfe, 1950.
Palenzuela, Nilo. *En torno al casticismo: Los exiliados españoles.* La Laguna, Spain:
    Universidad La Laguna, 2003.
Rainey, Reuben M. "Hallowed Grounds and Rituals of Remembrance: Union Regimental
    Monuments at Gettysburg." In Groth and Bressi, 67–80.
Reyes Cano, Rogelio. "Luis Cernuda y Sevilla: Entre la eternidad de Albanio y la
    temporalidad del desterrado." In Cortines, 17–37.
Richards, Mike. "'Terror and Progress': Industrialization, Modernity, and the Making of
    Francoism." In Graham and Labanyi, 173–82.

Sicot, Bernard. "Luis Cernuda, 'Variaciones sobre tema mexicano': el espacio y el tiempo recobrados." *Poesía y exilio: Los poetas del exilio español en México*. Ed. Rose Corral, Arturo Souto Alabarce, and James Valender. Mexico City: El Colegio de México, 1995.

Silver, Philip W. "Luis Cernuda en América: El poeta y el hombre." In Cortines, 97–110.

Taylor, John. "The Alphabetic Universe: Photography and the Picturesque Landscape." *Reading Landscape: Country, City, Capital*. Ed. Simon Pugh. Manchester: Manchester University Press, 1990.

Upton, Dell. *Architecture in the United States*. Oxford: Oxford University Press, 1998.

Williams, Raymond. *The Country and the City*. Oxford: Oxford University Press, 1973.

Zambrano, María. *Pensamiento y poesía en la vida española*. Madrid: Endymion, 1996.

◆ 11

Francoist Spaces:
Un hombre va por el camino (Manuel Mur Oti, 1948) and *Surcos* (José Antonio Nieves Conde, 1951)

Luis Mariano González

In a classic study, Henry Lefebvre remarked that each society and, particularly, every mode of production produces its own space (31). Thus, during the first years of Franco's dictatorship (1939–1975), in which its fascist ingredients appeared with more intensity, the "imagined community" of the regime was located in the rural world. With an economy mainly dependent on agricultural production and a small industrial infrastructure compared with the other European countries, the first stage of the dictatorship (1939–1957) aims to perpetuate a rural-based society marked by authoritarianism, patriarchy, and Catholicism.[1] It is in the countryside, untouched by the effects of Modernity, where Franco's regime will seek, and find, the ideal subject of the New Spain.

In this context, an important portion of Spanish cinema produced during the 1940s and 1950s, betraying its technological nature, presented itself as a refuge against the vicissitudes brought about by its main adversary, Modernity, while giving voice to the ideological agenda of the political and social conglomerate that constitutes Spanish Fascism.[2] In this essay, after analyzing the relationship between Fascism, Francoism, and Nature, I will explore how an important part of the cinema produced during Franco's dictatorship built a poetics of Francoist space with two complementary strategies toward Nature.

Un hombre va por el camino (Manuel Mur Oti; 1948) portrays a celebration of rural work as well as builds a social space dominated by Nature and its vital cycles. In *Surcos* (1951) (Furrows), the radical falangist José Antonio Nieves Conde, resorting to the newly born aesthetics of Italian Neorealism and American *film noir*, presents a demolishing criticism of life in big cities, the epitome of Modernity, so strongly opposed by those proponents of the ideological agenda of Fascism who idealized the Spanish rural universe. From a structural point of view, both films are articulated through what I define as a "mainstreaming narrative." As we will see in the analysis of the films, this "mainstreaming" strategy will be aimed at correcting an initial situation marked by an ideological conflict between some of the life occurrences or events chronicled in the plot and the philosophical universe of National Catholicism.

Fascism, Francoism, and Nature

It has often been said that the industrial revolution that occurred in Europe between the eighteen and nineteenth centuries played an important role in the development of Modernity. John McGowan points out the transformed modes of production and distribution brought about by capitalism, and the growth of towns and cities as indisputable components of Modernity (4). In other words, it is necessary to establish a strong link between Modernity and industrialization and demographic growth in the cities. From the beginning, voices condemning the perils of the industrial movement arose, desiring a return to a pre-modern state in which the individual had not yet broken his links with Nature, now severely threatened by industrial development. Many examples of this rejection can be found in Romantic literature as well as in some of the works of modernist writers. In the Spanish case, authors of the so-called Generation of '98 were the most vocal against the advances of Modernity and sang the praises of a pre-modern Castile, pure and untouched by the effects of the industrial revolution. Romantic and modernist writers alike resorted to a bucolic tradition that began with the *Georgics* by Virgil (29 B.C.) and extended to the *Menosprecio de corte y alabanza de aldea* (1539) by Antonio de Guevara.

With the rise of fascist movements in Europe in the first decades of the twentieth century, the relationship of the individual with technology and Nature was again at stake. Fascism, like Janus's face, looks both at the past and the future. On the one hand, it extends its gaze toward a mythical and idealized past, frozen in history and untouched by the liberating process triggered by the Enlightenment. On the other, fascinated by the technological advances brought about by capitalism, it aspires to transform the universalism of Enlightenment into a violent nationalism fed by the imperialistic rhetoric that converts war into the protagonist of a revolution aimed at stopping revolution. Regarding its contradictory character, in an article published in 1927, José Ortega y Gasset commented that whatever aspect we consider, Fascism is a certain thing and its opposite at the same time: it is A and it is not A (497).

British historian Mark Neocleous states that Nature plays an important role in the political agenda of Fascism, to the extent that some of its manifestations focus on the peasantry and agriculture as the most powerful expressions of the spirit of a nation (76). Similarly, Alice Kaplan notes that fascist literature shares with other movements opposed to Modernity a sense of reverence towards Nature and a desire to revolt against modern life (26). Like its contemporary European counterparts in Germany and Italy, Spanish Fascism resorted to a nostalgic longing for the rural way of life in order to suppress the fear provoked in certain sectors of Spanish society by the rapid changes of Modernity, particularly during the Second Republic (1931–1939). However, in the Francoist ideological universe, this obsession with ways of life distant from the social patterns imposed in big cities after the industrial revolution functions not only as a nostalgic revision of the past, but also as a future aspiration on which, at least rhetorically, the dictatorship insisted upon until its end.[3]

In this spatial Francoist imaginary, the local is privileged in opposition to the universal, open and barely populated rural spaces are favored over the dense city and its unmanageable crowds. And finally, in the face of an economical model based on industrial and technological development, agriculture is proposed as the basis for the autarchic program supported by Spanish Fascism. As Juan Cano Ballesta sums up:

> The utopia of Spanish conservatism, at least as it was understood by its most outstanding representatives like José Antonio Primo de Rivera, Agustín de Foxá and José María Pemán, among others, is a pre-industrial paradise of roses, corn spikes, lilies, fairies, and fresh nude young ladies, where all the traditional values and the grandeur of Empire flourish. Moreover, machines are depicted as sinister forces that destroy all the beauty and spiritual value of the Spanish cultural background.[4]
> (300)

Part of the filmography produced during Francoism will put into images this utopia of Spanish Fascism. The film *Un hombre va por el camino* by Mur Oti portrays the Virgilian topic of praise of the rural world by presenting appealing images of life in the countryside and of its inhabitants. In its National

Catholic version, the man (and the woman) of the New Spain fulfill their obligations to the Church while supporting a family model that becomes the fundamental unit of an organic and hierarchized social network. This exaltation of the countryside brings along a demonization of the city. In *Surcos* and in his other films as well, like the popular *Balarrasa* (1950), Nieves Conde presents Madrid as a metaphor of the dangers of Modernity, opposed by a significant part of the philosophical milieu of European Fascism. The crowd, about which Oswald Spengler and, in the Spanish case, José Ortega y Gasset had warned, dominates a city where the Church and its rituals have been substituted by the neighborhood patio, the bar, and the cabaret as spaces of social interaction, where, according to the spiritual tenets of the times, Christian morality and mores will be trampled. I will now analyze this in detail.

Alabanza de aldea (Praise of Village Life)

Manuel Mur Oti (1908–2003) is one of the most interesting directors of the first years of Franco's dictatorship and also one of the least studied.[5] Among the critics who have dealt with his work[6] is Nekane Zubiaur, who has pointed out "[Mur Oti's] expressed desire to endow his stories with a universal flair," and how "he never showed in public any interest in the socio-political conflicts of the country, and never gave an opinion on the matter, neither in personal declarations nor in his work" (6). Without judging Manuel Mur Oti's political agenda, I believe that *Un hombre va por el camino* both expresses and consolidates the ultra-conservative ideology of the hegemonic block of post-war Spain. From an economic point of view, the film defends the principles of an autarchic system (economic national self-sufficiency or autonomy) imposed by Franco's regime after the Spanish Civil War. From a social perspective, through what I call a "mainstreaming narrative," it builds a sociological universe ruled by the National-Catholic ideology that delimits the spaces of movement for men and women. By "mainstreaming narrative," I mean a structure shared by some texts (above all from popular culture) which reproduce the ultra reactionary ideology hegemonic at that time. In this narrative, there is an initial social and familiar situation considered "anomalous" from the ideological perspective of Franco's dictatorship. Through the development of the plot, this original "status quo" will be gradually amended until it becomes completely acceptable to the regime's value system.[7] As this process underlines, the Spanish society of the time was more complex and problematic than the official Francoist rhetoric intended to show when it depicted a monolithic and homogeneous image of Spain. In other words, if a "corrective" is needed, it is because there are deviations from the norms, and it is precisely these deviations on which I will focus. In short, the desire for absolute control of all the sectors of Spanish society purported by the ultra-conservative National-Catholic ideology in the first stage of Franco's dictatorship proves to be a fallacy.

Written and directed by Mur Oti, *Un hombre va por el camino* premiered on December 30, 1949. The film, produced by Sagitario Films, had Ana Mariscal and Fernando Nogueras in the leading roles. According to the Filmoteca Española (Spanish Film Library), it had an audience of more than three thousand spectators and earned two hundred and thirty-seven Euros in today's currency. Its plot can be summarized as follows: Luis (Fernando Nogueras) is a vagabond who wanders along rural paths with no fixed destination. Accidentally, he arrives at the house of a widow, Julia (Ana Mariscal), who, together with her little daughter, is trying to continue to work her land. Julia persuades Luis to help her, at least for a day. After an exhausting day, the vagabond leaves the farm the following morning, only to return in the summer to contemplate the fruits of this labor. At this point, the film becomes a romantic melodrama: we find that Luis is really a doctor who lost his wife when she died in a car accident with her lover, and lost his daughter, whom he could not save in the operation room. Disillusioned, Luis had abandoned his life in the city.

The opening scene in *Un hombre va por el camino* (1948) shows the main character, a tramp, reading Shakespeare's *The Taming of the Shrew* (1590–1594). This particular fragment refers to life in the city and material wealth against which Mur Oti's film takes a stand.[8] The fact that the film is set in an undetermined space (the first scene shows the main character at the crossroads of Tierra Vieja and Cabañuelas), and in an unspecified time (there is not enough textual evidence to know if the story occurs before or after the Spanish Civil War) all contribute to the universalism that, according to Nekane Zubiaur (6), characterizes Mur Oti's cinematography. Finally, after rejecting a job offer made by the mayor of Tierra Vieja, Luis arrives at Monte Oscuro's farm. Located in an inhospitable place, it astonishes the vagabond, who is awestruck by the immensity of the surrounding Nature, and triggers a real expression of the Kantian sublime. This first impression is corroborated by Julia, who points out that "behind these peaks there is an abyss that few men will dare to trespass" (Dialogue).

The first scenes of the film are panoramic shots of the fields, the mountains, and the land that the main characters are working. Simon Schama has remarked that it is possible to establish a synecdoche-like relationship between Nature and nation due to the fact that the West conserves a good dose of myths, metaphors, and allegories related to the landscape. Thus, according to this critic, the representation of rivers, forests, and mountains entails the representation of the nation (14). From my point of view, Monte Oscuro functions as an allegory of the Spanish nation and its reconstruction process after the Civil War. In order to achieve this difficult task, the participation of the entire social body is required. Highly influenced by organicist theories, above all those of Ortega y Gasset in the Spanish case, Fascism sees the nation as a body in which each organ needs to perform specific functions and which cannot be replaced by another. The beginning of the film shows a dysfunctional organism because it is the woman who is working the land. According to the National-Catholic ideology, women are not prepared to fulfill this task and, therefore, this "anomaly" needs to be fixed. The narrative of the film will correct this problem through what I call "mainstreaming narrative." In this case, it consists of a linear progression in the film that attempts to recover Luis as a productive social element by leaving behind his life as a tramp and becoming the village doctor, removing the female protagonist as an active social individual (by marrying Luis she becomes a traditional woman), and rectifying the scandalous relationship between Luis and Julia and leading to matrimony as sanctioned by the Catholic Church.

From the exterior space, characterized by a hostile Nature that the protagonists wish to domesticate, the film moves to the interior. It is a home dominated by the absence (although present in the form of constant remembrance) of Julia's husband, who is portrayed in a picture holding a pickaxe to emphasize his devotion to work. His library is beneath the picture. Luis cannot help taking a look to find the work of two philosophers, Friedrich Nietzsche (1844–1900) and Henri Bergson (1859–1941). Their presence cannot be innocent, since they are usually associated with the genesis of Fascism because of their anti-rationalistic philosophy. Finally, Charles Darwin's (1809–1882) volumes share the same shelf. Julia's deceased husband's latest book *Crítica de la relación humana* (Critique of Human Relationships) analyzed the works of the English naturalist, apparently from a critical perspective. Darwin's theory of evolution of the species could hardly be accepted by the hegemonic Catholicism of the times, supported in different moments in the film.

Julia attempts to compensate for the loss of her husband Enrique by transforming Luis into a resemblance of him. This metamorphosis materializes in the scene in which the vagabond dresses up in the dead writer's clothes. Contrary to what Julia thought, the clothes are too small for him. The new version of her husband is an improved one, bigger and stronger and without the intellectual pretensions of her previous one. Julia undergoes a similar process, too. She will replace Luis's wife, an excessively modern woman. As in the previous case, Luis gains by this transformation because, as it is stated close to the film's end, Julia is—unlike his first wife—"the strong woman capable of helping a man fulfill his dreams" (Dialogue). Therefore, while their former spouses are clearly shaped by the years of the Second Republic, to which Julia's husband's intellectualism and Luis's wife's adoption of certain female liberation principles attest, Julia and Luis present themselves as the ideal subjects of the New Spain.

Julia truncates Luis's intentions of returning to a wandering life, thus, according to Michel Maffesoli's portrait of the tramp (13), eliminating his latent Dionysian character capable of upsetting and rebelling against the established order. Moments before his departure, she persuades him to help her sow the last plot of land acquired by her husband and destined to cultivate the wheat that would produce the family's bread. After Enrique's death, Julia, with the help of Luis, takes the first step in order to achieve the goal of consuming bread entirely cultivated and elaborated at the farm. After they finish the first sowing season, Julia expresses: "[A wheat field in summer] is something beautiful. This piece of land will look like a golden sea in June. We'll do all the chores and, if you dare, we'll build a small mill to make the flour also, and then our daily bread will be completely ours" (Dialogue). This dream, first Enrique's and then Julia's, symbolizes the self-sufficient economic plan of Spanish Fascism. This system, ultimately declared inefficient in the 1950s, will effect the remodeling of the ministerial cabinet in 1957. This change led to the substitution of the Falange (the main group of the Spanish fascist conglomerate responsible for the economic policies of the country) with the technocrats of the ultra-conservative Catholic group Opus Dei.

Finally, Luis changes his mind and returns to his vagabond life. At this point, the film conjures images of the future and shows the summer harvest, while Mur Oti's camera lingers on scenes that exalt country life and its cycles, inhabitants, and traditions. These portraits appealed to the official rhetoric of the regime and its praise of rural life since, as it had been versified by the poets of the Generation of '98, it is in this nature and these landscapes that the true national spirit resides. In 1948 General Franco summarized this idea in the following way:

It is a real pleasure for me to travel through the Castilian villages and feel the warmth and honorability of its inhabitants, because the true Spain, the immortal Spain, the honorable Spain, the united Spain, emerged from these old Castilian villages, which have worn honorability as their coat of arms, and enthusiasm and patriotism as their emblem. (Vázquez Montalbán 136)

In the echoes of Luis's stream of consciousness we can hear Julia's remarks again regarding the bread being entirely produced by themselves. These memories make Luis return to the farm, this time for good. From here, the film follows a melodramatic path characteristic of much of the cinematographic production of the times. Being an eminently conservative genre, it served perfectly the ideological intentions of the dictatorship. The sudden illness of Julia's daughter forces Luis to return to his medical profession, which he had abandoned when he was unable to save the life of his own daughter in the operating room. This distrust towards science connects the character with the philosopher Henri Bergson, who, as I mentioned before, was one of the authors present in Enrique's library. After Julia's daughter's successful appendicitis operation, the film approaches a "happy ending," confirmed by Luis and Julia's wedding and the creation of a new family.

Thus, in addition to representing an apology of the self-sufficient economic program of Spanish Fascism, Mur Oti's film helps to consolidate a discourse in which the roles of men and women are fixed. Julia, unable to function in her feminine role because of her husband's death, will progressively manage to persuade Luis to perform the masculine role while she finally incarnates the fascist feminine ideal by remaining in the house, taking care of her husband and children. If at the beginning of the movie Julia is endowed with agency, at the end she is presented as a subject colonized by the patriarchal ideology, willing to assume her subaltern role in the society of the times. The nuclear family has been "happily" reconstituted, though soon it will face new challenges. In the early 1950s, the autarchic economic program of Spanish Fascism begins to prove inefficient, forcing peasants to leave the rural world and emigrate to the big urban clusters. *Surcos*, premiered in 1951 and discussed in the following pages, will deal with this reality.

Menosprecio de corte (Disdain of City Life)

At the beginning of the 1950s, an important turn in the course of Spanish cinematography took place. José María García Escudero, General Secretary of Cinematography, rated *Surcos* as a film of "National Interest" instead of granting the award to *Alba de América* (Dawn in America), directed by Juan de Orduña the same year. Nieves Conde's film is a realistic portrait of post–civil war Spain. By contrast, *Alba de America* is a bio-epic film in the same line as the official hegemonic imperialist rhetoric.[9] The polemic generated by his decision forced García Escudero to resign (he would return to office in 1962) and in some ways opened a new stage in the history of Spanish cinematography during Franco's dictatorship. The more pro-government films produced by CIFESA (Compañía Industrial Film Español S.A.), a semi-official producer, focused on Spanish history or on Spanish folk music, called "españoladas" and featuring the most important folk singers of the moment. On the other hand, films like *Surcos* prepared the ground for the turning point represented by the well-known Conversations of Salamanca, celebrated in this city in 1955, in the context of the incipient Spanish cinematography.

This change of direction in the themes and aesthetic of national cinematography coincides with the progressive estrangement of Franco's regime from the fascist rhetoric. At the end of the Civil War, and while the Axis forces had a chance to win the European war, the Falange was the political protagonist of Spanish Fascism. Later, with the eclipse of Fascism in Europe, Franco's regime had to hide its connections with Fascism, approaching instead a group of technocrats related to Opus Dei who would update Francoism in the face of the new economic needs imposed by the United States. From the 1950s on, and as a consequence of foreign impositions (for example the Madrid Agreements signed with Eisenhower in 1953), Franco's regime began a transformation of its external image. This change was not enough to disassociate it from the rest of the fascist movements of the twentieth century. Franco's regime, aware that its survival depended largely on its chameleonic capacity, managed throughout its prolonged existence to evolve without having to make substantial changes.

Surcos premiered in Barcelona on October 26, 1951 and two weeks later, on November 12, in Madrid. According to the National Film Library, the film was poorly received as the audience barely reached one thousand spectators, and the box office earnings merely amounted to around one thousand Euros in today's currency. Nieves Conde's film combined a cast of well-known actors and actresses (Luis Peña, Félix Dafauce, and Marisa de Leza) as well as new faces, in an attempt to endow the film with a realistic atmosphere. Here is a summary of its plot: the Pérez family arrives in the capital city, persuaded by the eldest son (who has come to Madrid to do mandatory military training) and by the promise of the city's enormous economic possibilities. Reality is, however, very different from their expectations, and the family is submerged into a spiral of illegal work and prostitution that ultimately leads to the death of the eldest son. Finally, the family resolves to return to their rural village to continue working the land.

Like *Un hombre va por el camino*, *Surcos* expresses a political agenda—the maintenance of Spanish traditional rural structures—which is in conflict with the gradual "desarrollismo" (economic development agenda) sponsored by broad sectors of Franco's regime. Thus, Nieves Conde's film represents one of the last attempts of the Spanish fascist intelligentsia to claim an anti-modern, patriarchal, and rural Spain. To achieve this, the production team—in contradiction with their self-sufficient political ideology—incorporated some of the aesthetic proposals of Italian Neorealism and American *film noir* while making use of some of the techniques associated with the cinematographic avant-garde. The result is a stark portrait of post-civil war Spain with an implicit criticism of Franco's regime, which could not, or simply did not wish to, achieve the "revolution" advocated by the most orthodox groups of Spanish Fascism. José Antonio Nieves Conde, director of the film, and Gonzalo Torrente Ballester, Eugenio Montes, and Natividad Zaro, as scriptwriters, belonged to the Spanish fascist intelligentsia.[10] They were all part of the fascist culture depicted by Jordi Gracia in his book *La resistencia silenciosa*, hegemonic in Spain between the Civil War and the early 1950s and, according to the critic, based on an active enmity against the ethical, civil, and political aspects of Modernity (385). In addition to this common fascist background, they shared a progressive distancing from Franco's regime and their subscription to what has been called "left Fascism" because of its positions against the dictatorship and in favor of the vindication of the original political agenda of Spanish Fascism and its national-syndicalist revolution.

If, from a thematic point of view, *Surcos* expresses the traditionalistic discourse of radical Falangism, from an aesthetic perspective it also introduces Neorealism in Spain. This use of neorealist patterns by a director clearly identified with fascist positions leads Marsha Kinder to wonder: "How are the conventions from a supposedly left-wing discourse like Neorealism ideologically reinscribed to serve an ultra-left-wing Falangist thesis film such as this?" (41). There is probably no simple answer, but I would like to present two hypotheses. One of them has to do with cinematographic aesthetics, and the other with socio-political notions. The fact that José María García Escudero, General Director of Cinematography, chose *Surcos* over *Alba de América* highlights the idea that pro-government cultural circles were already aware of the exhaustion of historical cinema (which had effectively expressed the ideology of the regime in the past) and of the need to provide the national cinematographic production with new aesthetic patterns. It is interesting to see how this change in perspective takes place at a moment in which the process of abandoning the self-sufficient economic program had begun to intensify. On the other hand, the confluence of the left wing of Spanish Falangism and of certain sectors of the traditional left is caused, in my opinion, by different factors. The attack on the industrial model proposed by capitalism on behalf of Marxism is explained by the socio-economic conditions imposed on workers. The criticism of Falangism is based on its belief that the exodus of peasants to industrial areas means the loss of traditional conservative Spain's influence. This falangist hypothesis will prove to be true since Franco's regime came to an end mainly because of the extraordinary pressure of the industrial centers and big cities which had grown in the 1950s and 1960s thanks to the rural exodus.

Surcos mirrors the tensions between rural and industrial Spain, and it resorts to *film noir* as the most appropriate aesthetic to achieve that goal. In his study on American *film noir* and the spaces of Modernity, Edgard Dimendberg pointed out that this genre, so popular in American theatres in the 1940s and 1950s, exposed the tensions between different social, geographical and cultural spaces. In this case, these tensions are caused by the clash between two ideological universes that are mutually exclusive—the countryside and the city— spaces that will collide in Franco's Spain, especially in the 1950s.

Nieves Conde's film shares many characteristics with American *film noir*: the inability of its protagonists, especially the two Manolos, to "live comfortably somewhere"; the avoidance of the happy ending, traditional in Hollywood productions; and finally, the depiction of the city as a threatening entity (Dimendberg 7–14). This leading role assigned to the city is also present in neorealist cinema, in which the city is one of the main characters, as "one of the most continuous concerns of neorealist cinema was with the city and with the processes of modernization—for example, post-war reconstruction, industrialization, secularization and rural-to-urban migration" (Shiel 15). Nieves Conde would acknowledge years later in an interview that: "in all my productions, I strove to follow two paths: the film of intrigue and social cinema. I generally combined both, neither creating a pure film of intrigue nor a pure social film" (Castro 263).

The negative depiction of the city has an ample artistic tradition that has been widely studied. The topic of "menosprecio de corte y la alabanza de aldea" (disdain of city life, praise of village life), developed by Antonio Guevara in 1539, is as old as art itself, and *Surcos* does not make any new contributions to it. However, I want to highlight Nieves Conde's obsession, as seen in the very first scenes of the movie, in showing the city of Madrid as dominated by huge and uncontrolled groups of people, the threatening masses against which Ortega y Gasset (whose texts had been essential readings for the Spanish fascist intellectuals) had warned. In *La rebelión de las masas*, Ortega y Gasset blames the masses for causing "the most serious crisis that peoples, nations, and cultures could suffer" (37). The image of unmanageable masses is repeated constantly in the film: during the family's arrival at the station; in the neighborhood where they live; during a fight at the entrance of a bar; and in the scene in which Manuel, the father, is detained for illegal sales. The masses are always depicted as negative actors. Let us focus in now on the following scene.

Manolo arrives at a park where children are playing and sets up his improvised stall. One of the children silently approaches the stall and through gestures conveys the idea that he wants some candy but does not have any money. Manolo, an honest and good-natured country man, gives him a piece for free. Immediately, the camera captures the faces of three other children, who, also silently, show that they too want candy but cannot afford it. Manolo sends them away. When the children do not move, he decides to change location. Before his stall is fully arranged, the three children are already there, still silent. Manolo tries to persuade them that "he cannot give candy to everybody." Defeated by the children's persistence, he gives a candy to each of them. In the following shot, the heads of eight children represent the crowd (shown in its entirety in the next shot) that has literally surrounded Manuel, shouting: "We want candy! We want candy!" Now the camera shifts to the left in order to include the shot of a policeman who is observing the scene from a distance. His presence, and not Manolo's remarks, will make the children run away, allowing the kindhearted Manolo to regain his "freedom." The camera focuses on the harsh face of the policeman, who is insistently looking at the street vendor. Unaware of the fact that he is breaking the law by selling merchandise on the streets, Manolo begins a conversation with the officer: "You know how kids are, but if you are too soft with them. . . ." His naïveté leads him to ask the policeman if he wants to buy cigarettes. By way of an answer, the officer requests his sales permit, which, of course, Manolo does not have. Understanding the situation, he dismantles the stall and accompanies the officer to the police station.

Manolo is a victim of the crowds. From my point of view, this fear of uncontrollable crowds, characteristic of the first decades of the twentieth century, plays an important role in the inception of the European fascist movement. One of its first goals is, precisely, the organization of those crowds, converting their revolutionary energies through a clear nationalistic purpose. The crowds will only become a people once they have been tamed and structured within the organic unit into which the national entity has evolved.

In a later conversation between Manolo and his wife, the audience learns that his merchandise has been seized and he has been threatened with having to pay fines should he reoffend. His wife is furious and makes him peel potatoes in the kitchen, a space reserved for women, as is that of the Church. She regrets not having left him behind in the countryside to work the land. For the first time in the film, Manolo states that they should have stayed there.

The gender tensions are evident in a film in which, with the exception of the puppeteer (whom I will discuss shortly), female characters are always negative. Immoral, dishonest, lascivious, and materialistic, they bring disgrace upon men. Nieves Conde's film connects in this way with the misogynist character of Francoism through female characters who consciously deviate from the path marked for the woman of the times by the Feminine Section of the Falange. The only exception to the rule is the puppeteer's daughter, who couples with the youngest son of the Pérez family.

The two oldest women, one of them the mother of the family and the other the relative who lives in the village and also owns the house they are living in, are blinded by the materialistic opportunities they see in a city in which, as one of them expresses, "If you are too scrupulous, you'll go hungry." Meanwhile, the two youngest women, Pilar and Toña, display an overflowing sexuality, distant from the official morals of the times. Pilar's character is based on the "femme fatale" of the American *film noir*, a genre with which the film has been associated. Toña, the daughter of the family, is conscious of her feminine power of seduction, and she exploits this throughout the film in order to obtain the favors of Chamberlain, one of the villains. Inspired by the model of the "nouveau riche," Chamberlain has made his money through illicit business in the black market during the first years of the dictatorship.

Life in the city does not go as well as the Pérez family had imagined when they left the village. They do not find steady work, the oldest son is connected with a mobster who deals in the black market, and, on top of that, the youngest daughter wants to start a career as a singer. Her failure as an artist, along with the fact that she becomes the lover of the black market dealer, causes Manuel (the head of the family) to put into practice the "narrative of mainstreaming" that I defined earlier. He will attempt to return to the village and restore the original order, disturbed as a consequence of their exodus to the city. In the ideological universe of the film, the restoration of values takes place too late, and the price paid by the family is the death of the oldest son. Ironically, this final sacrifice makes it possible for the peasants to return to the mythical place of the village, a paradise lost that they will ultimately recover.

The oldest son's death brings to the forefront one of the most habitual topics in the rhetorical repertoire of Francoism. For fascist thinking, death is an essential component of redemption. In 1946, Franco expressed that "there is no redemption without bloodshed; bless a thousand times the blood that has brought about our redemption" (Vázquez Montalbán 136). Therefore, the Pérez family expiates its sins through the death of the son. Their sin is none other than their attempt to change the social determinism that made them peasants in order to live a life that is not for them, in an environment they are not prepared for.

The film concludes with the scene of the burial, in which the soil that covers the son's coffin is a metaphor for the land they abandoned and now must reclaim. Originally, Nieves Conde and his scriptwriters intended another twist to the story. According to the script, the train that took them back to the village would cross paths with another going to the city, full of peasants who would face a destiny similar to the Perez's. Upon arriving at the station, Toña, the daughter, switches trains to return to Madrid and continue her life as a singer and a prostitute. The Francoist censorship did not approve of this ending.

Surcos underscores the contradictions and tensions of a regime in which two different ways of understanding the economic life of the country coexist: the falangist self-sufficiency economic agenda; and the capitalist perspective of the Francoist bourgeoisie, with its emphasis on industrial development. The autarchic-agrarian policies of the Falange will attempt to retain the peasantry in rural areas in order to maintain the structure of traditional Spain. On the other hand, the industrial sector surrounding the big cities will require a fast-growing, non-qualified labor force, thus highlighting the deep transformations that will eventually cause the failure of the economic principles of the radical Falange. The tensions between a traditional agricultural Spain and a modern industrial one will ultimately be resolved in favor of the latter. The late 1950s will see the appearance of television, the Seiscientos, and crowds of tourists who, with their arrival at the Spanish coast in search of the sun, will gradually open up the gilded cage in which the dictatorship had secluded Spanish society. This process, which brings positive economic consequences, is fundamental to the establishment of the foundations of a society that, by Franco's death in 1975, is prepared to begin its journey toward democracy.

To sum up, Francoism, in an attempt to erase (as much as possible) the modernizing effects of the Second Republic, represents its conception of the ideal space for the construction of the New Spain. It favors a rural world distanced from Modernity, with the city as the epitome of the latter. In this natural, rural Arcadia the ideal subject is far removed from all intellectual and material temptation in order to blend in with a Nature that, as Schama has pointed out, is a synecdochal expression of the national essence. Centering on the Church and the family as fundamental units of the national organism, this subject accepts a hierarchized society in which hard work and the capacity of sacrifice are presented as essential Spanish values. In this context, the cinematography produced during the first years of Franco's dictatorship, a time in which the fascist aspects of the regime intensified, idealized rural Spain with the same eagerness it combated the vices of big cities. Hence, the filmography of the period promoted a socio-economic viewpoint that supported an autarchic order in which the countryside played the leading role, and agriculture was the basis of the economic development of the nation. This rural and agricultural Spain was the depositary of the eternal values that supported the essential family structure on which the Spanish fascist social ideology was built. Reality, as *Surcos* had already hinted, was very different, and since the early 1950s more and more Spanish people leave an Arcadia that was not, in order to be part of a society that was becoming progressively more urban and industrial, and more conscious of the enormous gap between Spanish society and its anachronistic government.

Notes

1. In spite of the attempts of certain historians to minimize the fascist ingredients of Fascism, I agree with Paul Preston, Michael Richards, Jordi Gracia, and Carme Molinero and Pere Ysàs, among others, when they refer to a first stage in the dictatorship marked by a fascist political, social, and cultural discourse. While it may be easy to establish 1939 as the initial date of the period since it coincides with the end of the war, it is more complicated to set a specific date for the end of the autarchic-fascist stage. In fact, it is possible to mention a gradual abandonment of isolation through the 1950s, with three decisive moments. The first important date in this process is 1953, the year in which the pacts between the Vatican and the United States are signed. These agreements represent the most significant boost to the Francoist politics by the Catholic Church, loyal ally of Francoism, since the beginning of the insurgency, and from a superpower that regarded the visceral Francoist anti-communism as its best ally in the Cold War against the USSR. At the end of 1955, Spain completed its quest for international acknowledgment by becoming part of the United Nations, from which it had been excluded for supporting the Axis powers during World War II. From a domestic perspective, this abandonment of autarchic-fascist practices was completed by the ministerial cabinet reformation of 1957.
2. Francoism set in motion a series of ideological apparatuses that naturalized its reactionary ideology so as to consolidate the dictatorship. Among them, mass media (newspapers, radios, and, later on, television, besides all kinds of publications, including those for children) were widely exploited and helped establish its

hegemony for nearly forty years. Their disposition to express the dominant discourse in the years studied in this chapter leads me to believe that there was a cinematographic trend that derived from the ideological propositions of Fascism and, at the same time, contributed to their reproduction. In addition to the films analyzed here, one can mention *La aldea maldita* (Florián Rey, 1942), *Mariona Rebull* (José Luis Sáenz de Heredia, 1947), *Las aguas bajan negras* (José Luis Sáenz de Heredia, 1948) *Pequeñeces* (Juan de Orduña, 1950) and *Balarrasa* (José Antonio Nieves Conde, 1950), among others, as part of a trend of anti-urban cinematography that defended a utopic and pre-modern Arcadia on which to base the New Spain.

3.   From the period of the 1960s, the popular humorist Paco Martínez Soria is the best example of the Francoist veneration of rural spaces. In films such as *La ciudad no es para mí* (Pedro Lazaga, 1966) and *Abuelo Made in Spain* (Pedro Lazaga, 1969), among others, the privilege of rural spaces goes hand in hand with the demonization of urban spaces. In the early 1970s, Pedro Lazaga directed the popular Alfredo Landa in *Vente a Alemania, Pepe* (1971), another apology of rural life, this time not so much to demonize the city but to dissuade the Spanish people from laboral migration to Europe.

4.   All translations are my own.

5.   In addition to the film analyzed in this chapter, during the 1950s Manuel Mur Oti directed *Cielo negro* (1951), *Condenados* (1953), *Orgullo* (1955), *Fedra* (1956), *El batallón de las sombras* (1957), *La guerra empieza en Cuba* (1957), *Duelo en la cañada* (1959), y *Pescando millones* (1959). In 1992, Mur Oti was awarded with an honorific Goya to celebrate his career as director, writer, and producer. In 1993 he was awarded with the Gold Medal for "Mérito en las Bellas Artes."

6.   For a panoramic view of Manuel Mur Oti's work, see *Manuel Mur Oti: Las raíces del melodrama* by Miguel Marías.

7.   This structure is also shared by, among others, the following films: *Balarrasa* (José Antonio Nieves Conde, 1950), *Pequeñeces* (Juan de Orduña, 1950), *Cielo Negro* (Manuel Mur Oti, 1951), and *Condenados* (Manuel Mur Oti, 1953).

8.   Specifically, the quote is part of Gremio's speech in the second act. He enumerates his riches in order to support his request for Blanca's hand, also requested by Hortensio, who is unable to match his economic offer.

9.   Like Nazi Germany and Mussolini's Italy, during the 1940s Franco's dictatorship resorted to national history in order to legitimize the Spanish Civil War and the subsequent regime as the only possible outcome in an historical chain, unfolding in accordance with a strict causality. Establishing an official history also contributed to reconstructing national identity, gravely weakened after three years of Civil War. However, from my point of view, this attempt to recast the history of Spain as a homogenous and coherent narrative finally failed due to the internal ideological contradictions of Fascism, in general, and Franco's regime, in particular.

10. According to Gonzalo Torrente Ballester, he would be the only one responsible for

the script since Nieves Conde rejected a first draft by Natividad Zaro, because he considered her proposal too "arnichesque" (Vázquez Aneiros 63).

Works Cited

Cano Ballesta, Juan. *Las estrategias de la imaginación: Utopías literarias y retórica política bajo el franquismo*. Madrid: Siglo XXI, 1994.

———. Literatura y Tecnología. *Las letras españolas ante la revolución industrial (1890–1940)*. Valencia: Pre-Textos, 1999.

Castro, Antonio. *El cine español en el banquillo*. Valencia: Fernando Torres, 1974.

Dimendberg, Edward. *Film Noir and the Spaces of Modernity*. Cambridge, MA: Harvard University Press, 2004.

Gracia, Jordi. *La resistencia silenciosa: Fascismo y cultura en España*. Barcelona: Anagrama, 2004.

Guevara, Antonio de. *Menosprecio de corte y alabanza de aldea*. (1539). Madrid: Espasa Calpe, 1952.

Kaplan, Alice Y. *Reproductions of Banality: Fascism, Literature, and French Intellectual Life*. Minneapolis: University of Minnesota Press, 1986.

Kinder, Marsha. *Blood Cinema: The Reconstruction of National Identity in Spain*. Los Angeles: University of California Press, 1993.

Lefebvre, Henry. *The Production of Space*. Oxford: Blackwell Publishers, 1991.

Maffesoli, Michel. *Du nomadisme. Vagabondages initiatiques*. Paris: Livre de Poch, 1997.

Marías, Miguel. *Manuel Mur Oti: Las raíces del melodrama*. Lisboa: Cinemateca Portuguesa/Filmoteca Española, 1990.

McGowan, John. "Toward a Definition of Postmodernism." *Postmodernism and Its Critics*. Ithaca: Cornell University Press, 1991.

Molinero, Carme, and Pere Ysàs. *Anatomía del franquismo*. Barcelona: Crítica, 2008.

Neocleous, Mark. *Fascism*. Buckingham: Open University Press, 1997.

Ortega y Gasset, José. *La rebelión de las masas*. Madrid: Espasa Calpe, 1969.

Preston, Paul. *Franco 'Caudillo de España.'* Barcelona: Grijalbo Mondadori, 1998.

———. *La política de la venganza: El fascismo y el militarismo en la España del siglo XX*. Barcelona: Península, 1997.

Richards, Michael. *A Time of Silence: Civil War and the Culture of Repression in Franco's Spain, 1936–1945*. Cambridge: Cambridge University Press, 1998.

Schama, Simon. *Landscape and Memory*. New York: Alfred A. Knopf, 1995.

Shiel, Mark. *Italian Neorealism: Rebuilding the Cinematic City*. New York: Wallflower Press, 2006.

Surcos. Dir. José Antonio Nieves Conde. Perf. Luis Peña, María Asquerino, Francisco Arenzana and Félix Defauce. Atenea Films, 1951.

Un hombre va por el camino. Dir. Manuel Mur Oti. Perf. Ana Mariscal, and Fernando Nogueras. Sagitario Films, 1949.

Vázquez Aneiros, Aurora. *Torrente Ballester y el cine: Un paseo entre luces y sombras*. Ferrol: Edicions Embora, 2002.

Vázquez Montalbán, Manuel. *Los demonios familiares de Franco*. Barcelona: Random House, Mondadori, 2004.

Zubiaur, Nekane. "Un hombre va por el camino (Manuel Mur Oti, 1949): La llamada de la tierra." *Pausa* 5 (Diciembre 2007). Accessed 7 Feb. 2010. *www.revistapausa.com/pdf/n5/unhombrevaporelcamino.pdf*.

◆   **12**

The Spectacle of a National Trauma: Gaze, Space, National Identity, and Historical Memory in Democratic Spain

Carmen Moreno-Nuño

(Translated by Andre Moskow)

> Spatial practices in fact secretly structure the determining
> conditions of social life.
> —Michel de Certeau

As a consequence of the movement for the recovery of historical memory, in the last few years Spain's cultural sphere has produced a resignification of places that relate to the Spanish Civil War and the Franco period. It is a resemantification that mythologizes, consecrates and monumentalizes spaces that were essentially pragmatic—that is, spaces that until now had been considered important for their economic value and purpose (Tuan 17). This phenomenon is related to a desire to memorialize, which, according to Pierre Nora, characterizes our contemporary societies that are continually searching for places of memory. In Spain, there has been a memory boom of the Spanish Civil War and the Franco period. The current status of the problem of space is also due to the tension and subsequent malaise caused by urban development speculation beginning in the years immediately prior to the entry of the euro, and particularly since 1999–2000. The restructuring of spatial memory also stems from the real estate crisis in Spain and its influence on the serious economic crisis of 2008. The debate surrounding the complete demolition of the Carabanchel jail, an emblem of Franco repression, in order to build apartment buildings, or whether to preserve its dome as a place of memory, is an example of the confrontation between a vision that places a premium on land's economic value and one that defends the humanistic dimension embedded in the space.[1]

The digging up mass graves has also highlighted how in Spain places linked to the repression of the traumatic past have ceased to be anthropological—places where history is lived—and have become historical—places where history is made. In fact, mass graves paradigmatically embody the problem of placing symbolic value on spaces and places, given that in the dilemma over whether to leave the exhumed remains in a grave that for some have acquired a sacred status or bury them in a place that has traditionally been considered more dignified, lies the symbolic value that is imprinted on the place. This revalorization of place is at the heart of the films analyzed in this essay. In contrast to the sense of indifference toward places and places of memory, these cultural productions succeed in becoming the memory of specific places—instruments that re-create what took place—as they themselves stand in places of memory that are unavoidable referents of what took place. Moreover, in notable contrast to the repression of the gaze caused by the pragmatic nature of the loss of memory concerning the Spanish Civil War and the Franco period that dominated the first few decades of the post-Franco democratic period in Spain, these works develop a gaze that forces us to look at what we were unwilling to see.

The revalorization of space is especially important in a country in which places of memory are both scarce and space-negating constructions: failed attempts that, instead of memorializing a place, negate it and instead of building history, resist it.[2] It is not only that places of memory, such as monuments or museums, that serve to dignify and keep alive the memory of the vanquished in the Spanish Civil War have not been built during the first few decades of democracy. It is also that the iron-fisted discriminatory memory of the victors— preserved in cemeteries, churches, street names, and commemorative monuments—has repeatedly tried to prevent the exercise of symbolic justice that the dismantling of Franco statues entails. The monument in the Plaza de la Lealtad (Allegiance Square), the Valle de los Caídos (Valley of the Fallen), the Alcázar de Toledo (Toledo Fortress), and the Parque García Lorca (García Lorca Park) illustrate the paradox that the most paradigmatic places of memory in Spain are places of non-memory.[3] If the monument to all of the fallen in the Plaza de la Lealtad in Madrid is the epitome of a lack of memory, given that it is sadly unknown by the vast majority of Spaniards (Aguilar Fernández, *Memoria* 283–84), the Alcázar de Toledo, the Valle de los Caídos, and the Parque García Lorca are also failed places that exemplify how in Spain the transformation of political realities, historical conceptions, and cultural representations of the Civil War has not been matched by the conflict's monumental representations, thereby leaving us with a landscape that is dominated by historical anachronism (Cartwright-Punnet 5). In keeping with Baudrillard's notions in *Simulacra and Simulation*, we can say that these are monuments behind which there is nothing original nor any origin since what they refer to has disappeared thus obscuring the difference between the real and the imaginary.

At its root, the resignification of space promoted by the sociopolitical movement to recover historical memory, like the movement itself, is a search for sense and individual, social, and national identity, since the collective reference points have never been so fluctuating as in our contemporary period. Given that space is an expression of group identity—the roots, the telluric—it is therefore that which most needs to be defended from external threats or internal uncertainties so that the discourse on identity does not become meaningless. Space, despite being along with time the most universal category, has also become a subject of dispute due to the relationship that exists between space and power. As scholars of space have indicated, space and place do not have a unique meaning but are subject to interpretation by individuals and communities, thereby giving rise to a plurality of meanings that may be the cause of strife or consensus and harmony. Space is therefore political: "Place is also political because the way it is constructed means that it is occupied by some people's stories but not by others" (Sheldrake 20).

This political dimension of space explains the confrontational nature that the current debate on memory in Spain has acquired, since what is at stake with regard to the country's past and its places of memory is what we understand Spain to mean. On the one hand, we advocate a pluralistic and multiple resignification of spaces as the solution to the monolithic ideological constructions of the past, and propose accepting and moving beyond the fact that there is a lack of any basic national agreement on the meaning of the Spanish Civil War and the Franco dictatorship. On the other hand, historical manipulation is denounced in a society that is still divided as a result of the different senses of nationalism and the problem of the different versionsof history.[4] As demonstrated by the "archival war" that has been waged since 1995 over the civil war documents of the National Historical Archive located in Salamanca and claimed by Cataluña, "the Spanish Civil War's field of memory continues to be a minefield with regard to the difficult question of Spain's identity" (Ehrlicher 286). It is an identity that protects the union of the nation's monumental body from any internal claim that threatens its political dismemberment. We are also in a period in which the ashamed and inferiority complex- laden national sentiment that characterizes the young Spanish democracy has given way to an "intento de recuperación del patriotismo español y de renovación del discurso nacionalista procedente tanto de la derecha como de la izquierda españolas" (Castiñeira

70) (attempt at recovering Spanish patriotism and renewing the nationalist discourse coming from Spain's right and left), from which the discourse on the Spanish Civil War and the Franco period is not spared. The resignification of space must also strike a delicate balance between defending the political virtues of remembering the past (Margalit) and the dangers of victimization, since all stories about victims report the suffering by affirming the victims' undefined moral and political privilege (Todorov).

In the area of film production, the hyperrealism that characterizes the dominant mode of portrayal runs the risk of endorsing films on the Spanish Civil War and the Franco regime that replace the self-glorifying memory of Spain during the Franco period with a mere Republican martyrology on the victims of the repression.[5] This is why a critical, metafictitious self-reflection on why and how the creation of certain fictional places of memory that fulfill this purpose, yet at the same time denounce the perils of victimization and nostalgia for the past, is so important. In the remainder of this essay I shall analyze three films—*Soldados de Salamina*, *Para que no me olvides* and *En la ciudad sin límites*—which reflect on the relationship that exists between historical memory, identity, space and gaze. By reclaiming the public dimension of memory and, more specifically, the memory of the vanquished, these films bring about a resignification of places that is in essence a revalorization of them. The films in question deal with the "crisis of place in Western societies" (Sheldrake 2) because they portray the uprootedness, dislocation, and displacement that characterize a world which, in light of the challenges of globalization and postmodernity, seeks answers in the trauma of a silenced past.

They are also films that recover spaces considered worthless—even wastelands. By promoting a commemorative culture around historical memory, they seek to erect spaces that through (de)monumentalization, mythification, and consecration fetishize places by turning them into a sublimating locus of the historical event In contrast to the temptation of totality, the ideal of exhaustive interpretation, and the essentialization of culture, these works present everything from an all-encompassing construction of space to its complete deconstruction, depending on the degree to which they take into account both the intrinsically problematic nature of commemorative cultures and the critical value of cultures that remember. On the one hand, these films portray the contemporary world's anxiety and sense of guilt resulting from the thoughtless use of industrial and technological power over nature, and on the other hand, the problem of the city. The spectacular growth of the world population and its massive concentration in urban centers have made the city's future one of the most pressing problems of the modern world.[6] But above all, these cultural

productions denounce how the problem of space requires not only solid principles of economy, engineering, architecture, and urban planning, but also a
more complete and humanistic approach that is reminiscent of the value that
for centuries has been awarded to anthropological places—places that have become endangered by the deterritorialization of human life, the compression of
space, the homogenization of place, and the loss of historical memory. One
need only recall the literary genre of the *laudes civitatis*, poems that articulated
the utopian ideal of civic life. This cultural production's fundamental ideological proposal is the exhortation to use historical memory as an instrument to
rehumanize the space we live in. In the words of Yi-Fu Tuan:

> Many places, profoundly significant to particular individuals and groups, have little
> visual prominence. They are known viscerally, as it were, and not through the dis-
> cerning eye or mind. A function of literary art is to give visibility to intimate experi-
> ences, including those of place. (162)

Para que no me olvides

Para que no me olvides ("So that you don't forget me"), directed by Patricia
Ferreira, portrays space related to the Spanish Civil War's historical memory
as a totalizing construction based on myth. As Sheldrake has noted, the purpose of mythical space as an intrinsic part of a holistic cosmovision "is not to
illuminate questions of concrete context but to sketch a kind of utopian place
in which everything is properly ordered in terms of ultimate meaning" (41).[7]
Order is restored in *Para que no me olvides* when Mateo inserts the cut-out
page into the book of *Treasure Island* in the attic recovered from his childhood
home.[8] Within that restored cosmic order, the dedication "De tu padre, para que
lo regales a tus hijos y ellos a sus nietos" (From your father so that you may
give it to your children and they, in turn, to their grandchildren) starts to make
sense when David's girlfriend stands in for the lost grandchild. She receives
the diary in which Mateo has written David's life in a way that is analogous
to how David had written his grandfather's life, to save it from oblivion. In
addition, the three main symbols of the film—the home, the olive tree, and
the *Treasure Island* book—act as the bases of a community telluric dimension
built on the protection provided by the dwelling, the collection of the fruits of
nature, and the wisdom of the written word. The reconfiguration of the family
fabric as a result of David's death underscores that we are witnessing a story of
life and death, primordial mythical elements of human existence. In contrast to

the chronological, historical, and progressional temporality that is imposed by industrial forms of production, the mythical cosmovision in this film upholds a "non-productive" concept of time—David's girlfriend is "only" a cashier at a supermarket—a concept based on the value of the past and the subjectivity of historical memory.

The mythical framework of *Para que no me olvides*, however, does not advocate in favor of ahistoricity, since myth and historical trauma are allied in order to give space a political value. In the scene on the beach at Alicante, which commemorates the twenty thousand Republican refugees who futilely waited to be evacuated at the end of the civil war, the sea remains offscreen, a fact that hides and at the same time evokes the scene in which the 1939 tragedy took place. By remaining offscreen, it embodies the impossibility of portraying the horror as it is conceived of by trauma theorists. If the sea as an open space is a common symbol of freedom in the Western world, which suggests the future and spurs one to action, any open space is also a threat insofar as it exposes the vulnerability of the individual. This is why there is a need for a place that acts as a safe haven of established values, which is what the recovery of his childhood home represents for Mateo. The home also exemplifies how the memory that is embodied in a place goes beyond one's personal story, and one can speak of coexistence and textual permanence in a single space of a multiplicity of layers of stories and of history.[9] In this film, memory also appears linked to death (David's death, and the death of the generation that went through the civil war), in a double story of mourning that critically reflects on the two strategies democratic Spain has adopted vis-à-vis the past: forgetting and remembering. The film advocates for the importance of remembering in order to save the past from death.[10] The intertextuality with the play *The Seagull* by Anton Chekhov, in which the characters are blind, acts as a metaphor for mourning and an invitation to look at places laden with historical significance that, like Mateo's house, are all around us.[11] This rediscovery of space is especially important in a historical period in which the increase in life expectancy has caused the normal coexistence of three generations to be extended to four, thereby increasing genealogical, collective, and historical memory and multiplying the occasions when each individual may have the impression—like Mateo—that his or her story is part of history, and that the former is related to the latter:

> Sabía que tenía que acordarme de todo hasta que devuelvan el honor a los muertos sin nombre que se llevó por delante aquel régimen implacable, pero cada día que pasa me doy cuenta de que nos van a dejar morir sin pedir perdón, de que no van

a colocar los nombres de las víctimas en un lugar bien visible para todos, como durante más de sesenta años han estado los nombres de los caídos por Dios y por España, para que los jóvenes lo sepan. (*Para que no me olvides*)

(I knew I had to remember everything until the honor of the nameless dead that was taken away by that implacable regime is restored, but with each passing day I realize they are going to let us die without asking for forgiveness. They are not going to place the names of the victims in a clearly visible place for all to see, as the names of the fallen for God and for Spain have been for over sixty years, so that young people will know about it.)

Given that, in the postmodern world—characterized by tourism, travel, intersection, non-place, transit, and non-permanence—one is never "home," *Para que no me olvides* is a "return home" to a mythical space that is resemanticized by a traumatic historical memory.[12] This mythical space puts into dialogue the poetics of the home understood as a set of phenomenological images of intimacy (Bachelard), with the political awareness of the need to have an historical home in order to avoid the fragmentation and dissipation of identity. The redesignation of Mateo's former home as an historic preservation site is not directed at its monumentalization but to its claim as a commemorative text that is capable of transmitting a cosmovision from one generation to the next: the home as a place of memory according to the terminology of Pierre Nora. In fact, the film denounces the urban speculation of the consumer-capitalist society that has dominated construction in Spain for the past several decades, a speculation which, like the loss of memory, reincorporates place into the space of what is not differentiated by accumulating debris—pasts, languages, cultures, traditions—in the name of a creative destruction that tends toward human beings' progressive isolation.[13] The novel *Treasure Island* assumes the symbolic center in a series of concentric circles involving the interior patio of Mateo's house and an olive tree that stands in the middle of it. The tracking shot that envelops the tree where Mateo used to read Stevenson's classic metonymically marks the entire house as a protective space (Bachelard 31) of mythical significance (Tuan 150).

As a paradigmatically maternal space, the childhood home protects human beings from the fragility, future, chance and destruction that, accentuated by the snow and cold in *Para que no me olvides*, set their roots in the Spanish Civil War.[14] But above all the representation of the home as a mythical place that is primordial and therefore privileged proposes, through the act of poetic transformation of reality and the fruitfulness of thought that embodies the myth, a safeguard of a community emotion that to this day is still wounded by the horror of the Spanish Civil War and the Franco period.

Soldados de Salamina

David Trueba's *Soldados de Salamina* (Soldiers of Salamis) brings to the screen the critical eye of Javier Cercas's novel by the same name in a metafictional film that forces us to look at space as an inquiry or search, that is, as an incessant and never-ending quest for historical knowledge and memory.[15] As a metafictional discourse, *Soldados de Salamina* proposes a concept of history, specific to the Spanish Civil War, based on facts from the past that include the present conditions under which these facts are transmitted and remembered.[16] By destabilizing the idea of history through a memory that obsessively questions itself, this work questions conventional film productions about the Spanish Civil War. In so doing, and as a postmodern work, it becomes a work in progress that doubts itself, is self-reflective and has no ending. It also turns into an exploration of the dilemmas of representation and a compulsive questioning of the very possibility of production itself.[17] By continuously including archival footage, not as period pieces or anecdotal images but as an intertextual presence that invites the viewer to reflect on how film tells a story and thus creates history, the movie acquires the form of a flashback of historical memory that is abstract rather than concrete and historical rather than personal. It presents a series of events that are the same and yet also different, which, by making use of space to develop a story through film together with the original novel, can be considered as artistic paradigms of Spanish postmodernity.[18]

Soldados de Salamina represents the search for historical knowledge through the classic leitmotif of the voyage as an internal search, but from a postmodern sensibility that turns the purpose of the voyage, and of all cinema, into an exploration of resistance zones and, therefore, into an acknowledgement of the limits of historical knowledge. Thus, in both the film and the novel a search for knowledge and physical displacement go hand in hand and are part of the protagonist's overarching disorientation: "Recorrí bibliotecas, hemerotecas, archivos. Varias veces viajé a Madrid, y constantemente a Barcelona" (70) (I went through libraries, newspaper libraries, and archives. I traveled to Madrid several times and constantly to Barcelona). The voyage as both a means and an end to the search for historical knowledge multiplies and complicates the representation of space in Cercas's film. To intensify the displacements, location changes and highlight the contrast between formal spaces of knowledge—libraries, bookstores, universities, book fairs—and informal ones—cafes and restaurants—that determine the physical space. The film adds printed, technological and virtual spaces through photographic, film, television, and computer images. It also inverts the traditional fictitious relationship between gaze and landscape that defines voyages. Here the traveler creates the landscape and is therefore the spectator of his own spectacle (Augé *Los no lugares* 91). By recovering the historical memory of the shooting of the Falangist Sánchez Mazas, the protagonist's visits to Collell and Dijon serve to build a truer relationship between gaze and landscape than the relationship left to us by the Franco period and the first few decades of Democracy.[19]

By embodying the relationship between space and memory, the monument, which is a tangible expression of permanence, or at least duration, contributes to preventing history from being an abstraction in the eyes of the living. It is for this reason that the portrayal in *Soldados de Salamina* of two monuments, the sanctuary of Santa Maria del Collell and the cross commemorating the execution by firing squad, is important. The caption "Caídos por Dios y por España" (Those who died for God and for Spain) on the commemorative cross and the locals' negative opinion of it underscores and denounces, respectively, the monolithic monumentalization of history that for decades was imposed by the Franco side. In contrast to the monolithic centrality of the monument, *Soldados de Salamina* advocates for a decentering that turns the notions of itinerary and intersection into protagonists; that is, through the protagonist's continuous travels and displacements, the film emphasizes a search rather than an imposed truth. We are not confronted with an orderly and centered landscape, just as we are not confronted with an orderly linear temporality. The visits to the clearing in the woods where the massacre took place and to the commemorative monument make it clear that the recuperation of historical memory in Spain must come from a critical and distanced encounter with one's own identity; that is, from a cathartic trip mediated by mourning as understood by LaCapra: "Como si aguardara una revelación por ósmosis, me quedé allí un rato; no sentí nada" (70) (As if I were expecting a revelation by osmosis, I remained there for a while; I felt nothing).[20]

The forest acquires enormous importance in the story told by Trueba as the personification of the struggle for survival imposed by the life-death dialectic of Fascist Spain. Although "[s]paciousness is closely associated with the sense of being free" (Tuan 52), the subjective movement created by the hand-held camera that accompanies the claustrophobic foreground and middle ground in the forest illustrates how the land is both friend and foe in Sánchez Mazas's escape.[21] Just as in the novel, the forest presents itself to Sánchez Mazas as a possibility: "un espeso breñal de pinos y maleza promete una posibilidad de esconderse" (102) (a dense thicket of pines and underbrush that offers a possible hiding place). However, the threat of death resemanticizes the place when he is discovered by the soldier in "un agujero sin dignidad" (103) (a wretched hole). If space is a biological and psychological necessity, a condition for survival and a social prerequisite and spiritual attribute that connotes salvation and deliverance (Tuan 57), in *Soldados de Salamina* the civil war has imposed the unambiguous nature of death on the space's multiple meanings. In other words, we have the death of Spain at the hands of Fascism, which is what Sánchez Mazas's figurative blindness—the loss of his glasses—prevents him from seeing. Moreover, nature in the wilderness also produces a pantheist intuition of totality that wipes out history and time (Augé, *El tiempo* 46). To be sure, by transforming history through its representation of the forest into an eternal present that affirms the persistence of an unfinished past, Trueba's film reaffirms the importance, for current Spanish society, of recovering the historical memory of the Spanish Civil War's traumatic past through cinema.

The representation of space in *Soldados de Salamina* is also linked to the theme of the unfruitful search for a hero and, therefore, to the postmodern denial of the ending as closure and *telos* in a story that does not offer the narrative conclusion that stories with a moral traditionally end with.[22] If the fact that the anonymous soldier thought "Nada" (nothing) when he saw and did not kill Sánchez Mazas questions the instrumental rationality of the contemporary period, the refusal of the old man Miralles to acknowledge that he himself is that soldier underscores the inexistence of any moral ground, the lack of validity of any catharsis, and the impossibility of a rebuilt community in the wake of historical trauma. It also underscores the duty and moral necessity one has to tirelessly continue a historical search conceived of as a voyage. With his silence, Miralles refuses to be an accomplice to a society that, while it once condemned the Spanish Civil War to oblivion, now wants to turn it into a spectacle.[23] Analogous to the manner in which the leitmotiv of *Suspiros de España* transforms the space into a dance floor by exalting life in contrast to the military marches' invocation of death, the anonymous soldier/Miralles is affirmed as a subject of history because of his refusal to become part of it due to his ethical self-awareness vis-à-vis the world.[24] In this search for a hero, the representation of space unveils while at the same time deconstructing the unavoidable human tendency toward mythification, since the first image we have of Miralles is marked by failure or, what amounts to the same, victimization: the Estrella de Mar campsite and exile in Dijon.[25] However, when Miralles himself enters the scene, the space ceases to be an object of mythification and proceeds to demand the recovery of self-critical historical memory. In other words, it makes us conscious of the dangers of victimization. While in the novel "no era la sórdida habitación de asilo que yo esperaba, sino un pequeño apartamento limpio, ordenado y con luz: de un solo vistazo abarqué una cocina, un lavabo, un dormitorio y una salita de paredes casi desnudas, con dos butacones, una mesa y un ventanal que daba a un balcón abierto al sol de la tarde" (196) (the sordid room in a nursing home that I expected [is on the contrary] a small, clean, tidy, and well-lit apartment [with] a balcony that opens out onto the afternoon sun), the Nimpheas Residence of the film adds the clear and sunny verdure of an omnipresent garden to an apartment that is in fact clean, tidy, and well-lit. This apartment advocates in favor of a recovery of the past that does not give way to the postmodern destruction of the subject by means of a communication that is understood as testimony—in contrast to the solipsist fantasies of the female protagonist in the taxi—in defense of the constructive and open-to-dialogue nature of historical memory as the true and ultimate purpose of any voyage and any search.[26]

En la ciudad sin límites

The film *En la ciudad sin límites*, directed by Antonio Hernández, denounces the lack of historical memory that for years has characterized democratic Spain through a representation of space in which *non-places* predominate. The concept of a non-place has been developed by Marc Augé as an explanation of the changes that space has undergone since the birth of postmodernity. According to Augé, supermodernity's economic and technological globalization has produced a world that has seen a proliferation of places that lack territorial vocation and whose only purpose is to "facilitate circulation (and thus consumption) in a world of planetary dimensions" (*El tiempo* 101).[27] Unlike anthropological places, a non-place sets up a "space that can not be defined as a space of identity or as a relational or historical place" (*Los no lugares* 83), since its purpose is not to create single identities, symbolic relationships, or common heritage, but rather to multiply points of transit and temporary occupations. In the film the places marked by historical memory of the past are, however, distanced from the non-place and represented by the category of sacredness.

In *En la ciudad sin límites* the vast majority of the scenes are typical non-places: a hotel, a discotheque, an amusement park, a train station, trains, airplanes, airports, taxis, lobbies, elevators, and even a hospital, the place which best reflects the situation of anonymity and, therefore, the de-individuation that characterizes non-places. Shot from below, the vast illuminated mass embodies the discourse on power to the extent that elevated structures are indicative of social class and purchasing power.[28] In the hospital the majority of the scenes take place not in Max's room but in the hallway, just as the scenes in the hotel take place at the front desk and in the lobby, non-places within non-places, in a multiplication of Russian dolls that is further and further removed from real places, i.e., Max and Rancel's former house in Paris and Rancel's current apartment in Madrid. The amusement park criticizes the oversizing of the senses and the overabundance of supermodernity's events in a spectacular excess that leads to some disturbing images of gargoyles. It is the opposite of the euphoria of the spectacle and a metaphor for both Victor's adultery with his sister-in-law and the plot that is woven around the family's pharmacy business. The trips constantly being taken by different family members—non-places are both the facilities needed for the frenetic circulation of goods and people and the very means of transportation in their spectacular acceleration (Augé, *Los no lugares* 41)—denounce a present in which spatial overabundance, changes in scale, and the multiplication of imagined and imaginary references have come to displace the traumatic memory of the past. Victor and his girlfriend's worldliness actually hide the social dimension of the crisis of space that characterizes the contemporary period.[29] In addition, non-places also refer to the type of individual that these places generate. This is why the "cuadro psicológico cercano a la enajenación" (psychological make-up approaching alienation) that Max presents denounces the breakdown of an identity that is the product of both supermodernity's lack of roots and the loss of historical memory that a lack of grounding entails.[30]

In contrast to the de-individualizing cosmology of non-places, in *En la ciudad sin límites* Max and Rancel's home represents the permanence of a place that is not only anthropological—because historical memory runs through it—but has also acquired a sacredness as a result of having been kept hidden and immaculate by Max for forty years. In keeping with Mircea Eliade's theorization of the sacred, we could say that this house is, like all sacred places, an *axis mundi* or center of a world that reveres the past, with real and imagined borders that separate and isolate it from the secular and profane world of postmodernity (Sheldrake 5). In contrast to the acceleration of postmodernity—the accelerated montage of the taxi that takes Mateo away—there is the almost mystical quietude of the silent wait in the apartment. Together with the house, the cemetery plays with the sociological concept of a place that is defined by ethnological tradition as a culture that is set in time and space. Because few friends or acquaintances go there, the cemetery denounces the way in which the final resting place can become a non-place in our contemporary period. In stretching Augé's concept, it would be a nothing or non-place by being condemned by death to nothing, to non-existence, to the destruction of any reference and any meaning behind the referent. However, the cemetery encapsulates the paradox of also being an anthropological place insofar as it is the place of the long hoped-for (posthumous) meeting between Max and Rancel, the foundational moment of a new ethical family, and a space in which the truth—the homosexual relationship between Max and Rancel—moves into the public sphere and thus into the realm of what exists.

In *En la ciudad sin límites,* the non-place is the cause and result of the spectacle that characterizes the entire family, a spectacle conceived of not as a collection of images but rather as social relationships determined by images. In other words, it is the spectacle that accompanies the dominant class as an uninterrupted monologue of self-praise and self-portrait of power (Debord 19). Max's family exemplifies, beyond the society of well-being and globalization, the spectacle of democratic Spain's self-complacency that denies its past (Subirats). This is the spectacle of having and not being, a product of the alienation and breakdown of the dividing line between truth and lies, which obscures the true relationship between siblings who are fighting for control of the family business and reveals human relationships marked by betrayal, underscored by long hallways that impede communication. At the height of this spectacle of appearances is the myth that has been woven for decades by Marie regarding her husband's heterosexuality in order to, as Roland Barthes would put it, immobilize and perpetuate her bourgeois world (252). In fact, this is done for the purpose of hiding a betrayal that one would rather forget, just as one wishes to forget the historical framework in which it took place: the anti-Franco resistance by the Communist Party in exile during the first post–civil war period.

It is the title's metaphor, the city without limits, that offers a solution to the loss of historical memory caused by the uprootedness of the contemporary world's non-places, which in Spain is added to the spectacle of democratic self-complacency. It is also what solves this thriller's mystery. In the film, the clear exhortation to search out the memory of the past as a memory that is repressed and therefore liberating fortunately manages to escape a simple black-and-white separation of good and evil that the partisan issuing of the truth entails. Although Victor is the only one who searches for and finally discovers the truth that afflicts his father, his mother reminds him that "tú no eres el más apropiado para hablar de mentiras" (you are not the best person to be talking about lies). Or, in what amounts to the same thing, it is important to realize that, in the task of recovering historical memory that Spain is currently struggling with, there is no moral beacon illuminating a privileged position from which to judge history. Yet there is also no privileged position from which to judge the task of recovering the past's memory. In *En la ciudad sin límites* the only truth is that Max dies in the train station while fulfilling his desire to wait for a Rancel who never arrives. In other words, the reconstitution of the fragmented community that is the product of catharsis is only achieved at death. The recovery of historical memory, despite being an unavoidable imperative, is no guarantee of a definitive solution. In spite of this, we must try to escape from a past that Spain, like Max, is compulsively pursued by and which encloses it in a "ciudad sin límites" (city without limits), with no end, no exits, and no escape from itself, as evoked by the title's mysterious metaphor.

If for Michel de Certeau the city is always that which escapes us—"what ought to be, ultimately, the place but is only a name, the City" (103)—and requires a series of ongoing practices that have social significance to invent itself, in *En la ciudad sin límites* we witness the construction of the city of Paris—an emblem of all cities—as a mystery that, just like the past, needs to be unraveled in order to enable that inhabitable space that always escapes us to exist.[31] By lacking limits and therefore identity, the Paris of the past is as illusive and, by the same token, persistent as today's Paris. Max is unable to escape from the clutches of a city which, in his disturbed mind, is still the city occupied by the Nazis, just as he is unable to escape from the hospital's surveillance or from his paranoid memory of the past: "nos vigilan" (they are watching us). The stately monumentality of the city by the Seine is represented by buildings shot from below that are spread out by the depth of the field and illuminated by a ghostly light that makes them appear unreal in the present time. The distancing zoom in the aerial view of the city increases the dimensions of a metropolis that escapes our control due to its lack of borders. Rancel's novel titled *La ciudad sin límites*—without any preposition, since Rancel has in fact escaped from it—is an indirect acknowledgment of both the relationship between literature and film and the relationship between fiction and reality, since its protagonist, just like Rancel himself, does know where the city's exits are. Transformed into a gigantic prison—"todos creen que la ciudad no tiene límites" (everyone believes the city has no limits), "te matarán y la ciudad seguirá creciendo sin salidas para nadie" (they'll kill you and the city will continue to grow without any way out for anyone)—Paris becomes a symbol of that globalized world to which we belong without really belonging, and from which we cannot escape because we have lost the keys to a city and, thus, to a past that the cinema of historical memory now forces us to look at.

Conclusion

Recovering the past from the Spanish Civil War and the Franco repression is inseparable as a social phenomenon from its extensive media coverage. It is broadcast on 3:00 p.m. television news bulletins practically every day, as well as on the World Wide Web, and there are over two hundred associations for the recovery of historical memory. In other words, we are witnessing the creation of a new view that forces us to look at what we once tried to forget. Given that this extensive coverage is in an ideological struggle with the media that cover the large numbers of beatification processes for the martyrs that were murdered in the Republican zone, the historical memory effect may turn the memory of the past into a public spectacle: the Partido Popular has referred to this media phenomenon as a smoke screen meant to hide the economic crisis of 2008. However, it is especially prone to becoming an ideological spectacle in an age characterized by the end of ideologies.[32] On an academic level, the excess of memory may also lead to a squandering of memory, given that we have gone from vetoing doctoral dissertations on subjects that are considered especially controversial to a proliferation of them.[33] It is no wonder that the temptation of identity closure by imposing and patrimonializing a memorialistic canon leads to political and cultural battles, given that belonging to a national culture involves appropriating, internalizing, and sharing a specific set of social and cultural representations. But, even more importantly, it entails holding the interpretive key to understanding these representations: "Lo importante en la memoria nacional del pasado no es su verdad, sino su significación" (Castiñeira 66) (What is important about a nation's memory of the past is not its truth but its meaning).

A large part of recent cultural production in Spain is a reaction against the institutional loss of memory of the foundational violence that has characterized nation-states up through our current age. In contrast to the way the Spanish Civil War's memory has been discredited and how democracy's discourse itself is self-legitimized, Spain's recent cultural productions advocate for the transmission to new generations of a history that now wants to be written based on the values of freedom and tolerance. In this sense, by turning memory into a project, Spanish cinema seeks to narratively represent a new hermeneutics of the nation through the link between personal memory, collective memory, and historical memory. Moreover, it seeks to defend a public policy of historical memory that, by representing the stories of the vanquished, will lead to the recovery of that part of history which, because it tends to be rather subjective, has always remained outside the limits of historical objectivity. As we see in the films analyzed here, Spain's cultural sphere is producing a resignification of places that relate to the Spanish Civil War and the Franco period that is, in essence, a revalorization of these places. In one film (*Para que no me olvides*) these places are mythologized; in another (*En la ciudad sin límites*) they are made sacred; and in a third (*Soldados de Salamina*) they (de)monumentalize a space that used to be primarily pragmatic when approached from various degrees of self-criticism that advocate for the detotalizing construction of space. With the demise of the idea of progress, political utopias, and metanarratives, space, like time, has stopped being a principle of intelligibility and, therefore, has stopped being the center on which the principle of identity is inscribed. It is this self-consciousness that, in contrast to the romanticizing that is inherent in the recovery of historical memory, should most warn us of the insufficiency of culture itself as a locus for the search for lost unity. Thus, there is a caution contained in the title of this essay, "The Spectacle of a National Trauma," regarding the importance of critically looking at a past that has turned into a spectacle.

Notes

1. The Carabanchel jail, whose official name was the Provincial Prison of Madrid, was built by the Franco regime for the purpose of incarcerating its political opponents. During the fifty-five years it was in operation it was at the center of political claims as important as the struggle for amnesty, and it housed many of the main anti-Franco leaders as well as numerous artists and intellectuals. Despite opposition from some neighborhood groups and associations for historical memory, in 2008 the entire complex was demolished.

2. For Nora, a place of memory is an (symbolic, material . . .) object that embodies a memory that one does not want to lose in a historical period that, like the current period, has abandoned the cultivation of traditional forms of memory.

3. The Plaza de la Lealtad, located on the Paseo del Prado in Madrid and built during the reign of Isabel II, is known for its Monumento a los Caídos por España (Monument to those who died for Spain), where the ashes of the Madrileños who rose up in arms on May 2, 1808, and were shot the next day were deposited. The Valle de los Caídos is located in the Valle de Cuelgamuros in the Sierra de Guadarrama, near Madrid. Conceived by Franco as an homage to the fallen on the National side, the gigantic funeral monument actually pivots around only two figures, the Falangist José Antonio Primo de Rivera and Francisco Franco himself. By embodying the values of the dictatorship, the monument and its basilica continue to be a controversial reality, among other reasons, because they were built by

political prisoners. The military fortress of El Alcázar de Toledo is one of the most emblematic symbols of the National side. At the beginning of the Spanish Civil War, Colonel Moscardó defended the fortress against repeated Republican attacks, which (in the falsified Nationalist historical version) cost him his own son's life. The building currently houses the main branch of the Autonomous Library of Castilla-La Mancha and the Museum of the Army. García Lorca Park, located in the town of Alfacar in Granada, commemorates the poet's work while at the same time housing in one corner an olive tree under which García Lorca is supposedly buried.

4. Resina and Winter have studied the problem of places of memory from a Nationalist approach.

5. With regard to current film production, Jo Labanyi has stated that cinema "ha optado por un hiperrealismo que nos muestra el pasado 'tal como fue', sin ninguna exploración de los mecanismos de la memoria, y por tanto sin examinar los procesos que determinan la transmisión (o falta de transmisión) del pasado a las generaciones posteriores" (158) (has chosen a hyperrealism that shows us the past 'exactly as it was' without any exploration of the mechanisms of memory and therefore without examining the processes that determine the transmission (or lack of transmission) of the past to subsequent generations).

6. In 1950, 29 percent of the world's population lived in urban centers; in 1990 it was 50 percent; and it is estimated that in the year 2025 it will be between 60 and 75 percent.

7. In contrast to the displacement and uprootedness that characterize the postmodern world, a myth is put forward as a response to a desire for belonging that goes beyond the biological or the aesthetic and that relates to the very heart of our identity (Sheldrake 9).

8. The attic has been studied by Bachelard as the ascension to a place of greater tranquility and poetic solitude (26).

9. "It is appropriate to think of places as texts, layered with meaning. Every place has an excess of meaning beyond what can be seen or understood at any one time. This excess persistently overflows any attempt at a final definition" (Sheldrake 17).

10. Jacqueline Cruz has noted how the film warns us against both the acute memory loss suffered by the character of Irene and against the obsessive memory that haunts Clara.

11. Jacqueline Cruz has analyzed the intertextuality between this film and the work of Chekhov (37–38).

12. Jacqueline Cruz has studied the home in this film as a metaphor for the evolution of Spain in the twentieth century: the home and workshop of a typographer prior to the civil war; a bicycle shop during the Franco period; a somewhat abandoned and unhealthy mansion during the democracy; and a future apartment complex "para beneficio de especuladores, políticos corruptos y la clase media hipotecada" (34) (for the benefit of speculators, corrupt politicians and the mortgaged middle class) in the new century.

13. "Urbanism is the mode of appropriation of the natural and human environment by capitalism, which, true to its logical development toward absolute domination can (and now must) refashion the totality of space *into its own peculiar decor*" (italics in original, Debord 121).

14. "When we dream of the house we were born in, in the utmost depths of reverie, we participate in this original warmth, in this well-tempered matter of the material paradise. This is the environment in which the protective beings live. We shall come back to the maternal features of the house" (Bachelard 7).

15. "La intriga de la novela se sostiene como una búsqueda, una investigación, la persecución de un enigma, cuyo desvelamiento compromete al propio narrador, pero también el sentido total de la figuración literaria" (Pozuelo Yvancos qtd. in Martín 43–44) (The intrigue of the novel is sustained as a search, an investigation, the pursuit of an enigma whose discovery compromises the narrator himself but also the entire sense of literary imagination).

16. Both Mabrey and Ballesteros have analyzed the novel and the film by highlighting their connections to historical memory. Albert has framed the novel in the current commemorative enterprise that tries to break the spell of collective amnesia that was imposed by the transition period. García Jambrina has focused his comparative analysis of the novel and the film on the characters, time and structure.

17. Antonio Gómez has shown how the novel reacts against the literature of the Spanish Civil War as a literary subgenre in danger of becoming standardized or conventionalized due to the excessive application of literary formulas that have thus far been predominant and have been used *ad nauseam*. It is the epistemological superiority of this novel with its greater degree of self-awareness and self-reflectiveness that explains the fact that the strategy of anti-literariness becomes a paradoxical path toward a more effective literature (57–59).

18. The metafictional nature of this novel has been studied particularly by Richter, Grohmann, and Jünke.

19. In the novel, the visit to the Mas de la Casa Nova (Casa Nova farmhouse), transformed by the passage of many years into "una masía medio en ruinas" (55) (a farm that is half in ruins), shows how the ruins (as an invitation to experience time, Augé *El tiempo*) is also an invitation to discover the trauma of a past that has remained after the agreement to forget what is hidden from sight: "habrían sido sin duda tres casas muy distintas, pero el tiempo las había igualado, y su aire común de desamparo, de esqueletos en piedra entre cuyos costillares descarnados gime el viento en las tardes de otoño, no contenía una sola sugestión de que alguien, alguna vez, hubiera vivido en ellas" (71) (they had no doubt been three very different houses, but time had made them all the same, and their common appearance of abandonment, of stone skeletons through whose fleshless ribcages the wind howls during autumn afternoons, did not contain even a single suggestion that anyone had ever lived in them).

20. LaCapra opposes the act of working through (mourning) to that of reenacting or

repeating (melancholia). The former entails a distancing of oneself from a trauma, while the latter entails an identification of oneself as victim, bringing about a retraumatization, and retarding the progression of any healing.

21. If the forest as a saturated space is the antithesis of an open space with views, in contrast to the domesticated, safe and orderly space of a farm or human settlement, it is also a region of boundless possibilities (Tuan 56).

22. The representation of the hero is a topic that has garnered much attention from critics of *Soldados de Salamina*, whether from the viewpoint of the classical hero (Yushimito del Valle), the anonymous hero (Saval) or solidarity (Gagen). The moral dimension of this novel has also been studied by Robert Spires.

23. "The individual who in the service of the spectacle is placed in stardom's spotlight is in fact the opposite of an individual, and as clearly the enemy of the individual in himself as of the individual in others. In entering the spectacle as a model to be identified with, he renounces all autonomy in order himself to identify with the general law of obedience to the course of things" (Debord 39).

24. "As for the *subject* of history, it can only be the self-production of the living: the living becoming master and possessor of its world—that is, of history—and coming to exist as *consciousness of its own activity*" (Debord 48, italics in original).

25. In the novel, going camping, which is a social class marker, inserts Miralles in "una población flotante compuesta básicamente por miembros del proletariado europeo" (153) (a floating population that is basically composed of members of the European proletariat). The city of Stockton, California in John Huston's film *Fat City*, which provides the title and gives meaning to the third part of the novel, is a symbol of failure and a mirror in which Miralles sees his future reflected (178-79); Dijon is the "ciudad sin alegría y sin futuro" (181) (city with no happiness or future) where he has spent his long exile and where he will undoubtedly have a solitary death.

26. Gómez has analyzed this novel as a long, winding narration leading up to a final testimony that involves the culmination of the plot from a dramatic and thematic point of view. Lluró has also noted the role that testimony plays in this novel by bringing into question who in the novel is testifying for whom.

27. Augé considers supermodernity to be a new modernity that prolongs, accelerates and complicates the effects of modernity as it was conceived in the eighteenth and nineteenth centuries: "Supermodernity would be the combined effect of an acceleration of history, a retraction of space and an individuation of destinies" (Augé, *El tiempo* 59).

28. In today's cities tall buildings have inverted what used to be a symbol of prestige—living on the ground floor—since the problem of vertical distance, which has now been resolved by machines, has given way to the prestige of elevation: the wealthy not only purchase real estate but also possess and demand more visual space (Tuan 38).

29. "Another dimension of the contemporary crisis of place is social. People in the West are increasingly an exiled and uprooted people, living 'out of place.' Social

geographers suggest that while it is essential to have 'place identity,' since the Second World War we have de-emphasized place for the sake of values such as mobility, centralization or economic rationalization" (Sheldrake 8).

30. The representation of the conflict's consequences through the topic of insanity is characteristic of the literature and cinema of the Spanish Civil War (Moreno-Nuño 298–300).

31. For Michel de Certeau, the city is the social experience of lacking a place, since, as a space to walk around in, the city is an undefined process of countless minimum deportations, displacements and trips, and an interminable absence of place within the urban landscape. Three symbolic mechanisms organize the *topoi* of the discourses on the city--the legend, the memory and the dream—thereby making the space inhabitable, invoking the dead, and imposing a history and an identity. In light of the importance of these signifying practices as practices that invent spaces, de Certeau warns against the dispersion of stories as a dispersion of memory (*The Practice*).

32. Pope John Paul II beatified numerous Spaniards who were killed in the Republican zone during the civil war and who are considered martyrs, and Benedict XVI has done the same. The first beatification procedures were halted by John XXIII and Paul VI so as not to reopen old wounds. In March 2001, the John Paul II beatified 233 people, and nearly a thousand have been brought up to the altars.

33. While Moreno Gómez criticized how the Spanish university system had not encouraged the study of the resistance movement, and even boycotted it (25–26), during the last few years Luis Gómez and Natalia Junquera have noticed a proliferation of doctoral dissertations on the civil war and the Franco period: as of this writing, there are four being worked on that deal with repression by the Franco regime in Zamora, where the repression was not particularly noteworthy.

Works Cited

Aguilar Fernández, Paloma. "Guerra Civil, Franquismo y Democracia." *Claves de Razón Práctica* 140 (March 2004): 24–33.

———. *Memoria y olvido de la Guerra Civil española*. Madrid: Alianza, 1996.

Albert, Mechthild. "Oralidad y memoria en la novela memorialística." *Lugares de memoria de la Guerra Civil y el franquismo: Representaciones literarias y visuales*. Ed. Ulrich Winter. Madrid: Vervuert Iberoamericana, 2006.

Álvarez Junco, José. "Que no nos den una versión falseada de la Historia." *El País* 14 September 2008: 6.

Augé, Marc. *El tiempo en ruinas*. Barcelona: Gedisa, 2003.

———. *Los "no lugares" espacios del anonimato: Una antropología de la sobremodernidad*. Barcelona: Gedisa, 2006.

Bachelard, Gaston. *The Poetics of Space*. Trans. Maria Jolas. Boston: Beacon Press, 1969.

Ballesteros, Isolina. "La exhumación de la memoria histórica: Nostalgia y utopía." *Soldados de Salamina* (Javier Cercas 2001, David Trueba 2002). *Film-Historia* 15.1 (2005). *www.pcb.ub.es/filmistoria/filmistoriaonline1_2005.htlm.*

Barthes, Roland. *Mitologías.* Trans. Héctor Schmucler. Madrid: Siglo XXI de España editores, 2000.

Baudrillard, Jean. *Simulacra and Simulation.* Ann Arbor: University of Michigan Press, 1994.

Cartwright-Punnet, Lynn. "How Spain Sees Its Past: The Monumentalization of the Spanish Civil War." Unpublished B.A. honors thesis, Wesleyan University.

Castiñeira, Ángel. "Naciones imaginadas." *Casa encantada: Lugares de memoria en la España constitucional (1978–2004).* Madrid: Iberoamericana Vervuert, 2005.

Cercas, Javier. *Soldados de Salamina.* Barcelona: Tusquets, 2001.

Certeau, Michel de. *The Practice of Everyday Life.* Trans. Steven F. Rendall. Berkeley: University of California Press, 1984.

Cruz, Jacqueline. "Para que no olvidemos: La propuesta de recuperación de la memoria histórica de Patricia Ferreira." *Letras hispanas* 3.2 (Fall 2006): 31–40.

Debord, Guy. *The Society of the Spectacle.* New York: Zone Books, 1994.

Ehrlicher, Hanno. "Batallas del recuerdo: La memoria de la Guerra Civil" en *Land and Freedom* (Ken Loach, 1995) y *Soldados de Salamina* (David Trueba, 2002). *Miradas globales: Cine español en el cambio de milenio.* Ed. Jörg Türschmann. Madrid: Vervuert, 2007.

En la ciudad sin límites. Dir. Antonio Hernández. Perf. Leonardo Sbaraglia, Fernando Fernán Gómez. Zebra producciones, Icónica and Patagonik Film Group, 2001.

Gagen, Derek. "Heroism in Defeat: Alberti's *Cantata de los héroes y la fraternidad de los pueblos* and Cerca's *Soldados de Salamina.*" *Bulletin of Hispanic Studies* 83.4 (2006): 349–66.

García Jambrina, Luis. "De la novela al cine: *Soldados de Salamina* o 'El arte de la traición.'" *Ínsula* 688 (April 2004): 30–32.

Gómez, Luis, and Natalia Junquera. "Juicio a la barbarie." *El País.* 14 September 2008: 4.

Gómez López-Quiñones, Antonio. *La guerra persistente: Memoria, violencia y utopía: Representaciones contemporáneas de la guerra civil española.* Vervuert: Madrid, 2006.

Grohmann, Alexis. "La configuración de *Soldados de Salamina* o la negra espalda de Javier Cercas." *Letras Peninsulares* 17.2 (Fall/Winter 2004–2005): 297–320.

Jünke, Claudia. "'Pasarán años y olvidaremos todo': La Guerra Civil española como lugar de memoria en la novela y el cine actuales en España." *Lugares de memoria de la Guerra Civil y el franquismo: Representaciones literarias y visuales.* Ed. Ulrich Winter. Madrid: Vervuert Iberoamericana, 2006.

Labanyi, Jo. "El cine como lugar de la memoria en películas: novelas y autobiografías de los años setenta hasta el presente." *Casa encantada: Lugares de memoria en la España constitucional (1978–2004).* Madrid: Iberoamericana Vervuert, 2005.

LaCapra, Dominick. *Writing History, Writing Trauma.* Baltimore: Johns Hopkins University Press, 2001.

Lluró, Josep María. "Novela para una liquidación." *Lateral* (April 2002): 8–9.

Mabrey, María Cristina C. "Experiencia de la memoria o memoria de la experiencia: Novela y film, *Soldados de Salamina*." *Espéculo: Revista de estudios literarios.* Universidad Complutense de Madrid. 2008. *www.ucm.es/info/especulo/numero37/salamina.html.*

Margalit, Avishai. *The Ethics of Memory.* Cambridge: Harvard University Press, 2002.

Martín, Juan Carlos. "Historia y Ficción en *Soldados de Salamina*." *Ojáncano* (October 2005): 41–64.

Moreno Gómez, Francisco. *La resistencia armada contra Franco: Tragedia del maquis y la guerrilla.* Barcelona: Crítica, 2001.

Moreno-Nuño, Carmen. *Las huellas de la Guerra Civil: Mito y trauma en la narrativa de la España democrática.* Madrid: Libertarias, 2006.

Nora, Pierre. "Between Memory and History: Les Lieux de Mémoire." In "Memory and Counter-Memory, special issue, *Representations 26* (Spring 1989): 7–24.

Para que no me olvides. Dir. Patricia Ferreira. Perf. Fernando Fernán Gómez. Continental Producciones, Tornasol Films, 2005.

Resina, Joan Ramon, and Ulrich Winter, eds. *Casa encantada: Lugares de memoria en la España constitucional (1978–2004).* Madrid: Iberoamericana Vervuert, 2005.

Richter, David F. "Memory and Metafiction: Re-membering Stories and Histories in *Soldados de Salamina*." *Letras Peninsulares* 17.2 (Fall/Winter 2004–2005): 285–96.

Saval, José V. "Simetría y paralelismo en la construcción de *Soldados de Salamina* de Javier Cercas." *Letras Hispanas: Revista de literatura y cultura* 4.1 (Spring 2007): 62–70.

Sheldrake, Philip. *Spaces for the Sacred: Place, Memory, and Identity.* Baltimore: Johns Hopkins University Press, 2001.

Soldados de Salamina. Dir. David Trueba. Perf. Ariadna Gil, María Botto. Lolafilms and Fernando Trueba P.C., 2003.

Spires, Robert C. "Depolarization and the New Spanish Fiction at the Millennium." *ALEC* 30.1–2 (2005): 485–512.

Subirats, Eduardo. "Postmoderna modernidad: La España de los felices ochenta." *Quimera* 145 (March 1996): 11–18.

Todorov, Tzvetan. "Los dilemas de la memoria (Un texto para Valientes): Paper given at the Cátedra Julio Cortázar of the University of Guadalajara, Mexico." Trans. Dulce María Zúñiga. *www.74.125.47.132/search?q=cache:RImRmywg5MwJ:www.jcortazar.udg.mx/documentos/TODOROV.pdf+Tzvetan+Todorov+Los+dilemas+de+la+memoria&cd=1&hl=en&ct=clnk&gl=us.*

Tuan, Yi-Fu. *Space and Place: The Perspective of Experience.* Minneapolis: University of Minnesota Press, 2001.

Yushimito del Valle, Carlos. "*Soldados de Salamina*: Indagaciones sobre un héroe moderno." *Espéculo: Revista de estudios literarios.* Universidad Complutense de Madrid. 2003. *www.ucm.es/info/especulo/numero23/salamina.html.*

◆ Afterword

Tom Conley

In his dazzling study of Eduardo Zamacois Quintana's *Memorias de un vagón de ferrocarril*, a novel we can appreciate today as ephemera of the 1920s that literate travelers consumed to pass endless hours of transit on Iberian railways, Robert Davidson invokes the concept of "the thing-that-feels." For good reason: as the title indicates, the principal character is a railway car that speculates on its life that went from the chromed elegance of a first-class conveyance in its youth to a wood-worn and well-traveled third-class carriage in middle age before, finally, settling down in its golden years to become a restaurant. The *vagón de ferrocaril* becames the analogue of today's soon-to-disappear "diner," the eatery, parked on the streets of spacious Midwestern towns, crafted from the old wagons of the California Zephyr or the Twentieth Century Limited. Reminding moviegoers of scenes from *The Lady Vanishes*, *The Palm Beach Story*, or *The Narrow Margin*, memories of dining cars tell viewers how the international "café car," be it the Acela or the TGV, that serves fast food on cardboard places heated in microwaves, is a sign of a world going to pot.

Zamacois's personification startles because, for a first time, the thing-that-feels is not an animal-that-talks (as had been the dogs Cipión and Berganza in "El Coloquio de los perros") but a metaphor, a mode of transport that carries the reader across social and spatial divides. Zamacois's wagon inspires editors David Castillo and Bradley Nelson to remark that the "novelist's decision to explore modern subjectivity through the construction, movement and destruction of a luxury dining car shows that the subject is made like "this thing they call a place," *hecho como esto que llaman lugar*. The subject is a fabricated, moving object until, at the axis of Spain's railway network, it occupies a "dwelling"—Davidson appeals to Heidegger—where it "gentrifies the material and social difference that it had previously represented" in its descent from a cosmopolitan to a local condition.

The *vagón de ferrocaril* can serve as an emblem for this collection of twelve rich and varied essays that move to and away from the terms of its title. *Spectacle* is understood as a mechanism that links the collective memory it crafts to the geographical sites where it takes place. In this volume spectacle is understood in strongly ritualistic and ocular senses: ritual, because its makers seek to have participants share a common ground where social contradiction and class conflict are effaced for the duration of its performance; ocular, because those who take part see themselves being located within its machination. To see that one is actively "taking part" has much to do with what it means, in the topographical sense, for the event to "take place" or to make manifest the operation of its illusion. The editors appeal to *topophilia,* understood by Yi-Fu Tuan (whom Lawrence Buell has called "the greatest living intellectual who remains unknown to one and all") as being a sustained force of attraction to a locale prior to gaining access to a more intellectual and abstract sense of relation with the world at large. For the geographer of experience (Tuan often described himself in those terms) any existential rapport with the ambient world begins in propinquity. Sentient bodies identify with what is near; they collect sensory impressions of their surroundings and eventually they associate with what they claim to be their identity; what they learn about other places comes through intercessors or outsiders The editors and authors use these two compass points to study ideology and its relation to space and place in Iberian and Latin American cultures.

All of the essays examine ideologies of nation and identity through "third spaces," landscapes of sorts, through which readers and spectators are invited to move. Landscapes that depict given spaces concretize our understanding of ideology, not as a collected sense of various and often contradictory beliefs and practices but in the spirit of Louis Althusser's famous definition of the term: as the imaginary relations we hold with real modes of production. The landscape becomes an intermediate and mixed area where language and image are held together, often in conscious confusion; where spatial fantasies commingle prior to acceding to language or semiosis; where, as in the Freudian unconscious, oppositions know no contradiction; where, much as had been the vista of earth and hell and Bosch's "Garden of Earthly Delights" that hangs in the Prado, the spectator enters *in order to get lost*, that is, to discern other alternative spaces in wild pictorial fantasy.[1]

The contributions to this volume demonstrate that a variety of media build landscapes in order to negotiate issues they cannot resolve. Spatial constructions become complex objects—and these words differ slightly from those of the editors—that set in play, in mixed form, social, economic, political and aesthetic tensions and desires. They include the animated movie that has svelte Indian princesses scamper through the primeval American forests that David Castillo affiliates with the society of spectacle, in a world today that Guy Debord could never have imagined. After *Pocahontas* it suffices to watch any televised transmission of Sunday NFL football to see why: hundreds of cameras move about an arena of plastic grass on which buff athletes in Lycra display spectacular force of movement and collision: our eyes train on close-ups of undifferentiated masses of arms, thighs, calves and gigantic buttocks—all squirming and jawing below electronic cornices whose moving advertisements coordinate words and colors that match the game itself (images of blood-red bottles of Heinz ketchup speed about the stadium when a team reaches the red zone, and so on). Fans pay handsomely to paint themselves in team colors and to be seen flailing on-camera and perhaps, if one of them is noticed, to get a call from an advertising agency for the production of a "spot." Yet, in the midst of the spectacular landscapes, Castillo inserts "third-spaces" or uncommon vistas coming as if from nowhere, out of the early modern and contemporary canons. These are regressive zones that, as a historian with a keen political sense, he displaces into our own field. In this manner they become disquieting and enchanting memory-places that turn spectacles—operations that seek to eradicate the history that informs them—into multilayered forms, or what Gilles Deleuze has called "stratigraphies," where memory-places, archival matter, and the impetus that retrieves them come forth.[2] He locates their ideology in terms of the ways they are distributed and designed to shape future cognition of the ambient world.

Early on we also see how the most ideologically charged Iberian landscape, Andalusia, and its cultural icon, the Alhambra, become a layered space—a stratigraphic form—by which William Childers uses *topophilia* to coin the concept of *maurophilia*. The informed westerner's zeal to embrace the Muslim others finds a privileged place in the zone where Islam is felt to have been at its zenith. Yet the consequences of the retaking of Granada in 1492 (that historian Bernard Vincent qualified as an event no less major than the Columbian discoveries) remains a wound that the hispanophile must open and close over and again so as to remain, at an increasing remove from the event, in happy contrition, which might amount to the unavowed pleasure of knowing that Spain indeed *did* win.[3] The maurophile is part of a layered landscape in which contradictions are both distinguished and fused.

It would be a stretch to say that Cervantes's *Los baños de Argel* anticipates the bathhouses in northern California where Michel Foucault is said to have found heterotopia. Or would it? Moisés Castillo appeals to the shipboard- or island-landscape that the author of "Other Spaces" made famous in his work on the *Stultifera navis*. These are intermediate areas that welcome amphibious species where otherwise different things and beings commingle. For the reader of today the insertion of the space and place of *Los Baños* into a context that is not under control of literary history (such as the idea of the desperate utopia of seclusion in the landscape of pastoral literature) endows Cervantes with political effectiveness. The area that Castillo describes is of a third order, *between* a prison and an Elysian field, and between the composite landscape of the author's greater work and that in which we can project it for the good sake of using literature to discover other and unforeseen ways of practicing space.

The first three chapters of this volume find their spatial model in the mechanism of texts and images produced throughout the Golden Age. Bradley Nelson shows how the emblem, a genre born of the miscibility of images and idioms, changes at the moment of the Galilean revolution. It negotiates conflicting hypotheses concerning the shape and extension of the cosmos in both scientific and political circles. Often portraying landscapes in ornately miniature frames, the emblem weds wit with science and what is *here*, an emerging Iberian consciousness, to speculation about the machinery of the heavens. Thus it seems as if Colleen Culleton exploits the plasticity of the intermediate space that Nelson carefully disengages from the late and underappreciated manifestations of the emblem in order to move to and fro from one cartography of Catalonia to another. In doing so she crafts a stratigraphy. It is one by which the Catalan Atlas is a ground—but also a force of metamorphosis—for the mapping of a consciousness whose fortunes ebb and flow in contemporary literature. Appealing to Gilles Deleuze and Félix Guattari's concept of "striated" and "smooth" spaces, she shows how the fields of tension that result from the opposition of the two terms is in itself a way to discern the intermediate character of a "national" landscape in modern history. To obtain a view of a smooth space the geographer cannot do without striations of a frame or a grid delineating a zone that would be free of the lines of social contradiction.[4] Like Nelson's and other essays in the volume, Culleton demonstrates that what could be a "global" consciousness begins only from the perception of spaces whose distinguishing traits are felt to be local: the *here* of Catalonia cannot be attached to a greater entity, a *there* of world-space, without encountering various striations. Culleton moves deftly over and across those which would separate the time of the Catalan atlas from contemporary manifestations of the mapping of the space in literature. She turns a geographically and historically codified body of matter into one whose affect—vital to its self-definition—dismantles or at least calls its chronology into question.[5]

Justin Read's and David William Foster's essays convey similar tensions of striated and smooth surfaces in their treatments of Buenos Aires. Both begin with the city, in every manual of classical geography an emblem of what is local or topographical that stands in contrast to what is global. For Ptolemy and his commentators, especially Pieter Apian, the geographer from Ingolstadt who carried favor in the court of Charles V, made clear the distinction by juxtaposing a spherical world-map to the portrait of a king or of a sacred figure to show that the sum of the world, in itself invisible, can be fathomed by the view of the full portrait of a human being. By contrast, the sight of a city can be thought of as the analogue to the depiction of the sitter's eye or ear, the sentient organs that are best equipped to perceive the urban area shown adjacent to it.[6] The gap between the whole and the perceiver, on the one hand and, on the other, the city and two sentient organs that seek to "see" or "hear" it may be indeed what drives topophilia, the wish to know the secrets of a local place that gives rise to reflection on extension of unknown range and limit. The latter, what Nelson discerned in Juan de Borja's emblems about the earth becoming the entire cosmos at the same time as it is "tiny and insignificant," inspires the *topofilia porteña* that Justin Read describes by way of Borges's view of Buenos Aires. Taking it to be a border zone, a third or intermediate space that carries the legacy (from the east) of modern cosmopolitanism and (from the west) *criollo* spirit from the pampas, Borges *overlooks* Buenos Aires. He stands high above it as an omniscient geographer who sees the city from far above the earth at the same time he remains oblivious to "all the people that actually lived and migrated to Buenos Aires," populations that were in the throes of dependency in the "total theater" of modernity as Walter Gropius had conceived its architecture "circa 1930." Not dissimilarly, Horacio Coppola's photographs of Buenos Aires are taken, in the spirit of Yi-Fu Tuan, to be "intermediate divisions," at once documents of "high abstraction and specific responses" to the conundrum of the topographical image that sets forward a relation of doubt as to what might be the extent of the world in which it is found. The pictures are fragments, like Apian's eye and ear, that see and hear what they wish to identify as modernity—that "spectacular" development and sense of "spectacle" that willfully elides or overlooks the longer history of the origins and growth of the city.

What spectacles overlook happens to be the topic of Catherine Vallejo's study of the image of Spain in the 1893 Chicago Exhibition. Remembered at the time of the Columbian Quincentennial in 1992 as the display that juxtaposed Thomas Edison to Columbus, the event made clear that the illuminations the pragmatic genius had wrought were enough to leave in the shadow of penumbra the man who discovered the New World. Vallejo shows how Raúl Prebisch's theory of dependency, that Justin Read located in the history of the representation of Argentina, was manifest in a colonial spectacle that "redefined the symbolic world order, as the New World 'discovered' by Columbus was now represented by North America only, both South America and Spain relegated to a stagnant life immersed in a dead past." If José Rabasa's words about colonial narrative of Mexico pertain to the event of 1893, the Exposition was telling Spain and Latin America to "tell the story to the world of the way that the colonizer," now the personification of the United States, "subjugated them."

Implicit in the treatment is that the Exposition took place at the threshold of the advent of cinema, a colonizing and controlling medium par excellence. The reader of Goretti Ramírez's contribution on the pastoral world in Luis Cernuda's poetry cannot fail to see the presence of a *caméra stylo* that moves through a stratigraphy composed of "urban landscapes mostly in Anglo-Saxon settings, Edenic settings mostly in Hispanic setting, and Spanish historical landscapes." Each is an intermediate term in relation to the two others. Gardens and ruins call into question edenic milieus, which historical vistas no sooner unsettle by locating the objects that make them visible in terms of time. The poet's "conflictive, oscillating" rapport with Spain from the standpoint of exile—with an imaginary whole from the point of view of a site that allows it to be seen as a mix of topographies—owes to the ideology of Raymond Williams's landmark study of the "country and the city." The essay finds an ideal complement in Luis Marino González's treatment of the space of Franco's Spain as it is mediated by cinema of the 1940s and 1950s. The author treats of the ways that the landscape, the very object of topography, is portrayed both positively and negatively, respectively, in Manuel Mur Oti's *Un hombre va por el camino* (1948) and José Antonio Nieves Conde's *Surcos* (1951). The land that would be timeless and that is the seedbed of fascist ideals is *already* undone by the very nature of the cinematic medium—modernity itself—that portrays it. Much like Victor Erice's opening shots of *El espíritu de la colmena*, in which a movie truck goes from village to village in La Mancha—affiliation of the truck-that-feels with Quixote could not be more apparent—or much, too, like the opening shot of *Volver*, in which windmills in the same region have become electric turbines, the "man going on the road" is the man with a movie camera, a quasi-personification of the technology that brings time, history, and an extraordinary literary heritage into the landscape. Through the art of juxta-position González uses *Surcos* to make clear the way that the Franco's regime required exchange with urban and international spheres to maintain and even develop an ideology of Spanish topography. The city intervenes, and with it also *film noir*, a convention that decisively melds history and space in urban areas, thus opening a third or intermediate zone between pre-war reverie and the reality of Spain at a threshold of globalization.

Carmen Moreno-Nuño works on the same issue from the standpoint of the memory-place in contemporary Spain. Much in the line of works that deal with the Shoah, exhumed works and places allow their viewers to "develop a gaze that forces us to look at what we were unwilling to see."[7] Hence Patricia Ferreira's *Para que no me olvides,* a film in which allusion to Robert Louis Stevenson's *Treasure Island* and its cartography allows past time to be recovered through the perception of local space, in other words, through a gaze on landscapes that can be taken as stratigraphies or even layerings of "non-places" or "any-places-whatsoever," in which oblivion mixes with searing force of re-membrance. Moreno-Nuño shows how David Trueba's *Soldados de Salamina* disrupts an ideology of history (which would have as its memory-image a dia-grammatic timeline of specious events—elections and wars—that have caused the nation to be as it is) "through a memory that obsessively questions itself." Much like Chris Marker's *Sans Soleil* and *Level Five*, which study the pitfalls of any project that would construct a history, Trueba makes the very search for history the project of a filmmaker "que va por el camino," into archives and commemorative places that resist the pressure the historian applies to them.

It is a fitting irony that in her study of Antonio Hernández's *En la ciu-dad sin límites,* Moreno-Nuño appeals to Marc Augé's work on the non-place, which he alertly reminds us is that which lacks a space of identity, of history or, more important, of *relation*. The latter term has much to do with what the authors of this volume have located in intermediate zones, areas in which rela-tions of history and place are constituted through the mix of perception and memory. Through the construction of relations a prismatic sense of the past is retrieved, and so also are the motives that inspire oblivion, the necessary opera-tion that requires us to forget—in order to remember over and again—what we always prefer not to recall. In his brief *Casablanca: Movies and Memory* Augé shows how films that come out of the past, even if they are as schmaltzy as Curtiz's classic that no one fails to remember, force us to reconsider our relation with history. Thanks to the accruing distance between the time of their making and the here-and-now in which they are disinterred, films of the stamp of *Casablanca* spur a relation with history.[8] Hernández takes the issue a step further by shooting the film in hotels, airports, train stations, and other anonymous and anodyne places in which the recall of traumatic history, if recall there is, floats without any mooring. Objectivity gets lost, but subjectivity, what relates to topophilia, is recovered. How can we relate to non-places or construct sites that account for history where the architecture of spectacle would smooth it over? Such is the question that Moreno-Nuño asks at the end of her article, which the authors of every piece ask in one way or another in spaces that move to and fro from the New World to the Old.

Much like Zamacois's rusty *vagón de ferrocaril*, the thing-that-feels its history on the rails it traveled in a world in transition, the authors who study the sites, events, objects and films that are gathered in this volume reflect limpidly on situations and forces that cause us to be conscious of where we are and how we happen to be there. They work forcefully with the matter of space and place in ways that open new avenues of study by which a highly effective politics and aesthetics of analysis is brought forward: no small feat at a time when the acuity of the kinds of readings shown in this volume is needed more than ever.

Notes

1. In the first chapter of *La fable mystique* Michel de Certeau describes the ocular voyage that the viewer of Bosch's painting takes as one that leads to and from "places in which we get lost."
2. Gilles Deleuze, *Cinéma 2: L'Image-temps* (320–34). The term is applied to the mixed landscapes the philosopher finds in the films of Rossellini, Antonioni, Resnais and Straub-Huillet. They derive in a strong degree from the concept of the *lieu quelconque* or "any-place-whatsoever," a landscape in such decay or chaos that it could belong anywhere in the world at large.
3. See Bernard Vincent, *1492: L'Année admirable.*
4. It can be added that many of the essays use the distinction in order to discern the character of topophilia. The "smooth" space would that of the topophile— it welcomes all kinds of forces of different origin and trajectory—and might

hypothetically be compared to the surface of what Deleuze and Guattari (also in *Mille plateaux*) call the CsO, the *corps sans organes* or body-without-organs. By that the philosophers suggest that a body of this sort has no specific or privileged zones of affection. No single area has erotic privilege because the body, smooth in character, is sensitive to the ambient world everywhere, indeed *all over* its epidermal surface.

5. In *Cartographies of Time*, Daniel Rosenberg and Anthony Grafton note that any chronological distinction begins with the drawing of a line. Culleton redraws them so as to open historical analysis of space onto its memory and its invention.

6. Pieter Apian, *Libro de la cosmographia de Pedro Apiano, el qual trata la descripcion del Mundo, y sus partes, por muy claro y lindo artificio, augmentado por el doctissimo varon Gemma Frisio. . . . Agora nuevamente traduzidos en Romance Castellano*. Thirty editions of the work were published between 1529 and the end of the sixteenth century. The impact of the illustration in this popular manual cannot be underestimated. Like an emblem, it remains a memory-image for the study of the attraction that topography has for any treatment of space. In *Mapmakers of the Sixteenth Century and their Maps*, Robert Karrow offers a detailed survey of the fortunes of Apian's *Cosmographia*.

7. The force of the memory-images of the Holocaust from 1945 until now are the topic of two searing studies, both of French extraction, that apply to the films Moreno-Nuño takes up: Antoine de Baecque, *L'Histoire-caméra* and Jean-Michel Frodon, *The Shoah: An Art Confronts the Tragedy of the Twentieth Century*.

8. Marc Augé, *Casablanca: Movies and Memory*. It might be said that the title of Franco's (or J. L. Sáenz de Heredia's) classic film of 1941, *El espíritu de una raza*, which cinephiles might prefer to forget, can be glossed as "the spirit of an erasure." Its title is clearly recalled in Erice's *El espíritu de la colmena* of three decades later.

Works Cited

Apian, Pieter, and Gemma Frisio. *Libro de la cosmographia de Pedro Apiano: El qual trata la descripcion del Mundo, y sus partes, por muy claro y lindo artificio, augmentado por el doctissimo varon Gemma Frisio. . . . Agora nuevamente traduzidos en Romance Castellano*. Enveres (Antwerp): Gregorio Bontio, 1548.

———. *Cosmographia Petri Apiani, per Gemmam Frisium apud Louanienses Medicum & Mathematicum insignem, iam demum ab omnibus vindicata mendis, ac nonnullis quoeu locis aucta, figurísque novis illustrata. . . .* Antwerp: Gregorio Bontio, 1550.

Augé, Marc. *Casablanca: Movies and Memory*. Minneapolis: University of Minnesota Press, 2008.

Baecque, Antoine. *L'histoire-caméra*. Paris: Gallimard, 2008.

Certeau, Michel. *La fable Mystique*. Paris: Editions de Minuit, 1982.

Deleuze, Gilles. *Cinéma 2: L'Image-temps*. Paris: Minuit, 1983.

————, and Félix Guattari. *Capitalisme et schizophrénie 2: Mille plateaux*. Paris: Editions de Minuit, 1980.

Foucault, Michel. "Des espaces autres." *Dits et écrits 1954–1988*. Vol. 4. Eds. Daniel Defert and Franois Ewald. Paris: Editions Gallimard, 1994. 752–62.

Frodon, Jean-Michel, Anna Harrison, and Tom Mes. *Cinema and the Shoah: An Art Confronts the Tragedy of the Twentieth Century*. Albany: State University of New York Press, 2010.

Karrow, Robert. *Mapmakers of the Sixteenth Century and their Maps*. Chicago: Speculum Press, 1993.

Rosenberg, Daniel and Anthony Grafton. *Cartographies of Time*. Princeton: Princeton Architectural Press, 2010.

Sáenz de Heredia, J. L. *Raza: Espíritu de una raza*. (Videorecording). Edición especial coleccionista incluye las dos versiones de 1941 y 1950. Madrid: Divisa Ediciones, 2002.

Vincent, Bernard. *1492: L'Année admirable*. Paris: Flammarion, 1991 and 1996.

Williams, Raymond. *The Country and the City*. London: The Hogarth Press, 1985.

◆ Contributors

David R. Castillo is Professor of Spanish and Chair of the Department of Romance Languages and Literatures at SUNY Buffalo. He is the author of *(A)wry Views: Anamorphosis, Cervantes and the Early Picaresque* (2001), *Baroque Horrors: Roots of the Fantastic in the Age of Curiosities* (2010), and co-editor of *Reason and Its Others: Italy, Spain and the New World* (2006).

Moisés R. Castillo is Assistant Professor of Spanish at the University of Kentucky, with a specialization in early modern studies. He is author of *Indios en escena: La representación del amerindio en el teatro del Siglo de Oro* (2009) and has also published articles in *Bulletin of the Comediantes* and *Theatralia*. He is currently writing a book on Cervantes's theater.

William Childers is Associate Professor of Spanish at Brooklyn College. In addition to his book *Transnational Cervantes* (2006), he has also published a number of articles on Cervantes and other topics relating to early modern Spain. He is currently working on a book-length project entitled *Spain's Last Moors: A Cultural History of the Morisco Question*.

Tom Conley is Professor of Romance Languages and Visual and Environmental Studies at Harvard University. He studies relations of space and language in early modern culture and cinema. Recent publications include *An Errant Eye: Topography and Poetry in Early Modern France* (2011) and *Cartographic Cinema* (2007). Some of his translations include Marc Augé, *Casablanca: Movies and Memory* (2009), Christian Jacob, *The Sovereign Map* (2006), Michel de Certeau, *The Capture of Speech and Culture in the Plural* (1997), and Gilles Deleuze, *The Fold: Leibniz and the Baroque* (1993).

Colleen P. Culleton is Assistant Professor of Spanish at SUNY Buffalo. Her research explores the intersection of landscape, literature, and the cultural imaginary in modern Catalonia. Her publications can be found in scholarly journals, including *The Catalan Review*, *The Journal of Catalan Studies*, and *Romance Quarterly*.

Robert A. Davidson is Associate Professor of Spanish and Catalan at the University of Toronto. He is the author of *Jazz Age Barcelona* (2009) and is currently completing a second book titled *The Hotel: Space Over Time*, which will also be published by University of Toronto Press.

David William Foster is Regents' Professor of Spanish, Humanities, and Women's Studies at Arizona State University. His research interests focus on urban culture in Latin America, with emphasis on issues of gender construction and sexual identity, as well as Jewish culture. His many publications include *Violence in Argentine Literature: Cultural Responses to Tyranny* (1995); *Cultural Diversity in Latin American Literature* (1994); *Contemporary Argentine Cinema* (1992); and *Gay and Lesbian Themes in Latin American Writing* (1991).

Luis Mariano González is Assistant Professor of Spanish at Connecticut College. He specializes in contemporary Spanish literature and culture, and his research interests include film, drama, and television. He has published three books: *La escena madrileña durante la II República, 1931–1939* (1996); *El teatro español durante la II República y la crítica de su tiempo, 1931–1936* (2007); and *Fascismo, kitsch y cine histórico en España, 1939–1953* (2009). He is currently working on a book-length project on Spanish film produced during the first years of Franco's dictatorship.

Carmen Moreno-Nuño is Associate Professor of Spanish at the University of Kentucky, specializing in contemporary Spanish literature and film. She is the author of *Las huellas de la Guerra Civil: Mito y trauma en la narrativa de la*

España democrática (2006) and is currently writing on film and the globalization of historical memory. She is co-editor of *Armed Resistance: Cultural Representations of the Anti-Francoist Guerrilla*, for submission to *Hispanic Issues On Line* (HIOL).

Bradley J. Nelson is Associate Professor and Chair of the Department of Classics, Modern Languages and Linguistics at Concordia University (Montreal, Canada). He is the author of *The Persistence of Presence: Emblem and Ritual in Baroque Spain* (2010), and his current project is focused on the intersection of scientific and aesthetic paradigms in early and late modern contexts.

Goretti Ramírez is Associate Professor at Concordia University (Montreal, Canada), where she teaches literary and cultural studies of modern Spain. She is the author of *María Zambrano, crítica literaria* (2004) and over thirty publications on twentieth-century Spanish poetry and intellectual history, with particular emphasis on the Republican exile. She is currently finishing a monograph on the representation of space in the poetry of the Spanish Republican exile, as well as an edition of María Zambrano's autobiographical writings. She is a member of the Advisory Board of *Antígona: Revista de la Fundación María Zambrano*.

Justin Read is Associate Professor of Spanish and Portuguese in the Department of Romance Languages and Literatures at SUNY Buffalo. His primary research interest is the urbanization of the Americas, focusing on twentieth-century avant-garde poetry and modernist architecture. He is the author of *Modern Poetics and Hemispheric American Cultural Studies* (2009), and he is currently working on a second book, *Hemispherics: The Cultural Production of Space in the Americas*. Read is also co-founder of the Reading Group in Cultural Studies of Space at SUNY Buffalo.

Catherine Vallejo is Professor of Spanish at Concordia University (Montreal, Canada). Her research interests center on the contemporary Spanish-American short story, especially by Spanish-Caribbean women, and on nineteenth-century Spanish Caribbean women writers. She has published critical editions of texts by Cuban, Dominican, and Colombian writers, such as the *Poesías* of Mercedes Matamoros, the 1876 novel *Una holandesa en América* by Soledad Acosta de Samper, and *Obras* of Virginia Elena Ortea. She is currently studying nineteenth-century Spanish and Cuban women's writing on their visits to the Paris World Expositions of 1889 and 1900 and the Columbian World's Fair of 1893.

◆ Index

Compiled by Brian Phillips

VOLUMES IN THE HISPANIC ISSUES SERIES

38 *Spectacle and Topophilia: Reading Early Modern and
    Postmodern Hispanic Cultures,*
    edited by David R. Castillo and Bradley J. Nelson

37 *New Spain, New Literatures,*
    edited by Luis Martín-Estudillo and Nicholas Spadaccini

36 *Latin American Jewish Cultural Production,*
    edited by David William Foster

35 *Post-Authoritarian Cultures: Spain and Latin America's Southern Cone,*
    edited by Luis Martín-Estudillo and Roberto Ampuero

34 *Spanish and Empire,* edited by Nelsy Echávez-Solano
    and Kenya C. Dworkin y Méndez

33 *Generation X Rocks: Contemporary Peninsular Fiction, Film, and
    Rock Culture,* edited by Christine Henseler and Randolph D. Pope

32 *Reason and Its Others: Italy, Spain, and the New World,*
    edited by David Castillo and Massimo Lollini

31 *Hispanic Baroques: Reading Cultures in Context,*
    edited by Nicholas Spadaccini and Luis Martín-Estudillo

30 *Ideologies of Hispanism,* edited by Mabel Moraña

29 *The State of Latino Theater in the United States: Hybridity,
    Transculturation, and Identity,* edited by Luis A. Ramos-García

28 *Latin America Writes Back: Postmodernity in the Periphery
    (An Interdisciplinary Perspective),* edited by Emil Volek

27 *Women's Narrative and Film in Twentieth-Century Spain:
    A World of Difference(s),* edited by Ofelia Ferrán and Kathleen M. Glenn

26 *Marriage and Sexuality in Medieval and Early Modern Iberia,*
    edited by Eukene Lacarra Lanz

25 *Pablo Neruda and the U.S. Culture Industry,* edited by Teresa Longo

24 *Iberian Cities,* edited by Joan Ramon Resina

23 *National Identities and Sociopolitical Changes in Latin America,*
    edited by Mercedes F. Durán-Cogan and Antonio Gómez-Moriana

22 *Latin American Literature and Mass Media,*
    edited by Edmundo Paz-Soldán and Debra A. Castillo

21 *Charting Memory: Recalling Medieval Spain,* edited by Stacy N. Beckwith

20 *Culture and the State in Spain: 1550–1850,*
    edited by Tom Lewis and Francisco J. Sánchez

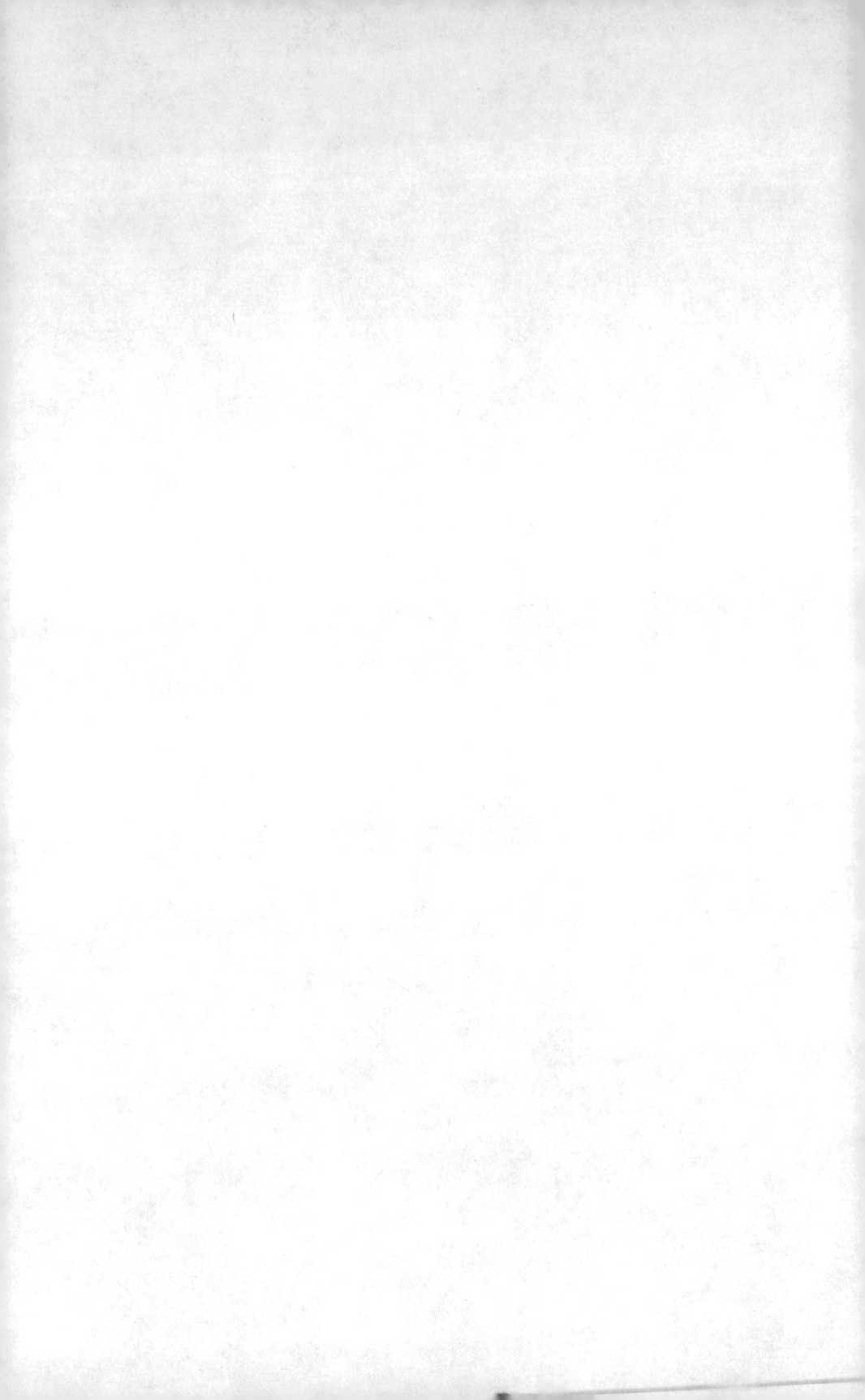

www.ingramcontent.com/pod-product-compliance
Lightning Source LLC
Chambersburg PA
CBHW030643270326
41929CB00007B/188